PARENTS, PER

PARENTS, PERSONALITIES AND POWER

WELSH-MEDIUM SCHOOLS IN SOUTH-EAST WALES

Edited by

Huw S. Thomas and Colin H. Williams

UNIVERSITY OF WALES PRESS
CARDIFF

www.uwp.co.uk

British Library Cataloguing-in-Publication Data.
A catalogue record for this book is available from the British Library.

ISBN   978-0-7083-2584-1
         978-0-7083-2585-8

Typeset by Dinefwr Press, Llandybïe, Carmarthenshire
Printed by CPI Antony Rowe, Chippenham, Wiltshire

Dedicated to one man from amidst the countless thousands of individuals who have been, or still are, part of the 'remarkable and spectacular' success story analysed in this volume. The late Gwilym E. Humphreys (1931–2012), school teacher, college lecturer, head-teacher of Ysgol Gyfun Rhydfelen, HMI, Director of Education for Gwynedd, chairman of a range of educational and cultural groups, worked unstintingly for the promotion of Welsh-medium education of the highest order. The outstanding success of Ysgol Gyfun Rhydfelen under his leadership (1962–75), with its richly rounded education in the academic, cultural and sporting fields, inspired the foundation of many more Welsh-medium schools, and thus made a contribution of immense significance to reversing the language shift in Wales.

Contents

Foreword

Colin Baker

Mae addysg cyfrwng Cymraeg yn arbennig is a statement often heard in connection with our experience. Yet is Welsh-medium education so special?

First, it cannot be claimed that Welsh-medium education is internationally special as minority language education, bilingual education, heritage language education, content and language integrated learning and immersion education are also found around the globe. Wales is not internationally different, as bilingual education has within a seventy-year period spread to most countries of the world.

Yet Welsh-medium education is internationally famed for its quality of education, its rapid and considerable spread in the last century, benefiting from the expertise of inspectors, pioneering headteachers and, not least, enthusiastic teachers and parents as advocates. Wales has an international reputation for successful bilingual education and for that education being a major ingredient in language revitalisation. Nevertheless, that success has developed in spite of the dearth of high-quality research and evaluation of Welsh-medium education.

Second, Welsh-medium education cannot claim to be special because it is internationally exclusive. There were early explorations of heritage-language education in Canadian education (e.g. Ukrainian and Hebrew), the United States (e.g. Yiddish and Native American Indian schools), Maori and Basque, Catalan and Irish. Particularly from the 1960s onwards, what Joshua Fishman calls the 'ethnic revival' and other elements such as language revitalisation enabled the rise of language minority education.

Yet modern Welsh-medium education is almost unique in that different models of bilingual education can be embedded in the same classroom. 'Welsh-medium education' contains within it much variety and we are special in successfully adapting and adjusting. For example, in contrast to the well-defined dual-language education in the United States and immersion education in Canada, Wales often combines different 'models' within one Welsh-medium classroom. For instance, a classroom may contain first-language Welsh-speaking children who follow a heritage-language approach whereby most of the curriculum is taught through the indigenous language. In addition, there are children from English-speaking homes experiencing immersion education whereby most of the curriculum is initially through Welsh. Recently, in a few Welsh-medium schools, the presence of children who speak first languages other than Welsh and English, requires additional consideration in terms of refugee education, asylum-seeker education and immigrant language support. Such children become fluent in both English and Welsh, and access the curriculum through English and Welsh. The result is that a modern teacher in Welsh-medium education is sometimes engaged in the language and curriculum development of children for whom English or Welsh or another language is dominant, with pressure for excellent curriculum outcomes as well as language competency outcomes.

Third, Welsh-medium education is not special in terms of being historic. Bilingual education goes back more than five thousand years to the Ancient World. In Luxembourg, bilingual education commenced in the 1840s and trilingual education in 1913. Although Wales is naturally proud of its history of Welsh-medium education, which is often dated back to 1939 for primary education and 1956 for secondary education, we do not have the longest history.

Yet Welsh-medium education is special because of the historic treasury of parents, personalities, power and politics that is so well represented in this book. What this collection reveals is that we are special in terms of grassroots movements as distinct from top-down language planning; there are special individuals who have made a unique contribution through ambition and vision, commitment and supervision. There is no understanding of Welsh-medium education except through politics and power, and through aspirations, assertiveness and ambition.

Welsh-medium education has been a foundational element in language planning and in fostering Welsh identity, a growing belief in self-government and self-regulation, and an ever-increasing self-respect among those whose forerunners had been disempowered by monolingual education, disadvantaged because their bilingualism was not celebrated and recognised and subjected to attacks on their self-esteem; they had experienced minimal self-regulation yet demonstrated maximal resilience.

The book portrays such paradoxes of Welsh education: sometimes special and definitely unique; once repressed but now resilient; powered by parents and personalities, yet surrounded by politics and power. The proud history of the movement has shaped a hope for the future in its contribution to language renewal, cultural diversity and, not least, the high-quality education of successive generations.

Welsh-medium education has a special place in Welsh-language history, hearts and hopes. 'Mae gan addysg cyfrwng-Cymraeg le arbennig yn hanes yr iaith Gymraeg ac yng nghalonnau a gobeithion y Cymry.'

Preface and acknowledgements

Colin H. Williams

I have previously described the growth of Welsh-medium education in Wales as one of the little miracles of post-Napoleonic Europe and as a gesture of faith that the world can be changed in some small, but significant, way. I am sure that many of the first generation of active promoters and parents for Welsh-medium education in the 1950s would be astonished at the subsequent growth in that sector that we have witnessed in the past generation. And yet, we cannot be fully confident that the merits of a Welsh-medium education and training are an undisputed shared value within contemporary Welsh society. There remains a constant need for evidence-based policy and innovative promotional work to sustain the message that quite distinct forms of value can be added to a person's socialisation through the acquisition of two or more languages and the reproduction of the associated cultures.

To that end the Language, Policy and Planning Research Unit, School of Welsh at Cardiff University was established to analyse and scrutinise developments in contemporary Welsh society within an international comparative context. The LPPRU has a long-standing interest in language policy and planning and in aspects of education practice and policy. In the past we have dealt with issues of bilingual education, second language acquisition, investigations into the needs of the Welsh for Adults sector and the potential for improving the adoption of Welsh as a language for instruction in a number of disciplines within the University sector.

This current volume is derived from a sustained research investigation of the development of Welsh-medium education in south-east Wales. Previous publications derived from the project have tended to be in Welsh (Thomas 2007; 2010). However, I was concerned that much of the evidence and the accompanying interpretation and recommendations, which could have a wider impact on parents, decision-makers and fellow travellers, was sustained by discussion of the themes raised by the research available in English; hence this volume. I am confident that similar investigations, both within other sub-regions of Wales and at the national and comparative international level, would pay dividends, for we tend to take for granted the self-evident nature of such education.

Yet as we know, having recently established a new language regime, undergirded by the Welsh Language (Wales) Measure 2011 and the Welsh Language Commissioner, April 2012, there will be newer and perhaps more challenging issues to face as we construct a bilingual society within an increasingly multicultural context in Wales. How we approach and seek to integrate 'new speakers' and convince recalcitrant or downright hostile opponents of the value of such trends will be a certain test of our ability to shape sustained arguments in favour of the developments reported upon in this volume.

A number of acknowledgements are in order. I wish to thank the contributors for their ready response when asked to prepare interpretations of the development of Welsh-medium education from their various perspectives. In addition thanks are due to Tim Pearce for preparing the maps, Professor Barrie Long and Dr Burt Sellick for stylistic improvements and Dr Guto Thomas for clarifying a number of European matters.

Generous financial support for the publication of this volume was provided by Councillor Phil Bevan, Caerffili; Cronfa Glyndŵr; the Caerffili branch of RhAG; and Cardiff University and its School of Welsh, and we are extremely grateful to the above for their encouragement of this work. We also wish to thank the staff at the University of Wales Press for their diligence in bringing this volume to publication. On a more personal note I am delighted to acknowledge the excellent convivial and productive relationship which Huw and I have shared these many years.

List of Maps, Figures and Tables

Maps showing location of Ysgolion Cymraeg in south-east Wales

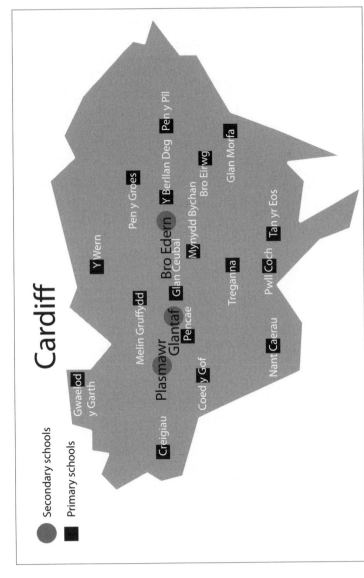

Map 1: Cardiff (1974–96 was part of South Glamorgan)

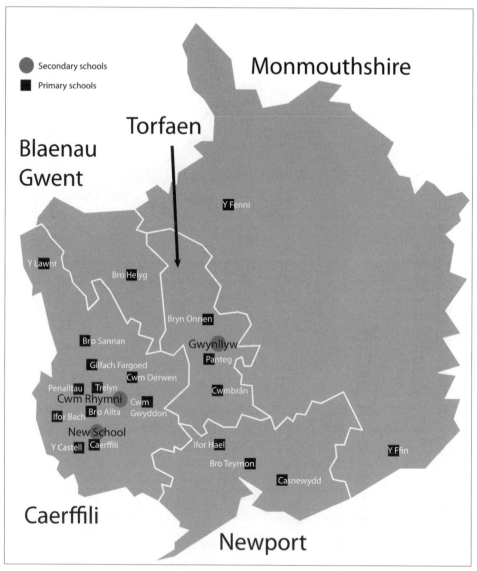

Map 2:
Newport, Monmouthshire, Torfaen, Blaenau Gwent (1974–96 constituted
most of Gwent) and Caerffili (1974–96 was part of Gwent
but mostly of Mid Glamorgan)

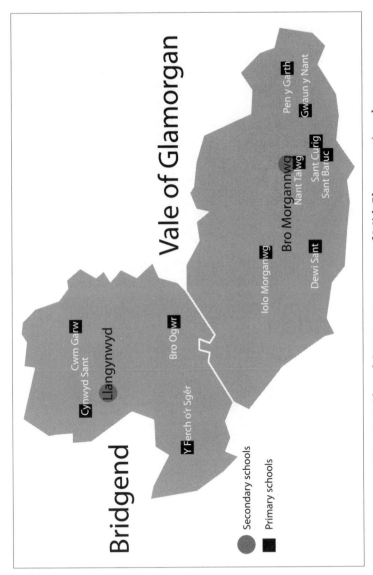

Map 3: Bridgend (1974–96 was part of Mid Glamorgan) and
Vale of Glamorgan (1974–96 was part of South Glamorgan)

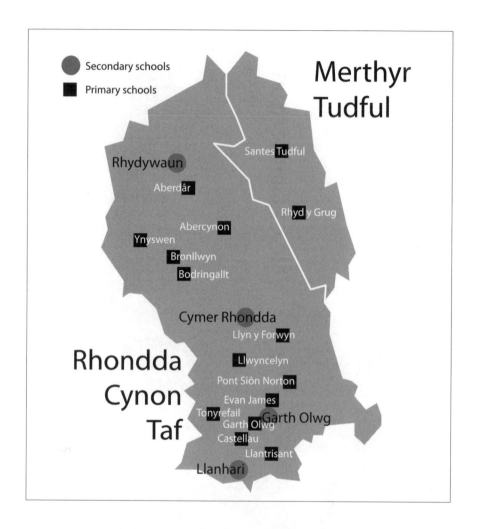

Map 4:
Rhondda Cynon Taf and Merthyr Tudful (1974–96 constituted
most of Mid Glamorgan)

Notes on Contributors

Colin Baker was Professor of Education and Pro Vice-Chancellor at Bangor University, Wales. He is the author of sixteen books and over sixty other texts on bilingualism and bilingual education, with specific interests in language planning and bilingual education. He is a past member of the Welsh Language Board.

David Hawker, an independent education consultant and Visiting Professorial Fellow at the Institute of Education, University of London, was formerly Director General of Education for Wales.

Meirion Prys Jones was Chief Executive of the Welsh Language Board until its demise in 2012 and an expert on Welsh-medium education and educational strategies in Europe. He is currently Chief Executive of the NPLD, the Network to Promote Linguistic Diversity in Europe.

Michael L. N. Jones practised as a solicitor in Cardiff for many years and is a former Chair and current Legal Adviser to RhAG (Rhieni Dros Addysg Gymraeg/ Parents for Welsh-Medium Education; see *http://www.RhAG.net*).

The Right Honourable *Rhodri Morgan* was Cardiff West MP (1987–2001), Assembly Member for Cardiff West (1999–2011) and First Minister of the National Assembly for Wales (2000–9).

Geraint Rees has been a leading Education Officer within Welsh local government at Cardiff County Council and is a former headteacher of Ysgol Gyfun Plasmawr, Cardiff. He is currently executive headteacher of the federation of two English-medium secondary schools in the city.

Jeni Price is a specialist in education who formerly worked at the Welsh Language Board, Cardiff.

Huw S. Thomas is a former headteacher of Ysgol Gyfun Gymraeg Glantaf, Cardiff and is currently a member of the Language, Policy and Planning Research Unit of the School of Welsh, Cardiff University. He is the editor of a Latin-Welsh Dictionary (UWP 1979), and in 2010 the same press published his acclaimed volume *Brwydr i Baradwys?*

Colin H. Williams is Research Professor and Director of the Language, Policy and Planning Research Unit at the School of Welsh, Cardiff University, and the author/editor of numerous volumes on sociolinguistics and language policy in multicultural societies, ethnic and minority relations and political geography. He is a past member of the Welsh Language Board.

Abbreviations

ACAC	Curriculum and Assessment Authority for Wales
ACCAC	Curriculum, Qualifications and Assessment Authority for Wales
ALN	Additional learning needs
AP	Average points
AS	Advanced Supplementary
BICS	Basic interpersonal communicative skills
c	Chapter
CAER	Cymdeithas Addysg Ewrop y Rhanbarthau/Education Society of the European Regions
CALP	Cognitive academic language proficiency
CCET	Community Consortium for Education and Training
CE	Council of Europe
CFR	Council on Foreign Relations
CIG	Cymdeithas yr Iaith Gymraeg/Welsh Language Society
CILAR	Committee on Irish Language Attitudes Research
COMEX	Committee of Experts
CP	County Primary
CSE	Certificate of Secondary Education
CSI	Core Subject Indicator
CSPM	EU Civil Society Platform on Multilingualism
CWIP	City-Wide Investment Plan
CYDAG	Cymdeithas Ysgolion dros Addysg Gymraeg/Association of Schools for Welsh-medium Education
CYPP	Children and Young People's Partnership
CYPSE	Children, Young People and School Effectiveness
DCELLS	Department for Children, Education, Lifelong Learning and Skills
DELLS	Department for Education, Lifelong Learning and Skills
DES	Department of Education and Science
DfES	Department for Education and Skills
DiDA	Diploma in Digital Applications
EBLUL	European Bureau of Lesser Used Languages
ELEN	European Languages Equality Network
ELWa	Education and Learning Wales
EU	The European Union
FE	Further education
FSM	Free school meals
FUEN	Federal Union of European Nationalities

GCE	General Certificate of Education
GCSE	General Certificate of Secondary Education
GIDS	Graded Intergenerational Disruption Scale
GP	General Practitioner
HABE	*Helduen Alfabetatze Berreuskalduntzerako Erakundea*
HE	Higher Education
HEFCW	Higher Education Funding Council for Wales
HMI	Her Majesty's Inspector
INSET	In-service training
JP	Justice of the Peace
KS	Key stage
LA	Local authority
LEA	Local education authority
LHR	Linguistic human rights
MEP	Member of the European Parliament
MLR	Minority language rights
MP	Member of Parliament
NAfW	National Assembly for Wales
NAW	National Assembly for Wales
NFER	National Foundation for Educational Research
NGfL	National Grid for Learning
NGfL Cymru	National Grid for Learning Wales
NGO	Non-Governmental Organisation
NPLD	Network to Promote Linguistic Diversity
NUT	National Union of Teachers
OED	Oxford English Dictionary
OHMCI	Office of Her Majesty's Chief Inspector
par.	paragraph
PDAG	Pwyllgor Datblygu Addysg Gymraeg/Committee for the Development of Welsh-medium Education
PFI	Private finance initiative
pl.	plural
PSI	Popular schools initiative
PTA	Parents' and Teachers' Association
QAIT	Quality assessor information and training
R	Reason
RCT	Rhondda Cynon Taf
RE2	A government record of educational data
REF	Research Excellence Framework
RhAG	Rhieni dros Addysg Gymraeg/Parents for Welsh-medium Education
RLS	Reversing language shift

S	Statement
s	section
SATs	Standard assessment tests
SEN	Special educational needs
SENTW	Special Educational Needs Tribunal for Wales
SHELL	Skills, Higher Education and Lifelong Learning
UCAC	Undeb Cenedlaethol Athrawon Cymru
UK	United Kingdom
USA	United States of America
WAG	Wales Assembly Government
WESP	Welsh in Education Strategic Plan
WG	Welsh Government
WLC	Welsh Language Commissioner
WO	Welsh Office
WJEC	Welsh Joint Education Committee
WLB	Welsh Language Board
Y	Year/years

Glossary of Terms

Additional learning needs (ALN)	The term 'additional learning needs' is used to identify pupils whose learning needs are additional to the majority of their peers. The term 'special educational needs' is a subcategory of additional learning needs, used to identify those learners who have severe, complex and/or specific learning difficulties as set out within the Education Act 1996 and the SEN Code of Practice for Wales. (Estyn, 2011)
Adferwyr	Members of Mudiad Adfer (Renewal Movement), a splinter group of Cymdeithas yr Iaith Gymraeg (Welsh Language Society) formed in the 1970s. They believed in creating a monoglot region (Y Fro Gymraeg) in predominantly Welsh-speaking areas of west Wales.
A level	General Certificate of Education at advanced level.
achievement	'[H]ow well learners are doing in relation to their ability and the progress they make.' (Estyn 2006a: 91)
AS level	Advanced subsidiary level: an examination taken between GCSE and A level.
attainment	'[H]ow well learners are doing, as measured in national tests and in the qualifications or credits they gain.' (Estyn 2006a: 91)
Core Subject Indicator	'This indicator shows the percentage of pupils who attain the level expected of them in each of mathematics, science and either English or Welsh as a first language.' (Estyn 2006a: 92)
Cwricwlwm Cymreig	'This is part of the National Curriculum [in Wales] that helps pupils to develop and apply knowledge and understanding of the cultural, economic, environmental, historical and linguistic characteristics of Wales.' (Estyn 2006a: 100)
Cymmrodorion	The Honourable Society of Cymmrodorion, a Society founded in 1751 which promotes the literature, arts and sciences of special interest to Wales, the Welsh people and those interested in Wales.

ethnolinguistic	'pertaining to the branch of linguistics concerned with the relations between linguistic and cultural behaviour.' (OED)
ethnolinguistics	'the branch of linguistics concerned with the relations between linguistic and cultural behaviour.' (OED)
GCSE	A UK public examination in specific subjects mainly for 14–16 year olds. It is generally taken in a range of subjects.
intergenerational	occurring between generations; from one generation to the next.
intergenerational transmission of language	one generation passing a language on to the next.
linguistics	the scientific study of language and its structures.
Llais Gwynedd	Llais Gwynedd (or Voice of Gwynedd) is a small centre-left political party based in Gwynedd in north Wales. Its ideology is Welsh nationalism and Gwynedd regionalism.
Local (Education) Authority (LEA, LA)	An administrative unit of local government that has responsibility for state education within its jurisdiction. Since 2010 the term LEA has ceased to be in official use.
Menter Iaith	'A Menter (pl. Mentrau) Iaith, or language initiative, is a local organisation which offers support to communities to increase and develop their use of the Welsh language. A Menter Iaith usually services a whole county and it reflects the wish of local people to make more use of the language. A Menter will offer advice and assistance to individuals, organisations and businesses, and will organise activities to raise the profile of the Welsh language.' (Mentrau Iaith Cymru website)
mutations	'In common with other Celtic languages, Welsh shows a phenomenon known as initial mutation in which the initial consonant of a word changes as a function of its lexical and syntactic context.' (Boyce, Browman and Goldstein 1987: 6). For example, ci (a dog), y ci (the dog), ei gi (his dog), ei chi (her dog), gwelaf gi (I see a dog), gallaf weld ci (I can see a dog), gallaf weld, weithiau, gi yn croesi'r stryd (I can see, sometimes, a dog crossing the street). Words starting with a vowel may also aspirate (add 'h' to their initial letter); for example, oren ac afal, ein horen a'n hafal (our orange and apple). (Thomas 1996: 704)

National Vocational Qualification (NVQ)	'A National Vocational Qualification is a work-related qualification that reflects the skills and knowledge needed to do a job effectively. These qualifications are organised into five levels based on the knowledge and skills needed for a particular job.' (Estyn 2007: 87)
normalisation (language or linguistic)	Originally popularised within Catalan and Spanish experience, the term has been applied to a variety of processes and contexts. The significant feature of the concept is that it seeks to suggest either a return to a previous state of a language's widespread use, or a future consideration as an 'integral' and 'normal' part of society. The term has become popular in Wales to describe a similar process of achieving co-equality between English and Welsh within certain contexts and, perhaps most intriguingly, as a psychological precept, whereby it is increasingly assumed that Welsh and English should be treated on the basis of equality.
percentage point	'For example, an increase from 30% to 33% is an increase of three percentage points, not a 3% increase (it is in fact a 10% increase).' (Estyn 2006a: 98)
reversing language shift (RLS)	Shift refers to a shift in the number of speakers of a language; in RLS it means a decline. Reversing the shift refers to language revitalisation, language revival and strategies by individuals or groups, private or state-funded, to achieve an increase in the number of speakers, thus reversing the decline or shift. RLS is a process or step along the way to save a language. RSL and saving a language are therefore not synonymous.
RhAG	Rhieni dros Addysg Gymraeg (Parents for Welsh-medium Education) is a pressure group with which government (local and central) consults regularly, and is often instrumental in the planning of Welsh-medium provision and the strategic location of new schools.
societal	'to do with a social mode of life, the customs and organization of a civilized society.' (OED)
sociolinguistic	'pertaining to language in its social functions.' (OED)
sociolinguistics	'the study of language in relation to social functions.' (OED)

Special educational needs (SEN)	This i a subcategory of Additional learning needs. (Estyn, 2011)
Tynged yr Iaith	The Fate of the [Welsh] Language "'Restoring the Welsh language in Wales is nothing less than a revolution. It is only through revolutionary means that we can succeed." This was the defiant message of Saunders Lewis in one of the most important broadcasts in the history of Wales, the BBC Annual Lecture delivered on 13 February 1962. His lecture had a dramatic effect. He called on the people of Wales to refuse to complete forms, pay taxes or licences if it was not possible to do so through the medium of Welsh . . . Although the number of Welsh speakers was falling, he proclaimed that the Welsh language could be saved'. (National Library of Wales)
Urdd	Urdd Gobaith Cymru (literally the Order of Hope for Wales), a Welsh-language movement established in 1922 for children and young people to socialise in Welsh. It provides a range of cultural and sporting activities both locally and in residential centres across Wales, and has announced the Message of Peace and Goodwill to the world since 1925.
value added	'Some children will always find it difficult to do well in tests and examinations. But all children are capable of making progress and it is important that schools are given recognition for the work that they do with these children. The progress that schools help individuals to make relative to their different starting points is usually referred to as value added. Value added measures are intended to allow comparisons between schools with different pupil intakes. For example, school A might show high percentages of pupils achieving five or more GCSE/GNVQs at grades A*–C, while school B shows lower percentages. But in value added terms, the pupils at school B may have made more progress than other pupils who were performing at the same level at KS2, and therefore have a higher value added 'score' than school A.' (DfES 2004)
Xish	A language under threat, for example Welsh. It may also be used adjectivally.
Xishness	The feeling of belonging to the Xish identity.

Xmen	Speakers of X.
XSL	Xish as a second language.
Yish	A stronger and therefore threatening language in a country or region, for example English in Wales. It may also be used adjectivally.
Yishness	The feeling of belonging to the Yish identity.
Ymen	Speakers of Y.
Ysgol Gymraeg	A Welsh-medium school (pl. Ysgolion Cymraeg).

Chapter 1

Ysgolion Cymraeg:
An Act of Faith in the Future of Welsh

Colin H. Williams

INTRODUCTION

Parents, Personalities and Power: Welsh-medium Schools in South-east Wales is written to encourage those engaged in the promotion of Welsh-medium activities to reflect on some of the underlying forces which animate the drive towards a more robust system of education in Wales. It is also written to inform parents and future parents who may be considering sending their children to Welsh-medium schools of the historical background and central issues which have shaped the current provision of schooling. Typically educational professionals focus on teacher-training methods, pupils' learning strategies, the cognitive processing of information and the acquisition of skills, class-room organisation, curriculum development, language policy across the curriculum, school management, budgetary issues and the like. Our focus in this volume is on the interaction between the structure of national and local authority control of education and the agency of parents and key individuals whose actions have helped shape the system of education we currently enjoy.

Education, the bedrock upon which the Welsh language movement has flourished, has fulfilled five functions.[1] Firstly, it has legitimised Welsh bilingualism as a social phenomenon within this most critical agency of socialisation.[2] Secondly, it has developed the value of bilingual skills in a range of new domains, especially in terms of meeting some of the demands of the burgeoning bilingual economy and largely public-sector labour market. Thirdly, for some it has been and remains a focus of a

1

national project of identity reformulation. For many engaged in the language struggle, education was the principal focus and justification for their involvement. For such individuals the advancement of Welsh-medium education was both a personal and a national cause. The growth of Ysgolion Cymraeg was not merely an extension of the state's education policy in Wales, but a struggle for recognition and the right to survive, the more so as it required tremendous energy, conviction and perspicuity in arguing the case for the provision of bilingual education, often in the face of a hostile and unsympathetic response from politicians, local authorities, fellow professionals and many parents.[3] Fourthly, the Welsh-medium educational infrastructure, from the nursery school level right through to the university sector, has provided a series of distinctive, interlocking, sociocultural networks, which have validated and reinforced developments at each level in the hierarchy. This has been crucial in the cultivation of a sense of national purpose for professional bodies such as Undeb Cenedlaethol Athrawon Cymru and Mudiad Ysgolion Meithrin, as well as for pioneering local education authorities such as Flintshire, Glamorgan and, since 1974, for Gwynedd Education Authority, which has had the most comprehensive bilingual system of all local authorities.[4] Fifthly, as bilingual education has been both academically and socially successful, it has served as an additional marker of the country's distinctiveness within both a British and an international context.

A great deal of work has been undertaken previously on the relationship between bilingual education and cultural identity, between the use of Welsh and English in the schools of Wales (Baker 1985) and in following the inspirational lead given by Professor Jac L. Williams, in popularising the results of educational enquires so as to inform the choice of parents in Wales (Jones and Ghuman 1995). Similarly cameos of the development of individual Welsh-medium schools, such as Ysgol Gymraeg Rhymni (Heulwen Williams 2005) or the Welsh-medium sector as a whole (Williams 2002; 2003) have provided an invaluable record of achievement.

But as education forms part of the common wealth of any society it is appropriate that it be constantly critiqued and evaluated, the more so when elements within the education sector are the source of some disquiet or overt hostility. Nowhere has this been more prevalent than in the growth of Welsh-medium education in south-east Wales, the subject of this volume.

2

Parents, Personalities and Power: Welsh-medium Schools in South-east Wales is an apt title for this volume as so much of the resultant and ongoing dynamism of Welsh-medium education derives from having to overcome inherent prejudice and structured opposition to the growth of this 'intrusive' element within the schooling of the nation's youth. As with other cleavages in society, a separate language is often depicted as an element which keeps people apart, the more so if young children attend different types of school from a very early age, thus reproducing the 'dialogue of the deaf' which is said to characterise so many bilingual or multilingual societies.

'A WEALTH OF LIBERALITY'[5]

The driving force for the establishment and mainstreaming of Welsh-medium education in south-east Wales has been the unstinting commitment of parents, teachers, political leaders and activists, Welsh speakers and non-Welsh speakers alike. While most of the parents initially involved were Welsh born, not all were fully convinced that a Welsh-medium education was the best option for their children. Even today, for some, the picture is clouded, the arguments confusing and the available pattern of education daunting if not entirely complex. Typically many parents have sent one or more of their children to a 'normal' English-medium school, while another child may have attended a Welsh-medium school. The home language use may be mixed, Welsh and English, with one or more child speaking Welsh to only one of the parents or a guardian or, more typically today, with a sibling or a grandparent.

Conscious that without the driving force of parental power Welsh-medium education in industrial, anglicised Wales would not have flourished, this volume is a tribute to the parents who have been the bedrock and dynamic pressure in the promotion and extension of Welsh-medium schools. I am a product of Ysgol Feithrin Y Barri (1952–5), Ysgol Sant Ffransis Y Barri (1955–62)[6] and Ysgol Uwchradd Rhydfelen (1962–9), one of the very few who entered the school in its first year of existence and thus 'enjoyed' or 'endured' the pioneering days of Welsh-medium education.

A word on my own parents, Islwyn Williams (1914–94) and Irene Margaret Haslehurst (1912–73). My father's family was from farming stock in Llanbadarn Fawr, Ceredigion and Alltwen, Glamorgan, while my mother's family were bourgeois merchants, designers and shipbuilders in Poole, Dorset. They met as young people in Barry, Glamorgan, where their respective families had relocated in the late 1920s. After their marriage in 1945 they became very active in the promotion of Welsh-medium education in south-east Wales and in the sociocultural life of Barry and Wales. My father, who worked in the Planning Department of the Port of Barry, was a talented and inspirational musician, *arweinydd y gân* in Tabernacle Chapel, Barry for many decades, conductor of many brass bands in south Wales, including Barry Town Silver Band, Tongwynlais and Vale of Glamorgan Band, secretary of the Brass Band Association and a tutor in the Glamorgan County Youth Music scene for over forty years. My mother and Mrs Ceinwen Clarke were the first voluntary teachers of Ysgol Feithrin y Barri and there, from 1950 until her death in 1973, my mother shepherded generations of children taking their faltering first steps in schooling and socialisation.[7] Both she and Mrs Clarke were tireless advocates of Welsh-medium education and my mother in particular was a joyful ambassador of the advantages of bilingualism as she, with many others, encouraged parents throughout south Wales to establish nursery and primary schools, initially in the 1950s and then, following their involvement in the establishment of Ysgol Uwchradd Rhydfelen in 1962, in the promotion of sister schools in Llanhari, Bargod (Cwm Rhymni) and Cardiff (Glantaf). My mother's convictions had little to do with formal politics or Welsh nationalism. For her the issue of the availability of Welsh-medium education was essentially a matter of social justice and quality of life, a perspective which I share.

But given that this volume has the central theme of parents, personalities and power running through it, looking back on my childhood I am acutely conscious of how people such as my parents were criticised by friends and others on a number of grounds. Typically a number of criticisms would be levelled against them for their choice and determination to live through the medium of Welsh, for 'wasting' their child's education on a dead language such as Welsh, for making young children travel long distances to school, for taking them out of their community so that they would have few friends in the local area and for breeding 'nationalists' in adulthood as a result of having had a separate education in a poorly resourced school with no reputation compared with the excellent local grammar school at

4

Barry. In many ways my mother's response is captured in this chapter's title; hers was an act of faith, of conviction and of hope.

THE STRUCTURE OF THIS VOLUME

This volume is a product of the Language Policy and Planning Research Unit of the School of Welsh, Cardiff University.[8] The School of Welsh has had a long interest in the development of Welsh-medium and bilingual education, whether at statutory education, further and higher level, Welsh for Adults or in-service training of professionals such as teachers and medical practitioners. Earlier research related to bilingualism in the school has focused on threshold levels of Welsh (Jones et al. 1996), the reorganisation of ELWa and bilingual education policy (Williams 2001), the growth and development of Welsh-medium schools in south-east Wales (Thomas 2007) and the impact which legislative devolution and the Welsh Language Measure (2011) has on the construction of a bilingual society (Williams 2011).

Demographic trends, migration patterns and Welsh-language learning trends also add to the mix and inform parental choice as to the type of school to which they would wish to send their children, and of the consequences for educational achievement and attainment, linguistic diversity and community integration. Hardly any of these choices are informed by authoritative, sustained analysis and debate. There have been some earlier volumes which seek to record the achievements of the Welsh-medium schools in Wales, such as that edited by Professor Iolo Wyn Williams, *Our Children's Language* (2003), but nothing recently and certainly nothing which purports to bring together in a single volume the views of several of the key agencies and partners in the development of Welsh-medium and bilingual education. Thus I am confident that this volume will have a significant impact and contribute in a timely fashion to the public debate as well as helping inform perspective parents as to the advantages and perceived disadvantages of maintaining the current level and type of provision of Welsh-medium and bilingual education.

A specific concern of the editors and all participants in this volume was how to diffuse the findings of our research so that its main results, insights and recommendations would generate the interest and attention of two target audiences, namely parents and future parents of school-aged pupils in Wales and decision makers at national and local levels. We have consciously designed this volume so that it appeals to the interested lay reader, the informed parent and others who share an interest in social developments in Wales and beyond.

The editors first met in the 1960s when we were both involved, in markedly different ways, in the formative days of the development of Ysgol Uwchradd Rhydfelen. I attended as one of the first cohort of pupils who entered the school in September 1962 and Huw Thomas, who taught Latin, later became my sixth form master. In 1981 Huw Thomas left Rhydfelen to become the first headteacher of Ysgol Gyfun Cwm Rhymni and he decided that Welsh would be the medium for all subjects at all levels, a natural progression from his previous school where all subjects bar mathematics and sciences were taught in Welsh. He subsequently became headteacher of Ysgol Gyfun Gymraeg Glantaf, Cardiff in 1985, from which influential position he retired in 2003. Having been exercised by the need to pursue in-depth research on the context within which such schools operated, he joined me in the School of Welsh at Cardiff University to undertake a detailed study of the influences on the growth of the Ysgolion Cymraeg in south-east Wales. The results of that investigation were published in Welsh as *Brwydr i Baradwys?* (Thomas 2010).

I was conscious that the very fine empirical evidence and the strategic recommendations which derived from this work would not be readily available to much of the target audience for Welsh-medium education, as many of the parents and well-wishers are unable to understand Welsh. My time as a member of the Welsh Language Board (2000–10) with a particular interest in policy and strategy also convinced me that many members of the general public with whom we interacted at WLB open days, public meetings and in dealing with their complaints had a misguided or exaggerated view of where power lay, and of who was responsible for what in terms of educational matters.[9]

Consequently this volume consists of two parts. Part one analyses the structures and processes which have shaped the development of Welsh-medium education in our region, while part two provides the opportunity for key players within the education system and political life to offer their own perspectives on the state of play of Welsh-medium challenges and advances of late.

PART ONE:
ADVANCES IN WELSH-MEDIUM EDUCATION

Rather than provide a summary history of the education sector as a whole, we have chosen to interrogate the more significant variables which have influenced the resultant pattern of Welsh-medium provision. As will be demonstrated in chapters 2 and 3, we were convinced that the growth of the Ysgolion Cymraeg in south-east Wales (from 3 in 1949 to almost 80 today, including growth from 1 comprehensive in 1962 to 12 by 2013, 15 if one includes the whole of the original Rhydfelen catchment area) could not be critiqued without due attention the evolution of the Welsh language in terms of its demographic and geolinguistic growth, the increase in a feeling of Welshness and the concomitant acquisition of Welsh as a marker of such identity, the political maturation of the NAfW as a legislative body and the increased relevance of the Welsh Government to the quality of life of all residents in Wales.

The interdependence of language, identity, education and political momentum thus required a more holistic approach to policy critique than had hitherto been attempted. Earlier work emanating from the very fine advances of Joshua Fishman (1991) and Stephen May (2001)[10] had drawn attention to the need for systematic approaches to critiquing influential models of language revitalisation, such as reversing language shift (RLS), as illustrated by Fishman's Graded Intergenerational Disruption Scale (GIDS). But such attempts had also been severely criticised for not fully understanding the internal dynamics of Welsh-medium education, both in terms of analysing power and ideology as detailed by Glyn Williams (Williams 1987) and Colin Williams (Williams 1988; 1999) and in terms of the personalities who animated the structures and systems as portrayed by the material in Iolo Wyn Williams's significant collection of original source material (Williams 2002; 2003).

Thus chapter 2 sets out some of the key characteristics of the growth of Ysgolion Cymraeg and comments on their contemporary vitality in terms of the pupils' home language background, school organisation, the standards of teaching and learning and considerations of value added to the school's overall performance by its management and teaching strategies. Huw Thomas tackles head on the much-heard criticism that such schools 'over-achieve' precisely because a significant proportion of the children come from a 'privileged' social background. Remember that we are describing industrial south Wales, thus 'privilege' is a relative concept and the suburbs of Cardiff, Bridgend or Pontypridd cannot be compared with Epsom, Alderley Edge, Wilmslow, Knowle or Bearsden in terms of median income, life style or intergenerational transfer of wealth. This is slightly disingenuous though as in the latter areas a much higher proportion of children attend fee-paying schools and we are thus not comparing like with like in terms of examination results league tables or any other comparator indices. Nevertheless the study does reveal that the Welsh-medium schools do indeed add value as a result of their dynamic nature and academic aspirations. But recall that a large proportion of children are being formally examined in a language that is neither their mother tongue nor the language of the educational support system which reinforces the hegemony of English in the provision of teaching materials and specialist information derived from the mass media and available as a result of advances in IT and interactive learning developments.

Chapter 3 deals with the interdependence of language, identity and education. The contribution and impact of the Ysgol Gymraeg to this social psychological interplay is evaluated by reference to Joshua Fishman's framework for measuring ethnolinguistic vitality. His Graded Inter-generational Disruption Scale (GIDS) is a standard means of measuring progress in theories of Reversing Language Shift (RLS). Thomas applies the framework to the schools in his study region and suggests that teaching all subjects through the medium of Welsh exemplifies Welsh as a dynamic, evolving language and consequently the schools function as symbols of modernity and progress. He is particularly taken with Fishman's concentration on the role of key actors in the RLS framework and suggests that Fishman's greatest contribution to language planning in Wales is the manner in which his probing and insights have sharpened our intellectual understanding and reflections on the whole of the system per se and not just its constituent elements. I would concur with this, even if my own interpretation of RLS efforts has been more critical in the past (Williams 2005).

One of the difficulties which both RLS efforts and the discursive literature have is with the concept of linguistic normalisation. Originally popularised within Catalan and Spanish experience the term has been applied to a variety of processes and contexts. The significant feature of the concept is its normative implications, in that it seeks to suggest either a return to a previous state of a language's widespread use, or a future consideration as an 'integral', 'normal' part of society. Mar-Molinero (2011) has characterised the term thus:

> Besides implying the promotion of Catalan, Basque and Galician to equal status with Spanish, 'normal' is also understood to refer to their previous historical status. This is especially true for Catalan, a high prestige language in the Middle Ages and widely used during the1930s. In this way, then, normalization encompasses both the idea of linguistic equality for minority Spanish languages, and their role as identity markers for their communities.

The term has become popular in Wales to describe a similar process of achieving coequality between English and Welsh within certain contexts and perhaps most intriguingly as a psychological precept, whereby it is increasingly assumed that Welsh and English should be treated on the basis of equality. The implications of Welsh navigating into the mainstream are treated here and more specifically in the closing chapter.

The interpretation concludes with an affirmation that as a result of political maturation the Welsh education system is now more professional and secure as a result of having abandoned ad hoc pragmatism to embracing evidence-based policy making. However, as successive chapters will demonstrate, even within this climate of planning and strategic overviews, the local application of policy, as in the case of Cardiff's Welsh-medium schools, can remain problematic and conflictual.

Chapter 4 goes to the heart of the volume, namely the many faces of power which are at work in the construction and maintenance of a parallel, separate, but equal education system. By adopting some key principles from structuration theory (Giddens 1984) Thomas is able to demonstrate how power is distributed throughout the education system, particularly in terms of various actors' ability to allocate resources. He writes, of course, as a former headteacher who is well used to grappling with budgetary requirements, the demands for capital expenditure on new buildings, the equipping of science laboratories and the like, let alone the dominant unit of expenditure, namely teachers' salaries.

A critical element of the exercise of power is social communication and a central feature in the strengthening of the Welsh schools movement has been the attempt to understand the parameters of the exercise of power by decision makers and civil servants. The bulk of the chapter details how various key actors have each interpreted their own role in the exercise of collective power and the application of strategic government guidelines such as those articulated in 'Iaith Pawb' (Williams 2004b) and the current Welsh Government education strategy (Williams 2011). In the new era of legislative devolution, the exercise of discretion by the Welsh Government in its policy application processes will doubtless increase. Thus it is vital for educational professionals and school managers to understand, as much as they are able, the institutional culture of governance, for thereby they are able to interpret the signs, seek to influence the agenda, and better represent their own sectoral interests.

Chapter 5 deals with the articulation of power in the real-world settings of Mid Glamorgan and Cardiff County Councils. In seeking to promote the development of Welsh-medium schools, directors of education, head-teachers, teachers' union representatives, and, most critically, parents' associations, were faced with the double helix of strong political leaders and county councillors and the initially overwhelming opposition of many parent groups to the establishment of Welsh-medium schools in their local area. What concerns us here is less the blow-by-blow account of how each and every Welsh-medium primary and secondary school was established, and more the recognition that all too often the pristine arguments of professionals and the demands of Rhieni dros Addysg Gymraeg (RhAG) (Parents for Welsh-medium Education) had to be filtered through powerful individuals within the Labour Party caucus if they were ever to be realised as bricks and mortar in the linguistic landscape of south Wales.

However questionable this background of party-political struggle or infighting may have been at times, this is the reality of policy debate and political calculus. The chapter pays due regard to the championing of the Welsh-medium schools by a variety of visionaries and political pragmatists, I would call them intelligent operators, from several party political back-grounds. Thus influential articulators such as Haydn Williams (director of education, Flintshire, 1941–65), Gwyn Daniel, Keith Price Davies, Gwilym Humphreys,[11] Gwilym Prys Davies, John Morris, Wyn Roberts and Emyr Currie-Jones[12] have each been lightening rods through which the energy of the Welsh schools movement has been channelled. Without these actors and their convictions, no amount of favourable goodwill towards the establishment of Welsh-medium schools would have produced the same results. Inherent in the exercise of power is a strong element of discretion and persuasion and both secretaries of state referenced above, John Morris and Wyn Roberts, exercised a great deal of coercion as well. As Hart (1963: 75) avers in the context of a different subject, namely the relationship between law and morality: 'this distinction between the use of coercion to enforce morality, and other methods which we use to preserve it, such as argument, advice and exhortation, is both very important and much neglected in discussions of the present topic'. I would seek to stretch this and suggest that enforcing a Welsh-medium education system and preserving it is a current topic of great import. I say this for there are real dangers that systemic erosion of the salience of the current strengths of the Welsh-medium pattern of education may be on the horizon as a result of government policies, local government school closure or amalgamation policies, legislative changes and, of course, the collective decisions of parents as will be discussed in the next chapter and in part two of this volume.

Chapter 6 draws out several strands which influence the immediate future of Welsh-medium education. They are an admixture of the pragmatic issues which face every parent or guardian, such as how to cope with homework and help at times to encourage greater motivation of their children as they experience the necessary difficulties of navigating their way through formal education, together with the more systemic and strategic issues, such as marketing the advantages of bilingualism within a Welsh-medium sector and planning for a balanced and exciting curriculum. Recall that the minister of education, Leighton Andrews, and the former director general of education, Dr Emyr Roberts (2010–12), have both committed themselves and their organisation, the DfES, to 'raising performance and standards' so that every child can reach its potential. Some of the change has to do with the restructuring and renaming of DCELLS (DfES since 1 April 2011) into two distinct parts, Children, Young People and School Effectiveness (CYPSE) and Skills, Higher Education and Lifelong Learning (SHELL), while other changes have involved clearer strategic aims and more backroom support for the realisation of education goals.[13]

Chapter 6 also contains a discussion of several of the challenges which DfES is attempting to overcome, such as the nature of the linguistic continuum in Welsh schools, the appropriate role of foreign-language teaching, the calibration in Wales of UK wide and European trends as regards pedagogy, the turn towards multilingualism rather than an over-reliance on bilingualism, official or otherwise, the specification of a linguistic and educational rights agenda in the light of the developing remit of the Welsh language commissioner for Wales and, of course, the articulation of power within the education system over the medium term.

Part one has treated the issue of Welsh-medium education, individual and societal bilingualism and power in nine distinct senses. It is, I think, probable that what Huw Thomas conceives as the several, separate instances of power, are in reality open to a variety of criticism if one does not share the ideological and cultural commitment to the Welsh language which he espouses. Here a certain discrimination is needed. But first, what are his nine vertices of power? In part one he has demonstrated that:

1. Parental power has been the main force driving the growth of the Ysgolion Cymraeg. The Ysgolion Cymraeg create their own identity, a bond of relationship with similar schools and the confidence that develops with success and being accepted as part of the normal provision. The 'movement' of Welsh-medium schools is micro-centred, in the sense that it campaigns for the next school in the locality. This is a bottom-up influence, from the micro level to the meso or local government level. It is also a counter-negative phenomenon, since parental power is determined to overcome any negativism or indifference on the part of the LA, or lack of vision by central government. His evidence has suggested that the parents' main reasons for choosing the Ysgol Gymraeg are a combination of commitment to the Welsh language, the Welsh identity, and the ethos and standards of the schools. However, the combination of reasons is extremely complex. (He recalls that in all parents recorded twenty-six different reasons.)
2. The power of the schools is that they have created a society that focuses parental aspirations on three vital elements: language and identity, a family relationship and ethos, and high standards and expectations.
3. Political power is one of the supportive forces, which varies in its influence not only during different periods of development but also from locality to locality.
4. The power of the centre to encourage further growth is the substantial potential which should be developed in the near future in order to realise the vision and aims of 'Iaith Pawb', a seminal document published by the government in 2003 and updated in 2011's language strategy. The Welsh Government Welsh-medium Education Strategy (2010) is central to further development of the Ysgolion Cymraeg.

5. The power of governance is the apparatus that should be used in order to develop a knowledgeable civic society which could promote a bilingual Wales.
6. The power of the Welsh language and identity is the spiritual force which unites supporters in a long and difficult struggle to save the language.
7. Potential power is the ability to plan in a coordinated, holistic way to serve the linguistic needs of the nation.
8. The power of the individual is the force that can inspire others to move mountains.
9. The power that has driven the Ysgolion Cymraeg has been a multilayered power.

Thus it is that we can reiterate the three main conclusions of the research described in part one to be:

1. that parent power and high quality education are the major factors in ensuring the success of the Ysgolion Cymraeg
2. that support by a variety of agencies varies over time and locality
3. that within political parties it is individuals, not the groups to which they belong, that have been the driving forces for change.

Parents, Personalities and Power: Welsh-medium Schools in South-east Wales thus makes the case for a greater appreciation of, and analysis by, the several actors who animate the system. Let us turn now in part two to several representative voices who have been asked to reflect on the findings of part one, to offer some criticism from their own valuable experience and to suggest future avenues for further work and improvements in the development of the educational sector in Wales or parts thereof.

PART TWO:
CRITICAL RESPONSES AND PERSPECTIVES

The results of our investigations are interrogated from a variety of perspectives so as to prompt a reaction to the strengths and weaknesses of the current Welsh-medium education provision from the viewpoint of parents, politicians, national and local decision makers, education policy implementers, strategists and government advisers. The resulting blend of professional and social reactions offers a very strong interpretation of 'where we are at' as regards current practice. We have encouraged the contributors to be as open and frank as they can be and to mix their professional with their personal observations.

This is an especially opportune and challenging time for the field of education. On a positive note, the recent legislative empowerment of the National Assembly for Wales guarantees that the twin issues of education and training and the Welsh language will receive a great deal of scrutiny in the coming years, the more so perhaps as the Welsh-language policy portfolio was transferred in the Cabinet changes of May 2011 from the heritage minister to the minister of education. This will doubtless impact on the current implementation of the Welsh-medium Education Strategy announced by WAG in 2010 and the greater role given to education as the cornerstone of the government's reformulation of its earlier 'Iaith Pawb' strategy to construct a bilingual society in 'A living language: A language for living' (2011). More contentiously there are the uncertainties associated with budgetary reductions and fiscal tightening at national and local authority level. This has already occasioned public debate, and some tension/anger at school closure and school amalgamation, relocation, and redesignation proposals in many parts of Wales.

One virtue of part two is the quality of the personnel we have assembled, who write in a clear, engaging manner with authority and insight but are always accessible and conscious of what Huw Thomas has written, so that the end result is a tightly organised collection of ideas, perspectives and responses to the core material presented in part one. It is evident that the contributors have been very influential decision makers in terms of the contours of Welsh-medium Education Strategy and its implementation.

That the position of Welsh-medium education has been strengthened is a significant development in its own right and is recorded in much more positive attitudes towards bilingualism and the construction of a bilingual society per se. However, beneath this positive trend there remains for many a grumbling doubt as to the real worth of bilingualism, for it is argued that once many pupils have left the confines of the school classroom there is little economic and instrumental justification for maintaining fluency in Welsh. Such judgements have far less purchase now than a decade ago for, as we shall see below, there has been a corresponding growth also in the value of bilingual skills within the workplace.

In chapter 7 David Hawker, the former head of DCELLS, places the future challenges of Welsh-medium education within the wide gamut of influences on both the demise and the current growth of the Welsh language. For Welsh-medium education to really make an impact on the nation, Hawker argues:

> [A] critical mass must be reached in the education system. In my view, the proportion of children who are educated wholly or mainly in Welsh will need to double, from the current 20 per cent plus, to around 40 per cent, if Welsh is to have a secure future as a genuine *lingua franca*. This is a tall order, and rather beyond the target of 30 per cent set out in the Welsh-medium Education Strategy (WAG 2010a).

Amongst the drivers and levers of power are parental demand and political will, but the question posed and discussed is whether it will last. Parental motivation, high achievers, a sense of pride and passion in the idea of Wales and Welshness all have their place. But over and against these positive elements he identifies a number of barriers, chief of which is that 'the political vision in some local authorities has not always matched these aspirations, with the result that they tend to lag behind parental demand in creating new Welsh-medium schools and housing them in decent accommodation'. He detects a weakening of the resolve of parents as many of these structural barriers seem too difficult to overcome. Consequently he believes that the national government should shoulder a far greater share of the responsibility and articulate a more convincing vision of how to achieve the goal of creating a bilingual society. He argues:

> This is why one of the key planks of the Government's Welsh-medium Education Strategy is a challenge to local authorities to become more ambitious in planning their Welsh-medium provision, on the basis that when the provision appears, the demand often increases as a result. By the same token, if there is a lack of such planning (perhaps due to lack of resources for building or converting schools), there is a danger that the impressive growth in provision which we have seen over the past fifteen to twenty years will slow to a standstill.

The chapter ends with a discussion of a different approach to Welsh-language education, but the author concludes with the difficult and challenging question as to whether Wales has the confidence to stand on its own two feet and to face the challenge of sustainability in Welsh-medium education.

Welsh-language education schemes have been renamed Welsh in Education Strategic Plans (from April 2012). The title change is far more than a tinkering with titles, as the questions posed (annually) by Welsh Government are strategic, probing, demanding, robust and detailed. The whole thrust of the documentation suggests a government that is determined to see its Welsh-medium policy succeed.

In chapter 8 Michael Jones reflects on parental power. His essay is a consideration of the historical contribution of parents to the development of Welsh-medium education since the 1930s. Important case study evidence is contained herein which leads the lawyer/writer to place the parents into two classes derived from legal philosophy, those whose contribution was a *sine qua non*, an underlying cause of development, an essential circumstance and those whose contribution was a *causa causans,* an exciting cause of development. At each and every turn the author cites the influential role of RhAG and of powerful individuals, many of whom went on from their campaigning days to become local authority officials, councillors, politicians and even judges. What is most revealing in the analysis is the number of times that local government reorganisation has occasioned difficulties. This difficult terrain is also explored by Geraint Rees (chapter 9) who corroborates Michael Jones's message that local government boundary changes have, in the main, slowed down the growth of the Ysgolion Cymraeg. Opportunities have, however, been created by such reorganisation, as Huw Thomas argues in chapter 4, when he discusses the establishment of new schools in the Vale of Glamorgan, Caerffili and Bridgend LAs. Michael Jones's chapter illustrates the rich and noble historical battles for Welsh-medium education, encapsulated in the final, provocative sentence: 'Parents favouring Welsh-medium education must always make a nuisance of themselves, enough of a nuisance to make it easier and cheaper to provide enough Welsh-medium places than not to do so.'

In chapter 9, Geraint Rees provides a local authority (LA) perspective. This chapter deals with the interaction of parents, LA officials and local councillors and illustrates a challenge that has emerged since 2010, caused by reorganisation and new policies that appear to have largely disregarded the needs of Welsh-medium pupils. The author analyses the responsibilities of LAs in the provision of Welsh-medium education. The main challenge facing Welsh-medium schools is to ensure that new political and administrative structures do not impede the growth of such schools.

While in the past the LAs were chiefly concerned with the provision of a sufficient number of places in Welsh-medium education, both the agenda and the expectations have changed. Rees argues that LAs and their partners now need to do more than plan a sufficiency of school places; the range of statutory and non-statutory targets included in the Welsh-medium Education Strategy also needs to be achieved. Demographic impulses notwithstanding, school reorganisation, as we shall see in relation to Cardiff Council in chapter 10, poses severe strains on the ability of a local authority to plan in a coherent and resource-efficient manner for the diverse educational needs of its constituent groups.

So much has been heard of the declining role and influence of local government as a result of increased centralisation and the pursuit of neo-liberal policies at the UK level that it is significant that Rees underlines the continued purchase which LAs have for the implementation of a range of policies designed to promote and regulate the interests of Welsh. A key role is to obtain consent and consensus in the planning of school provision and in the implementation of statutory consultation processes. Rees argues that:

> Because of the high profile given to the statutory consultation processes necessary to plan for the opening or closing of schools, it easy to under-estimate the significant wider contribution made by local authorities to the well-being of the Welsh language. The local authority contribution is crucial, not only in its planning and provision of sufficient school places, but also in its role in supporting leadership and management of schools, staff develop-ment, school transport and a plethora of other key roles.

This supportive infrastructure is essential in the consideration of education as a public good. But there are strong hints in the contribution that, once again, structural reform and systematic reorganisation of the functions, if not the statutory responsibilities, of public bodies, might slow down the growth in Welsh-medium education. He concludes, optimistically, that 'this challenge will be a considerable one to overcome'.

In chapter 10 Rhodri Morgan provides a rich cameo relating to school reorganisation in Canton, Cardiff. His subtitle reveals the line of argument in that it provides 'a lesson in how not to do it'. The ramifications and intricacies of educational, social and politically expedient considerations within the complex process of school closures are exemplified in this chapter, which centres on the issue of providing a replacement school for Ysgol Treganna, Cardiff. It underlines the need for proactive and politically astute decisions, particularly within local government. It also underlines the need for specialist advice and evidence-based critiques of future educational and demographic trends. The latter in particular is a central point with which all those responsible for educational provision in the UK would agree. What is most revealing about this authoritative interpretation by the former first minister for Wales, is the deft handling of the interplay between actors at different sites and levels within the political hierarchy, city and neighbourhood, local authority and Welsh Government, national assembly and political party. The direct intervention in the long-running dispute of the current first minister, Carwyn Jones, on 26 May 2010, effectively put an end to several years of speculation over the possible closure of Lansdowne Primary School. Rhodri Morgan argues that:

> in upholding the appeal by the parents, teachers and children of Lansdowne Primary to keep their school open, in effect he announced the rejection of the Liberal Democrat/Plaid Cymru administration's proposals for school reorganization in western Cardiff. Since that date, the campaigners' decision to stand firm in opposing the Council's various flawed proposals to deal with surplus places in English-medium and lack of places for Welsh-medium primary education in the west of Cardiff has been totally vindicated. Carwyn Jones's decision has also been totally vindicated despite the Council's threat of going to judicial review over it.

Now, of course, there is a central party political thread to all of this, which is why we invited Rhodri Morgan to contribute his perspective on the vicissitudes of education policy in south-east Wales. He chose to focus on developments within his own city and has provided an analysis which relates to changing tactics, to the issue of funding school reorganisation and resources at the Cardiff Council level in general, as well as the delicate balance between local authority responsibilities and national assembly powers. Leading national politicians, and indeed former ministers of education, have not previously sought to intervene overly in local educational issues, even if in reality the result of their financial deliberations often directs LAs to act in certain ways. This is precisely the exercise of the nuanced power, not to say coercion, which part one sought to explicate.

In a volume which celebrates the central role of parents and activists it is entirely fitting to highlight Morgan's final tribute to those who stuck to their guns. He concludes that 'the most remarkable aspect of this entire episode is the resolute refusal of the parents in the Lansdowne catchment area to withdraw their children from the school'. Clearly not all the parents involved would champion this intransigence, but in a democracy, where the deliberative element at times is valued over and above the outcome, this is a refreshing reminder of the exercise of real grounded power at the local level, the most intimate context within which the quality of life chances experienced by our own children is paramount. Of course, the sad element in this affair is the manner in which policy changes and political manipulations and U-turns pitted parent against parent and advocates of the expansion of Welsh-medium education against defenders of the status quo, a scenario anticipated more than twelve years ago in Jones and Williams's (2000) analysis of Cardiff's education policy, so aptly titled 'Reactive Policy and Piecemeal Planning'.

A strong case can also be made for the manner in which parents who supported the establishment of Ysgol Treganna as a Welsh-medium school exercised their power and influence on the city's authorities. The fact that a decision to establish a new Welsh-medium school with excellent facilities was announced by Cardiff Council in the spring of 2011 suggests that ultimately both sides in this dispute gained a victory. Some might argue that in a system which is ostensibly charged with creating a bilingual society, this sort of fractious and acrimonious debate between parents, interest groups, and national and local authorities should not be entertained. Yet this is precisely how the experience of opening Welsh-medium schools has been tempered as a baptism of fire, a trial of faith and a struggle for recognition, as well as for coequality of funding and resources, staffing and infrastructure. Yet to perceive this struggle in terms of language as the prime operative variable is to overshadow a number of other considerations, not least of which is party political competition for the control of posts and the allocation of educational resources, together with fidelity to the perceived interests of one's own constituency, whether at the level of MP, AM or city councillor. When Welsh-speaking politicians from one party are pitted against other Welsh-speaking politicians from opposing parties, the argument that it is an English-Welsh or indigenous-migrant cleavage just does not hold up. This is precisely why the argument advanced in part one is cogent: one needs both the robust analysis of the education system at work, and the intelligent, not to say intimate, understanding of how the key personalities who animate the system, actually operate and justify their decisions and causes.

In chapter 11 Jeni Price deals with the critical factor of how to encourage an increased use of Welsh in the social language-use patterns of pupils in Welsh-medium education. From its earliest days, Welsh-medium education has been criticised for not guaranteeing an automatic transfer of the classroom use of Welsh into the school corridors, playing fields and surrounding home area where English tends to dominate. Opponents of Welsh-medium education use such language practices as evidence of the insufficiency of Welsh to command loyalty and instrumental attachment and of the 'forced' nature of schooling, when the 'natural', 'default' and 'normal' language would be English. All these apparently common-sense terms belie a value system and an ideological predisposition which have had far reaching consequences. Almost thirty years ago Glyn Williams (1987) tackled the inherent power differentials in the discourse used to describe the relationship between Welsh and English in social life. We now recognise that education is central to the cultural reproduction of minority groups because it serves as the basis for ideological formation and the legitimisation of values and positions within society. Many of these power differentials have been unwittingly incorporated or blithely ignored in the broader field of language policy and planning according to Williams and Morris (2000).

It thus seems evident that the apparent success of the Ysgol Gymraeg has not been matched by an increase in the numbers of current or former pupils who speak Welsh in their daily lives. This chapter analyses an innovative project funded and steered by the Welsh Language Board aimed at changing pupil attitudes. Pupils' academic and social language proficiency and their linguistic confidence are probed and an evaluation concludes that better planning is needed for the social use of Welsh. Both planning and strategic initiatives rely on supporting the social use of language at school and on measuring the impact of whole-school approaches and strategies to encourage social language use. The lack of linguistic confidence so often identified in past social surveys (Williams and Evas 1997; 1998) starts at a very early stage in the socialisation process of some bilinguals and, as Price notes, this lack of confidence is one of the main obstacles preventing pupils from using Welsh naturally and informally around the school. Two elements of a proposed strategy to reverse some of these tendencies are the balancing of negative and positive methods of encouragement which have significant ramifications for the social psychology of language-use patterns and a greater awareness of the role which the attitudes of teachers and auxiliary staff and their language-use practices can have on language-switching behaviour throughout the whole of the school. One very distinct feature noted during the initial research period in the three schools surveyed was the influence of the attitudes and language use of teachers and auxiliary staff on pupils' language use. A number of comments were made about the lack of informal use of Welsh among teaching staff, and these issues should be discussed openly, sensitively and yet unambiguously. It is clear that there is further work to be done in the schools to increase staff awareness of their duties and responsibilities with regard to their use of Welsh.

Given that both the family and the community have been overtaken by the school as the main vehicle for creating a truly bilingual country where everyday use of the language becomes increasingly common across all areas, Price argues that a robust school system has a vital role in equipping all pupils with the necessary skills and confidence to use the language for both formal and informal purposes. We are used to the advocacy of a stronger role for planning in language matters, but Price avers that precise planning and sociolinguistic intervention are also required so that school pupils may change some of the practices that had been embedded since primary education. This will be effective as a behaviour-modification strategy only if the parallel reform of the attitudes of the schools' management team, teaching and auxiliary staff is undertaken in tandem. This again highlights the need for holistic analysis and action to redress some of the more deleterious patterns and processes in Welsh-English interaction. The social psychology of language switching and the often very rational response by pupils to a range of stimuli should not be underestimated or overly criticised if a real increase in the use of the Welsh language within the social interplay of the pupils at the project's schools is to be achieved.

In chapter 12 Colin H. Williams and Meirion Prys Jones anticipate how current reforms and trends might play out in relation to Welsh-medium education over the next few years. They take account of the new Welsh-medium Education Strategy, the transfer of the functions of the Welsh

Language Board to other agencies and the impact which the Language Measure (2011) and the office of Welsh language commissioner are likely to have. Their analysis throws light on new ways to answer the question I asked in 1988 when I provided the plenary opening lecture for Bangor University's Language Centre, 'Bilingual Education in Wales or Education for a Bilingual Wales?' Several of the challenges facing Welsh-medium education force a rethink on the manner in which this sector has been run and how it achieves its goals. Issues of sustainability, standards and achievement, teacher training, partnership activities, linguistic normalisation and the relationship between the Welsh-medium sector and the education system per se all deserve close scrutiny. The delicate balance between preserving the best of the past and the urgent desire to innovate, to break new ground, is the final concern of this concluding chapter. The finding of solutions is made more acute when trends elsewhere in Europe and beyond force us to reconfigure our concern with bilingualism and reconsider the emergent reality that for many residents of Europe multilingualism is a more accurate description of their individual and societal experience. Learning and education, as we have seen, do not just take place within formal institutional spaces, in a linear fashion from the cradle to the grave. Learning is far more dynamic, episodic, idiosyncratic and opportunistic, especially if the individual is released from the confines of a curriculum and assessment regime, to explore the riches of cyber space in a mélange of word, vision and sound. Huw Thomas appreciates the liberalism of developing multilingualism but draws our attention to the challenge of timing such a development, arguing that the Welsh language must be firmly embedded as a social communicative medium before Wales pushes the boundaries of multilingualism. He argues that this is pragmatism rather than regression, and takes the view, like Fishman and others, that saving a language is a long-term process. Hans Sakkers from Utrecht has summarised the dualisms we face in navigating a course through this multilingual space when he suggests (King et al., 2011, 41) that:

> Europeans are slowly being squeezed between the tensions of two cultures: between openness and closure, between the challenge of diversity and the attraction of uniformity; between inclusion and exclusion; between learning by exchange and learning by introspection and self-absorption; between the joy of curiosity and the safety of home; between reaching out and holding on to what is known.

He concludes:

> Perhaps we could learn something from those cultures which have a tradition of combining innovation with legacy – there are no dead traditions. In Europe, multilingualism could play an important role in calming emotions and tensions. Perhaps it is a hopeful sign of congruency that (as the Utrecht survey shows) multilingual people do not feel less connected with the culture they grew up in than do monolinguals. It could mean that multilingualism could help us to reach out to the other without losing a sense of who we are.

Notes

[1] Were it not for the dedication of committed schoolteachers and their parent associations in promoting bilingual education, the Welsh language would today be in a parlous state.

[2] For an analysis of bilingual education as a social phenomenon, see Colin H. Williams (1982; 1988); see also Colin Baker (ed.) (1987).

[3] This was certainly the case until relatively recently, and even today certain local authorities are reluctant to service the demand for bilingual education in their areas. It also increased the determination of those parents who, angered by the perceived injustice in the educational system, became involved in broader linguistic and political issues.

[4] See Gwilym Humphreys (1987). For an excellent overview of the system up until the early 1980s, see Colin Baker (1985).

[5] The phrase comes from 2 Corinthians 8.2.

[6] Ysgol Gynradd Gymraeg Y Barri, Sant Ffransis-ar-y-Bryn, Y Barri, was officially opened by Mrs Dorothy Rees JP on Friday, 5 October 1956. Among the guest speakers and participants were the Mayor of Barry, W. East JP, the minister of Tabernacl, Capel yr Annibynwyr, the Revd T. Huw Griffiths, Glamorgan County Council architect E. A. E. Evans, Alderman Llewellyn Heycock JP, Alderman R. A. Thomas, Alderman P. J. Smith JP, Councillor J. Haydn Thomas, Councillor B. L. Williams, and the Revd R. H. Lomas.

[7] Active participants in south-east Wales included Dorothy Rees JP, Gwyn Daniel, Cassie Davies, Maxwell Evans, Lily Richards and Raymond Edwards, while pioneering teachers at nursery and primary level in one location, Barry, included Ceinwen Clarke, Irene Williams, Rachel Williams, Eluned Bere, W. R. Evans and Elwyn Richards among others.

[8] The substantive research may be read in its original in Thomas (2007). We are grateful to the Cardiff Humanities Research Institute and the School of Welsh, Cardiff for their co-funding of a conference devoted to the Ysgolion Cymraeg in an international context held in Cardiff University in April 2010 which enabled many of these issues to be debated by a lively audience of education and language-policy professionals.

[9] The kernel of the debate and some of the various contributions have been trialled by us by sharing the key ideas and perspectives with a range of parents who currently have children in the bilingual education sector. The response has been very positive and encourages us to believe that this type of 'popularising' of the subject matter will go a long way to inform public opinion.

[10] The empirical adaptation of Fishman's GIDS method involved a triangulation from in-depth interviews with a representative sample of 28 parents, politicians and professionals, questionnaires returned by over 600 parents and 100 teachers, and an analysis of almost 200 Estyn (Schools Inspectorate) reports and other government based data, in particular over 300 value-added government analyses for the 103 comprehensive schools in south-east Wales from 2003 to 2005.

[11] See Humphreys (2000) for his account of his first headship and Davies (2008) for his interpretation of political events since 1945.

[12] For a different perspective on Emyr Currie-Jones, see the comments by M. Jones in chapter 8 below.

[13] For reactions by stakeholders to this set of changes, see the special report in the *Western Mail*, 3 March 2011.

Chapter 2

A Dynamic Profile: Perceptions and Facts

Huw S. Thomas

It is generally acknowledged that the Ysgolion Cymraeg (Welsh-medium schools) have flourished in south-east Wales both in terms of numbers and achievements (Thomas 2007: 232). Little research has been undertaken into the reasons for their success, while publications (mainly occasional articles or single chapters) referring to such schools have tended to concentrate on sociolinguistics, using Welsh-medium or bilingual education and schools to exemplify a point or to prove a thesis. This volume sets the schools at the heart of the study, and is written for a widely diversified audience: parents and politicians, practitioners and academics, as well as the general public, all of whom will, I hope, find material that disentangles the complex reasons for the expanding school movement whose develop- ment has been described as 'remarkable' and its success as 'spectacular' (Williams 1994: 168–9). Stephen May (2001: 266) described the growth of Welsh-medium education, particularly at the end of the last century and the beginning of this century, as 'nothing short of spectacular'.

Audiences across the world are interested in themes exemplified by the Ysgolion Cymraeg, topics such as minority language issues, bilingualism or human and linguistic rights. It is therefore appropriate to contextualise the Ysgolion Cymraeg and to include a few definitions. Some readers may find this unnecessary, but they will be tolerant of the needs of a global readership. Wales is a small country whose population (according to the 2011 census) has crossed the three million mark for the first time. A little over a fifth of the population was able to speak Welsh, according to the 2001 census. In south-east Wales the figure was 10.7 per cent. The corresponding figures for those able to speak, read and write Welsh were 16.3 per cent and 8.4 per cent. The entire population (except for a few immigrants) is able to speak English, the language of its immediate geographic neighbour, England. Wales is sometimes called a Celtic nation and as such has an affinity with Scotland and Ireland.

What exactly is an Ysgol Gymraeg (singular form of Ysgolion Cymraeg)? It may be a nursery, a primary (Y1–6) or a secondary (Y7–13) school, occasionally other ranges, all located in Wales, apart from Ysgol Gymraeg Llundain in London. The official language of all such schools is Welsh, and, except for English as a subject and foreign languages (where the target language is used extensively) Welsh is, on the whole, the sole language of instruction. English is introduced into the primary curriculum when pupils are seven years of age, and one or two subjects may be taught through the medium of English in some secondary schools. In south-east Wales, it is rare for any subject to be taught in any language other than Welsh. Baker and Jones (2003: 66–7) describe the variations in models on an all-Wales basis. The following sentences exemplify the complexity of provision. If one includes Swansea (where Ysgol Bryn Tawe was established in 2003) in a definition of south-east Wales, the last Welsh-medium secondary school to be established in the rest of Wales was over twenty years ago, namely Ysgol Gyfun Preseli, Pembrokeshire, in 1991. In the last twenty years few Welsh-medium primaries have been established outside south-east Wales, in stark contrast to the growth within the south-east discussed in this volume. In north-east Wales, which has three Welsh-medium comprehensives, growth has been limited: Ysgol Glan Clwyd was established in 1956 and Ysgol Maes Garmon in 1961, both in Flintshire. Ysgol Morgan Llwyd in Wrecsam was opened in 1964. I have not researched the comparative growth of Ysgolion Cymraeg in this anglicised area of north-east Wales, but one factor is that Welsh-medium education in this part of Wales was a top-down development, led by directors of education such as Dr Haydn Williams and Moses Jones. However, the overall national picture is difficult to analyse, as Hywel M. Jones describes in his excellent analysis of Welsh in education (2012: 64–80). Bilingual, dual-stream and Welsh-medium secondary schools are increasing their Welsh-medium provision, but county by county data are currently not available for analysing the exact nature of linguistic provision, in other words, which subjects are taught and assessed through the medium of Welsh at 16 and post-16 years of age. That will have to remain for another study, hopefully in the near future. What is indisputable, however, is the steady growth on a national basis in primary classes where Welsh is the sole or main medium of instruction, from 15.9 per cent (38,404 pupils) in 1990–1 to 22.0 per cent (53,479 pupils) in 2008–9 (WG, 2009, tables 7.7, 7.8). In secondary schools the percentages of pupils taught Welsh as a first language increased from 9.7 per cent (21,458 pupils) in 1979–80 to 16.0 per cent (28,320) in 2008–9 (WG, 2009, table 7.15). Pupils come from a variety of language backgrounds, but English is the dominant or only language spoken in the vast majority of homes. The schools are therefore immersion schools. All pupils are fluent in both Welsh and English. Immersion and first-language nursery education is provided either in state schools or by Mudiad Ysgolion Meithrin (MYM) groups, a voluntary movement subsidised until 2012 by the WLB and now by Welsh Government. Parents make a contribution to their Meithrin group. (In 2011 MYM was rebranded as Mudiad Meithrin.) All Ysgolion Cymraeg are state schools; private and independent schools are a minority sector in Wales.

THE GROWTH OF THE YSGOLION CYMRAEG IN SOUTH-EAST WALES

The first three schools to be established in south-east Wales by local education authorities were Tyderwen in Maesteg, Ynys-lwyd in Aberdâr, and Ysgol Gymraeg Caerdydd in Cardiff. The three were opened in 1949. By 2006 the area (then served by ten local authorities) had 49 primary schools, 5 units or two-stream schools (also primary), and 9 secondary (comprehensive) Welsh-medium schools. By September 2008 a further 6 primaries and 1 comprehensive were established; by September 2012 the number had approached 80. All the schools are listed at the end of this chapter.[1] The pattern of growth is complex, as Ysgol Gyfun Rhydfelen was the only secondary school serving the whole of south-east Wales between 1962 and 1974, the year that Ysgol Gyfun Llanhari opened. A notable feature is that the number of Welsh-medium pupils in, for example, Cardiff and the Vale of Glamorgan in 2006 (2,644) had grown from an initial 34 (19 in Cardiff in 1949 and 15 in Barry in 1952). See Table 2.1.

While 1949 is a landmark date in the history of Welsh-medium schools in the area, Dr Sian Rhiannon Williams (2002: 120) refers to the establishment of an Ysgol Gymraeg about a century before Ysgol Lluest in Abersytwyth

TABLE 2.1

Population growth of the Ysgolion Cymraeg, comparing the original number
of pupils in the first primary school in the geographic area of every one
of 9 secondary schools by 2006

Primary school	Year established	Numbers that year	Secondary school	Year established	Numbers 2006
Tyderwen Maesteg	1949	45	Llanhari	1974	1,091
Ysgol Gymraeg Caerdydd	1949	19	Glantaf	1978	1,082
			Plasmawr	1998	781
Ynys-lwyd Aberdâr	1949	28	Rhydywaun	1995	903
Ynyswen, Treorci	1950	36	Cymer	1988	945
Pont Siôn Norton Pontypridd	1951	16	Rhydfelen	1962	910
Sant Ffransis Y Barri	1952	15	Bro Morgannwg	2000	781
Rhymni (Gwent)	1955	12	Cwm Rhymni	1981	1,140
Risca Unit	1967	15	Gwynllyw	1998	785

The data are based on a range of statistical sources: the Welsh Office (1980, 1985, 1990, 1998), NAW (2001, 2003–6), Iolo Wyn Williams (2003), and information provided by individual schools and LEAs.

(1939) or Ysgol Dewi Sant Llanelli (1947): '[O]ne could argue that a school established in Llanwenarth, Monmouthshire, by the Abergavenny Cymreigyddion Society in 1837 was really the first.'

An analysis of every individual school's growth could be a valuable study, given the variations in size and speed of their growth. Sometimes the differences are significant, probably due to the influences of sociological, economic, political and demographic factors, as well as the level and efficacy of parental pressure and campaigning. What is possible within the parameters of this study is an overview of the growth over time and locality, as shown in Table 2.2.

Since the establishment of the first three schools in 1949 growth has been steady across the area; by the end of the quarter of a century 1950–75

TABLE 2.2

Ysgolion Cymraeg (primary schools, primary units or two-stream schools, and secondary schools): number of schools/units 1975–2006

Year	Gwent	Mid Glamorgan	South Glamorgan	South-east Wales
1975	4	19	5	28
1980	4	23	7	34
1985	6	28	9	43
1990	7	32	11	50
1995	8	35	12	55
2000	8	35	17	60
2006	9	36	18	63
2008	10	38	22	70

Schools have been allocated to their LEA areas as they existed prior to local government reorganisation in 1995. This facilitates the analysis of trends in growth. For example, Ysgol Trelyn, formerly in Gwent, was (from 1995 on) in Caerffili, while Gwaelod-y-Garth in Mid Glamorgan was subsequently administered by Cardiff. Ysgol Bryntaf in Cardiff was closed in 1981, not due to insufficient demand; on the contrary, it developed into four primaries in locations across the city.

The analysis is based on a range of statistical sources: the Welsh Office (1980, 1985, 1990, 1998), NAW (2001, 2003–6), Iolo Wyn Williams (2003), and information provided by individual schools and LEAs.

there were 28 schools, and over the next twenty-five years the total increased to 60 and the pupil numbers to 21,763 (Thomas 2007: 536). An examination of pupil numbers in Table 2.3 shows a general increase year on year. The apparent decrease in Gwent is due to the inclusion of pupils in the Schools Council Bilingual Project in the official data; in reality, pupil numbers in all the Ysgolion Cymraeg grew. Between 95 per cent and 100 per cent of primary pupils continue their education through the medium of Welsh at secondary level, without the significant, but decreasing, drop-out rates experienced in south-west Wales. In south-east Wales the annual increase in secondary pupil numbers was steady, from 6,901 in 2000 to 8,409 in 2006.[2]

Growth has been steady when viewed across the whole of south-east Wales but uneven over time and locality, with Mid Glamorgan at the forefront until the mid 1980s, with its impressive and dramatic growth rate

TABLE 2.3
Pupil numbers in the Ysgolion Cymraeg (primary) 1975–2005

Year	Gwent	Mid Glamorgan	South Glamorgan	Total numbers in south-east Wales
1975	858	3,018	1,382	5,258
1990	784	6,153	1,978	8,915
Numerical change from 1975 to 1990	-74	3,135	596	3,657
Percentage change from 1975 to 1990	-8.6%	103.9%	43.1%	69.6%
1995	1,179	6,970	2,707	10,856
2005	1,393	8,038	3,942	13,373
Numerical change from 1995 to 2005	214	1,068	1,235	2,517
Percentage change from 1995 to 2005	18.2%	15.3%	45.6%	23.2%

The data are based on a range of statistical sources: the Welsh Office (1980, 1985, 1990, 1998), NAW (2001, 2003–6), Iolo Wyn Williams (2003), and information provided by individual schools and LEAs.

of 104 per cent from 1975 to 1990. One should not forget decisions taken by the former county of Glamorgan to establish Ysgolion Cymraeg with low initial pupil numbers, for example, Tonyrefail (1955) with 11 pupils (Morgan 2003: 42). Until fairly recently, South Glamorgan and Gwent trailed far behind. However, between 1995 and 2005 the primary increases were Gwent 18.2 per cent, Mid Glamorgan 15.3 per cent and South Glamorgan 45.6 per cent. Between 2000 and 2006 the secondary population increased at the following rates: Gwent 14.6 per cent, Mid Glamorgan 12.6 per cent and South Glamorgan 47.4 per cent (Thomas 2007: 528). Growth in Gwent is encouraging, considering its low initial base, although its large geographical spread has impeded the rate of growth, due to the time spent by pupils (and their parents) travelling to its one secondary school (Ysgol Gyfun Gwynllyw) in Pontypŵl. Since 1980 the number of schools in Gwent has more than doubled and, while pupil numbers are fairly low, the percentage increase is notable. Growth is apparent also in Caerffili, where a second comprehensive school was scheduled to open in 2012. However, the change in 2011 from 70 per cent central government funding and 30 per cent from the LA to 50 per cent from both sources has caused financial challenges to the LA and consequently delayed the establishment of this school until September 2013. Parents are actively promoting the advantages of Welsh-medium education, one method being leaflet-dropping in targeted homes in the area.

The geographic area of South Glamorgan, currently Cardiff and the Vale of Glamorgan, saw an increase of eight schools between 1990 and 2006, which is equivalent to one new school every other year. This is where the greatest increase has been seen in the last ten years, while Mid Glamorgan appears to have reached a plateau, with only one new primary school established in that area between 1990 and 2006, namely Ysgol Bro Sannan in Aberbargod, Caerffili. By September 2008, six new primaries were established (four in Cardiff, one each in Newport and Caerffili), and a secondary in Bridgend. A further six schools have been established since 2008 (one each in Caerffili, Cardiff, Newport and Torfaen, and two in the Vale of Glamorgan). Being up-to-date with such dynamic data is a welcome challenge. A comprehensive (Ysgol Bro Edern) opened in Cardiff in 2012 and another one, mainly for pupils aged 11–16, will open in Caerffili in 2013.

The recent dramatic growth in Cardiff and the Vale of Glamorgan reflects the growing importance of Cardiff as Wales' capital city, with an ability to engender an increased sense of national pride and confidence within its citizens. National institutions such as the assembly, with its Senedd building, the Wales Millennium Centre and the Wales Millennium Stadium, are housed in iconic buildings, attracting large numbers of visitors from all over Wales and the world.

Rhondda Cynon Taf is at the heart of the former Glamorgan and Mid Glamorgan local authorities. Its Welsh education scheme (2008) shows good intentions with regard to measuring demand for Welsh-medium education, and aims to be inclusive in its planning, for example by bringing RhAG on board as members of a planning group. However, it has failed to meet the needs of parents in the Abercynon area. While it is true that parents in Mid Glamorgan have battled for their linguistic rights for over half a century, new parents should not feel battle-weary. Possibly, there needs to be a revitalising of forces with new leadership or catalysts within the parent body. Michael L. N. Jones's remarks in chapter 8 (addendum 1) suggest that the linguistic tide has at last turned in this area. Statistically, Rhondda Cynon Taf had in 2006 the highest proportion of Welsh-medium pupils in south-east Wales in the primary sector (18.3 per cent), followed by Caerffili (11.7 per cent). Both figures are lower than the national average of 20.1 per cent, as Table 2.4 shows.

TABLE 2.4
Percentages of classes and pupils in Welsh-medium teaching
in the schools of south-east Wales, 2006

LEA	% classes	% pupils
Blaenau Gwent	4.3	4.8
Bridgend	8.6	8.4
Caerffili	11.8	11.7
Cardiff	10.8	11.2
Merthyr Tudful	10.3	10.6
Monmouthshire	2.8	2.4
Newport	2.9	2.9
Rhondda Cynon Taf	17.0	18.3
Torfaen	6.2	6.6
Vale of Glamorgan	10.5	10.2
Wales	21.5	20.1

Source: National Assembly for Wales (2007: Table 8).

Rhondda Cynon Taf should be particularly proud of the catalytic contribution made by the first Welsh-medium secondary school in south-east Wales, Ysgol Gyfun Rhydfelen, in the Pontypridd area. Originally housed in wooden prefabricated structures with later more appropriate additions, the school was relocated (from Rhydyfelin to Church Village, a few miles away) into a brand new building in 2006. However, in spite of an impressively coordinated campaign to keep its original and iconic name, local politicians succeeded in changing it to Ysgol Gyfun Garth Olwg. The following paragraphs are taken from a letter that I sent to the Council (27 June 2006); it was not acknowledged:

Rhydfelen has historical and cultural significance in that it was the first Welsh-medium secondary school in south Wales. It was Glamorgan that felt the pain over a few generations of seeing the language come to within an ace of dying, and it was a strong affinity for the language as a badge of identity that started a long and successful reversal of that language shift. It was Glamorgan's practical support for the establishment of Welsh-medium schools that saved the language, not only in south-east Wales, but, in my opinion, in the whole of Wales. Rhydfelen set the standard for the rest of Wales.

Rhydfelen has been, and still is, an inspiration for the whole of our country in its aspirations to become a bilingual country. Without the success of Rhydfelen, we would not have seen the wide-scale endorsement of the policy document, 'Iaith Pawb', which is the basis, at a planning stage, for the language revival, and is the policy document of the Welsh Assembly Government on saving our language.

In brief, I urge the Council to look further than the geographical or conceptual vision of a community school, and celebrate the enormous significance of Rhydfelen, not only in Wales, but in so many bilingual countries across the globe.

The influence of well-organised and active groups within RhAG should not be underestimated, and their intelligent interaction with education officers nurtures mutual respect and, very often, practical outcomes. Political goodwill and far-reaching long-term planning by local authorities are two major factors that explain the significant development in some areas of south-east Wales. Historically, the establishment of an Ysgol Gymraeg has been seen as a result of parental pressure and lobbying. Two recent developments appear to buck that trend. While one cannot deny many years of lobbying by parents before the decision was taken to establish Ysgol Gyfun Bro Morgannwg in the Vale of Glamorgan in 2000, the campaign was more muted than usual and was marked by astute political strategies and tactics, as well as pragmatic, carefully designed solutions to basic matters of finance and buildings. Even more muted on the national scene was the way that Ysgol Gyfun Gymraeg Llangynwyd was established by Bridgend LEA in 2008. I will discuss the strategic implications of its establishment in chapter 4.

THE LINGUISTIC BACKGROUND OF THE YSGOLION CYMRAEG

The decline of the Welsh language is well documented and is illustrated by the data in Tables 2.5 and 2.6. The 2001 Census recorded the first upturn in Welsh speakers in a century (Table 2.6), an event of both historic and emotional significance.

TABLE 2.5

Percentages of Welsh speakers in south-east Wales, 1901–91

Area	1901	1911	1921	1931	1951	1961	1971	1981	1991
Glamorgan	43.5	38.1	31.6	30.5	20.3	17.2	11.8	10.0	
Mid Glamorgan									8.4
South Glamorgan									6.5
Monmouthshire	13.0	9.6	6.4	6.0	3.5	3.4	2.1	2.7	
Gwent									2.4
Wales	49.9	43.5	37.1	36.8	28.9	26.0	20.8	18.9	18.6

Source: adapted from Aitchison and Carter (1985: 8, 2; 1994: 89).

In 1941 there was no census because of the Second World War. I have not included similar statistics for 2001 to avoid unfair comparisons due to the reorganisation of local government in 1996.

TABLE 2.6

Numbers of Welsh speakers within Wales, 1901–2001

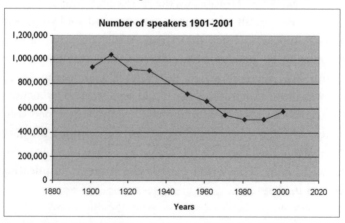

Source: adapted from Aitchison and Carter (1985: 8, 2; 1994: 89).

The percentage range of speakers within the LEAs in south-east Wales is small, from 9.0 per cent in Monmouthshire to 12.3 per cent in Rhondda Cynon Taf (Table 2.7). Percentages of those able to speak, read, and write Welsh are lower, ranging from 6.6 per cent in Blaenau Gwent to 9.8 per cent in Rhondda Cynon Taf (Aitchison and Carter 2004: 38–39).

TABLE 2.7
Numbers of Welsh speakers (3 and above) in the LEAs of south-east Wales, 2001

Area	Area population	Numbers	Percentages
Blaenau Gwent	67,795	6,141	9.1
Bridgend	124,284	13,155	10.6
Caerffili	163,297	17,825	10.9
Cardiff	294,208	31,944	10.9
Merthyr Tudful	54,115	5,428	10.0
Monmouthshire	82,351	7,428	9.0
Newport	131,820	12,608	9.6
Rhondda Cynon Taf	223,924	27,505	12.3
Torfaen	88,062	9,425	10.7
Vale of Glamorgan	115,116	12,734	11.1

Source: numbers from Aitchison and Carter (2004: 50).

According to Aitchison and Carter, the distribution of speakers shows the key importance of the towns and cities in revitalising the language (2004: 56):

> [W]hile it is customary to identify the Welsh-speaking community with rural areas of north and west Wales (y Fro Gymraeg), the actual heartland of that community in terms of absolute numbers lies in south Wales, embracing the long-standing Welsh-speaking communities of the former western coalfield and the burgeoning regions of the east, with Cardiff as a powerful focal point.

A detailed chart of the increases may be seen in Table 2.8.

TABLE 2.8
Welsh speakers (3 and above) in Wales and the south-east, 1991 and 2001

Area	1991	2001	1991 %	2001 %	Growth % points	Growth %
Blaenau Gwent	1,523	6,141	2.2	9.1	6.9	303.2%
Bridgend	10,159	13,155	8.2	10.6	2.4	29.5%
Caerffili	9,714	17,825	6.0	10.9	4.9	83.5%
Cardiff	18,080	31,944	6.6	10.9	4.3	76.7%
Merthyr Tudful	4,237	5,428	7.5	10.0	2.5	28.1%
Monmouthshire	1,631	7,428	2.1	9.0	6.9	355.4%
Newport	2,874	12,608	2.3	9.6	7.3	338.7%
Rhondda Cynon Taf	20,042	27,505	9.0	12.3	3.3	37.2%
Torfaen	2,128	9,425	2.5	10.7	8.2	342.9%
Vale of Glamorgan	7,755	12,734	6.9	11.1	4.2	64.2%
South-east	78,143	144,193	5.7	10.7	5.0	84.5%
Wales	508,098	575,640	18.7	20.5	1.8	13.3%

Source: adapted from Aitchison and Carter (2004: 50; 2003/04: 56).

The percentage increase in speakers from 1991 to 2001 is impressive, with actual numbers across south-east Wales almost doubling, from 78,143 to 144,193. This number represents just over a quarter of Welsh speakers in Wales. ('In Wales' in the previous sentence is not a tautological phrase, since many Welsh speakers live outside Wales and were not counted in the census.) Differences in percentage points and percentages have to be treated with caution, given the low starting base of a number of communities, especially in Gwent. However, the first increase in speakers in a century is an accomplishment to be celebrated.

Before examining the linguistic background of the Ysgolion Cymraeg in detail, it is important to see how they fit into the age profile of Welsh speakers on a national basis. The highest percentage of speakers (irrespective of their ability to read and write Welsh) is in the 10–15 age range. The percentage

TABLE 2.9
All-Wales distribution of Welsh speakers in age bands,
according to the 2001 census

Age	Population	Percentage able to speak Welsh	Percentage able to speak, read and write Welsh
All	2,805,701	20.5	16.3
3–4	70,519	18.5	4.7
5–9	185,325	36.2	27.7
10–14	195,976	42.6	38.6
15	37,951	42.1	39.0
16–19	146,753	27.4	24.5
20–24	169,493	17.3	14.8
25–34	364,658	15.8	12.8
35–49	592,140	14.5	11.4
50–59	385,188	15.5	11.9
60–64	152,924	16.6	12.6
65–74	264,191	18.0	13.5
75 +	240,583	21.0	15.4

Source: Welsh Language Board (2003c).

in the age range 5–9 is comparatively high, followed by the 16–19 group (Table 2.9). These three groups correspond closely to the statutory education age of 5–16 and reflect the influence of compulsory Welsh in the National Curriculum and as a medium of instruction.

The next question is, 'How many of these children speak Welsh at home?' One answer is provided by government statistics that analyse the home language of 11–15-year-olds. These statistics also suggest the enormous challenge faced daily in the Ysgolion Cymraeg to encourage their pupils to speak Welsh in a social interactive milieu outside the classroom. Data for 2004 (Table 2.10) show that only 1.5 per cent of 11–15-year-olds in south-east Wales spoke Welsh at home. Equally challenging are the implications in the low national percentage of 7.6 per cent.

The percentages for the following three years were:

	South-east Wales	Wales
2005	1.7%	7.9%
2006	2.2%	8.8%
2007	2.1%	8.6%

TABLE 2.10

Pupils aged 11–15 in south-east Wales speaking Welsh at home,
according to their parents, 2004

Local education authority	Total population in age range (all schools) 2004	Numbers speaking Welsh at home 2004	Percentages speaking Welsh at home 2004
Blaenau Gwent	4,480	1	0.0
Bridgend	8,518	12	0.1
Caerffili	12,234	93	0.8
Cardiff	19,228	517	2.7
Merthyr Tudful	3,833	7	0.2
Monmouthshire	4,823	6	0.1
Newport	9,250	6	0.1
Rhondda Cynon Taf	16,484	466	2.8
Torfaen	7,195	11	0.2
Vale of Glamorgan	8,174	264	3.2
South-east Wales	94,219	1,383	1.5
Wales	189,516	14,377	7.6

Source: National Assembly for Wales (2006a).

The data for 2006 is skewed by the abnormal increase of speakers in Torfaen: 11 (2004), 19 (2005), 203 (2006), 62 (2007). Where did most of these speakers disappear to in 2007? This example is a salutary lesson for compilers and interpreters of statistics. It is more than likely that the 2006 numbers are incorrect. When one analyses the age ranges of speakers in individual LEAs in the south-east, one realises that the opportunities afforded to children and youngsters to communicate in Welsh with adults outside the school community are limited. For example, adult speakers of

Welsh in Newport aged 20–50 (1,006 in the 2001 census) represent a mere 2.0 per cent of the city's population in that age range.

Finally, how does one discover parents' language skills, short of getting a high rate of return from questionnaires sent to all parents of children attending Ysgolion Cymraeg in the area? A similar challenge faces the researcher in trying to describe the language or languages used at home by the entire family. Three studies conducted between 1988 and 2007 suggest that the number of families where Welsh is the home language is very low. Aitchison and Carter's study in 1988 also drew attention to the dependability of evidence, and their 1994 study (based on PDAG statistics collected in 1991) showed that the percentages of 5–11-year-old children speaking Welsh at home were 0.5 per cent in Gwent, 1.0 per cent in Mid Glamorgan, and 1.3 per cent in South Glamorgan. My own research between 2004 and 2007 revealed that only two families from a representative sample of 178 recorded that Welsh was the only language of the home. A subsequent piece of my research based on a further 189 families showed the following pattern:

Welsh only	5.3%
Mainly Welsh	12.2%
Half Welsh and half English	20.1%
Mainly English	41.3%
English only	20.6%

It is difficult to interpret these statistics, unless far more detailed research is conducted. For example, some Welsh is used in almost 80 per cent of homes, which is encouraging, but one does not know the extent or depth of that language interaction. There is hope in the fact that almost a fifth of homes in the sample maintain that they use Welsh solely or mainly.

People's use of languages and their attitudes towards them are critical factors in reversing language shift. Indeed the desire to see their children speak Welsh and develop into bilingual citizens was the main reason by far why parents opted for an Ysgol Gymraeg. For example, open-ended questionnaires returned by parents in 2004 showed that of the twenty-five different reasons noted by them, 62 per cent of all respondents included the Welsh language in their choices. A fairly similar response rate was recorded by Hodges (2010a, 2010b, 2011), who based her analysis on fifty in-depth interviews with Rhymney Valley parents aimed at discovering why they had chosen Welsh-medium education for their children. A half of her sample noted cultural reasons as the main stimulus for their choice. Two salient patterns of language use by parents emerged from my own research. The first revealed that of sixteen families where Welsh was the mother tongue of both mother and father, only four families used Welsh as the only language of the home. Failure to transfer language between generations is one of the foremost reasons for language death. Significantly different language expectations between home and school usually lead to tensions and frustrations, exemplified by the evidence of a primary head-teacher who recorded that a Welsh-speaking mother would speak English daily to her child when she brought him to school. In other words, language transference had become a transfer of 'responsibility' from mother to teacher, from home to school. The other language pattern that emerged is in stark contrast. Only ten families (twenty parents) from the research sample of 189 noted that Welsh was the sole language of the home. English was the mother tongue of twelve of the twenty parents. In two families, English was the mother tongue of both parents. Such determination and commitment need to be celebrated, while mother-tongue Welsh speakers need to be made more aware of the importance of intergenerational transmission of the language.

PARENTAL ATTITUDES TOWARDS THE LANGUAGE AND WELSHNESS

Attitudes were measured by analysing responses to a range of statements regarding the language, with some of the same attitudes being repeated later in the questionnaire in a negative form. Correlation of data showed that respondents thought before answering. Whilst a range of attitudes has been described in the preceding section, a strong tendency emerged from the data collected for parents to be keen to join a learners' class or to improve their fluency. Over a half of the mothers and over a third of the fathers had started learning Welsh. In response to the following statement in a questionnaire, almost 90 per cent of respondents (a figure that included 85.3 per cent of parents) agreed with its message: 'There should be a campaign to persuade parents to learn Welsh and to improve the fluency of those parents already learning it.' Statements about adult classes elicited an overwhelming response in favour of free classes. Some parents mentioned the difficulty of attending classes at convenient times, which is an important consideration in planning adult learner classes.

Extremely mixed responses came to the following statement: 'The children who attend a Welsh-medium school are not at a disadvantage that the vast majority of those parents do not themselves speak Welsh.' Of the respondents, 44.2 per cent agreed, 39.4 per cent disagreed and a further 15.1 per cent agreed, more or less. Markedly significant differences in opinions were not common in the questionnaires, which sought views on ninety statements on a seven-point scale. I would argue for research into parental perceptions regarding mixed language experiences, particularly regarding homework, a topic to which I return later in this volume. Parents showed strong feelings in favour of the Welsh language. For instance, Welsh was the most popular reason in Questionnaires 1 and 3 for choosing the Ysgol Gymraeg, with bilingualism top in Questionnaire 4 and Welsh in second place. Statistically, 50.3 per cent of parents agreed very strongly and over a quarter agreed strongly with the following statement: 'I hope that our children, when they are themselves parents, will speak Welsh to their own children.'

Respondents' depth of feeling and optimism were probed by the next statement: 'I chose Welsh-language education so that my child would be immersed in Welsh language and culture, not necessarily so that he would achieve high standards in his schoolwork.' This received the support of 94.7 per cent of parents and, given that it was a multilayered statement, it was not surprising that agreement was evenly spread across the three categories of 'very strongly agree', 'strongly agree' and 'agree'. This is solid evidence of parental commitment to the language.

Opinions about the social roles of language were also measured; for example, in the case of the statement 'Unless there are opportunities to speak Welsh outside school, the Welsh language will die', four out of every five parents agreed, underlining the importance of extracurricular activities in Welsh. Teachers contribute immensely to pupils' extended experiences in Welsh, and language and socially enriching experiences were placed eighth in order of importance out of twenty-six reasons suggested for choosing an Ysgol Gymraeg.

Urdd Gobaith Cymru is one of the foremost youth organisations that have responded to the language challenge. According to Baker (1990: 80):

> [I]ts effect on the Welsh language, Welsh culture and attitudes to Welsh has been, in terms of an international perspective on the fate of minority languages, a remarkable, important and uniquely Welsh factor in halting the fast decay of the indigenous language.

Only 7 per cent of parents disagreed with the statement which said, 'As far as our children in our family are concerned, the Urdd has given them the opportunity to speak Welsh, or it will in future.'

Practical issues relating to preserving the language, such as the Mentrau Iaith, the media, and teaching and learning resources were included in the survey. Response patterns suggest that research needs to be undertaken to probe parents' understanding of the Mentrau Iaith. In contrast, clear and unequivocal messages emerged agreeing that, without a wide range of teaching materials, novels, and television and radio programmes in Welsh, the success of Welsh-language education would be limited.

Finally, respondents were asked about the role of the Ysgol Gymraeg in reversing the language shift in the following terms: 'It is foolish to believe that the Welsh-language schools on their own can save the language.' Teachers have worked so hard preparing teaching materials, using language-bath methodology unsupported by academic research, and pushing forward the boundaries of extracurricular activities that they have little time to extend their own horizons in the field of language reversal and preservation. That had been my own experience as a practitioner. Over a half of teachers realised that they could not save the language on their own, over a quarter were undecided, but 18 per cent believed that they could. Just over a quarter of parents also believed in the all-powerful ability of the school to reverse the language shift. The majority, however, agreed with sociolinguists such as Fishman, whose ideas will be explored in the next chapter.

THE SOCIO-ECONOMIC BACKGROUND OF THE YSGOLION CYMRAEG

No study of the Ysgolion Cymraeg would be complete without setting them in their socio-economic milieu. Khleif, for example, referring to the late 1970s, wrote (1980: 124): 'Welsh-medium schools predominantly serve a Welsh-speaking middle class – parents and pupils . . . whose home language is Welsh or whose aspirations are more Welsh than "British"'. He contradicted himself, since he had written on the previous page:

> [A]lthough the early Welsh-medium schools did rely heavily on Welsh-speaking children as a nucleus for their enrolment, many later Welsh-medium schools had actually to 'create' Welsh children out of English-speaking ones. At present, the overall rate of children from English-speaking homes who attend Welsh-speaking schools is close to 80 per cent.

His claims (ibid., 217) that the Ysgolion Cymraeg were viewed as snob schools, where the best people and the professional classes sent their children, are still echoed today. To what extent, if at all, do such perceptions reflect reality? How does one measure, without the support of grants and researchers, the socio-economic profile of some seventy Welsh-medium schools? Small-scale research projects by Morgan (1969), Bush (1979), Evas (1999) and Thomas (2007) all point to an above average representation in socio-economic classes 1 and 2. Iorwerth Morgan, for example, researching in the 1960s, found that all the parents in his small sample belonged to classes 1 or 2. 'You have a veritable Eton here' was the comment made at the time by a well-known educationist; Morgan would not name him in an interview in 2006. Bush, Atkinson and Read (1981a: 43–4; 1981b) refuted claims that the parents in their survey were an ambitious elite when they analysed their sample of 104 families in Gwent. Evas's sample comprised 106 parents of Y12 students in four Welsh-medium comprehensive schools in Mid Glamorgan and Gwent. My own sample represented 336 mothers and 339 fathers, spread across south-east Wales. Initial analyses appeared to confirm an impression that the Ysgolion Cymraeg are predominantly middle class: 41.7 per cent of mothers and 28.9 per cent of fathers in the sample belonged to Social Class 1. How representative were these parents? In reality, my research reflects the views and opinions of my sample, nothing more, and nothing less. However, my personal experience of almost forty years in Ysgolion Cymraeg in a variety of socio-economic settings informed me that the schools' socio-economic profile needed further probing.

One of the indicators most frequently used in comparative studies of school backgrounds is that of free school meals. I chose 2005 as my sample year since it coincided with the major period of my empirical research. Considerable variations occur across the ten LEAs in south-east Wales, ranging from 8.8 per cent (secondary) to 27.6 per cent (primary). Generally, percentages in the south-east are above the national average and suggest substantial social deprivation. Percentages for individual LEAs can be seen in Table 2.11.

TABLE 2.11
Free school meals: Individual LEAs in south-east Wales, 2005

Local education authority	Primary	Secondary
Blaenau Gwent	25.9	20.7
Bridgend	20.0	15.3
Caerffili	20.0	17.2
Cardiff	20.8	18.1
Merthyr Tudful	27.6	24.8
Monmouthshire	9.2	8.8
Newport	22.6	18.3
Rhondda Cynon Taf	26.2	20.1
Torfaen	21.4	13.9
Vale of Glamorgan	11.9	9.3
South-east Wales	20.8	17.1
Wales	18.0	15.3

Source: National Assembly for Wales (2003–6; 2006b).

In 2005 in the primary sector the difference between the Ysgolion Cymraeg in the south-east (14.9 per cent) and the whole of Wales (18.0 per cent) was 3.1 percentage points, exactly the same as the secondary difference. On this basis it could be argued that the population of the Ysgolion Cymraeg in south-east Wales is fairly similar socio-economically to the national profile. Data for the primary schools are in Table 2.12.

Since post-16 provision in some areas is in FE Colleges only, and since the percentages returning to Y12 (sixth form) vary significantly from school to school, it follows that some skewing may have occurred in the secondary data. It therefore appeared better to use primary data, as shown in Table 2.12. However, an interesting anomaly appears in the secondary data (Table 2.13), where schools are grouped either in their LEA or in an amalgam of three LEAs (where cross-boundary provision would make exact comparisons difficult).

First of all, let us examine socio-economic trends that emerge in the wider geographical context of the area. The first is that the percentage of

TABLE 2.12

Free school meals (primary sector) in south-east Wales, 2005

Local education authority	Every school	English-medium	Welsh-medium	Percentage points difference
Blaenau Gwent	25.9%	26.2%	20.1%	-6.1
Bridgend	20.0%	20.2%	17.3%	-2.9
Caerffili	20.0%	20.4%	16.7%	-3.7
Cardiff	20.8%	22.1%	10.2%	-11.9
Merthyr Tudful	27.6%	28.6%	19.6%	-9.0
Monmouthshire	9.2%	9.3%	6.4%	-2.9
Newport	22.6%	22.7%	17.3%	-5.4
Rhondda Cynon Taf	26.2%	28.2%	16.8%	-11.4
Torfaen	21.4%	21.6%	18.9%	-2.7
Vale of Glamorgan	11.9%	12.2%	9.6%	-2.6
South-east Wales	20.8%	21.5%	14.9%	-6.6

Source: National Assembly for Wales (2003–6; 2006b).

TABLE 2.13

Free school meals (secondary sector) in south-east Wales, 2005

LEA or amalgam of LEAs	English-medium	Welsh-medium	Percentage points difference
Caerffili	17.2%	17.7%	+0.5
Cardiff	18.1%	7.9%	-10.2
Gwent	15.7%	12.0%	-3.7
Bridgend, Merthyr, and Rhondda Cynon Taf	20.0%	13.6%	-6.4
Vale of Glamorgan	9.3%	6.2%	-3.1
South-east Wales	17.3%	12.2%	-5.1

Source: National Assembly for Wales (2003–6; 2006b).

free school meals is lower in the Ysgolion Cymraeg in every LEA and in both sectors (except for one anomaly), 6.6 percentage points higher in the primary sector and 5.1 in the secondary. The general trend corroborates the widely held perception that the socio-economic background is higher than in the English-medium sector. This gives the Ysgolion Cymraeg an image or brand, though the differences are not as high as some people might have thought. The second trend is that there are substantial variations across the Ysgolion Cymraeg. In the primary sector, the difference between the Welsh and English sectors is fairly small in half the LEAs (less than 4 percentage points). In the other half, the range of differences goes from 5.4 to 11.9 percentage points. The greatest differences are in Cardiff and Rhondda Cynon Taf, a pattern reflected in the secondary sector. It appears that the anomaly in the Caerffili secondary schools data (the only positive difference recorded) is not a statistical aberration. Ysgol Gyfun Cwm Rhymni's free school meal indicator of 17.7 per cent is half a percentage point above the LEA indicator. Might this statistic be significant in any way? I would suggest two possible explanations. Firstly, that Welsh-medium education might be on the verge of normalisation in the Caerffili area, and secondly that Ysgol Gyfun Cwm Rhymni has a sixth form returners rate which is twice as high as for the other sixth forms within the LEA (Thomas 2007: 610). This suggests a wider range of ability and background post–16 in this Ysgol Gymraeg than is the norm within the LEA English-medium schools. The school is the only major provider of vocational courses through the medium of Welsh in the area.

The third trend is that the range of free school meals is smaller in the Ysgolion Cymraeg than in the English sector. For example, the range for all English-medium comprehensive schools in the south-east is from 3.5 per cent to 47.5 per cent, while that for the Ysgolion Cymraeg is from 6.2 per cent to 17.7 per cent. Such a smaller range helps to create a brand image, which is advantageous from the point of view of marketing and promoting growth. The fourth trend is that about a third of the Welsh-medium primary schools have a free school meals percentage that is higher than the national average, a statistic that undermines the belief that the Ysgolion Cymraeg have elitist intakes of pupils. Conversely, of course, two thirds are below the Welsh average.

However, LEA raw data can hide significant differences between schools, even within the same LEA, irrespective of their language of instruction.

For example, one of the LEAs had a range of between 3.4 per cent and 51.7 per cent, though that LEA's percentage was below 20 per cent. An LEA in a post-industrial valley had a range of between 8.4 per cent and 42 per cent. Neither figure belonged to an Ysgol Gymraeg. Consequently, one needs to be circumspect before making broad-brush statements about the socio-economic profiles, whether at sector or LEA level. In brief, the free school meals indicator shows that the Ysgolion Cymraeg are only three percentage points above the Welsh average. While there are variations in the entitlement to free meals, the percentage range is smaller than in the English sector, thus giving the Welsh sector a more homogenous image. At the same time it is misleading to brand the sector as being elitist, particularly as there are exceptions and substantial variations, not only in the Welsh sector but in the English sector as well.

STANDARDS ACHIEVED BY THE YSGOLION CYMRAEG

This section will examine standards achieved, with particular attention given (in interpreting those standards) to the socio-economic features of the schools. My observations are in two parts: perceptions about standards, followed by objective measurements, which are applied to critique standards and perceptions held about those standards.

Perceptions create images – in the case of the Ysgolion Cymraeg a popular image of high standards. Whether one agrees or disagrees with the image is another matter. For example, Gorard (1998: 462) refers to 'the . . . sustaining myth, that Welsh-medium schools are more effective than their "English" counterparts'. He further argues (2000: 144): '[T]here is an indication that the Welsh-medium schools in south Wales are not especially effective.' A different view was exchanged in the House of Commons six years earlier (Hansard 1992: 8):

> Mr. Butler: Did my right hon. Friend see the survey in The Sunday Times which showed that some Welsh-medium schools offer excellent education . . . some of the best education in the whole of the United Kingdom? Is not that a tribute to the quality of education within them?

> Sir Wyn Roberts: I agree with my hon. Friend and with the comments in the article to which he referred. The Welsh-medium schools provide a first-class education.

My own research sought the views of a cross-section of interested parties, interviews with 28 individuals between May and August 2006, and data processed from questionnaires filled by 524 parents and 96 teachers from the Ysgolion Cymraeg (45 primary and 51 secondary teachers) between spring 2004 and summer 2005. (Outcomes from a control group in English-medium schools are discussed in chapter 6.) The unanimous opinion of the interviewees was that the Welsh-medium schools had flourished, numerically, educationally, and academically. High standards of teaching, staff commitment and outstanding examination results were the main reasons offered for their success. Eirlys Pritchard Jones, a former headteacher of Ysgol Gyfun Cymer Rhondda, underlined the impossibility of separating the rights inherent in parental choice from the high quality of teaching.

For parents responding to the open-ended questionnaires, the ethos and high standards of the schools came second in order of importance after the Welsh language from a total of twenty-six reasons volunteered by them. They were uninhibited in their comparison of standards between local schools, maintaining (in their opinions) that standards in the Welsh sector excelled, a reason ranked fourth out of twenty-six. While academic standards as such were barely mentioned by these parents, their counterparts answering the structured questionnaire ranked this benchmark as the third most important reason for choosing an Ysgol Gymraeg. The reasons for the apparent differences in response are discussed in Thomas (2007: 232–7). One of the most important messages that emerged from the question-naire data was the high expectation of the parent body that their children should achieve their academic potential in the Ysgolion Cymraeg, and a parallel professional view amongst the teaching staff. Almost a half of teachers in the sample agreed strongly or very strongly with the statement that 'more potential parents would choose English-medium education unless the Welsh sector achieved high standards amongst local schools.' This shows that teachers are aware of the competitive nature of attracting (and retaining) pupils, a factor that gives the lie to the well-spun comment that schools in Wales are not competitive. When asked whether they thought that the Ysgolion Cymraeg would become less popular in their area should their examination standards drop, 43 per cent of secondary teachers agreed strongly or very strongly, contrasting with 29 per cent of parents, though 80 per cent of parents actually agreed with this statement to some extent or other (on a seven-point scale). The variations were more prominent in the degree to which respondents felt strongly about matters. On the whole, in the sample, teachers showed stronger feelings than parents.

We now turn to objective measurements regarding standards achieved. The interpretation and comparison of standards is a challenge referred to by Dylan Vaughan Jones (1997: 9):

> To prove that Welsh-medium education provides education of a superior quality to comparable English-medium schools is not easy and even to claim as such is clearly contentious. There is no doubt, however, that Welsh-medium schools have gained from their reputation, rightly or wrongly that they provide a better standard of education . . . From a position of relative strength there is now, however, a need to subjected [sic] current practice to closer scrutiny.

Little empirical research appears to have been conducted (or published) into the standards of teaching and learning in the Welsh-medium sector, nor into pupils' achievement and attainment. An exception is *A Competitive Edge* (Reynolds et al. 1998), in which its limitations as a research project are acknowledged (six OHMCI reports on Welsh-medium comprehensives in south-east Wales, thirty-eight on the English-medium comprehensives, and a comparison of two Welsh-medium and two English-medium comprehensives in the same area). The mean inspection ratings in the report showed that the Welsh-medium sector was (1998: 15) 'clearly rated as more effective in every area studied by the inspectors' (ibid., 15).

My own research examined standards of teaching and pupil achievement at both primary and secondary level, and pupil/student attainment at GCSE and A Level. Statistics on both teaching and achievement were based on Estyn Inspection reports on individual schools (2001–6), as well as three of Chief Inspector's Annual Reports (2003–6), making a total of 189 sources. Estyn used a five-point scale from 2004 on, with 1 meaning 'good with excellent features' and 5 'many important weaknesses'. According to Estyn (2006a: 59), the number of level 4 and 5 grades at primary level was so low that they had no statistical significance. My own analysis revealed that no significant differentiation appeared when grades 1–3 were used, leading to my aggregating grades 1 and 2 as a performance indicator. The pattern for secondary schools was fairly similar, though 3 per cent of grades (for all schools) were at level 5. After an initial trial, it was concluded that the primary methodology was appropriate at the secondary level as well.

A variety of samples was used in a range of comparisons, and one of the main conclusions was that grading is very closely matched for quality of teaching and pupil achievement. Statistics in this section refer to both teaching and achievement, unless they are specifically applied to one aspect or the other. Between 2001 and 2005, standards of teaching (grades 1–2) in the Ysgolion Cymraeg in south-east Wales were 9 percentage points above the national average for all primary schools inspected, 77 per cent compared with 68 per cent. On the whole, the range of grades was narrower in the Ysgolion Cymraeg, thus creating a more homogenous image of standards within the sector. This image or brand is important for potential parents, many of whom have to make a range of decisions before choosing the Welsh-medium sector.

Variations in quality of teaching occur between LEAs. For example, the percentage of grades 1 and 2 in the 8 Welsh-medium schools inspected in LEA B was 88 per cent, compared with 75 per cent for the 77 English-medium schools in the sample, and 68 per cent nationally. Both differences are marked, and confirm the impressions formed of high standards. Within the same LEA the range of grades between language sectors varies as well: 25 percentage points (73–98 per cent) for the Ysgolion Cymraeg, and 68 percentage points (32–100 per cent) for the English-medium sector. In LEA C, while the Ysgolion Cymraeg were 12 percentage points above the national average, their score of 80 per cent was only two percentage points above that for the LEA. This time the sample was 5 Welsh-medium compared with 53 English-medium primary schools. At secondary level, the sample is much smaller, but all Welsh-medium comprehensive schools except for one scored above the national average of 75 per cent by three percentage points. In LEA B the Welsh-medium sector (2 schools only in the sample) was 20 percentage points above the LEA average of 69 per cent.

Finally, Estyn evaluations of the quality of teaching in the Ysgolion Cymraeg are closely matched by Reynolds et al., who used the QAIT system, which (ibid., 18) has four main dimensions: quality of instruction (i.e., the effectiveness of teaching); appropriateness of instruction (i.e., the matching of the material to the needs of the pupils); use of incentives (i.e., promoting desired outcomes); and time usage (i.e., maximising effective time use). The authors' informed speculation regarding the teachers in Welsh medium education was that they had been 'more distinctive in the following ways':

- by being risk takers and pioneers of the new system in many cases, and being therefore more self confident than 'all' teachers taken together
- by having more ownership of their school, since they generated their own curriculum material in the early days of the schools, and their own curriculum material in the case of sixth form materials currently
- by having a strong sense of 'mission' and a firm 'identity' in a profession where both may be in shorter supply than formerly
- by having an exceptional regard for the Welsh language, and being correspondingly likely to work very hard to establish the schools. (ibid., 24–5)

One of the study's main conclusions (ibid., 21) was that: '[T]he Welsh medium schools are more effective schools and they are slightly more effective than English medium schools *even if one takes account of their advantaged intakes.*' The phrase *advantaged intakes* echoes the findings recorded earlier regarding the socio-economic nature of the Ysgolion Cymraeg, as well as the occasional innuendo that the Ysgolion Cymraeg, because of their intake, are not adding much value to their pupils' achievement or attainment. Before investigating value added in terms of pupils' attainment (in examinations), it is worth including the following quotation from Estyn's Inspection Report (2005a) on Ysgol Gyfun Gymraeg Glantaf, a Cardiff comprehensive often denigrated as a leafy suburb school. (Numbers in brackets at the end of every paragraph refer to page numbers in the Report.)

- The economic, social and linguistic background of the pupils is very varied. (6)
- [S]ixty eight per cent of pupils come from homes where Welsh is not the first language. (6)
- Pupils and students of all abilities, regardless of gender, social or linguistic backgrounds, achieve very good standards. Pupils with special educational needs achieve good standards. Gifted and able pupils achieve very good standards. (19)
- Pupils' and students' progress in their learning is very good. Pupils of all abilities acquire knowledge and new skills. They understand what they need to do to improve and they develop a high level of independence in

their work. They develop very good creative, personal, social and learning skills. All these are outstanding features. (10)

- The educational support centre is a very appropriate place for a small number of pupils with special complex educational needs. The progress pupils make, particularly in their communication and personal and social skills, is outstanding. (30)
- Pupils' learning experiences are an outstanding feature. (12)
- The County's 'added value' analysis shows that pupils of all abilities make very good progress at key stage 3 and key stage 4. (9)

The next section examines pupils' and students' attainments, and develops the theme of value added mentioned above. An analysis of pupil attainment needs to evaluate indicators used to measure the degree of attainment. Let us start with Y11. The most commonly used indicator for the GCSE, particularly by the media, is the percentage of five grades A*–C achieved in the context of the entire Y11 population. It is a crude indicator, like the five A*–G indicator, since it fails to differentiate; for example, a hypothetical school achieving all its grades at C level would have the same percentage of A*–C grades as a school achieving all its grades at A* level. Another indicator, the percentage achieving at least a C grade in Mathematics and Science and either Welsh or English (the Core Subject Indicator) ignores a good half of the students' curriculum. The remaining indicator, apart from value-added scores, is the average points score, which at the time of my research would allocate 8 points for an A*, 7 for an A, and so on, and divide the total for Y11 by the number of pupils on roll in Y11. The result-ing sum is the average points score.

The Ysgolion Cymraeg as a group of schools in south-east Wales scored above the national averages every year, by an average of 6.9 points. One could argue that the inclusion of Welsh and, to a lesser extent, Welsh literature in the core curriculum, skews the average points score. The counter argument is that all schools have the same contact time and that the indicator measures outcomes at the end of the same number of hours of time-tabled lessons. As one would expect, there are significant differences between the nine Welsh-medium schools, with the range of points going from 36 to 60. On a national level, the Ysgolion Cymraeg scored above the national average annually, except for one school. However, when every school's attainment was analysed in the context of the attainment of all comprehensive schools in its locality, every Welsh-medium school scored substantially above its neighbourhood cluster, as may be seen in Table 2.14. The average points score for the 101 comprehensives schools in south-east Wales in 2004–5 was 39.1, compared with 46.7 for the Ysgolion Cymraeg. The methodology used is described in detail in Thomas (2007: 250).

TABLE 2.14
Average points score of the Ysgolion Cymraeg in south-east Wales
and of all schools in their locality, 2004–5

Ysgol Gymraeg	School's average points score	Local schools' average points score	Comparison
1	51	46.5	4.5
2	60	39.1	20.9
3	46	37.4	8.6
4	43	36.8	6.2
5	37	33.8	3.2
6	44	40.6	3.4
7	48	39.3	8.7
8	44	35.0	9.0
9	47	38.2	8.8

Source: RE2 reports on individual schools.

The following paragraphs analyse the attainment of Y13 students, namely those who were 17 years of age at the beginning of the academic year 2004–5 and who took two or more subjects at A/AS level or equivalent vocational qualifications. Only sixth-form students are included in this study. Though the analysis of 2005 results showed that the Ysgolion Cymraeg scored above the average for south-east Wales, the difference was insignificant (+0.1). Compared with national statistics, their score of 19.5 was one point lower. Two schools scored significantly below their average for the period 2002–5. While one might expect results to be nearer the norm, given the (apparently) more homogenous nature of sixth forms, it was still notable that the profile was different from all other attainment profiles for the Ysgolion Cymraeg. Over a longer period (2002–5) their average points score was 20.1 compared with the south-east score of 19.2. Five of the eight schools scored above their locality clusters (from 0.8 to

3.6) and one was equal; the other two schools were 1.3 and 1.6 points below their locality score. Given the outstanding scores in Estyn inspections for the quality of teaching and pupil/student achievement, one needed to delve more deeply into such an abnormal profile. An analysis of prior attainment at GCSE gave an initial strong indication that their sixth form students represented a greater range of ability and attainment than those in local schools. One Welsh-medium school for example accepted into the sixth form in 2003 73 per cent of all students who had achieved at least 5A*–C grades in their GCSE, compared with 53 per cent for the remaining local schools. Another salient feature of sixth-form provision in the Welsh-medium sector was that it had a greater proportion of vocational students, given that local FE Colleges provide few courses through the medium of Welsh. Comparisons of attainment are therefore difficult to make in the post-16 sector, and like all comparisons have to be treated with caution.

Another interpretation is that the Ysgolion Cymraeg are showing signs of normalisation, not only of the Welsh language but of educational provision. For example, Professor David Reynolds was highly critical of Welsh-medium schools' GCSE results in 2005 (Blake 2006a: b). Though he was using the 5A*–C indicator (which I argued above was a crude indicator), and though his comments are directed at the GCSE results, nevertheless the following remarks made by a number of commentators at the time have a cross-phase relevance (Blake 2006a, b):

> Increasingly, Welsh-medium schools are local comprehensive schools serving a surrounding community. That is how it should be. One of the consequences of this expansion is that more and more parents now see Welsh-medium education not only as a desirable option but also a practical one. (Gethin Lewis, Secretary NUT Cymru)

> If there are good and not so good English schools, there will be good and not so good Welsh schools. Comparing one Welsh-medium school with another is as difficult as comparing apples and pears. (Geraint Rees, Headteacher Ysgol Gyfun Gymraeg Plasmawr)

> With the full spread of pupils now making up our school populations maybe just maintaining the excellent results has been a remarkable success story. (Geraint Rees)

> Although one of the arguments for Welsh-medium education in the past has been its higher standards it was always likely that this would be difficult to

sustain, particularly as the number of pupils attending Welsh-medium schools expanded. (Peter Black, AM south-east Wales)

I now turn to the final section on standards: value added, whose significance is described thus by the Department for Education and Skills (2004):

> Some children will always find it difficult to do well in tests and examinations. But all children are capable of making progress and it is important that schools are given recognition for the work that they do with these children.

> The progress that schools help individuals to make relative to their different starting points is usually referred to as value added. Value added measures are intended to allow comparisons between schools with different pupil intakes. For example, school A might show high percentages of pupils achieving five or more GCSE/GNVQs at grades A*–C, while school B shows lower percentages. But in value-added terms, the pupils at school B may have made more progress than other pupils who were performing at the same level at KS2, and therefore have a higher value added 'score' than school A.

Value added may also be defined as the difference between actual performance and estimated performance. The estimate is based on prior attainment and on other indicators such as gender, month of birth, or percentages of free school meals in a school. Positive scores mean that performance is greater than anticipated, while negative scores mean under-attainment. Significant positive or negative scores mean that 'it is 95 per cent certain, taking into account the number of pupils in the calculation, that the difference is unlikely to arise by chance' (WAG 2006). The complexities of value added analyses are discussed in Saunders's comprehensive review of the field (1999).

All in all, the Ysgolion Cymraeg appear to be performing well above the norm. However, some critics explain this by referring to the nature of the intake into the schools, high innate ability and privileged social background. How valid is this explanation? Here are five of the seven main findings in a National Assembly for Wales statistical analysis of Welsh-medium schools' examination results on a national basis (2001):

- A greater proportion of 15-year-olds in Welsh-medium schools achieved five or more GCSEs grade A*–C or vocational equivalents, (59 per cent compared with 47 per cent in English-medium schools).

- The average GCSE/GNVQ points score of 15-year-old pupils in Welsh-medium schools was higher than in English-medium schools (45 compared with 36).
- A greater proportion of 16–18-year-olds who were entered for two or more A levels or who achieved vocational equivalent achieved two or more A levels grade A–C or vocational equivalent than in English-medium schools (65 per cent in Welsh-medium schools compared with 58 per cent in English-medium schools).
- A smaller proportion of pupils in Welsh-medium schools were entitled to free school meals, (12.2 per cent compared with 19.0 per cent in English-medium schools).
- Analysis of levels of examination performance . . . in comparison with levels of free school meal entitlement shows that most, *although not all,* of the difference can be explained by the different levels of free school meals entitlement (used as an indicator of deprivation).

The report includes the following sentence, which I would argue belongs to the main findings: '[However,] further analysis suggests that, taking into account levels of deprivation, there was still a statistically significant difference of about 3 per cent between examination performance in Welsh-medium and "similar" English-medium schools.'

This view contrasts with that of Gorard (1998, 460): '[T]here is no evidence that Welsh-medium education per se leads to any advantage in schooling.' Gorard takes a limited perspective of the Ysgolion Cymraeg, without taking into account their linguistic background. He appears ignorant of the fact that some schools have an entire intake from non-Welsh-speaking homes, since he tends to refer to Welsh mother tongue parents (ibid., 462). Gorard appears not to accept the Welsh sector's critical role in reversing language shift, and his language verges on the vitriolic (ibid., 470):

> According to one account, there may be at heart a community, or 'Welsh class', linking nationalism with language, behaving as a status group in Weberian terms . . . producing changes by agitation which 'have been of most benefit to members of this status group', and attempting to monopolize resources through social closure . . . By remaining vociferous on [this] issue of effectiveness, the community may also hope to silence predictions about language '*apartheid*' and racism . . . the difficulties of comparative assessment . . . and lack of choice.

It is difficult to find any empathy in his writings with the Welsh language and identity, and he appears to reject linguistic inclusion, basing his arguments on a misconception that pupils are mainly from Welsh-speaking homes (2000: 144): '[The conspirators] . . . skew current choices, encouraging the use of Welsh-medium schools by non-Welsh-speaking families – a policy with potentially serious equal opportunity implications for ethnic minorities in Wales.' In another article, while arguing for parental choice of schooling, he does not include language-medium choice. He defends choice on religious grounds but not on linguistic ones (1997). Part of his paper focused on:

> The problems caused to this minority [families with minority religions], among others, by the implementation of a bilingual programme based on the principle of territoriality in a region where the majority of Welsh speakers now live in predominantly English-speaking areas such as Cardiff.

It was clearly necessary to include empirical research into value added data, and a full account may be read in: Thomas (2007: 258–65, 436–47), including an appraisal of various models, a discussion of some dangers inherent in value added analyses, such as the skewing that may be introduced by alternative qualifications (DiDA for example). The data used was from 307 information sheets on value added scores at key stages 3 and 4 provided by NAW, and covered the three academic years from the beginning of 2003 until the end of 2006. Data representing 94 English-medium schools and 8 Welsh-medium (9 from 2004 onwards) were processed. Considerable variations were noticed, not only between sectors, schools and different indicators, but also from year to year (in the case of individual schools). This pattern underlines the danger of overdependence on any one indicator. However, a school that has every score in the significant positive or significant negative category two years running would appear to have obvious outstanding features or weaknesses. Small numbers may also skew outcomes. In this study no statistically significant outcomes are recorded, merely trends.

Four indicators were analysed, based on progress made between key stage 3 and key stage 4: the average points score, 5 GCSEs A*–C, 5 GCSEs A*–G, and the Core Subject Indicator (CSI). Table 2.15 shows that the positive scores[3] for the Ysgolion Cymraeg are substantially higher than those for English-medium schools, both basic positive and significant positive scores. The significant positive scores over time are roughly from twice to four times better.

TABLE 2.15

A comparison of average points scores (value added) in both sectors

Year	Sector	Percentages: Positive scores	Percentages: Significant positive scores	Percentages: Negative scores	Percentages: Significant
2003/4	English	19.4%	23.4%	22.3%	35.1%
	Welsh	–	75.0%	12.5%	12.5%
2004/5	English	20.2%	22.3%	18.1%	39.4%
	Welsh	33.3%	41.7%	19.4%	5.6%
2005/6	English	17.2%	23.7%	28.0%	31.2%
	Welsh	11.1%	88.9%	–	–

Source: Thomas (2007: 442).

Such excellence reflects the high standard of both teaching and pupils' achievement and attainment, rather than any curricular factors, which I dismissed earlier in this chapter.

The second indicator, 5 A*–C or equivalent, recalls criticisms made by Reynolds (Blake 2006a, b). Unfortunately, the raw indicator is the one most commonly used by the media in reporting GCSE results. Results are higher in the Welsh-medium schools, even when background and other factors are taken into account, as can be seen in Table 2.16. The gap between sectors for the significant positive score is 35 percentage points in 2003/4, 16 in 2004/5, and 51 the following year.

Table 2.17 shows data for the 5 A*–G or equivalent indicators. The 25 per cent significant negative score is the worst value-added score for the Ysgolion Cymraeg in this trio of tables, and is matched by the CSI in Table 2.18. However, an annual improvement emerges, with no negative scores at all by the summer of 2006, whereas the English sector has just over 50 per cent of its scores in the negative section every year. The 100 per cent positive scores for the Welsh sector show that lower ability pupils are

TABLE 2.16
A comparison of 5A*–C scores (value added) in both sectors

Year	Sector	Percentages: Positive scores	Percentages: Significant positive scores	Percentages: Negative scores	Percentages: Significant
2003/4	English	33.0%	14.9%	34.0%	18.1%
	Welsh	–	50.0%	37.5%	12.5%
2004/5	English	29.8%	17.0%	30.9%	22.3%
	Welsh	55.6%	33.3%	11.1%	–
2005/6	English	28.0%	15.1%	34.3%	22.6%
	Welsh	33.3%	66.6%	–	–

Source: Thomas (2007: 443).

TABLE 2.17
A comparison of 5A*–G scores (value added) in both sectors

Year	Sector	Percentages: Positive scores	Percentages: Significant positive scores	Percentages: Negative scores	Percentages: Significant
2003/4	English	35.1%	23.4%	24.5%	17.0%
	Welsh	37.5%	25.0%	12.5%	25.0%
2004/5	English	33.0%	17.0%	29.8%	20.2%
	Welsh	44.4%	11.1%	44.4%	–
2005/6	English	36.6%	17.2%	30.1%	16.1%
	Welsh	44.4%	33.3%	22.2%	–

Source: Thomas (2007: 444).

improving their attainment annually, which should go some way towards answering critics who describe the Ysgolion Cymraeg as elitist academies or grammar schools.

The final analysis is of the Core Subject Indicator performance in value added terms. The fact that the Ysgolion Cymraeg have four core subjects rather than three, as in English-medium schools, means that the Welsh sector allocates less teaching time to the core subjects. Nevertheless, by the summer of 2006 the Ysgolion Cymraeg were scoring more than five times better in the significant positive section (55.6 per cent compared with 9.7 per cent).

TABLE 2.18
A comparison of the Core Subject Indicator in both sectors

Year	Sector	Percentages: Positive scores	Percentages: Significant positive scores	Percentages: Negative scores	Percentages: Significant
2003/4	English	30.9%	17.0%	28.7%	23.4%
	Welsh	–	37.5%	37.5%	25.0%
2004/5	English	29.8%	16.0%	30.9	23.4%
	Welsh	22.2%	33.3%	22.2%	22.2%
2005/6	English	25.8%	9.7%	37.6%	26.9%
	Welsh	22.2%	55.6%	11.1%	11.1%

Source: Thomas (2007: 444).

In brief, many educational observers believe that standards of teaching, achievement and attainment in the Ysgolion Cymraeg are high. My research showed that parent and teacher expectations too are high. The extensive data analysed revealed a substantial level of success across the sector, thus creating a brand of which parents, pupils and teachers are rightly proud. It became evident in the value added study that the myth created by opponents of the Ysgolion Cymraeg had been shattered: the truth is that standards are outstanding. Another cautionary note: recently published value added lists of school attainment, family groups of schools with similar socio-economic backgrounds and performance bands, need intelligent interpretation. In particular, the weighting given to some qualifications within a plethora of courses may well disadvantage some schools in their perceived performance. It is not the courses that are called into question, but the comparative weighting given to different types of disciplines.

To conclude, the Welsh-medium schools are characterised by their dynamic nature: their growth, their changing linguistic and socio-economic background, their increasing popularity and their academic and cultural success.

Notes

[1]   Ysgolion Cymraeg in south-east Wales, 2003–6.

Numbers of registered pupils. Schools opened since 2006 are also included, but without details, as they did not feature in the research. Some of the earliest schools are not named as such in this table. (Ysgol Bryntaf, Cardiff, was opened in 1949 and Ysgol Sant Ffransis, Barry, in 1952. Their subsequent closures due to oversubscription led to the establishment of a number of schools serving the same areas.) Secondary schools are printed in italics.

LEA	School	Date of opening	Number of pupils			
			2003	2004	2005	2006
Blaenau Gwent						
	Brynmawr (Bro Helyg, Blaenau, since 2010)	1971	..	303	304	301
Bridgend						
	Cynwyd Sant	1949	292	306	321	315
	Bro Ogwr	1962	390	402	396	382
	Y Ferch o'r Sgêr	1982	..	179	192	198
	Cwm Garw	1988	..	145	149	145
	Llangynwyd	*2008*	..	..	..	..
Caerffili						
	Y Lawnt, Rhymni	1955	..	168	168	161
	Ifor Bach	1961	..	213	199	187
	Gilfach Fargoed	1963	..	247	227	197
	Caerffili	1970	287	314	318	310
	Cwm Rhymni	*1981*	*1,021*	*1,064*	*1,135*	*1,140*
	Cwm Gwyddon	1985	..	182	186	193
	Bro Allta	1993	289	287	290	315
	Y Castell, Caerffili	1994	..	357	369	358
	Trelyn	1967	..	220	209	213
	Bro Sannan	2004	..	21	32	95
	Cwm Derwen	2008	..	..	..	..
	Panalltau	2009				
	New comprehensive	*2013*				
Cardiff						
	Gwaelod-y-garth++*	1968	108	106	128	116
	Creigiau++*	1977	137	148	149	150
	Glantaf	*1,978*	*1,106*	*1,098*	*1,075*	*1,082*
	Melin Gruffydd	1980	344	347	339	334
	Coed y Gof	1981	350	343	321	303
	Y Wern	1981	..	462	451	442
	Bro Eirwg	1981	..	434	436	449

Treganna	1987	..	172	161	170
Pencae	1990	..	195	195	200
Mynydd Bychan	1994	..	246	254	244
Pwllcoch	1996	..	313	338	364
Y Berllan Deg	1999	..	203	260	319
Plasmawr	*1998*	*688*	*735*	*743*	*781*
Glan Morfa	2005	..	..	..	14
Pen y Pîl	2007	..	..	..	..
Nant Caerau	2007	..	..	..	..
Tan yr Eos	2007	..	..	..	..
Pen y Groes	2007	..	..	..	..
Glan Ceubal	2009	..	..	..	..
Bro Edern	*2012*	..	..	..	..

Merthyr

Santes Tudful	1972	401	380	389	380
Rhyd y Grug	1976	..	218	188	183

Monmouthshire

Y Fenni	1994	97	104	111	109
Y Ffin, Caldicot	2001	..	36	45	61

Newport

Casnewydd	1969	..	387	392	397
Ifor Hael	2008	..	..	..	..
Bro Teyrnon	2011	..	..	..	..

Rhondda Cynon Taf

Aberdâr	1949	..	356	364	388
Ynyswen	1950	..	398	372	351
Llwyncelyn	1950	..	306	299	298
Pont Siôn Norton	1951	264	267	263	259
Tonyrefail	1955	..	197	199	191
Garth Olwg	1960	234	247	268	281
*Rhydfelen****	*1962*	*923*	*924*	*938*	*910*
Dolau ++*	1971	195	191	197	183
Heolycelyn +*	1971	113	110	108	107
Llanhari	*1974*	*1,115*	*1,062*	*1,091*	*1,081*
Penderyn +*	1976	104	105	104	96
Llantrisant	1976	..	225	212	219
Bodringallt	1979	..	216	218	209
Llyn y Forwyn	1985	238	235	246	221
Evan James	1985	..	425	434	429
Castellau, Beddau	1985	..	167	165	167
Cymer Rhondda	*1988*	*919*	*935*	*921*	*945*
Abercynon	1989	..	306	323	327
Bronllwyn	1990	255	251	262	266

	Rhydywaun	*1995*	*863*	*882*	*893*	*903*
	Llanhari (primary)	2013	..	..	..	..
Torfaen						
	Cwmbrân	1971	..	298	311	319
	Bryn Onnen	1985	..	230	230	231
	Gwynllyw	*1988*	*768*	*791*	*779*	*785*
	Panteg	2010	..	..	..	..
Vale of Glamorgan						
	Pen y Garth	1971	345	333	326	310
	Sant Baruc	1974	232	233	227	230
	Iolo Morganwg	1978	139	148	144	152
	Sant Curig	1992	400	401	406	382
	Gwaun y Nant	1996	118	116	128	134
	Bro Morgannwg	*2000*	*368*	*533*	*674*	*781*
	Dewi Sant	2011	..	..	..	..
	Nant Talwg	2011	..	..	..	..

Source: NAW (2006), 'Summary report on every school', *www.npd-cmru.gov.uk*

.. signifies that numbers were not recorded.
* signifies that the data were provided by either the school or the LEA.
** Officially Ysgol Gyfun Rhydfelen is now known as Ysgol Gyfun Garth Olwg.
+ Unit.
++ Two-stream school (one English stream and one Welsh stream).

[2] Sources: NAW (2000–2), RE2 returns; NAW (2003–6), Summary Data on Schools, National Pupil Database.
[3] A crude calculation was devised, aimed at showing broad trends: 1 point was allocated to a positive score, 2 to a significant positive, –1 to a negative, and –2 to a significant negative.

Chapter 3

The Shifting Impact of Language and Identity

Huw S. Thomas

The growth of the Ysgolion Cymraeg cannot be critiqued without due attention to three contemporary phenomena: the evolution of the Welsh language in terms of the number of speakers, the increase in a feeling of Welshness, and the incremental strengthening of powers granted to the Welsh Assembly Government. The interdependence of language, identity and education is therefore the first reason for allocating a substantial proportion of the volume to a critique of reversing language shift (RLS), with particular attention to Fishman's Graded Intergenerational Disruption Scale (GIDS). Equally important is that (for the first time in any breadth and depth) the Ysgolion Cymraeg are placed on a global conceptual stage. The third reason is to deepen an understanding, particularly within the educational sector in Wales, of the challenges of RLS, and the fourth is to show that the Welsh-medium school is no narrow, nationalistic, introverted institution, but part of a worldwide movement. The final reason is probably the most important: teachers and others who are daily engaged in (hopefully) saving the language for posterity should be encouraged to see that they are not 'fighting' on their own. Doubtless, the growth of the Ysgolion Cymraeg cannot be separated from the improved well-being of the Welsh language.[1]

Nationhood, culture, psychology, feelings and history are, for some (Mitchell 2009, for example), intrinsically linked with language and ethno-cultural identity. For others, (for example May 2001: 8), the connections between these elements are far more complex:

> Language is but one cultural marker among many and not even a particularly important one at that . . . or at least so it seems. This position immediately

problematises the intrinsic link between language and identity that is normally presupposed in many sociolinguistic discussions of language loss.

In Wales patriotic phrases such as *I'r gad! Safwn yn y bwlch! Coron gwlad ei mamiaith* or *Cenedl heb iaith, cenedl heb galon*[2] are well known, and are imbued with one of the most important features of reversing language shift, namely a rock-firm determination that Welsh will survive. Such firm resolution, if not credo, may be found across the nations of the world. According to Fishman (interview with Holson and Holt, 1994), the Mayans think that a nation that loses its language loses its identity; the Irish say that their language gives them the roots of the Irish tree; and the Sumatrans believe that without its language a nation disappears. On the other hand, Mac Giolla Chríost and Aitchison (1998) argue that the national identity of the Irish does not depend on the Irish language. Towards the end of the sixteenth century interest in the language increased to the extent that it became, in the end, a 'defining feature of ethnic identity' (ibid., 305). Towards the end of the twentieth century the link between language and identity weakened; the authors quote a number of sources (ibid., 306), including Northover and Donnelly (1996: 45): '[T]hose who do not learn Irish are not essentially different in their self-perception of ethnic identification from learners.'[3] Whatever view one takes, as Fishman said (Holson and Holt 1994: 83): 'It is hard to tell the truth about language and culture because anything that one says about the relationship between them is likely to be perspectival, that is, it is likely to be influenced by the "teller's" imbeddedness in the very relationship that is being discussed.' He continued: 'Most cultures, and minority or threatened cultures in particular, have very definite views of the relationship between languages and cultures in general, and, most specifically, about the relationship between their language and their culture.' He concluded: 'Accordingly, any commentator on the relationship is very likely to be influenced by the cultural view of that relationship into which he or she has been socialized.'

According to May (2005: 327), a generally held social and political theory is that language is at most only an element that impinges on identity, and he quotes in support Edwards (1985; 1994) and Eastman (1984). He goes on to say that 'our social, political (and linguistic) identities are inevitably plural, complex, and contingent' (2005: 329), and that 'while language may not be a *determining* feature of ethnic identity, it remains nonetheless a *significant* one in many instances' (2005: 330). Another approach, according to Smolicz (1979; 1993; 1995), is to consider language as a core cultural value,. While the following reference to Smolicz by May (2005: 341) is made in a footnote, it is particularly relevant in unravelling the complexities of Welsh identity:

> [W]here language is a 'core cultural value' – the *sharing* of that language may engender particular solidarities. Certainly, ethnic and nationalist movements have seen the potential this connection offers – often choosing language as a rallying point for the alternative histories, and associated cultural and political rights, that they wish to promote.

In Wales, with between a fifth and a quarter of the population able to speak Welsh, 'I'm as Welsh as anybody, though I don't speak the language myself, I'm sorry to say' is a frequently heard comment which incorporates that complexity of identity. While the cities in south Wales have been cosmopolitan for at least a century, England has been the main influence on the Welsh language and identity. According to Colin Williams (1990: 19), anglicisation – 'the process by which non-English people become assimilated or bound into an English-dominated cultural and ideological system'– is an enormously complex process, and one that transformed large swathes of the country and the majority of the population into monoglot English-speaking people. The allegiance of the majority was to the Crown and the idea of a British state. The complex links between Welsh language and identity were surveyed by Coupland et al. (2006: 22), who concluded:

> [O]ur regression analysis results show that levels of self-reported competence in Welsh do not predict subjective Welshness. That is *not* to say, however, that there is *no* association between these factors . . . Rather, that association is not sufficiently strong or consistent for the regression to have found it to be a significant predictor.

Harold Carter is another distinguished academic who has examined the Welsh people's desire to retain their Welshness and see it survive, against the odds, in the face of anglicisation, globalisation and multiculturalism (Carter 2010). He investigates the dilemma of the Welsh language as a marker of identity.

My own research into feelings of Welshness and Britishness amongst parents and teachers of the Ysgolion Cymraeg (2007: 70–1, 391–4) showed a strong, though not exclusive, preponderance towards Welsh identity. Whilst a little over a half of parents recorded that they were not warm-hearted British citizens, just over 30 per cent did, with a further 18.5 per cent 'agreeing more or less'. The data corroborates research by Coupland et al. (2006: 17): 'The overall pattern . . . suggests that no division into the categories of 'Welsh-identifying' and 'British-identifying' (the two categories used by Balsom) is tenable.' Of particular interest in analysing responses to research statement 31, 'Wales is my nation' (Thomas 2007: 391) was the relationship between 'my nation' and parents' country of birth (2007: 460). A little over 80 per cent were born in Wales and over 12 per cent in England (14.3 per cent of mothers and 10.1 per cent of fathers). Only four parents out of 378 were born outside the United Kingdom; 84 per cent of mothers born in England and 100 per cent of fathers born there recorded that Wales was their nation, thus showing that they had put down their roots so deeply in Wales that they elected Welsh-medium education for their children. Ninety-one per cent of them also recorded that they were warm-hearted Welsh people.

Where does the Welsh language fit into the global linguistic map? Only about 4 per cent of the world's population speaks 96 per cent of the world's languages, according to Crystal (1999a, b). There are approximately 6,000 languages in the world, according to Krauss (1992: 10), and it is forecast that only some 600 will survive. Whatever the academic prognoses, the general trend is clear (Grenoble and Whaley 1996; 1998; 2006; Crystal 2000): languages will die. There is no doubt that most threatened languages exist on the social and political periphery of the world. They are often spoken by ethnic groups or minority national groups. Another global pattern is that of the nation state. Of the 200 or so nation states, 120 have adopted English or French or Spanish or Arabic as their official language. The local language is the official language of 50 of them (Colin Williams 1996: 47). At the moment, less than 1.5 per cent of the world's languages are acknowledged officially by nation states. The nation state is the basis of the political framework across the world; it is powerful, ruling thorough politics and legislation. It creates an image of modernity and progress, and in political terms represents the triumph of universalism over regionalism. Of particular relevance to Wales is the emergence of one 'common' national language. According to May (2001: 6):

> This process usually involves the *legitimation* and *institutionalisation* of the chosen national language. Legitimation is understood to mean here the formal recognition accorded to the language by the nation state – usually, by the constitutional and/or legislative benediction of official status.

He continues:

> Institutionalisation refers to the process by which the language comes to be accepted, or 'taken for granted', in a wide range of social, cultural and linguistic domains or contexts, both formal and informal . . . At the same time, the chosen 'national' language comes to be associated with modernity and progress, while the remaining minority languages become associated with tradition and obsolescence.

It is essential that Welsh is represented in those language domains which are associated with modernity and progress. For example, mathematics and science taught through the medium of Welsh are symbols of modernity and are quoted as examples in the immediate context of legitimation and institutionlisation. Some readers may need to be reminded that this is happening in a country that has two languages with coequal status.

When one progresses the argument into the field of human rights, and defines the collective rights of linguistic communities compared with those of the individual, it would be illuminating to compile an attitude profile based on researching the following groups, to name some of the most obvious: Welsh speakers in the Bro Gymraeg (predominantly Welsh-speaking areas in the west of Wales); members of Cymuned (a Welsh communities pressure group in north-west Wales); Adferwyr; Llais Gwynedd; Welsh speakers in the capital city, non-Welsh speakers in the south Wales valleys; Welsh speakers in Carmarthenshire; immigrants; asylum seekers; the national assembly; or the monoglot English-speaking majority of the population of Wales. Individuals belonging to these groups are likely to have their own opinions, so that compiling a group profile would only be approximating to the true profile. Additionally, one needs to ask how the nation state is evolving linguistically within a multi-ethnic, multilingual, and multicultural context. These are difficult questions, but ones that need to be debated as Wales consolidates its initial reversing of the language shift.

Sociolinguists have long debated the factors that affect language shift. May, for example, summarises them (2001: 146) as:

- who speaks the minority language, and why [cf. Nelde at al., 1996]
- the degree of state recognition of the minority language
- the extent of support for the minority language within civil society
- the low status of minority groups and their social, cultural and economic marginalisation.

Wales, at the moment, scores highly on the second and third factors, while the status of Welsh speakers is often seen as high status, drawing criticism from some for elitism and belonging to the *crachach* [both Welsh-speaking and non-Welsh-speaking middle-class or 'posh' people associated with influential groups within Wales]. The growing determination of adults to learn Welsh is encouraging, while the number of school-age speakers reflects the growth of the Ysgolion Cymraeg and of compulsory Welsh. That many pupils do not speak the language outside the classroom is cause for concern, and is discussed elsewhere in this volume. Some commentators such as J. Edwards (1984a: 289–91; 1985: 17–18) believe that the most that can be hoped for a minority language is the reception of some of its symbolic or totemic symbols. Aitchison and Carter argue (2000:158) that the Welsh identity could develop on the strength and symbolism of its national institutions, with the language and traditional culture being interim means of keeping that Welsh identity. Linguistic and social Darwinians would argue that only those languages with the greatest communication currency are going to survive. Considerable importance is given in Wales to communication in Welsh in the public sector, the media and the national assembly. Sometimes tensions arise, as when debate centres on whether the Welsh Hansard should be totally bilingual. Failing to use Welsh as a language with strong communicative values would lead to diminution of status and the emasculation of any hope of saving the language.

Where does the truth lie? It seems to be somewhere between Gramsci's spiritual optimism of the will and an incisive intellectual pessimism. No one can foretell, but one factor is of paramount importance: the will of the people. Grenoble and Whaley (1996: 1998) believe in a bottom-up movement, while May (2001: 146) believes that 'it is regionally specific or even community-specific factors that dictate the ultimate patterns and effects of language shift in any given context'. Poor intergenerational transmission of language in Wales has led to a critical gap in the language's development;

currently intergenerational transmission is a line of defence. A critical mass of speakers must be maintained in west Wales, otherwise the country will be caught in a vicious circle of attrition. Faced with globalisation, electronic communication and American and English media, even majority languages are concerned about their future well-being. For example Ostler (2010: 2012) argues that the global transcendence of English may not be maintained. Across the world, there are systematic efforts to save minority languages, some of them indigenous languages and others spoken by immigrants. Joshua Fishman, one of the world's leading sociolinguists, is an emeritus professor on the medical campus of Yeshiva University in New York. It is understandable therefore that the well-being of body and soul is of fundamental importance in his theories regarding the reversal of language shift. Medical terms appear often in his voluminous publications: the patient, diagnosis, prognosis, medication, the spirit and the soul (2001: 1):

> What the smaller and weaker languages (and peoples and cultures) of the world need are not generalised predictions of dire and even terminal illnesses but, rather, the development of therapeutic understandings and approaches that can be adjusted so as to tackle essentially the same illness in patient after patient.

Wales has adopted many strategies to increase understanding of RLS and develop appropriate therapies: language planning, strategic analyses and planning, academic theorising, international cooperation, language in the community, language in social and leisure settings, and language through education. As it tries to close the gap between academia, the Welsh Language Board (1993–2012), the language commissioner and other strategic agencies on the one hand, and day-to-day language deliverers, particularly, though not exclusively, in the schools, on the other, Wales is trying to develop a coordinated therapy.

One of the challenges for the Ysgolion Cymraeg is to achieve a greater intellectual understanding of the more far-reaching implications of RLS, and then to adapt that understanding in promoting the social use of Welsh outside the classroom. In practical terms, the views of young people need to be central to the planning process, the recruitment of more adult participants (ideally from outside the teaching profession) needs to move apace, overseas patterns such as the Basque *ulibarri* (Aldekoa and Gardner, 2002) need to be critiqued, and the role of the Urdd and the Mentrau Iaith strengthened. The WLB had already started working on these challenges, but a greater focus is needed on marketing the aims and the events associated with developing the social use of language. The challenge is immense, but must be progressed successfully. Jeni Price's commentary in chapter 11 is illuminating, challenging and encouraging:

> If the Welsh-medium education system is to continue to be the main vehicle for creating a truly bilingual country, where everyday use of the language becomes increasingly common across all areas, then it has a specific and vital role to equip pupils with the necessary skills and confidence to use the language for both formal and informal purposes.

Wales has evolved strategies to reverse the language shift on many fronts contemporaneously, much against Fishman's belief (1991: 1): 'Let's try everything we possibly can, and perhaps something will work.' Theories may assist in RLS, but the human spirit is a stronger factor, as data from Thomas's research showed time after time (2007; 2010a *passim*). For example, the statement that 'Welsh needs to evolve in every aspect of life if it is to survive as a living language' elicited a 93.5 per cent agreement from parents, 96 per cent from secondary teachers and 100 per cent from their primary colleagues.

Following this brief introduction to language and identity, let us examine Fishman's GIDS (Fishman 2001: 466) and start with an explanation of it. (The conventions/shorthand are explained in the glossary of terms.) Every stage represents the seriousness of the intergenerational dislocation, and it is customary (though not obligatory) to read the levels from the bottom up.

STAGES OF REVERSING LANGUAGE SHIFT
SEVERITY OF INTERGENERATIONAL DISLOCATION
(read from the bottom up)

1. Education, work sphere, mass media and governmental operations at higher and nationwide levels.
2. Local/regional mass media and governmental services.
3. The local/regional (i.e. non-neighbourhood) work sphere, among both Xmen and Ymen.
4b. Public schools for Xish children, offering some instruction via Xish, but substantially under Yish curricular and staffing control.

4b. Schools in lieu of compulsory education and substantially under Xish curricular and staffing control.

II. *RLS to transcend diglossia, subsequent to its attainment*

5. Schools for literary acquisition, for the old and for the young, and not in lieu of compulsory education.
6. The intergenerational and demographically concentrated home-family-neighbourhood-community: the basis of mother tongue transmission.
7. Cultural interaction in Xish primarily involving the community-based older generation.
8. Reconstructing Xish and adult acquisition of XSL.

I. *RLS to attain diglossia (assuming prior ideological clarification)*

Fishman does not suggest abstracting ethnocultural identity (almost as if one were to encapsulate Welsh culture in a St Fagans museum-of-life context), nor does he suggest that it is possible to keep identity in a pure, unchangeable, permanent condition. Rather, he suggests that every human community tries to define its history and work towards an acceptable model of its future in accordance with that definition. This approach is echoed in 'Iaith Pawb' ('Everybody's Language'), a central government national action plan which aims at mainstreaming Welsh in the development of its national policies:

> The Welsh Assembly Government believes that the Welsh language is an integral part of our national identity. The Welsh language is an essential and enduring component in the history, culture, and social fabric of our nation. We must respect that inheritance and work to ensure that it is not lost for future generations. WAG (2003: 1)

The action plan builds on earlier policy commitments 'to the cause of reviving and revitalising the Welsh language' (ibid.), including *Betterwales.com* and 'Plan for Wales 2001'. The only sentence in 'Iaith Pawb' to be printed in bold underlines the strength of the government's commitment to reversing the language shift (ibid., 12): 'All Assembly members and their officials must share responsibility for the future of the Welsh language and take ownership for identifying and addressing language issues in their policy areas.' The Welsh Government's determination to increase the number of speakers reappears in its most recent policy statement, 'A living language: A language for living' (WG 2011a), and is discussed later in this volume.

Fishman believes (1991: 35) 'that both RLS-efforts and anti-RLS-efforts are essentially value based. They are philosophically and ideologically determined and are neither confirmable nor disconfirmable on a purely objective basis alone.' Developing a philosophy and ideology is another challenge that Wales is facing in a positive way, but that ideology and philosophy must not be the preserve of elite groups; fostering a wider appreciation of why and how the Welsh language is being saved should be a major target for government. Central government believes in local democracy, and should take heart from the following quotation, which sets RLS in a world-wide context (ibid.):

> RLS appeals to many because it is part of the process of re-establishing local options, local control, local hope and local meaning to life ... It espouses the right and the ability of small cultures to live and to inform life for their own members as well as to contribute thereby to the enrichment of humankind as a whole.

We will now examine, stage by stage, some aspects of Fishman's GIDS, starting with stage 8.

Stage 8

This stage is represented by old people who retain vestiges of their mother tongue; however, they are not part of the local community. It is the last stage before language death. It is possible to rebuild Xish based on the evidence of small vocabulary and language patterns, and by attempting to make the old people recall more. Rebuilt Xish can then become a basis for teaching it to younger people. While Welsh on a national (macro) basis is very far from Stage 8, it could be argued that at local community (meso) level Welsh was at this stage in, for example, some east Wales communities, but that the advent of the Ysgolion Cymraeg (micro) started the language revival in those communities. There is a fine line of distinction between this stage and the next.

Stage 7

At stage 7 most speakers of Xish are societally integrated, ethnolinguistically active and past child-bearing age. The Xish culture is an oral one, and young Xmen have the opportunity to experience the old Xish culture thorough the medium of Yish. One of the aims at this stage is to turn children and young people into second-language (XSL) speakers, and to persuade them to speak Xish. They will then be able to have children of their own and transfer Xish to their own children. Creating activities where Xish is the social language for families of child-bearing age is essential, as Canadians in New Brunswick have realised.

Stage 7 rings true for many areas of Wales, particularly east Wales, where there is still a need to organise social activities in Welsh for young families, and to persuade them to participate. The economic demands on young families, with both parents working full time, leading to little time for leisure, is a challenging one in terms of RLS. For children and young people, the Urdd and the Mentrau Iaith are two excellent examples of institutions that provide compensatory language experiences, now that the traditional linguistic, religious and cultural life of east Wales has been dissipated to a large extent. Some Xish activities such as the Cymmrodorion do not impinge on the under-fifties, and take place for the benefit of the older community. They do not contribute to intergenerational transmission of Welsh and can lull participants into believing that the well-being of the language is greater than it really is. This critique is not meant as a criticism of the Cymmrodorion activities but merely underlines the potential isolation of some groups within the Welsh-speaking community (cf. Fishman 1991: 92).

Stage 6

While 'language-in-culture' at stage 7 is for older people, stage 6 represents 'language-in culture waiting for young people to create their own families and for intergenerationally diverse families to achieve demographic con-centration of communities' (ibid., 93). Stage 6 is a difficult stage particularly since (ibid., 93) 'some of the families that it contains may not be entirely constituted of Xish speakers or of Xishly fluent speakers.' The greater the demographic concentration of Xish speakers, the greater the opportunity to transmit Xish to XSL learners through social norms and interactive situations. It is easy to apply this stage to the Welsh scene from two perspectives, one historical and the other contemporary. In the counties of Carmarthen and Ceredigion, for example, half a century ago speaking Welsh was the norm within families and between families in communities, as well as in places of worship. Within education, it was widely used in primary schools, but hardly at all in the secondary, further or higher sectors, apart from a few courses. The majority of the population would write and correspond in English, even from one member of a Welsh-speaking family to another, while Xish (Welsh) was totally acceptable for everyday life, religion, cultural events and small businesses. Yish was largely the language of bigger business, higher education and the media. The influence of Yish (English) was so strong that Welsh speakers would code-switch to English at the appearance of a Yish speaker. In short, English was the language of progress, of 'getting on in the world', while Welsh was fine within the local community spoken mode.

In spite of significant steps taken to reverse the language shift at a national level, including education, the number of speakers, according to the 2001 census, has continued to decline in the predominantly Welsh-speaking counties of Ceredigion and Gwynedd. (One needs to factor in the influence of the mainly monoglot English-speaking student populations in the universities of Aberystwyth and Bangor.) The lack of mother tongue transmission within families in Carmarthenshire, in spite of initiatives taken by the WLB, is particularly worrying. Since RLS involves enormous effort and commitment, it is doubtful whether the energy and emotion generated by language reversers in east Wales could be replicated in other areas of Wales. Keeping a critical mass of speakers in the Bröydd Cymraeg (plural of Bro Gymraeg) is essential not only for those Welsh-speaking areas, but also for the well-being of the whole nation. If west Wales came to depend on education, the media and the economy to keep Welsh alive, then the language might well have reached the point of no return. Such a pessimistic view must be seen in the context of Stage 6, with its focus on demographic concentration. There is a more optimistic interpretation, namely that small numbers of people can constitute a critical mass and switch from being a minority to a majority within communities. Cardiff is a good example, with concentrations of Welsh speakers in many wards or streets. There are concentrations as well in the media, the Ysgolion Meithrin and the Ysgolion Cymraeg, a good spread of places of worship, the Welsh-language societies, Welsh Government, and smaller institutions such as the WLB, or departments within colleges or universities. In all these milieus the language thrives, naturally, creating an identity and a feeling of belonging through the medium of Welsh. Such a reality counteracts the theory that unless at least 10 per cent of the population speak the language it is a lost language. According to Ambrose and Williams (1980: 69–70):

> [T]he pure fact that language may be in a numerical minority may not be particularly significant, since the evidence has shown that the language is not necessarily 'safe' in place where over eighty per cent of people can speak it, and that it is not necessarily 'lost' or 'dead' where only ten per cent can do so.

Where there are low numbers of minority-language speakers, inter-action may be through exchanging tapes, letters, video-conferencing, the phone, e-mailing or visiting (Fishman, 1991: 93–4). Wales uses all these media, but had the country concentrated on intergenerational and family strategies rather than on education, it is doubtful whether the decline could have been stemmed. The reason underlying this belief is that arranging sociolinguistic interaction (especially informally) is far more challenging than arranging an education system. Enhancing the social use of Welsh is the big linguistic challenge facing Wales. Numerous examples exist across Wales of activities aimed at encouraging the informal use of Welsh, activities that exhibit great commitment from volunteers, individuals, schools, societies and councils. Within education, there have been notable examples of originality – evening classes with overnight accommodation for pupils during the formative years of Rhydfelen (early 1970s), and social activities for all pupils integrated into the school timetable at Ysgol Gyfun Cwm Rhymni between 1981 and 1985, when all members of staff contributed. Ysgol Gyfun Rhydfelen bought an old school at Cwrt-y-Cadno in the middle of the Carmarthenshire countryside, facilitating study weekends or leisure activities. Many schools still follow the example set by Rhydfelen of arranging a residential summer course for new entrants, and whole cohorts of students will enjoy similar activities at any time of the year, particularly in Urdd camps. However, the new conditions of service and the ever-growing pressure on teachers to achieve incrementally better standards could well jeopardise such activities, unless the holistic purpose of education, particularly within minority-language communities, once again becomes a focus for school development.

The participation of Yish adults in promoting Xishness is one of the reasons for the success of the Ysgolion Cymraeg. While many adults become

XSL learners and fluent speakers, it is rather the feeling of Welshness, Xishness, through Yish that is the strong spiritual force driving forward RLS in east Wales. Personal experience confirms that the vision for increasing the number of speakers is clearer and more efficacious in the valley communities of south-east Wales than it often is in the Brӧydd Cymraeg or amongst native Welsh speakers in the capital city. The valleys have seen the dire consequences of stages 8 and 7, while complacency or short-sightedness in other communities can lead to branding campaigners as extremists. As the percentages of Welsh speakers drop in west Wales, and as family life disintegrates further with the migration of young citizens to towns and cities, the continued decline of the language in those areas calls for radical thinking within language and economic planning.

Intergenerational transmission of Welsh was one of the WLB's many forward-thinking and successful projects and is called Cynllun Twf (Growth Plan). According to the 1991 census, it appeared that 22.8 per cent of families had the potential to transmit Welsh, since at least one parent was a Welsh speaker. However, only 16.5 per cent of those families used Welsh with their children (WLB 2003a). An evaluation project (Edwards and Newcombe 2003: executive summary) recorded that:

> The national and international importance of Twf should not be under-estimated. While various language-minority communities are addressing language transmissions in a piecemeal way, the Twf project represents the first serious attempt to tackle this issue on a strategic level.

A further assessment of Twf (Irvine et al. 2008) suggests a number of ways of broadening the base for strategic improvements, including firming up *modi operandi* (health boards, midwives, and Twf personnel), enhancing publicity and marketing, highlighting the advantages of Welsh-medium and bilingual education and of intergenerational transmission, and improving the fluency of speakers. There is also reference to strengthening community developments. All in all, this latest evaluation encapsulates many aspects of RLS which are dealt with in this volume. It is encouraging to see a multi-focused improvement plan, which reflects Wales's growing (and successful) tradition of making progress on several of Fishman's stages contemporaneously. However, one is constantly reminded of Fishman's warning (1991: 95):

> Without an intimate and sheltered harbor at stage 6 an RLS movement tends towards peripheralization from personal and emotional bonds and faces the danger of prematurely tilting at dragons (the schools, the media, the economy) rather than squarely addressing the immediate locus of the intergenerational transmission of Xish.

It appears that Wales is developing an integrated approach to language revitalisation, though securing joined-up and coordinated thinking, planning and execution is challenging in itself.

Stage 5

This stage is reached when there is Xish literacy in the home, the school and the Xish-speaking community, but without consolidation of that literacy outside the Xish community. Historically, from the Renaissance onwards, the greatest influence on Welsh-language literacy nationally was the printed word as it appeared in the Bible. By today, Wales has a flourishing Welsh-language publishing industry across a wide range of fact and fiction. However, it could be argued that the Welsh-speaking nation is in essence a collection of Welsh-speaking communities: homes, schools, institutions, societies, areas of government and whole localities across the country. Outside such communities, the printed word has been normalised by the Welsh Language Acts, with indexical examples on street and road signs, for instance. The whole nation contributes towards the cost of such signs and the printed word receives government subsidies. Ymen rarely object to this strategy. But one should not call non-Welsh speakers Ymen, since they are strongly imbued with Xishness: they are Xmen without Xish, or Xmen through Yish. Though Wales has developed its literacy beyond stage 5, half a century ago this was barely the stage that Wales had reached within the sphere of text-books for schools, colleges and universities, since there were very few books printed in Welsh for these audiences apart from literature. The next quotation by Fishman (ibid., 98) is included since it locates the efforts of generations of teachers in the Ysgolion Cymraeg who produced their own teaching materials:

> It may seem unfair that the poor should have to tax themselves for their own betterment, but that is the way of the world and if Xmen do not labor on behalf of Xish before the world as a whole is changed, no one will do it (or pay someone else to do it) for them, or even believe that Xmen themselves really believe that it is worth doing.

He continues:

> The road to RLS is a long and difficult one and most of the road must be paved with self-sacrifice. There is no other way, really, for no language-in-culture can endure if it is dependent on another for the minimal essentials of its intergenerational continuity.

In spite of significant improvements and the addition of electronic materials, especially through NGfL Cymru, deficiencies remain, in particular a comparative dearth of resources in vocational fields, additional learning post-16, and further and higher education.

Stage 4

Stage 4 represents Xish in education, on lower levels which meet the demands of compulsory education statutes. At this stage efforts to promote the Xish community promote in turn the growth of Xish and the feeling of belonging to the community. All costs are paid from state taxes. It is possible to have Xish schools using Yish as a co-medium of instruction, while Xmen are given the right to formulate the curriculum. In 1991 Fishman believed that LEAs could withdraw their permission, thereby refusing to support Xish schools. Equal opportunities legislation and the Welsh Language Acts do not allow such a regression. At this stage, Fishman differentiates between schools he calls types 4a and 4b.

Type 4a Schools

These are schools which comply with compulsory, statutory education but are maintained mainly by the Xish community itself. Such schools are not part of the Welsh tradition. There have been two exceptions, the first being the private school established by Ifan ab Owen Edwards and Welsh-speaking parents in Aberystwyth in 1939. They anticipated or feared that the impending influx of evacuees would destroy the minimal amount of Welsh-medium primary education available in the university town. The significance of the first Ysgol Gymraeg is encapsulated by Iolo Wyn Williams (2003: 10):

> The establishment in 1939 of a private Welsh-medium school in Aberystwyth by Ifan ab Owen Edwards and his friends was a turning point in the history of education in Wales, comparable with the setting up of schools by Griffith

Jones and Thomas Charles, the Treason/Treachery of the Blue Books [Marvin 1908; Morgan 1991; Roberts 1998] and the 1889 Welsh Intermediate Education Act. By 1939 many rural schools used Welsh as their natural mode of instruction, thanks to the early efforts of O. M. Edwards, but the establishment of a Welsh-medium school in an anglicised town or industrial region was a revolutionary concept.

In Cardiff a similar move led by Gwyn Daniel to establish a private school failed. According to Iorwerth Morgan (2003: 25–6) this was due to the council's promise to establish a Welsh-medium class in an English-medium school, coupled with the fear that increased bombing raids on the city would lead to many Cardiff children being evacuated. He adds that many Welsh-speaking parents were not convinced that such a school was necessary, a calculated opinion that was replicated in the early days of Rhydfelen when some of the potential Cardiff pupils were not enrolled there (Humphreys, 2000: 70). Another development during the war was the oral encouragement given by R. A. Butler, president of the Board of Education, to the teaching of Welsh. Morgan documented the development in detail (2003: 26–7), underlining the importance in strategic terms of UCAC's letter of congratulation to him, and 'also calling upon him to send that encouragement in written form to the county councils of Wales.' Morgan continues:

> It arrived in October 1942, in the form of Circular 182: 'The Teaching of Welsh'. The significance of the Circular lay in its insistence that the Education Authorities draw up plans to promote the teaching of Welsh in their schools, and it called upon them to discuss their plans with teachers' unions and other relevant bodies. This was significant because it meant that the whole of Wales was obliged to discuss how to improve the status of Welsh and the teaching of Welsh in 1943, at precisely the same time as the Government was preparing the Education Bill that became the Education Act of 1944.

The 1944 Education Act created opportunities for the promotion of the Ysgolion Cymraeg, as it did for Welsh as a subject. In particular it advised LEAs to consider parental wishes with respect to their children's education. It is interesting that, in Fishman's typology, we can observe how the insight of a Yman, possibly/probably influenced by enlightened Xmen, led to practical implementation by Xmen. Such a pattern has been replicated within Welsh education on more than one occasion when Xmen have seen opportunities to progress Xish and Xishness through Yish patterns; the introduction of Welsh into the 'national' curriculum is one of the more obvious examples.

The second example of a type 4a school was Ysgol Glyndŵr in Bridgend, established in 1968 under the inspiration of Trefor and Gwyneth Morgan. According to Lord Gwilym Prys-Davies (2001: 11), this private Welsh-medium school was innovative and its establishment was an open criticism of the tardiness of some of the LEAs in south-east Wales in providing secondary Welsh-medium education. Shortly after Trefor Morgan's untimely death in 1970, Ysgol Glyndŵr's existence also came to an end.

Type 4b Schools

Type 4b schools are those that are given permission by the Yish government and its education authorities to teach in part through the medium of Xish, using a partial Xish definition of which elements of education are desirable and sufficient. They are taxed and funded from the state purse (Fishman 1991: 100). Type 4b schools provide 'an Xish component in the definition of minimally adequate and desirable education, but . . . are entirely funded from general tax funds' (ibid.).

According to Fishman, Xmen participate in a Yish education system. Ymen, representing a macro power, possess the political authority to educate according to Yish policies and programmes of study. In the 1980s, for example, it was England's national curriculum that created a framework which included a curricular and assessment structure for Wales, except for Welsh as a subject. The content of the curriculum reflected Welsh history and culture, and the Cwricwlwm Cymreig emerged as a national policy. While the general shape of state-school education was delineated by a Yish power, Xish politicians and educators, particularly the schools inspectorate, nevertheless seized the opportunity to make Welsh a statutory subject. As Fishman says (ibid., 99), 'public education involves an implicit social compact, just as does government itself'. In other words, had Wales not embraced such an opportunity, then any attempts to legitimate and institutionalise the language would have failed. Since the devolution of powers, including responsibility for education, from Westminster, the Yish government no longer has the power to grant or refuse permission to the Xish authorities to teach in part or wholly through the medium of Xish.

Such a change leads us to consider another type of school, which I have called type 4c. Later in this chapter an argument is made that there are no Yish schools at all in Wales.

Type 4c Schools

The Ysgolion Cymraeg could be called type 4c, since they do not fit into either of the two types described so far; they are not maintained by the Xish community (type 4a), and while the state funds type 4b, the curricular and assessment structures are basically the same for both Welsh-medium, bilingual, and English-medium schools. In 4c type schools, the Welsh language is far more than 'an Xish component' in learning and teaching; Welsh creates the school ethos, Welsh is the schools' official language, Welsh is the language of instruction for an ever-increasing number of subjects, and is thereby making a unique contribution towards RLS. Using Welsh for the sciences, mathematics, psychology, sociology, technology, child care and so on ensures that Welsh is progressive and modern, a theme developed elsewhere in this volume.

Before the advent of devolved powers it could be argued that the Ysgolion Cymraeg were type 4b schools, teaching partly through the medium of Welsh. The model established in 1981 by Ysgol Gyfun Cwm Rhymni of teaching the entire curriculum in Welsh from Y7 to Y13 has been replicated by every secondary Ysgol Gymraeg established since then. Schools in south-east Wales established prior to Cwm Rhymni have also followed Cwm Rhymni's lead, as have schools in north-east Wales. In fact, bilingualism and diglossia were confused in the early days of Welsh-medium education. Schools teaching some subjects in Welsh and others in English were diglossic: English for some defined tasks and Welsh for another set of defined tasks. Teaching what are often viewed as more important, higher level and more difficult areas of the curriculum (physics, chemistry, biology, mathematics) in English was a correct policy decision in the early sixties, as parents would not have accepted the viability of teaching those subjects in Welsh. In reality, sentence patterns are simpler in sciences than in the humanities. The similarity between English and Welsh scientific terms reflects their Latin or Greek origins; according to the *Geiriadur Termau* (Williams 1973: xi), they 'appear in large numbers in the dictionary'. These two points regarding terminology and sentence structure pose a fundamental question: why should learning sciences in

Welsh be more difficult than in any other language? My argument is that it is a perceived difficulty, which reflects aspects of language status. The argument is developed later in the chapter under language functions and compartmentalisation.

There has been a significant increase in the number of candidates taking their GCSE sciences through the medium of Welsh across the nation, as Table 3.1 shows.

TABLE 3.1

Number of candidates taking science and mathematics examinations in Welsh

O level/CSE/GCSE (WJEC only)				
Description	*1976*	*1986*	*1996*	*2006*
Sciences	69	902	2,642	3,991
Mathematics	23	962	2,597	3,049

Source: WJEC, Statistics Department.

It is equally significant to note the changes across the entire curricular assessments (Table 3.2). Both tables of statistics were produced by WJEC and do not include examinations taken in Welsh but assessed by examination boards based in England. The true numbers are therefore higher.

TABLE 3.2

Number of candidates taking Welsh-medium examinations (WJEC only)

Description	*1976*	*1986*	*1996*	*2006*
O Level/CSE/GCSE	2,553	7,356	14,607	22,684
AS	–	–	121	2,709
A	179	623	1,343	2,484
Total	2,732	7,979	16,071	27,877

Source: WJEC, Statistics Department.

The increase in external examinations through the medium of Welsh is encouraging, particularly at school level. There are four main reasons for the increase: the growth of the Ysgolion Cymraeg, in which pupils are assessed almost exclusively in Welsh; the evolving process of more Welsh-medium teaching in older Welsh-medium schools; a (slow) change in bilingual schools to more external assessment in Welsh; the confidence that comes from the normalisation of Welsh. The Ysgolion Cymraeg are accepted as a natural aspect of educational provision in Wales, increasingly supported by Welsh, British, and European legislation. The normalisation of the Ysgolion Cymraeg contrasts with considerable opposition towards them during their earlier formative period.

Fishman often refers to difficulties encountered on the road towards RLS, but his exemplification is often from minority communities in large cities and industrial areas and may lead to a somewhat pessimistic outlook. For example (1991: 102):

> [S]chools that are maintained from general tax funds . . . may elicit more public animosity and opposition than they are worth in terms of what they contribute to RLS . . . Even if implemented 4b schools must be 'indigenized' in *fact* (i.e., in their operations, in personnel, in program definition, revision and control, and in budgetary design and approval) . . . rather than merely in principle or in law.

However, one cannot digress too far from Fishman's warning that RLS calls for *constant vigilance*, as so many Xish developments within education are still influenced by Yish policies. Teachers' conditions of service and salaries, for example, are not devolved; curricular models are often not indigenous Welsh models, and are unacceptable when the language and ethos of education in Wales may be compromised by imported ideology, as in the 14–19 rationalisation. Sometimes the needs of Welsh-medium students appear to be marginalised, for example the Rhondda Cynon Taf County Borough Council draft plan for post-16 reorganisation (2009). This LEA has four Welsh-medium schools, all with sixth forms; the plan was to rationalise post-16 provision by creating three bilingual centres. Welsh-medium provision would be diluted, and the comparatively small numbers of students in Welsh-medium groups would probably lead to pruning of Welsh-medium provision, and to a smaller curricular spread for them, rather than a broader choice, which was the original *raison d'être* for the reorganisation. Creating one or two Welsh-medium centres would not be practical, due to the geographic spread of communities and the consequently long hours spent travelling. At the time of writing, the scheme appeared to be on hold.

In his concluding paragraph on stage 4 (1991: 103), Fishman argues that the influences of macro Ymen in the education system can create 'a process that inevitably destroys the vision of Xmen-via-Xish, even the vision of "Xmen with Xish who also know Yish and participate in Yish economic and political life"'. Welsh political life is a dynamic and ever-evolving process, making an objective evaluation based on Fishman's GIDS extremely difficult, if not impossible. Compromise, emulation, opportunism and pragmatism have certainly been patent aspects of the Welsh-language and education scene in Wales. Thomas and Egan's concluding paragraph on the inspectorate in Wales is a good example (2000: 166):

> [T]he overall experience of change appears to be another example of that 'incremental devolution so characteristic of Welsh education [*sic*, "educational history" according to Jones] over the past century' (Jones 1977: 192). Any differences between Wales and England arose as the actors in Wales used what scope they had, on the margins of policy formation, to reshape what had been designed in and for England.

One of the conclusions of this volume is that the Welsh language and education scene is complex. For example, there are many references to Wales's pluralistic language topography, which is mirrored in the nation's schools. Ken Hopkins (2006a: 14) alludes to the 'variety of linguistic provision in our schools' and to the need for parents to understand its linguistic nature and outcomes. It can be argued that Wales has no Yish schools, but rather a mixture of the following types:

- Yish-medium schools teaching Xish as a discrete subject, and promoting a feeling of Xishness through the Cwricwlwm Cymreig
- Schools that are mainly Yish-medium, teaching Welsh as a discrete subject but with some subjects taught through the medium of Xish to those who opt for that choice
- Schools that are mainly Xish-medium, teaching a subject or some subjects or a module or some modules within a subject or subjects through the medium of Xish
- Xish-medium schools teaching a subject or subjects through the medium of Yish to those who opt for that choice
- Xish-medium schools teaching a subject or subjects through the medium of Yish. The main reason for this pattern is historic (diglossic provision); there have also been statutory difficulties that make a change to total Xish-medium difficult

- Xish-medium schools teaching Yish as a discrete subject (English), as well as by Yish reading and communicative electronic methods

From such diversity let us resume the analysis and move to stage 3.

Stage 3

Using Xish in the lower work domains (spheres) outside the Xish neighbourhood or community and in interaction between Xmen and Ymen is the definition of stage 3 (Fishman, 1991: 103–5). Stage 3 is not totally necessary for RLS and is often outside the grasp of RLS movements, which should concentrate on stages 6–4. Wales does not believe in ignoring this stage, in spite of (or because of) the dire statistics that emerge regarding learning activities in the workplace. For example, of the 215,330 activities published in 2007 (WAG 2007b, overview: 5), a mere 0.2 per cent were taught through the medium of Welsh and 1.0 per cent bilingually. Opportunities to speak Welsh in the lower work domains vary across Wales, from the negligible and sporadic in the east of Wales to almost universal in some parts of the west.

The trading and economic limits of the business community have been extended in the west of Wales, taking Xmen into greater contact with Ymen across Europe while at the same time consolidating their business ventures within the Welsh-speaking communities. Economic and demographic planning in tandem with language planning is essential to Wales's efforts to stabilise (and increase) its communities of Welsh speakers, and is at the heart of government's 'Iaith Pawb'. It is not so much Yish per se that is threatening the Xish communities in Wales, but rather the immigration of Ymen and globalisation through the medium of English. English influences languages across the world due to its slickness and the ease with which other languages adopt new English words and phrases; the influences of the English media are considerable; English happens to have its home next door to Wales; and lastly, there is the hoary argument that the Welsh are able to speak English.

The next stage also deals with lower domains (spheres).

Stage 2

The lower, rather than the higher, domains of government and the media provide the focus for this stage. Few RLS movements reach this stage, according to Fishman. Wales, however, does operate comparatively success-fully at stage 2 within national and local government, radio and television, and (increasingly) information technology. Attempts to establish a daily national newspaper in Welsh have so far failed. 'Stages 2 and 1 represent the government itself or are most closely governmentally regulated because of their importance in the formation and preservation of integrative attitudes, opinions, identities and the topmost skills and statutes.' (Fishman 1991: 106) This is why assembly government support is crucial in many language-related developments: the Welsh Language Board, the education system through a range of agencies, particularly the Ysgolion Cymraeg, Welsh for Adults, language legislation, equal opportunities and the develop-ing field of language rights, to name but a few examples. Implementation by a civil service that mainstreams Welsh in its thinking processes and central planning is vital, though it is arguable, but not that critical, whether the civil service comes into stage 2 or stage 1. The answer is likely to depend on the level of responsibility.

Fishman says that stages 2 and 1 are the most difficult to influence. Wales has had notable successes, such as the Cwricwlwm Cymreig and obligatory Welsh within the national curriculum, or Welsh education schemes drafted by LEAs. The first two examples help to normalise Welsh (though delivery of Welsh as a second language in the classroom is generally poor), while the third raises awareness amongst planning personnel in county halls of the needs of Welsh-language learners and of their expectations (if not rights) within the local service. Cardiff City and County Council has opened its third Welsh-medium secondary school, without undue pressure having been brought on them by protest meetings and lobbying groups. The development is a good example of cooperation with RhAG and of proactive planning by the local authority, and suggests the normalisation of Welsh within the capital city. The planning of school places tends to be controversial, though citizens opposed to the develop-ment of the Ysgolion Cymraeg and/or to rationalisation of school places would disagree with this epithet. Jones and Williams, analysing Cardiff's reactive and piecemeal planning of Welsh-medium education during the last century (1939 onwards) referred to 'the delicacy of language revitalization' (2000: 168). It cannot be denied that the growth of the Ysgolion Cymraeg in the capital city is impressive, as has been detailed elsewhere in this volume. On the other hand, logistical and political challenges exist, with the third comprehensive (Ysgol Gyfun Bro Edern) being housed for its first year of existence in the buildings of Ysgol Gyfun Gymraeg Glantaf, while the overcrowding of one of the Welsh-medium primary schools (Treganna) led a parent to say (2007) that nothing had changed since the constant campaigning of her parents' days. Rhodri Morgan's essay (chapter 10) is illuminating in cataloguing the difficulties experienced in trying to resolve both English-medium and Welsh-medium provision in Cardiff West. Michael Jones (chapter 8) concludes his observations like this: 'Parents favouring Welsh-medium education must always make a nuisance of themselves, enough of a nuisance to make it easier and cheaper to provide enough Welsh-medium places than not to do so.' I am reminded of Emyr Lewis's lecture at the Newport National Eisteddfod entitled 'Minority languages in a new Europe – a bit of a head-ache for those who believe in order?' In his probing analysis of Europe's minority languages under international law, Lewis stated (1984: 7) that they can indeed be 'a bit of a nuisance for those who believe in order'. David Hawker uses the same phrase ('a bit of a nuisance') in chapter 7, when he reflects on minority-group perceptions of the power of central government and its civil service.

Fishman believes that governmental agencies and local services should be encouraged to operate bilingually, using Xish or Yish according to customers' wishes. Wales has lived through an evolving period from the 1950s, when Trefor and Eileen Beasley (affectionately known as the mother of direct action in our country and the Rosa Parks of Wales) insisted on receiving their rate demands in Welsh and were severely punished for their stance by having their furniture appropriated by bailiffs; members of Cymdeithas yr Iaith Gymraeg continued the campaign for normalisation of public services such as the post office and were incarcerated; those of a more pacific nature kept asking for Welsh-language forms and information leaflets or refusing to write cheques in English. More Welsh speakers should make use of those Welsh-language services that are available, but one is aware of the evolutionary nature of normalisation, the inhibiting effects of lack of confidence among users of threatened languages, and the confusion of extremism and narrow nationalism with what is nothing more than the right of the speakers of a lesser-used language to practice that language in all spheres.

Progress has been made in Wales by both campaigners and government, particularly through the agency of the Welsh Language Board. The interrelationship of individuals at micro level with services at meso level and with central government support at macro level is a subtle but essential process, where balances are constantly being struck between inputs at the three levels. When the balance goes awry, political friction arises, which can lead to frustration and, in extreme cases, to negativism and entrenched attitudes from both dominant and dominated parties.

Stage 1

Stage 1 represents some use of Xish at the higher levels of education, occupation, government and the media, but 'without the additional safety provided by political independence'(Fishman 1991: 107). It also means independent culture for Xmen-via-Xish. Xish becomes a language of coequal status with Yish. Representatives from education, the occupations, government and the media are responsible for planning, executing and evaluating the linguistic activities and the implementation of Xishness. Any assumption that one has reached nirvana at this stage would be a total misconception, since it represents the end of a long, difficult and tiring journey, but not the end of problems and matters of concern to RLSers. Fishman lists a number of these concerns (ibid., 108):

- Xish is not the only official and ethno-national language in the region
- many Xmen living outside the Xish language strongholds have a poor grasp of the language
- language standards may fall as more Xmen move from the periphery of the language strongholds to live in the Xish region's central area or main town
- Yish may continue to pressurise Xish
- Yish is the *lingua franca*, pressurising higher education, industry and technology.

It is easy to empathise with these concerns, such as the migration of Welsh speakers to towns and cities, particularly to the capital city, with the consequential loss, in some instances, of a critical mass of speakers within the traditional Bro Gymraeg. The 2001 census revealed a decrease of people able to speak, read and write Welsh in two of the heartlands of Welsh-speaking Wales (Gwynedd and Ceredigion). However, as Lewis (1981: 395–402) showed, college and university populations can skew data, and by 2001, for the first time, all UK students were registered in their college domicile, not in their parents' home.[4] Some commentators such as Carter (2002) argue that concentrating on maintaining the Welsh heartland could be counterproductive in the long term, considering that migration, particularly to south-east Wales, takes place for social and economic reasons. A counterargument is that losing a critical mass of speakers could be dangerous for the well-being of the Bro Gymraeg.

It is important, however, to underline that central government language policies, particularly those that originated from the WLB, appear to be successful, in that the downturn in the number of Welsh speakers was stemmed for the first time in a century, as was previously shown in Tables 2.5 and 2.6 in chapter 2 and in Table 3.3 in this chapter. These simple data are of great significance, according to Aitchison and Carter (2003/04: 55), 'for they confirm the predicted . . . turning of the tide – at least in terms of crude numbers.'

TABLE 3.3
Numbers of Welsh speakers in Wales (including Monmouthshire)

1901	1911	1921	1931	1951
939,830	1,043,421	922,100	811,329	714,700
1961	1971	1981	2001	2011
656,002	542,425	508,207	508,098	575,640

Sources:
1901, 1911, 1921, 1931, 1951: Welsh Language Board (2004); 1961, 1971: Aitchison and Carter (1994: 55); 1981: Aitchison and Carter (1994: 58); 1991, 2001: Aitchison and Carter (2004: 50)

There was no census in 1941, due to the Second World War. 'Welsh speakers in Wales' is not tautological, since there are considerable numbers of Welsh speakers in other countries, within the UK and across the world, who are not counted in the census.

When one examines the use of Xish or Welsh in further and higher education, Cen Williams's analysis (2003) shows that it is sparse. Current Welsh-medium courses show a modest increase, in spite of ongoing efforts by numerous committees and working parties. S4C (the Welsh-language television channel) broadcasts in Welsh for 23 hours a day during week-days and 17 hours at weekends (May 2011 analysis). Scheduling includes 6½ hours a day of programmes for young children (*Cyw*), a proportion of repeats (between 4 and 6 hours daily), some 6½ hours of events in the National Assembly for Wales (from midnight to 6 a.m.), while music programmes with a limited Welsh commentary are counted as totally Welsh broadcasts. Very little Welsh is used across the country in industry and technology. However, the Coleg Cymraeg Cenedlaethol (Ffederal) became operational in by September 2012, and central government stated in 'Iaith Pawb' that Welsh was to be part of every minister's portfolio. Yes, 'eternal watchfulness is the price of RLS' (Fishman 1991: 108).

Finally, let us examine briefly language functions and compartmental-isation, two principles that help one to understand the flow and status of the Welsh language, particularly within education.

Language Functions

During the first half of the twentieth century Welsh people believed that English was the language of 'getting on in the world'. Put another way, it was largely the language of the professions, business, education and government. Welsh knew its place in everyday life, religion and traditional cultural events. During the third quarter of the century a shift began in language status and functions, and those who chose to use Welsh in higher-level functions were not as widely regarded as extremists as formerly. The clear division of functions still influences education policies in some parts of the Welsh-speaking strongholds.

Fishman differentiates between the more powerful functions (P) such as employment, media or government and the other functions (n-P) such as the family, friends, and the community, or pre-school or primary education under the control of the community itself. Until the 1960s P functions tended to be conducted through the medium of the non-threatened language (n-Th), English. Within the school curriculum, the shift towards using Welsh, the threatened language (Th) as the main medium stopped when it came to science and mathematics. I believe that these subjects were regarded as more important and powerful learning areas than the humanities and the arts, which strengthened the perceived link between P functions and the n-Th language (English). That is why some language functions have become compartmentalised in some areas of Wales, causing considerable frustration for progressively minded people in Welsh-medium secondary schools in west Wales. Fishman explains thus (2001: 11): 'From the perspective of RLS, Th languages tend, at best, to become compartmentalised (i.e. functionally fixed), whereas n-Th languages tend to break out of any pre-existing functional compartmentalisation and to spread into new functions.' The Welsh language has nurtured its own self-confidence, so that by the beginning of the twenty-first century it refused to be compartmentalised and acquired new functions just like its non-threatened neighbouring language, English. Its status, psychologically, is now that of a non-threatened language.

Compartmentalisation

Fishman does not believe that RLSers should dissipate their efforts by trying to apply the language in every possible sphere, and urges them (ibid., 12):

> to reinforce recurringly the compartmentalisation of the n-Th language, so as to keep the latter from constantly generalising to new functions . . . The constant vigilance and insistence required by the n-P community of Th language users in order to compartmentalise continually and successfully the n-Th language of the P community is so substantial and unattainable that it also constitutes a reason why it is so difficult to strengthen threatened languages.

Compartmentalisation of the non-threatened language can easily lead to a parallel compartmentalisation of the threatened language, and a confusion of powerful and less powerful functions. Current practice in Wales is to extend the use of Welsh into all domains and spheres rather than keep some functions in English only. Such an approach may be exemplified by one of the country's Mentrau Iaith, Menter Cwm Gwendraeth in Carmarthenshire, as Campbell explains (2000: 253):

> One of the main aims of Menter Cwm Gwendraeth at the outset was to consolidate and support existing domains, establish new domains of language use and extend the use of Welsh to those domains which functioned mainly through the medium of English, concentrating mainly on community activities.

The pattern set by Ysgol Gyfun Rhydfelen in the early1960s of teaching the entire curriculum in Welsh except for the sciences and mathematics was an instance of diglossia, not of bilingualism: some spheres of activity in a person's life are in one language and some in another. Gwilym Humphreys, the school's first headteacher, argued the case for teaching these areas through the medium of English. His most valid argument (1973: 18–19) was that most parents would not have accepted a curriculum taught entirely through the medium of Welsh. In other words, his decision on the balance of medium and of the curricular areas was correct at the time, and reflected the pragmatism which helped shape Welsh-medium education. He does not discuss language status or the implications of using modernity of Welsh to promote the future viability of the language. It was rare to use such arguments in Wales in the 1960s. It is equally fair to record that a gradual evolution towards using Welsh in these subjects happened during the latter period of his headship, which suggests that his views were changing. Indeed he made it clear that had he listened to his heart Welsh would have been the medium from the outset (ibid., 19).

Unfortunately, the original Rhydfelen pattern influenced the language policies of secondary Ysgolion Cymraeg in west Wales, policies that are difficult to change even today, possibly because science and mathematics are often perceived by parents as high-level subjects, psychologically equated with power and prestige. Nevertheless, it is encouraging that Wales has seen a shift towards Welsh-medium science and mathematics over the years, as the statistics in Table 3.1 show. There is little discussion within Wales of the linguistic and sociocultural implications of teaching mathematics through the medium of a minority language.[5] Iolo Wyn Williams is one of the exceptions. His argument (1987: 42) is one with which I concur: 'If we designate important endeavours such as science and technology as being the concern only of majority cultures we diminish our own cultural identity.' He makes a similar point in arguing against teaching sciences and mathematics through the medium of English (ibid.):

> The most telling point to be made against such a policy is that it effectively defined English as being technical, vocational, and marketable, and has clear negative implications for the Welsh language, therefore undermining the very philosophy which the schools were established to foster.

CONCLUSION

All stages of Fishman's graded stages exist in contemporary Wales. For example, Welsh may be just about alive on elderly people's lips in some communities in east Wales; areas that have lost the language or are in danger of losing the language may be striving to re-establish it as a social language; the education system makes a significant contribution to the statistical increase in speakers; the language has official status; Welsh is the natural language of local government in some parts of west Wales such as Gwynedd; it is used intensively in some departments within higher education, and not at all in others; it is the language of S4C, but remains a minority language within the media in Wales. Secondly, the language shift is not a one-way process in Wales; there is language attrition in some areas and language reversal in others. The demographic movement of Welsh speakers to conurbations and particularly to the capital city is but one aspect of the current shift, but a significant one nevertheless as noted by Aitchison and Carter (1987: 492): 'a revolution of potentially considerable consequence for the survival of one of Britain's oldest languages'. The increase in speakers, notably those of statutory school age, in the south Wales valleys is almost totally due to the education system. On the other hand, there is insufficient intergenerational transmission within families in the Welsh heartland, for example in Carmarthenshire. The WLB's initiatives aimed at stemming language loss in the heartland (the language continuity project, for instance) are to be welcomed. Thirdly, Wales's language policies focus on all stages, the pre-school nursery phase, statutory and non-statutory education, intergenerational transmission, the Mentrau Iaith, Welsh for adults, Welsh-language schemes for businesses, institutions and councils, with the WLB steering and monitoring. Fishman might be critical of Wales's trying to do everything and think it likely to fail.

My view is that contemporaneous development on every front or stage is critical in a country that is characterised by its linguistic plurality, pragmatism and determination. On the lowest or micro levels, the language has to take root and show green shoots, particularly in the social milieu. Wales needs to endeavour more to encourage speakers to use their Welsh language. Activities at the higher stages do not lead inevitably to a language flourishing at the micro levels (Fishman 1991: 4). Fishman argues that social language which uses the medium of a minority language for insignificant, everyday matters is in a difficult position. Practitioners in schools would agree wholeheartedly with him. Nevertheless, successfully developing pupils' social language is essential. Their vocabulary exemplifies the difficulty: they know the technical terms in Welsh for *equation, gravity,* or *secondary,* but stumble over the Welsh for everyday words such as *knife and fork, windy,* or *a pair of gloves.* Jeni Price's chapter provides an insight into the psychological and practical ramifications of this complex challenge.

Fourthly, though Fishman might appear to be a structuralist and a promoter of systems, he never underplays the importance of the spiritual element, which is essential in reversing a language shift. Wales has depended heavily on such an element, which (with a strong sense of identity and patriotism) has inspired countless citizens to enter into a sacrificial mode in their total commitment to saving the language. Without the collective soul of the people and of individuals acting as catalysts, without an intense enthusiasm and a high degree of professionalism within the teaching profession, without the endless support of parents, governors, some local government officials and some civil servants, without leadership at critical points by school inspectors and politicians at a national level, and without language planning (though the structure is imbued with a strong element of personal commitment), there would not have been a reversal of the language shift in Wales. Fifthly, developing every partner's understanding of the implications of national initiatives and strategies is one of the greatest challenges facing Wales, along with a well-thought-out list of priorities and coordinated action. Adopting such a mindset would encourage the formation of a holistic vision shared by campaigners and the Welsh Government. Even during a recession, appropriate funding will be needed, but it should not add to to a growing national expectation that any initiative has of necessity to depend on additional central funding.

One of the characteristics of the Welsh psyche is unremitting self-criticism. While one accepts that success in one domain does not of necessity transfer into other domains, staff in the Ysgolion Cymraeg grapple with the daily challenge of how to make it natural for their pupils to speak Welsh in social milieus, including the school playground. One should not forget that English is the mother tongue of the vast majority of pupils in the Welsh-medium schools. One needs to respect the bilingual fluency of pupils, while at the same time working towards that linguistic nirvana.

'Working towards' is a crucial phrase to bear in mind when critiquing the success of the Ysgolion Cymraeg and the readiness of learners to use their adopted language in social settings. Over-planning and theorising is a dangerous route to take, particularly when the effects of strong central or European or global politics appear to be increasing, influencing the economies and languages of the world. That is why I find it comforting that RLS in Wales has depended to a large extent on a bottom-up move-ment, fortified by top-down government initiatives. For example, Baker and Jones (2000: 136), criticise the ad hoc, bottom-up influences on language and Welsh-medium education, and call for a greater input, vision, strategy and guidance by the National Assembly for Wales. That is now incorporated in the Welsh-medium Education Strategy (2010) and the Welsh Language Strategy (2011). Delivery of these strategies poses a different challenge. However, keeping a delicate balance between such divergent sources of power is crucial, since an overstatement of central influence can be counter-productive as, according to Gardner et al. (2000: 352), can be seen in Catalonia:

> Another problem which works against the normalization of the Catalan language is the loss of militancy in favour of Catalan, derived from a general feeling that Catalan is already 'normalized', or at least that it is no longer in danger. Indeed the important presence of Catalan in public life, chiefly in public organizations, corroborates this feeling.

On the road towards a bilingual Wales, will we see a balance between structures and policies on the one hand and, on the other, the will of the people to stimulate ideas and actions? As the known world appears to shrink and the influences of globalisation increase, will the lesser-used languages cooperate in a desire to keep variety? Fishman's final sentence in his volume *Can Threatened Languages be Saved?* (2001: 481) is: 'The languages of the world will either all help one another survive or they will succumb separately to the global dangers that must assuredly await us all (English included) in the century ahead.' Fishman's greatest contribution to language planning in Wales is the way in which he is able to stimulate and sharpen our intellectual understanding of RLS. As in all other disciplines, fashions and trends appear in sociolinguistics, but Fishman appears to transcend the temporal value of structures through his deep understand-ing of actors, their feelings and passions, their weaknesses and foibles.

In the earlier pioneering days of the Ysgolion Cymraeg, any planning for their expansion was basically pragmatic, but an embryonic process is slowly emerging of planned pragmatism, particularly the national strategy for Welsh-medium education, a development of massive potential for safeguarding the language and inheritance of Wales more securely than has ever been done before.

Notes

[1] Readers are encouraged to read in tandem with this chapter Colin Williams, 'The case of Welsh/Cymraeg in Wales (2005: 35–114), particularly the (substantial) section, 'A stage-by-stage analysis of current RLS efforts on behalf of Welsh', which gives a comprehensive overview of language planning in Wales at the beginning of the twenty-first century.

[2] *Take up your arms! Stand in the breach! A nation's crown is its language. A nation without its own language has no heart.*

[3] According to Mac Giolla Chríost and Aitchison (1998: 306):

> [T]he relationship between Irish ethnic identity and the Irish language in the Republic of Ireland, couched in terms of a separatist national identity (Ó Murchú 1997–81), may also be in decline (Ó Riagáin and Ó Gliasáin 1984; 1994). The result of the three national surveys of the language in the state (in 1973, 1983 and 1993) indicates a progressively lower level of ethnic and cultural identification with the language.

[4] The advantages and limitations of interpreting the 2001 census data are discussed by Higgs et al. (2004).

[5] Cf. articles by Khisty (1995), Dylan Vaughan Jones (1997), Adler (2001), Moschkovick (2002), Setati (2005), Evans (2007) and Gutstein (2007), some of whom discuss teaching mathematics through the medium of Welsh.

Chapter 4

Understanding Power

Huw S. Thomas

A simplistic analysis of the influences on the growth of the Ysgolion Cymraeg would suggest that power over their steady (and sometimes dramatic) growth lies in the hands of the parents. Since attendance at such schools depends on parental choice, there is no doubt that parents are basically the main driver in their growth. However, this chapter argues that the nature of power affecting their development is far more complex. I have aimed at striking a balance between an objective, academic analysis and, in the following chapter, a description of the power that has inspired the spirit and soul of individuals to change the historic course of language and education in Wales.

To avoid producing a disparate list of power factors, I have explored two fundamental theoretical frameworks, structuration and discretion, which appear to accommodate both human processes (the micro level) and policies and structures (the macro level). The first part of this chapter will define both theories, after which I will analyse examples of influencing powers, which, without the theoretical framework, might appear rather anecdotal. Machiavelli, Hobbes, Nietzsche, Gramsci, Foucault and Giddens are some of the thinkers who could provide the interested reader with further reading on the subject of power. I will restrict myself to Giddens.

STRUCTURATION

Structuration is a concept that will be new to many readers. It was developed by Giddens in order to explain the difference between structure and agency.[1] He defines the term (1984: 376) as 'the structuring of social relations across time and space, in virtue of the duality of structure'. His definition of structure (ibid., 377) is: 'Rules and resources, recursively implicated in the reproduction of social systems. Structure exists only as memory traces, the organic basis of human knowledgeability, and as instantiated in action.' Agency is an abstract noun, its concrete form being agent. An agent is someone who does things, accomplishes acts, an actor, or a person. System and systems are two other critical terms to understand within structuration. According to Giddens (ibid., 25), the words mean 'reproduced relations between actors or collectivities, organized as regular social practices'. Systems and structures are correlated concepts, but Giddens differentiates between them. Systems are patterns of relations within groups of every kind, ranging from small, closely-knit groups to large organisations; these could include families, peer groups, institutions, communities or cities. According to Gingrich (2000: 3),[2] structure for Giddens means something far more detailed and specific, such as habits and practices structured along clear lines. A structure has four main elements: rules of behaviour, rules of morality, material resources and the resources of authority.

Two essential elements come together in Giddens's work: his seminal writing on a highly theoretical level, and the concrete, as he forces us to perceive the actions of actors within the confines of time and space. Neither element can exist independently (1984: 2): 'In and through their activities agents reproduce the conditions that make these activities possible.' In other words, it is essential to perceive, understand and interpret the interaction between people and structures. Even more important is the particular way that structuration conceptualises structures and agencies, especially those processes that occur in the interface between structure and agent. Fundamental to the interrelationships and interdependencies between them are phenomenology (study or description of phenomena), hermeneutics (methods of explanation), and praxis (conduct and practice). According to Stones (2005: 4), 'These provide the hinge, if you like, between structure and agency.'

I have attempted a brief definition of the duality of structure, which is the basis for Giddens's theory of structuration (Giddens 1979: 5; 1984: 25). His argument was that structure is a significant medium as agents act. According to Stones (2005: 5), 'There is a complex and mediated connection between what is out-there in the social world and what is in-here in the phenomenology of the mind and body of the agent.' At the same time, structure is an outcome, the result of the actions of the agents. For example, the decision by a group of Aberystwyth parents at the beginning of the Second World War in 1939 to establish their own Welsh-medium school led to the current provision of Ysgolion Cymraeg. The Welsh-medium school has become part of the norm within educational provision and is recognised by law (for example, the Education Act of 1996). The Ysgol Gymraeg is a structure per se as a phenomenon, and is also part of larger structures, such as schools, education, or the Welsh language.

The importance that Giddens placed on locating his theory within time and space is outlined above. This is useful in empirical research when one considers the role of networks at the meso level.[3] How relevant therefore are Giddens's ideas in helping us to understand the influences on the growth of Welsh-medium education in south-east Wales? It seems to me that a focus on systems and structures as patterns of enacted conduct is one way to unravel the complicated weave between the micro, meso and macro levels in this study.[4] How relevant is a more evolved theory of structuration to the current analysis? Stones, for example, believes that structuration is at a crossroads (2005: 2), arguing for clearer, tighter and more systematic definitions. While he builds on Giddens's core concepts, he is also severely critical of him (ibid., 35), noting 'his [Giddens's] sheer lack of appreciation of the subtleties and complexities in any use of structuration theory at the empirical level'.

It seems to me that the prime value of Stones's critique within empirical research is twofold: firstly, his focus on the main arguments and counter-arguments regarding Giddens's theories[5] and secondly, his discussion of some of the dangers that could result from an unbalanced methodology. The first danger is overemphasis on either of the two main elements within structuration (ibid., 7):

> Depending upon where the emphasis was placed, structure or agency, it could be presented as either an overly voluntaristic theory – one that overestimates the knowledge and power of agents and their consequent ability to 'make a difference' – or an overly fatalistic and deterministic theory, where the structures make all the running.

Secondly, there is a danger of seeking justification for ontology-in-general rather than ontology-*in-situ*; in other words, of giving greater emphasis to concepts than to questions. The cornerstone of strong structuration, according to Stones (ibid., 38), is 'methodological reflexivity in relation to all of the relationships involved in the process of "finding out".' The third danger is the failure to realise the complexity of the interrelationship between agents and structures at different periods over time, and the different standpoints and conditions from which the agent and the structure begin interacting. For example, a new member of a committee will bring along a different point of view, no matter how rigorously he or she will have been briefed or read the minutes.[6]

The diagram in Figure 4.1 is another useful tool for unravelling the complexities and the divergent and overlapping features of actions.

FIGURE 4.1

Giddens' adaptation of Gregory's structural flow and interaction diagram

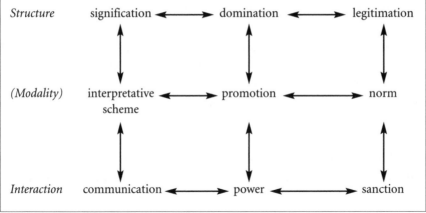

Adapted by Giddens (1984: 29) from Gregory (1982: 17).

Later in the chapter I discuss the centrality of power, interpreted as the ability to distribute resources. In Figure 4.1 one can see the flow between the various aspects of power. The terms 'signification', 'legitimation' and 'domination' also appear in the figure. 'Signification' may be interpreted at various levels: it refers to visual, material signs and to symbolic commands. However, in this discussion it means a clearer understanding of a concept or a perception of its significance for society. It may also mean that the concept loses its significance over time. 'Legitimation' means that the concept becomes more acceptable as part of the status quo. Its opposite is the open questioning of the concept, such as occasional letters in the *Western Mail* opposing the Welsh language. 'Domination' is reached when the concept becomes imbued with power by increasing both 'signification' and 'legitimation'. This stage depends on the acquisition of resources, both material and human.

Let us now consider Welsh-medium education within the framework delineated by the diagram. I would argue that it has reached 'signification', as demonstrated by a comparatively large number of visual, material signs, such as schools or teaching and learning materials. Symbolic commands are represented by statute, which recognises the Ysgol Gymraeg, and by public bodies which support Welsh-medium education. 'Communication' may be represented by the Welsh Government, county councils and various bodies including pressure groups such as RhAG. Welsh-language education schemes, written by the LEAs, are good examples of an 'interpretative scheme'. It is not necessary, however, to move from step to step in order to arrive at a particular point (in the diagram). Take 'signification', for example. In the formative period of the Ysgolion Cymraeg it would have been difficult to find an 'interpretative scheme' beyond the decision by LEAs and central government that such schools should be established. One could argue, however, that section 76 of the 1944 Education Act was an 'interpretative scheme', reflecting discussions between UCAC, particularly Gwyn Daniel, and R. A. Butler. It stated that 'Pupils are to be educated in accordance with the wishes of their parents.' Section 76 established the right to Welsh-medium education, not the right to establish a Welsh-medium school, as is explained by Iorwerth Morgan (2003: 30).

Equally important in the process is the movement along the lines of communication, a pattern that suggests discussion and agenda-setting by a variety of actors (people). An essential feature of any process is its dynamism, which varies in the energy that it produces. This holds true for the lines of communication. For example, while there is interaction between CYDAG or RhAG and Welsh Government, communication between the public and central government regarding Welsh-medium education has barely started. Lately, for example, marketing Twf has become more prominent, and there was widespread consultation in the draft strategy for Welsh-medium education (WAG 2009a). However, there were only 23 private individuals in a total of 152 responses; 82 per cent of all respondents agreed with the six strategic aims (WAG 2009b). Communication in the sense of marketing or advertising the Ysgolion Cymraeg as a national phenomenon is virtually non-existent.

The lines of communication between 'power' and 'legitimation' via 'norm' are not simple. For example, while the Welsh Government supports and has begun to promote Welsh-medium education, it tends to avoid the term Ysgolion Cymraeg. 'Norm' means that the Ysgolion Cymraeg are a natural and normal part of the educational landscape, though they represent a minority in statistical terms. When one considers Welsh-medium education in the context of 'domination', I would argue that it is not possible, as yet, to achieve the full level of 'domination' since 'signification' and 'legitimation' have been achieved only to a degree. More significantly, there is a gap in the line that flows directly from 'power' to 'domination', since it is difficult to find evidence of central government promoting the Ysgolion Cymraeg. One could argue that models trialled in immersion classes in Y6–7 support and promote the language within education, and schools' experience suggest that this is an additional method of allowing pupils to enter the Welsh-medium system (Estyn 2006b). However, the investment on the part of schools is considerable. It is also true that the draft strategy supported very strongly 'designated Welsh-medium education' (2009a: 42) in the east of Wales.

To conclude, aspects of structuration may be utlilised in empirical studies in order to delineate the complex interrelationship, not only between individuals and between structures, but also betweens structures and people, or agents; since agents are an essential part of structure, as structures would not exist without agents, a key question emerges regarding the role of individuals within a structure. The degree to which individuals change or influence the structure is a critical matter, which leads the study to subjective areas, assessing the effects on the structure of an individual's vision, discretion and ability to achieve practical outcomes. Do catalysts create opportunities and then steer them in a particular direction in the process of turning potential into success? The opposite is also true, namely the negative attitudes of individuals, which – intentionally or unintentionally – hamper the growth of the Ysgolion Cymraeg. Power may thus be used in a negative way by withholding resources. In the next section I will show how research into intentional discretion can explain negative attitudes amongst individuals (in politics or the civil service) who appear to be indifferent, if not opposed, to the Welsh language, Welsh culture and Welsh-medium education.

DISCRETION

A sound basis on which to explore the concept of discretion within decision-making as it affects the growth of Welsh-medium education and the Ysgolion Cymraeg may be found in Galligan's paper (1995) about discretionary powers and the principle of legality. For example, he maintains (1995: 17–8):

> in applying a standard to the facts, the decision maker has to settle both the meaning of the standard and the characterization of the facts in terms of that meaning . . . In . . . finding facts and applying standards, the senses of discretion are somewhat specialized; they derive from characteristics inherent in decision-making, in the need to select and classify evidence, and from our limited understanding of the cognitive process involved.

Galligan continues:

> it is discretion that results from the inherent qualities, in a sense, imperfections, of human decision-making, as well as from the elements of subjective judgement and evaluation which are irremovably part of the search for facts and the appliance of standards.

Standards or guidelines or rules are never complete, since they are an incomplete reflection of a more comprehensive and complex normative system. Before they can become specific, detailed and appropriate to specific circumstances, people's opinions have to be sought. Discretion inevitably becomes part of that process (1995: 19).

Both governance and administration call for professional and expert opinion, and reasonably clear authoritative standards are needed in order to avoid arbitrary decisions. Galligan develops a theory which may be a key to extending Welsh-medium educational provision (ibid., 28):

> The general importance of having authoritative standards which are reason-ably clear and settled need not be elevated into a rigid principle, since

situations can occur where the absence of prior standards opens the way for imaginative action on the part of the administrator which achieves the best outcome for all concerned.

Galligan's theory is illustrated by the example of schools' (historical) difficulty in evolving their language medium to the point of teaching the entire curriculum in Welsh. The main problem appeared to be the fact that they were labelled bilingual schools when they were established. In a detailed analysis of three cases in Carmarthenshire (Thomas 2007: 597–602), I argued that a study of discretion could lead to three main strands of development, particularly when considering the administrative influences on the growth of Welsh-medium education. They were:

1. Avoiding polarisation between the values of law and statute and the values that Galligan calls (1995: 31–5) contextualised considerations such as parents' commitment to Welsh-medium education and their campaigns to develop (or maintain) a school's language policy.
2. Developing a strategy which encourages productive interaction between agents in different structures. This in turn leads to legislation or guidelines or rules that allow people to be treated fairly and not arbitrarily, an example, according to Galligan (ibid., 35), of 'how administrative discretion can be a form of legitimate authority'.
3. Raising the awareness of agents who are outside government of the power and potential of laws and guidelines as they develop an ability to negotiate, whether formally or informally.

The argument was developed that lessons learnt from the Carmarthenshire case study were particularly appropriate to the nature of the growth of the Ysgolion Cymraeg across Wales. Many defects remain. The way to eradicate such defects also remains. There is a need to:

1. develop a better understanding between various actors
2. avoid polarisation
3. plan and draft guidelines in a coordinated, holistic way to ensure that from now on regulations will promote rather than hinder the aims of 'Iaith Pawb', 'A living language: A language for living' and the national strategy for Welsh-medium education. There is no evidence, however, to suggest any negativism behind the process of drafting the existing regulations reviewed. It is more a case of the wisdom of hindsight.

4. improve the effectiveness of some government departments
5. develop a sensitivity within the civil service to the subtleties of Welsh-medium and bilingual education
6. ensure sufficient time for drafting, consulting and responding to matters that arise from consultation.

The theme of intentional discretion is expanded by Huber and Shipan (2002), who developed a theory regarding the manner in which politicians frame statutes that will affect the discretion of agents. Their theory is based on the argument that considerations arising from policies are the main drivers that induce politicians to act.[7] Whatever the variables in the discretionary interaction between administrators or bureaucrats and politicians, people outside these two groups (pressure groups or societies or individuals) need to be aware of what these variables are, to understand them and to analyse the possibility of utilising them for the benefit of their own agenda.

The significance of such theorising is that the special nature of institutions affects, in a systematic and foreseeable way, the manner in which politicians utilise laws in order to frame the process of policy making. Wales has just crossed the threshold of primary law-making within the twenty-two devolved areas of responsibility, which include education. While Wales has had an apprenticeship in shaping measures, a process dependent on receiving approval to proceed from London-based governments, the democratic will of the people of Wales, expressed in the referendum of 2011, made it unequivocally clear that Wales wished for the freedom to create acts. This will be a new experience. One needs to be aware of the implications of the processes involved and particularly of their outcomes. Laws can be characterised by considerable dependency on discretion, or they can go to the other extreme. In other words, a legislative body might adopt laws characterised by detail and specificity in an attempt to control policy-making processes at the micro level; on the other hand, more general laws might be adopted which would allow both actor and bureaucrat considerable discretion. One aspect connected to structuration and discretion remains, namely setting the agenda. Before one has a legislative corpus the political agenda has to be set.[8]

THE POWER OF AGENDA-SETTING

The complexity and dynamics of setting a national agenda were explored by Kingdon (2003); while his arena was the USA agenda, one may adapt his theory to the politics of Wales, Britain or Europe. His theory was that problems, solutions and politics converge in order to move a subject into the agenda of public policy. The convergence, or coupling, does not happen accidentally: 'Successful policy entrepreneurs know how to pull together these diverse forces, but it is difficult to accomplish . . . independent policy streams "flow" through the system all at once, each with a life of its own' (2003: viii). The message for the development of Welsh-medium education that I draw from Kingdon's work is the need for policy makers, be they civil servants, politicians or educationists, to take a holistic overview of the forces that 'flow' from various directions, while the public body, whether individuals or pressure groups, is faced with a similar challenge, which appears to be of considerable magnitude. Kingdon describes the process as organised anarchy, and any agent or actor who hopes to influence the agenda needs insight and relevant information. Campaigners for Welsh-medium education therefore need to accumulate a store of expertise because, as yet, sufficient momentum has not been generated by the power of central and local government. The expertise needs awareness of problems, political processes and participants, both those that are in the public domain and those that are not.

Wales has the advantage of being a small country, which facilitates networking (to some degree). However, one still needs a comprehensive reservoir of people with the ability to see the flow of concepts within one holistic picture. According to a senior civil servant in the field of education (December 2005), there was no central vision (i.e., no civil service and government vision) with regard to the development of Welsh-medium education. The publication of 'One Wales' (May 2007; WAG 2007a) saw a change of attitude, leading to a draft strategy in May 2009 (WAG 2009a). The timetable was tight and ambitious. The document is an excellent example of ideas flowing, and of a comprehensive and holistic description of Welsh-medium education. The process of formulating the strategy with widespread consultation was an impressive exercise in governance, which enhanced the flow of ideas between a variety of agents and structures. The challenge will be to maintain the conceptual flow and ensure that the strategy becomes central to the understanding and vision of the civil service within education and beyond. Firm action by central and local government will need to follow.

Many aspects of the relationship between structure and agency are complex; that is also true of the various networks which exist both within and outside government. Marsh (1998) develops a concept that is one of the fundamental theses of this work, namely that macro, meso and micro levels cannot exist nor evolve without interaction between them. At the meso level I will examine patterns of communication by pressure groups; these are the policy networks. I will concentrate on matters concerned with the structure of the networks and the patterns of communication within them. The micro level is represented by the actions of individuals and the decisions of actors/agents within the networks. The present study does not provide a critique of structuration nor of the interaction between different levels of analysis; however, it does exemplify an awareness of these concepts. It is also important to note the danger of overemphasising the agent or the structure, without finding the power that drives discussion and creativity.[9] According to Marsh (ibid., 11), a critical question is to what extent, and in what ways, do policy networks affect policy outcomes. In the field of Welsh-medium education, now that ACCAC and ELWa have become part of central government, the accountability of the civil service and of politicians has become a key factor, paralleled, at best, by inclusive, open governance.

I have argued that policy makers in the field of Welsh-medium education need to take a holistic overview of the forces 'flowing' from various directions, while the parallel challenge for the public is substantial. Any influential agent or actor needs considerable insight and relevant knowledge. The challenge for Welsh-medium education campaigners will be to develop a reservoir of expertise, with an active awareness of problems, politics and stakeholders. One of the advantages of a country like Wales is that networking becomes easier, but sharpening the intellect and improving the level of debate is also necessary to ensure that the micro, meso and macro levels evolve as a result of the interaction between them.

WELSH-MEDIUM EDUCATION – WHERE DOES THE POWER LIE?

Power is a multilayered word encompassing strength, energy, vigour, ability, authority, government and the law, as well as personal, institutional, moral and spiritual influences. In the interaction between macro, meso and micro levels, power can influence in ways that are constructive as well as negative and destructive. According to Giddens (1984: 257–8):

> power is the capacity to achieve outcomes; whether or not these are connected to purely sectional interests is not germane to its definition. Power is not, as such, an obstacle to freedom or emancipation but is their very medium – although it would be foolish, of course, to ignore its constraining properties . . . Power is generated in and through the reproduction of structures of domination.

Mac Giolla Chríost (2003) discusses the connection between language, identity and conflict in his volume on that subject, and quotes Giddens's explanation of administrative power, which equates to the state's institutions (1985: 46):

> In all societies, traditional and modern, administrative power is the core of domination generated by authoritative resources, although it is not the only such resource that exists (there is in addition power deriving from control of sanctions and from ideology).

In this chapter I will analyse the interaction between the various levels of power in the development of the Ysgolion Cymraeg, and will adapt Mac Giolla Chríost's perception (2003: 172), 'power understood as the capacity to allocate resources' to the community of parents, who are seen as a powerful element, not only producing pupils but also insisting on Welsh-medium provision for them in the state's schools. Analysis, rather than description, will be the main element in my discourse, since other authors have recorded the campaigning and the consequential growth of the schools.

From the very beginning, parental power was the main impetus for establishing Ysgolion Cymraeg, and parental aspirations gave birth to real provision, due to practical support from LEAs along with centralist political influence: a combination of input by the civil service, the schools' inspectorate and politicians. The intensity of parental campaigning depended on the response of local politicians and the vision and support of professional officers. In other words, the greater was centralist negativism, the greater the passion shown by parents and pressure groups (such as RhAG or UCAC) in the campaigning. The history of establishing secondary schools is more complex, since pragmatic elements (particularly finance) would often stimulate LEAs to establish another Welsh-medium school or open their very first. For example, in the former county of Glamorgan Ysgol Uwchradd Rhydfelen reached capacity and Ysgol Gyfun Ystalyfera was established in 1964 for pupils living in the west of the original (immense) catchment area. By 'immense' I mean the whole of south-east Wales, the geographic area that is currently served by eleven LEAs (there are twenty-two in the whole of the country). Historical evidence suggests that some parents would inform their LEA that their children were living with relatives closer to Ysgol Uwchradd Rhydfelen than their actual home in order to circumvent the law, which forbade children from travelling to and from school for more than three hours a day. Oversubscription at Ysgol Gyfun Ystalyfera in turn led to the establishment of Ysgol Gyfun Gŵyr at the southern end of the catchment area. After further growth at Rhydfelen, Mid Glamorgan County Council opened in turn (every seven years) Ysgolion Cyfun Cwm Rhymni, Y Cymer and Rhydywaun. Oversubscription at Llanhari in Mid Glamorgan forced the LEA to refuse to accept pupils from the neighbouring local authority of South Glamorgan. That LEA was obliged to establish its own school, Ysgol Gyfun Gymraeg Glantaf, in Cardiff, the capital city of Wales. The establishment of Ysgol Gyfun Gwynllyw followed the traditional pattern; oversubscription in Ysgol Gyfun Cwm Rhymni forced Gwent LEA to make its own secondary provision. As pupil numbers at Glantaf grew, rather than establish a second school the LEA decided to make it a split-site school, with Y7–8 educated in buildings vacated by Cantonian Comprehensive. As numbers in Glantaf exceeded 1,500, the LEA decided to make the Glantaf lower site, less than two miles away, a separate institution, Ysgol Gyfun Plasmawr. At the time, both these schools provided for pupils from the neighbouring LEA, the Vale of Glamorgan.

Two challenges faced Glantaf as a result of the opening of Plasmawr in 1998. Staffing was the first, since it had to cope with the loss of a substantial number of experienced teachers or those around thirty years of age who had considerable potential to develop professionally at leadership level. Finance was its second challenge, namely the effect of significant financial cuts brought about by a drop in its pupil numbers. Plasmawr opened with Y7–9, taking a good third of the usual Glantaf intake. Though the LEA (after considerable negotiation) alleviated the problem to some extent by providing additional finance, the difficulties did not disappear. Only two years later, Ysgol Gyfun Bro Morgannwg was established in Barry, in the Vale of Glamorgan, a development that intensified the challenges to Glantaf. The fact that the school created an ethos of stability and improved its academic achievements during this potentially unsettling period is another story.

In this long line of development, the history of the establishment in 2000 of Ysgol Gyfun Bro Morgannwg does not fit in all respects the traditional pattern described above. Firstly, there were sufficient places in both secondary schools in Cardiff to accommodate pupils from Cardiff and the Vale LEAs for a further four or five years. Secondly, parents in the Vale campaigned diligently and intelligently for a school in their own locality; in this respect, the pattern was traditional. Thirdly, relationships between the Cardiff and Vale LEAs were not always good and a (negative) motivation developed, forcing the Vale to establish its own school. Fourthly, support for the new school came from the WLB, which may well have seen the expansion of the Welsh-medium school network as a positive step forward towards increasing the number of Welsh speakers, since the geographical proximity of a school increases parental support. On the other hand, two campaigners told me in an interview (22 June 2006) that the board gave no support at all, and that the WLB chairman's promise of financial support for the publication of a pamphlet came to nought. As far as the school inspectorate was concerned, my impression at the time was that it supported the development, though I have no primary evidence to support this assertion beyond the fact that when I raised the question of the effect on Glantaf, the only response was that establishing a new school was 'a good thing'.

The purpose of this analysis is an attempt to facilitate the process of establishing schools in the future, since lack of coordinated planning across LEAs can have a detrimental effect on existing schools. It is unlikely that Ysgol Bro Morgannwg would have been opened as early as 2000 had the same LEA existed for both Cardiff and the Vale (namely the former South Glamorgan, abolished during local government reorganisation in 1996). My argument is directed not against the establishment of the school, but against the failure of Cardiff LEA to make adequate provision to compensate for the negative impacts on Ysgol Gyfun Gymraeg Glantaf. In terms of power analysis, parental power in the Vale of Glamorgan succeeded, the local county council exercised its power by allocating resources (some £16 million) to establish the school and extend the buildings according to a well-defined timeline, and the Welsh Assembly Government agreed to the proposal to establish the school. On the other hand, Cardiff County Council withheld its resources by refusing further admissions to Vale pupils. Relationships between the Vale and Cardiff became so bad that a 'private' meeting was organised between senior officers and councillors of both LEAs with the then under-secretary of state for Wales, Peter Hain. This meeting took place in a hotel in Cardiff in the academic year 1998/99 and aimed at a compromise or some form of acceptable outcome. It was only partially successful.

This brief sketch is a good example of power at its various levels, including both positive and negative elements. One of the ever-present elements in the development of Welsh-medium education is the de-energising effect of the tension between different sources of power, which weakens the efficacy of the resources (both human and material) of all partners who contribute towards the decision. While one may argue that there was widespread, democratic governance at work in the process of establishing the school, those human resources could have been used in a far more effective and efficient way.

Cross-border coordinated planning was still lacking when Bridgend County Borough Council decided to open its own Welsh-medium secondary school in Llangynwyd, Maesteg, in 2008. Until then, Bridgend pupils had received Welsh-medium education at Llanhari, in neighbouring Rhondda Cynon Taf. There was no overcrowding in Llanhari to stimulate Bridgend to make its own provision. In fact, its Welsh Education Scheme (2006a) quoted a surplus of 250 places in Ysgol Gyfun Llanhari (par. 14.8.1). The scheme also detailed lack of growth of demand (at the time) for Welsh-medium education within Bridgend County Borough (par. 6.3; 13.9.2; 3.4.7; 13.10.1). An explanation for the proposed intra-authority provision is suggested by the following statement from the LEA (par. 3.2.3):

> Parental and student choice is clearly a key principle in determining how
> and where expansion in Welsh-medium education takes place within the
> County Borough. Increasing awareness of the opportunities that are offered
> will be critical in extending provision. It will be important to be flexible in
> planning this expansion . . . to ensure that strategies can be tailored
> appropriately to meet local needs.

Indeed, Bridgend's scheme was far more than a piece of bureaucracy; it
showed a determination to promote Welsh-language education. For
example (par. 3.4.1), it would provide 'a practical programme to promote
awareness of opportunities for Welsh-medium education and to "market"
the language in the County Borough, through education'. It would also
(target 1a, p. 55) 'undertake an annual review of parental preference and
intention' and increase the percentage of pupils continuing their Welsh-
medium education at secondary level to 100 per cent. Such intentions have
since become part of the national Welsh-medium Education Strategy. It
can be seen therefore that Ysgol Gyfun Gymraeg Llangynwyd too was
established without the process being crisis-driven by oversubscription. In
many areas, however, the battle continues, in spite of campaigning and
insufficient pupil places in appropriate settings. For example, Ysgol Cwm
Derwen in Oakdale, Caerffili, was opened in September 2009 after a hard
struggle by enthusiastic parents, as reported in the community newspaper
Tua'r Goleuni (2007). The campaigners, according to a local RhAG champion, Ben Jones, were former pupils of the area's Welsh-medium schools. In
the same month Ysgolion Ifor Hael in Newport, Tan yr Eos, Y Dderwen
(now renamed Pen y Pîl), Cefn Coed (now renamed Nant Caerau) and
Penygroes (all four in Cardiff) were established, the fruits of intense efforts
by parents and RhAG.

The battle for the continued viability of Ysgol Gyfun Llanhari has been
alleviated to some degree by the decision (spring 2011) of RCT Council to
change the age range of the school from 11–18 to 3–18. Its pupil numbers
had begun to fall significantly after the establishment of Llangynwyd in
2008. The emergence of a body to oversee provision of Welsh-medium
schools and plan an intelligent geographical network is one of the aims of
the national strategy, reflecting a stipulation in the European Charter for
Lesser-used Languages, and is discussed later in this chapter under
'Governance and European Dimensions'. Finally, another advantage for
Bridgend was that using the Llangynwyd site for Welsh-medium education

facilitated its new (and much needed) English-medium, one-site, secondary provision in Maesteg. This pattern is similar to the process of establishing Ysgol Gyfun Cwm Rhymni in the Bargod area in the early 1970s; the Welsh Office allocated finance for the reorganisation of secondary provision in the north of the Rhymni Valley, but most of the allocation was spent on building a new (and again much needed) English-medium comprehensive to serve Rhymni town and its environs. Ysgol Gyfun Cwm Rhymni was established in five old buildings on a multi-split (affectionately called 'splintered') site. This was the best option of three offered to prospective parents, and is a good example of inter-level power: parental at the micro level, opting for a five-site school; the council's political power at the meso level, offering three options (all of them poor ones); and the macro central government providing funding and approving the meso plans. In the Maesteg reorganisation plan one may draw obvious parallels with the Rhymney Valley scheme, particularly the power to allocate resources. There are however some subtle differences. Firstly, macro central government had already agreed to the reorganisation plan (Bridgend 2006b) before the statutory consultation on establishing Ysgol Gyfun Gymraeg Llangynwyd. Secondly, meso local government power appears to have been more pivotal than in the Rhymney Valley experience, where micro (parental) power was the main driving force for new Welsh-medium provision.

In short, the patterns that I have described are characterised by three important elements: the interaction between different powers in public life; the efficacy of local government power in its ability to agree or not to the establishment of schools; and the efficacy of people power through market forces that produced 'customers' who demanded to buy 'goods'. These elements may be summed up in one word: governance.

Governance is a process, and Welsh-medium education is an essential part of that process. Quinn (2005) is one author who discusses in detail the differences between government and governance. She refers to Osborne and Gaebler's emphasis on process as opposed to instrument.[10] Quinn's synthesis below (2005: 13) of Goldsmith's critique (1997) of the main characteristics of governance is a good snapshot of the process of governance in contemporary Wales:

> the characteristics of governance include 'an emphasis on vertical co-operation between institutions and tiers or levels of government, and on

horizontal co-operation between public, private and voluntary sectors' (Goldsmith 1997: 9). Such co-operation leads to the establishment of regimes or networks with shared values and visions. The creation of such networks raises issues of accountability, accessibility, openness and transparency.

Quinn goes on to emphasise that governance is a dynamic process which adapts to different circumstances, and that this reflects the constantly changing role of governments (2005: 3–4). The theme of a dynamic process is discussed by many other authors. In their treatment of the evolution of government to governance Stoker (2004) and Denters and Rose (2005) maintain that a number of factors are responsible for the change in the relationship between citizens and government (local): a significant decrease in the number who vote, other ways of expressing one's opinion outside the electoral system, a strengthening of the roles of executive officers, the creation of a cabinet system and the concentration of power in the hands of a smaller number of councillors, in spite of the role of scrutiny committees. The opposite may happen as well: a weakening of officers' roles as councillors increase their experience and power. Even more complex is a situation where a new ruling party comes to power after many years in opposition, without its members having been given any experience of sharing responsibility for government. Such a situation may lead to an increase of power within the executive, as executive officers use their discretion in the professional advice that they offer.

Before answering the question of where the power lies, it is fitting to see how Welsh-medium education sits in the broader context of the British political scene. One cannot appreciate the contemporary influences on the growth of the Ysgolion Cymraeg without an understanding of the influences on the British government and economy over the last sixty years. During this period the British political scene has changed under the influence of market fundamentalists, originally right-wing Tories and subsequently New Labour. One of the contemporary political scientists writing about the harmful effects of the private market on democracy and the well-being of the public domain, particularly from the point of view of citizenship, equality and services, is David Marquand. Throughout his volume, *Decline of the Public: The Hollowing-out of Citizenship* (2004), he emphasises that the public domain is not synonymous with the public sector. He makes three fundamental points regarding the future of the public domain.

First of all, Marquand argues that the public domain has its own culture and rules regarding decision-making. Action is generated by the pride that comes from fulfilling one's duties well or the feeling of civic responsibility (or a combination of both), and these take the place of profit-making or the fear of making a loss. The argument is that the public domain is very special and fragile and needs to be carefully nurtured (over time). The British state, he argues, has interfered aggressively in the public domain, thereby weakening its institutions and the very practices that nurtured the state. The state is by now in crisis. The most important element exhibited by the new right wing in the 1980s and 1990s was an unyielding and unsympathetic *Kulturkampf* that planned to eradicate the culture characterised by civic responsibility and services to others. Public trust in politicians and the whole political process has declined, fewer citizens vote in elections, and political sleaze increases through personal contacts, favouritism and sponsorship. In brief, British citizens do not show much interest in the public domain, except when they suffer as a result of its weaknesses, such as aspects of the health service or inconvenience caused by ineffective school transport. According to Marquand, the neo-liberal revolution is still with us, and leading the field are 'market mimicry, populist governance and central control' (2004: 139). How does this contemporary landscape look in Wales? I would argue that in government it varies as much as our physical landscape.

I will begin by referring to imitating (or not) strategies that belong to the market. The Welsh Assembly Government discontinued school league tables; the Welsh Government strives to promote partnerships between educational establishments, for both educational and financial reasons; emphasis is put on self-evaluation by establishments; and great importance is attached to the accountability of schools to the pupils, parents and government. The challenge is to find the right balance between professional autonomy and civic accountability, without regressing to comparatively unlimited freedom to do as you like. In the schools of Wales headteachers have been obliged to write a limitless series of policies, a process which has gradually led to emotional pressure and tension. In the Ysgolion Cymraeg in particular there are additional expectations: linguistic immersion, a Welsh ethos, extracurricular activities, the production of teaching and learning resources and the development of national strategies within political frameworks, often due to the inadequate treatment or even absence of Welsh-medium issues in draft schemes. Consequently it is not surprising that applications for headships are dangerously low. This is a challenge for the Welsh Government as it works towards achieving targets in both 'A living language: A language for living' (2011) and the national Strategy for Welsh-medium Education (2010).

Secondly, Marquand deals with populist governance. Consultation with the public, the professions, the pressure groups and the civil service was (he maintains) a pretence, as central government announced new policies. This attitude led to cynicism and negativism. In Wales, we need to make certain that politicians listen to people, to the various bodies and their various opinions but, in the complex and difficult process of political decision-making and policy development, to listen critically. After all, as Marquand says, people are not a homogeneous mass, and they can be wrong as well as right. Democratic self-government depends on tolerance, on the readiness to listen to others, and on the ability to differentiate between private interests and those of the public body. Individuals, groups representing particular interests, professional bodies and a powerfully effective local government all need to develop a national vision for Wales and interact with AMs and MEPs and (to a lesser extent in future) with MPs, so that together we can engage in genuine consultation as we jointly mould our ideal state. In Wales such a pattern, though ambitious, is achievable. Joint planning and development of common aspirations need to be nurtured by a balance between laymen, professionals, civil servants and politicians, but without the extremes of a Byzantine representative structure or elite select groups. At the moment, following the bonfire of the quangos, the future development and accountability of democracy is not altogether clear.

The third theme is the power of central government, one of the major factors that characterised public life in the last quarter of the twentieth century. In education, for example, one of the tactics adopted by the Tory government was the creation of grant-maintained schools, a policy that weakened local government. In Wales, very few schools opted for this new status, which would have freed them from the power of their LEAs and given them substantial new money. The state of school buildings, particularly, though not exclusively, in the case of the Ysgolion Cymraeg, was generally poor, and the new status facilitated new build or quality extensions or refurbishment. The appeal of improved buildings was strong.

However, with a few exceptions, Wales kept the status quo. The main reasons for such conservatism were the closeness of local government, a broad allegiance to the Labour Party and the overtones of private schooling which emanated from the new Tory model. In short, moving power from the centre is one of the basic elements in Marquand's vision, but I do not believe that the structures outlined by him are achievable, since they would be too time-consuming. Over-centralisation is harmful to the democratic process, and Wales needs to secure the right balance between the various actors who play their role in democratic politics. A substantial change is happening in local democracy at the moment, not only in Wales but also across the countries of western Europe.[11]

With regard to the Ysgolion Cymraeg, parents' commitment to their school is not in doubt, but I would argue that they need to be more aware of policies and trends in order to develop a better understanding of the future needs of their communities and country. I will quote from two sources to substantiate the lack of parental involvement (from every category of school) in the governance of Wales: results from Q4 in my doctoral research (Thomas 2007; 2010a) and the report by the Welsh Assembly Government, *School Governance and Improvement in Wales: Executive Summary* (2005). Statement 49 (Q4) stated: ' "Iaith Pawb", the Welsh Assembly Government's official policy on increasing the number of Welsh speakers, is essential in spreading the network of Ysgolion Cymraeg.' An analysis of parental response showed that 23.8 per cent of them had insufficient knowledge to respond. Had the statement asked whether respondents had read the document, the expectation would be that a very low number had done so. One may argue that 'Iaith Pawb' is not an essential element in the process of establishing more Welsh-medium schools, but that was not the point of the question; it aimed rather at measuring respondents' awareness of the policy laid down in 'Iaith Pawb'. One parent responded as follows (this is a translation of the original):

1. The questionnaire made me feel ashamed when I realized how ignorant I am of Assembly policies etc. and the way Councils work – I suppose that many (the majority?) are the same as me!
2. The Parents' Association in our school – its only function is fund-raising – there is no discussion on policy or anything like that – which disappoints me.

A strong suggestion emerges that there is a need to raise awareness among parents and teachers in Wales of far-reaching developments that could affect the development, or lack of development, of the Welsh language and Welsh-medium education.

The second source of evidence (WAG 2005: 2) underlines the fact that school governing bodies are unrepresentative:

> School governors who responded to our survey have a distinctive profile: they are likely to be white, middle aged, middle class and middle income public service professionals and managers. In this respect they are not representative of the population of most school catchment areas. School governance is class biased, with the under representation of ethnic minorities and parents from disadvantaged communities a serious concern.

The report continues (ibid., 3): 'Many governors believe recruitment in particular and also sometimes retention are problematic.' One could quote instances of Ysgolion Cymraeg where elections to the governing bodies are unnecessary because too few parents have been nominated. One also finds an imbalance between the percentages of governors who are Welsh-speaking, sometimes very high percentages, compared with the percentages of parents whose main language at home is English.[12] In short, Marquand's ideal of revolutionising civic interest in governance, even in the context of schools and communities, appears to belong to the distant future. However, the challenge of invigorating civil society remains.

GOVERNANCE AND EUROPEAN DIMENSIONS

As I have already demonstrated, the lack of both a holistic, coordinated planning process across county borders and a national overview of provision have been major weaknesses in delineating the provision of Ysgolion Cymraeg. The assembly government's Welsh-medium Education Strategy (2010a) seeks to address this deficiency, with the DfES (formerly DCELLS) assuming the coordinating roles. While the existence of appropriate legislation to allow that to happen is arguable, there is sufficient political will to set the agenda and to modify legislation, as the proposals in the draft Schools Standards and Organisation (Wales) Bill 2012 (WG 2012b) and Michael Jones's critique of it in chapter 8 show.

One of the purposes of Article 7, 1, i of the European Charter for Regional or Minority Languages (Council of Europe (CE) 1992: 5) is:

> to set up a supervisory body or bodies responsible for monitoring the measures taken and progress achieved in establishing or developing the teaching of regional or minority languages and for drawing up periodic reports of their findings, which will be made public.

The British Parliament became responsible for implementing the Article when it signed the agreement in March 2000 and that responsibility remained with it, according to the European Committee of Experts (CE 2004: par. 134), after devolution. Paragraph 34 of the document is a good example of interaction between governments, European macro, British meso, and Welsh micro:

> The devolution of responsibilities has the advantage of ensuring that the policies and measures for implementing the Charter are adopted close to the speakers of the relevant language. A difficulty that sometimes arises in states that have a strong tradition of local self government, in federal states, or where there is an allocation of powers to devolved administrations, is that the central state may not feel responsible for implementation of certain international commitments that it has undertaken, which expressly point to the level of government responsible. While fully recognising the value of such structures, the Committee of Experts nevertheless underlines that the United Kingdom remains responsible under international law for the implementation of treaties it has ratified.

Wales does now have its national strategy (including a supervisory body), and its first annual review has been published (WG 2011b). Historically, it seems that prevarication since 2000 (when the European agreement was signed) is a good example of some of the difficulties that have militated against inclusive Welsh governance: lack of mid- and long-term vision; lack of publicity for policies that already exist; the need to develop an understanding of policies at macro, meso and micro levels; the comparatively small size of the civil service, particularly sections with direct responsibility for Welsh-medium education and bilingualism; and the difficulties of keeping a balance between giving proactive advice, accomplishing daily pragmatic tasks, and dealing reactively with difficulties, many arising from an initial lack of proactive planning. We need to develop a more sophisticated level of debate in Wales, based on a good grasp of information, sharper thinking and mutual trust in open debate. There are, however, increasing opportunities for professional and pressure groups to interact with central and local government. CYDAG is an example of how a professional body may influence the shaping of national policy, by reacting to draft policies, but also by participating in regular discussions with the minister of education and (separately) the head of DfES. It is also represented on Estyn fora, WJEC committees and (formerly) on WLB steering committees.

The evolution of Welsh-medium education is dynamic and remarkable. In written evidence to COMEX in 2005, I appeared critical of many aspects of Welsh governance but some five years later the national Welsh-medium Education Strategy appeared, a historical declaration of centralist determination to improve provision. The following quotes (from 2005) need to be considered in this new context. For example, in July 2009 there were consultations on legislating for all LEAs to measure the demand for Welsh-medium education. Referring to the bonfire of the quangos, I wrote (Thomas, 2005: 5):

> Governance in Wales with its impending assimilation of ACCAC, ELWa and the Welsh Language Board, while not denying rights of access to central government, nevertheless has shades of judge, jury and even law-making, all in the hands of centralist government. CYDAG expresses serious concerns with the possible misuse of power, and sees a body as an external, objective participator in, hopefully, consensus governance. We are concerned that macro governance could become a monolithic, self-congratulatory institution with a perceived monopoly of the truth. That is dangerous.

Other points made that are central to the development of successful governance in Wales were:

> Another danger that could lead to conflict government is the tension caused by paradoxes between macro policy and meso implementation of those policies. I am equating meso government with LEAs; we have 22 such Unitary Authorities in a country with a population of some 3 million. Let me exemplify that tension. Macro government sets targets for increasing the number of Welsh speakers, and it acknowledges that Welsh-medium education, particularly immersion schools, is the most effective way of producing those speakers. However, macro government tells meso government that it is not

to create a demand for Welsh-medium schools, only to respond to the demand. We believe that such a policy is in direct conflict with the spirit of the language policy as expressed in 'Iaith Pawb'.

Here is another instance of the need for a central body to promote joined-up thinking. However, we ought to mention a recent macro guideline (CE 2005a: 22), which states that LEAs will in the near future have to show strong evidence that they have measured parents' wishes as to the language in which they would like their children to be educated. We understand that data on recent births will be made available in order to facilitate such market research. We applaud central government's initiative, and are ready to cooperate fully in their planning strategies. At the same time, publicity for this initiative is thin on the ground, and we cannot be blamed for thinking that this is an instance of government running with the hares and the hounds: supporting the language, without alienating non-supporters. We realise that policy makers are avoiding conflict by taking a neutral stance, but a more positive attitude needs to be developed, particularly with the marketing of Welsh-medium education.

'Iaith Pawb' seems to avoid referring to the . . . Ysgolion Cymraeg; instead, the report appears to deconstruct the schools as it were, and subsume them under the abstract term Welsh-medium education. There appears to be little promotion of the Ysgolion Cymraeg as a successful model.

The Welsh-medium Education Strategy in 2010 was followed some eighteen months later by the Welsh Assembly Government's draft Strategy for the Welsh Language, 'A living language: A language for living'. A massive shift in centralist government policy and stance since the 1990s and earlier may be exemplified by the following quotation (2011a: 20): 'The new standards proposed in the Welsh Language Measure will impose a duty on local authorities to promote the Welsh language more widely.' However, there is still little evidence of the local authorities promoting Welsh-medium schools, though such schools have been the main driver in increasing the number of Welsh speakers. Political will needs to ensure that policies are put into practice. That determination is encapsulated in the heritage minister's preface to the draft strategy, which includes the following sentence: 'Our strategy will reflect the vision of a Government determined to see the Welsh language thrive.'

In a theoretical discussion about concepts such as models and structures it is easy to neglect one of the most important elements that leads to success or failure, namely the nature and qualities of those people who create, adapt and put into practice the aims of those models and structures.

Before critiquing the influence of individuals in promoting the Ysgolion Cymraeg let us briefly consider the role of policies in the development of such schools. The production of policies is a *sine qua non* of contemporary practice.

POLICIES

At a macro level, commentators such as Rees (2004) maintain that a strong British regime still exists in the field of policy-making since the establishment of the national assembly. Within education, it is easy to quote examples of Wales developing her own system, for example, the foundation stage, the deletion of league tables, or higher education funding structures, particularly tuition fees. The question of convergence and divergence within education policies is extremely complex, again according to Rees (ibid., 36): 'to the extent that 'policy learning' between the territories of the UK develops as a major element in policy-making, then this is likely to reinforce tendencies towards policy convergence'. Of course, Wales's experience of policy-making at macro national level is a short one, so that one should not be surprised to see macro British policies influencing substantially its inspection system, the shape of the curriculum, funding systems and fundamental aspects of further and higher education, while agreements on working conditions and salaries are totally British. Some thirty years ago the challenge was greater, according to John Brace (1982, 68):

> Strangely enough, Mrs Nancy Trenaman in her review of the Schools Council saw little or no difference between the schools of Wales and those of England. It would appear that she saw Wales as an extension of England and only recommended a stay of execution for the Schools Council Committee for Wales because of that eccentricity that refuses to go away, the Welsh language.

The Welsh language and the Cwricwlwm Cymreig are of course unique to Wales, and are differences that arise from our national identity. It is expected that pupils are given opportunities within the curriculum to develop and apply knowledge and understanding of cultural, economic, environmental, historical and linguistic features (ACCAC 2003: 3). Estyn's report on the Cwricwlwm Cymreig (2005c) made a number of positive comments on its delivery and thirteen recommendations at the end of the report were aimed at deepening pupils' awareness of the nation's identity. The report reflects the inspectorate's influence, and is a good example of individuals within the inspectorate and the body corporate using their discretion to promote identity.

Within the political parties, the Liberal Democrats' policy on a bilingual Wales was explained by Jenny Randerson AM (now Baroness Randerson of Roath Park) in an interview on 18 August 2006:

> The Liberal Democrats have an extensive policy on the Welsh language and a commitment to a bilingual Wales. We have a long-standing policy to ensure that it is easier to establish Welsh-medium schools. In practice, it is like water building up behind a dam, which eventually breaks, and the local authority has to establish a new Welsh-medium school. Local authorities have an obligation to plan, but they are not proactive enough about it.

Some interviewees thought that the existence of policies expedited action (Geraint and Carys Evans, 22 June 2006), while language planners might query the sustainability of progressive growth for the Ysgolion Cymraeg if action were based on the status quo, namely ad hoc and incremental growth. Others, such as Keith Price Davies (21 June 2006), doubted the efficacy of policies. According to one headteacher (Alun Davies, 21 August 2006), parents tend not to be aware of strategies and policies, but are alive to influences on their own children. The last two comments suggest that pragmatism, good practice and fruitful interaction between people have been the key to the success of this education sector. Policy can certainly contribute towards encouraging further growth, but 'a policy may be an excuse for not taking action. It is the person who counts in the end' (Keith Price Davies, 21 June 2006). This point is developed later under 'Individual Discretion'.

INCREASING THE NUMBER OF YSGOLION CYMRAEG – WHOSE RESPONSIBILITY?

What have been notable aspects of policies in the field of Welsh-medium education at the micro level, here taken to be the county councils? Their Welsh education schemes are not discussed here, since they perceived as subsidiary to policy levels. Evidence from interviews made it clear that policies to promote Ysgolion Cymraeg and to be proactive in planning for them did not exist. According to the Chief Executive of the WLB (10 July 2006), six of the eight LEAs were following 'some sort of Welsh language education policy' in 1996. When asked who planned proactively in Gwent, Lilian Jones (former headteacher of Ysgol Gyfun Gwynllyw) laughed and mockingly suggested that I could not be serious (2 August 2006). The Chief Officer for Schools in the capital city, Hugh Knight, argued (12 July 2006) that Cardiff did have a policy, in the sense that its Welsh education scheme aimed at having at least one Ysgol Gymraeg in every ward. One could argue that the practice across LEAs to react to parental demand for provision has been some sort of de facto policy.

Research respondents were asked whether county councils should be neutral and avoid adopting any policy that promoted the Ysgolion Cymraeg. Three quarters of respondents disagreed, a not unsurprising result considering that they were already involved with such schools. A similar number agreed that local government should actually promote parental demand for Ysgolion Cymraeg, a strategy that goes beyond measuring the demand. Eighty per cent of respondents believed that the Welsh Assembly Government should set targets for every LEA to increase the proportion of pupils receiving Welsh-medium education. Such target setting (but on a national basis only) was included in the draft strategy for Welsh-medium education, but the actual targets were criticised by a number of respondents for being overcautious. The final strategy reflects the substantial difference between LEAs in that DfES will negotiate targets with individual local authorities (WAG 2010a: 24).

Responsibility for promoting the Ysgolion Cymraeg should lie with school governing bodies, the Welsh Assembly Government, the Welsh Language Board, or MYM. That was the clear message from almost four out of five respondents (78.5 per cent). Parents have been the obvious campaigners historically, but several interviewees maintained that parents were not as fired with enthusiasm as in the past, a view that appears to be corroborated by the research data. Is this the price one has to pay for a degree of normalisation, or does the response reflect a more self-centred society? A small majority of respondents (57.6 per cent) thought that not even RhAG should spearhead any campaigning for establishing further schools. When asked to respond to the statement 'It is wrong to expect parents and voluntary groups to have to fight for the establishment of more Welsh-medium schools', 77.6 per cent agreed that it was. While this response is in stark contrast to past action by parents, it could be argued that such an attitude is a healthy one, reflecting the fact that Welsh-medium schools have won their natural place within the country's educational provision and that one should not have to fight for what is justifiable, rightful and equitable. According to Dylan Phillips (Abley 2005: 264), it is possible that the Welsh psyche is responsible for lack of action by Welsh speakers: 'When Welsh speakers have their backs against the wall, they tend to be quite militant. Otherwise the vast majority are apathetic . . . The Welsh come out of their shells only when they have to, and maybe when it's too late.'

CHAPEL AND CHURCH INFLUENCES

Never too late to foster, in my view, is the influence of religion on our culture and education and the traditional interlinking of the Welsh language and places of worship is briefly described here. Many Welsh-medium schools evolved from nursery or starter classes held in the vestries of Welsh-language places of worship. This suggests a strong link between language and religion. However, over a third of families surveyed noted that there was no Welsh-language place of worship in their locality, a further quarter said that the Welsh-language place of worship had not offered their children an opportunity to speak Welsh, and 11 per cent maintained that they had no knowledge of a Welsh-speaking place of worship. Response to the statement 'As far as our children in our family are concerned, the Welsh-language chapel/church has given them the opportunity to speak Welsh, or it will in future' showed that there had been a decline in frequency of worship over the decades, with only 27.6 per cent of parents agreeing with the statement. However, the image of the traditional Welsh-speaking chapel remains strong, since 63 per cent of secondary and 51 per cent of primary teachers did agree with the statement. The reality is different.

THE HISTORICAL INFLUENCE OF VOLUNTARY GROUPS

The history of parental campaigning has been chronicled in the volume *Our Children's Language: The Welsh-medium Schools of Wales, 1939–2000* (Williams 2003). The saga has been well described, but new evidence (letters between voluntary bodies and Cardiff County Council during the 1970s and 1980s shown to me by the late County Councillor Emyr Currie-Jones) reveals a number of recurrent themes. Currie-Jones was chairman of the education committee at the time.

Firstly, meticulous research by RhAG, MYM, UCAC and Merched y Wawr forecast pupil numbers and produced appropriate and focused statistics, thus pragmatically underpinning their vision for the future of Welsh-medium provision. Secondly, their arguments were cogent and penetrating, quoting apposite legislation, discussing principles such as inclusion, and stressing a fair representation of parental views. Thirdly, the arguments from all pressure groups showed a high degree of consistency. Fourthly, one feels people's strong conviction emanating from the printed word. Fifthly, the collated views represented individuals who, according to Michael Jones (20 June 2006), 'knew that there was a latent need, and would set about proving that need'. No one suggested in the interviews that success in establishing and expanding the Ysgolion Cymraeg was due to any strategies or tactics by Cymdeithas yr Iaith Gymraeg. According to Derek Rees (1 July 2006), a Cardiff county councillor: 'It was not the sort of movement that politicians warm to.'

The strengths outlined above remain today, as does parental pressure for adequate provision. RhAG appears to be the most influential pressure group and shows political maturity in its dealings with local government and other agencies. The group is in tune with pragmatic strategy, and its negotiations are a good example of micro and meso interaction and cooperation and effective governance. Michael Jones, RhAG's legal adviser, publishes up-to-date accounts of the development of the Ysgolion Cymraeg in Cardiff in the capital city's Welsh-language monthly newspaper, *Y Dinesydd*. Caerffili is another area that sees considerable activity with a constant increase in demand; Ben Jones, the retired headteacher of an Ysgol Gymraeg, acts as an inspiring catalyst. RhAG was praised in *Yr Hogwr* (a local Welsh-language monthly paper) for its successful campaigning for a new secondary school in Llangynwyd, Bridgend (2008), and a new primary, Ysgol Ifor Hael, in Newport (2008). During an interview with Michael Jones, one noticed the sharp contrast between the association's meticulous research and Rhondda Cynon Taf's vague proposals for a new school in the Cynon Valley. He was proud of the fact that RhAG had influenced the Welsh Assembly Government to make progress on ensuring that LEAs measure the demand for Welsh-medium school places. The first meeting took place in March 2011 of a representative group to advise the minister of DfES on progress in implementing the Welsh-medium strategy, 'in particular the coordination of planning of Welsh-medium provision.' Its first annual report was published in July 2011 (WG 2011b). This may be a step in the right direction; the note of caution is sounded since its remit is the planning, not the delivery of school provision. RhAG has a secure unofficial finger on the political pulse of the country at the local level. When there is enlightened discourse between RhAG and an LEA, growth ensues.

One of the dangers of the rationalisation of language planning through political channels is that it leads to the institutionalistion of the activities. In the Basque Country, for example, once HABE (Institute of Basque-language Learning and Literacy for Adults) was established in 1981, the level of language awareness dropped as commitment to the language weakened. According to Montaña (1996: 235): 'although part of the individual responsibility had remained in the personal sphere or was lost (absence of commitment), a great part was assumed by public institutions.' It appears that the data regarding parental attitudes towards campaigning can be interpreted in similar vein. The clear message from a representative sample was that government, at both local and national levels, should take the lead in promoting Welsh-medium education, not the parents themselves.

One of the aims of fieldwork research was to measure the balance between the power of people and that of policy, or the comparative importance of structure and actors. For example, when respondents were asked for their opinion on the statement 'Documents like "Iaith Pawb" are OK as far as they go; parental pressure is the big influence on providing more Ysgolion Cymraeg', two out of every three agreed with the statement, which incorporates a feeling of power and of belonging to the wider community of the Ysgolion Cymraeg. In short, while parents believe that they have power, they are not minded, on the whole, to campaign. It is the choice of school that reveals their personal power, and the power of coercion on the LEA to provide places. Parental campaigns tend to be part of a reactive process (to the need for another school), rather than part of a long-term strategy.

'IAITH PAWB' (2003)

'Iaith Pawb' ('Everybody's Language') has been the Welsh Assembly Government's seminal policy on promoting the Welsh language in all spheres of life and thereby increasing the number of speakers. Its title is symbolic of linguistic inclusion, and it has developed in importance as a pivotal point of reference within debate on the future of the language. However, many interviewees, including leading (and successful) advocates for Welsh-medium education, had not read the document. From over seventy stimuli in a series of questionnaires, statement 49 – '"Iaith Pawb", the Welsh Assembly Government's official policy on increasing the number of Welsh speakers, is essential in spreading the network of Ysgolion Cymraeg' – achieved the highest score for 'lack of information'. The significance of this statistic is that it suggests a marked lacuna between information and knowledge held by language planners (whether politicians, civil servants, officials or academics) and the population at large, the voters within civic society. Historically, the Ysgolion Cymraeg were established (almost universally) as a direct result of parental demand. In future, whether ad hoc pragmatic development or coordinated, structured planning prevails, improving the level of knowledge and awareness of all actors is essential in a civilised democracy.

THE POWER OF INFORMATION AND FEELINGS

Respondents who believed that they lacked sufficient information to reply on a seven-point scale were required to add another (eighth) code. Table 4.1 lists the statements that scored highly for lack of information. It is notable that eight of these represent the fields of policies, legislation and central government. Local government is the focus of another three, and the remaining one shows the declining role of the Welsh language within worship, one of the traditional strongholds of the language.[13]

TABLE 4.1
The highest levels of lack of information

Statement number	Short description	Parents	Secondary teachers	Primary teachers	All respondents
49	'Iaith Pawb': essential?	23.8%	21.6%	15.5%	22.1%
60	Equal opportunities	28.5%	0.0%	2.2%	19.3%
66	New language law?	23.9%	9.8%	4.4%	18.2%
50	Parents more influential than policies	20.6%	13.7%	8.9%	17.5%
48	Publicity	19.0%	5.9%	2.2%	14.0%
47	Labour party support	18.5%	2.0%	4.4%	13.3%
68	European law	18.5%	2.0%	2.2%	13.0%
45	Welsh Education Schemes	16.4%	5.9%	2.2%	12.3%
65	A view of extremists	14.8%	3.9%	2.2%	10.9%
6	Welsh language place of worship	11.1%	5.9%	0.0%	8.4%
74	Local officers	10.6%	7.8%	0.0%	8.4%
73	County Councillors	10.1%	7.8%	2.2%	8.4%

Source: Thomas (2010a: 151).

Without sufficient information (let alone understanding and interpretation based on information), people's partial insights make it more difficult for them to influence planning and decision-making. Greater involvement with local and national politics needs to be nurtured.

Respondents' strength of feeling was measured on the extremes of a seven-point scale (1 'very strongly agree' and 7 'very strongly disagree'). There is a fine line between score categories, but it was argued that the extreme scores did reflect people's strong convictions. It is accepted that differentiating between opinion and emotion can be difficult. Therefore no attempt was made to do so. The seven statements that elicited the highest extreme scores are analysed below. (A significant gap between the seventh and eighth statement scores provided the cut-off point.) The results may be seen in Table 4.2.

Respondents' strength of feeling was measured to see whether a pattern emerged to corroborate a belief that people's will and feelings are critical

TABLE 4.2

Statements achieving the highest scores for agreeing or disagreeing with them[14]

Statement number	Short description	Parents	Secondary teachers	Primary teachers	All respondents
1	No point speaking Welsh	72.55	96.1%	88.9%	79.3%
31	Wales is my nation	59.8%	80.4%	88.9%	68.1%
2	Intergenerational transmission	50.3%	92.2%	75.6%	61.8%
39	Welsh in FE/HE	47.6%	76.5%	86.7%	58.9%
33	Warm-hearted Welsh	43.45	70.6%	80.0%	54.0%
63	Buildings	40.2%	68.6%	77.8%	51.2%
35	Everything bilingual	43.4%	68.6%	60.0%	50.5%

Source: Thomas (2010a: 152).

features in any movement aiming at reversing a language shift. According to Mark Abley (2005: 4): 'A minority language always depends on popular will'; 86.6 per cent of respondents agreed with this view. Lord Roberts of Conwy (1995: 13) underlined the sustaining force of people's goodwill as one of the conditions for the continued growth of the language. Fishman is but one sociolinguist who has written extensively about the importance of popular will:

> RSL efforts . . . are unwelcome testimony to shortcomings of the mainstream and to the tremendous will of the neglected and the 'different' to lead their own lives and to find their own satisfactions, regardless of outside pronouncements that nothing can or should be done for them. (2006: 80)

> RLSers are . . . change-agents on behalf of persistence. (2006: 85)

Since all respondents were involved in the Ysgolion Cymraeg, one hoped for a high score on the first statement in the bank: 'There's no point in learning Welsh, since everybody in Wales can speak English.' One was not disappointed. In reality, it was a test run on the reliability of the respondents understanding the scoring system. Four general points emerged.

Firstly, respondents felt very strongly that being monolingual English was unacceptable, a significant shift in attitude compared with the 1950s and 1960s. Secondly, very strong feelings in support of a bilingual Wales reflected the importance of Welsh and bilingualism when respondents were asked for their reasons for choosing an Ysgol Gymraeg. The consistency of response is noted. Thirdly, response to statement 1 (quoted in the preceding paragraph) accounted for the most consistent 'extreme' response (agreement) across the three groups of respondents. Fourthly, the teachers' strength of feeling was especially noteworthy, showing a clear vision for the future of their language, their country, and the importance of inter-generational transmission. Parents' agreement with statement 2 ('I hope that our children, when they are themselves parents, will speak Welsh to their own children'), with 27 per cent agreeing strongly, and only 1.7 per cent disagreeing, may appear hopeful. However, further analysis showed lack of intergenerational transmission, even in families where both parents' mother tongue was Welsh. (This was discussed in chapter 2.) Across the seven statements, teachers showed more enthusiasm and commitment than the parents, a pattern repeated across questionnaires 4, 5 and 6.

It is significant that three of the statements are concerned with the Welsh language, and two with Welsh nationhood. The data reveal a strong empathy with Welsh nationality. One could argue that strong feelings, particularly those connected with language and nationality, are a prerequisite in the Welsh-medium schools movement, and that parents' strong emotional ties with their language and identity help engender a feeling of belonging. According to historian John Davies (2007: 708–9):

> In the wake of the establishment of the National Assembly for Wales, nation building became a widely discussed issue. In that discussion, the experience of the Scots was again an important consideration. It argued that the Scots viewed their nationality in legal and constitutional terms, while the Welsh viewed theirs in social and cultural terms.

Research data (Thomas 2007) showed parental disinterest in legal and constitutional matters, while 93 per cent of them noted that they were warm-hearted Welsh people. Teachers in particular scored highly in the warmth of feeling towards their country, with 71 per cent of secondary teachers and 80 per cent of primary teachers recording that they agreed very strongly that they were warm-hearted Welsh people. When asked about their feelings towards British nationhood, 45 per cent of secondary and 51 per cent of primary teachers disagreed with the statement that they could be warm-hearted British citizens, compared with 19.6 per cent of parents. The difference in strength of feeling between teachers and parents has already been noted.

The current data suggest the possibility of a strong teacher influence on pupils' identity, an outcome fostered by official government policy through the Cwricwlwm Cymreig. In the past, the theme of Welshness has led to a misguided political interpretation that the Ysgol Gymraeg was a breeding ground for young nationalists. Such a link in people's minds between language, identity and Plaid Cymru led to prejudice and antagonism, but a more mature understanding of nationhood and language has slowly evolved within Wales.

Lastly I return to the theme of power that is generated by relevant knowledge, and exemplify it with particular reference to a long-standing challenge within the Welsh-medium school movement, the generally poor quality of buildings. The reader will not be surprised that this final section revives thematically one of the central themes of the chapter, Giddens's distribution of resources.

KNOWLEDGE ABOUT THE EFFECT OF BUILDINGS ON EDUCATIONAL STANDARDS

'Buildings don't make a school' was said so often by a governor of Ysgol Gyfun Cwm Rhymni during the early 1990s that it seemed to have become his mantra. His words, while true, offer but a partial insight into the connection between the standard of school buildings and the quality of experiences offered to its pupils. According to Estyn (2007a), standards of teaching, attainment, achievement and behaviour had improved in almost all schools that had new or refurbished buildings. A key sentence from that report summarises the enormous challenges faced by so many Welsh-medium (as well as English-medium) schools: 'Inadequate buildings make improvements in standards of achievement more challenging.'

Unsurprisingly 78 per cent of teachers agreed very strongly with the statement 'Our children deserve the best possible buildings', compared with 40 per cent of parents. That statement in a questionnaire was paired with the following one, 'Without good buildings, Welsh-medium education will fail.' Almost three quarters of all respondents disagreed, which pays tribute to the valiant efforts of teachers, headteachers and governing bodies to overcome decades of difficulties that arose from inadequate accommodation. Ysgol Gyfun Cwm Rhymni for example was accommodated (until its move to a brand new, purpose-built home in 2002) in what Councillor Phil Bevan described as 'a splintered site' of five separate buildings, divided by main roads and the valley town of Bargod. On its upper-school site pupils and staff had to cross roads when moving between lessons and science equipment had to be carried across the same highways. Thankfully, due to the determination of school leaders, parental lobbying and the support of local and central government, many improvements in accommodation have been effected in a number of schools, especially over the last two decades. However, challenges remain in some localities.

One of the most memorable experiences in my professional life was on St David's Day 1995 when I announced to the entire school in Bedwas Workmen's Hall that we were going to have a new building. The occasion was the school's annual eisteddfod, held off campus as we did not have a school hall (apart from two miniscule marching halls). I had no news or intimation of an impeding announcement; ironically, it was on the first morning of my headship in Glantaf, six months later, that a senior civil servant from the Welsh Office telephoned me to announce the good news that money had been allocated for a replacement school through PSI funding. My maverick announcement in Bedwas had arisen from sheer brinkmanship and optimism, or, in less emotional terms, from what Colin Williams refers to in chapter 1 as my 'ideological and cultural commitment to the Welsh language'. Early in my volume *Brwydr i Baradwys?* (2010: 2) I described the inevitable effect on my research of a lifetime's involvement in linguistic and minority rights, and quoted Stephen May on the subject (2001: xiii): '*All* positions that are taken – academic or otherwise – involve a moral dimension, reflecting the particular values and ideologies of their exponents.' I went on to say that a moral dimension is more than ideas; it means action. These few sentences partly explain my action in the school eisteddfod, which takes the narrative back to Bedwas as I recall the pupils' reaction to my announcement. Their enthusiasm and sense of justice erupted into ecstatic clapping, cheering and whistling, which lasted a good five minutes. They knew that they deserved better, but an entire generation of Cwm Rhymni pupils were destined to remain in dire buildings until 2002. Sheer determination from all members of the school community refused to allow the buildings to affect adversely the high standards achieved.

SUMMARY

The aim of this chapter was to articulate theories, particularly structuration (as developed by Giddens and later theorists), that offered a framework on which an analysis of the complex interaction between structures, agencies and actors could be developed. Of particular interest to the interpretation of the influences on the growth of the Ysgolion Cymraeg is the pivotal importance of individual discretion. Governance and the decline of democratic input into political decisions were explored as part of an applied critique of Marquand's seminal volume *Decline of the Republic: The Hollowing-out of Citizenship*. Treating Welsh-medium education as a public good necessarily requires a great deal of sensitivity to the question of democratic accountability and public participation in decision-making. How parental desires and group aspirations are represented within the political arena, both formally and informally, is a key issue. Consequently the influence of places of worship, voluntary groups, civil society networks and the power of relevant information have all been contextualised within the structuration framework. Power, according to Giddens, is the 'capacity to achieve outcomes', the outcomes in the current analysis being the establishment of more and more Ysgolion Cymraeg. The next chapter is an applied analysis of power, and articulates the range of individual powers that have influenced the growth of the Ysgolion Cymraeg. Having identified the key components we need to be reminded that it is the collective synergy which acts as the dynamo providing momentum for the Welsh schools movement, which is always far greater than the sum of its individual powers.

Notes

[1] Structuration was outlined in his seminal volume *The Constitution of Society: Outline of the Theory of Structuration* (1984). Anthony Giddens was one of the foremost British sociologists and a former director of the LSE, credited with inspiring the intellectual foundations of PM Tony Blair's Third Way philosophy.

[2] Gingrich observes:

> Structures and educational institutions . . . are formed by structured practices – that is, they do not just exist in and of themselves and they cannot exist without enacted conduct. While we may abstract these structures, and refer to them as large-scale structures that affect us, Giddens forces us to consider how they are reproduced.

He continues:

> It is enacted human conduct in the form of structured practices that maintains and reproduces these structures. But if these enacted forms of conduct change, either because individuals make conscious decisions to change, or through less conscious forms of adjustment, adaptation, and practice, then this can result in structural change as well. Social movements, collective action, or parallel changes by many individuals could have this result.

³ As Stones says (2005: 6), 'Between large historical, spatial and social forces, on the one hand, and the situated practices of individual agents, on the other, it is useful to identify meso-level networks of relations and practices.'

⁴ Giddens discusses the weakness of differentiating between the micro and the macro in the section 'Against "Micro" and "Macro": Social and System Integration' (1984: 139–44).

⁵ Cf. his comments on the works of Cohen (1989), Craib (1992), Archer (1995), or Loyal (2003).

⁶ Stones develops this aspect when he refers to 'the web-like nature of interdependencies' (2005: 126–7).

⁷ They say (2002: 78):

> [O]ur theory is built on the simple premise that politicians are motivated by policy considerations. The policy motivations could stem from electoral considerations – politicians may want to produce the policy outcomes that will get them re-elected. Alternatively, politicians might simply have an intrinsic interest in policy itself, either for selfish or altruistic reasons. Regardless of their origin, these policy motivations create a challenge for politicians, who must decide how to use legislation in the pursuit of desired policy outcomes.

⁸ According to Easton and Lasswell, for example, as Thurber says in his foreword to Kingdon (2003: vii):

> [Easton and Lasswell's] theories of policy making are based on a stages metaphor, the phenomenon of the political environment giving rise to wants that are converted into demands by interest groups, the public, and individuals . . . They argue that each of the stages in the policy process involves distinct periods of time, political institutions, and policy actors.

⁹ According to Daugbjerg and Marsh (1998: 71):

> Overall, we need to recognise the utility and the limitations of network analysis. It can't explain policy outcomes simply by reference to the structures of the network or the behaviour of the agents. We need to know why the networks take the form they do, how they relate to the broader political system and how network structures and actor behaviour affect outcomes and restructure networks.

¹⁰ 'Governance is the process by which we collectively solve our problems and meet our society's needs. Government is the instrument we use.' (1992: 24)

¹¹ Amongst British academics who have been observing the shift from government to governance are Rhodes (1997) and John (2001). Denters and Rose agree that this is an international phenomenon and perceive three substantial changes: the widespread development of New Public Management and public-private partnerships; the involvement of organised local societies, interest groups and private actors in policy partnerships; and the introduction of a new form of civic involvement.

The reader is given firm advice regarding the careful interpretation of trends such as the ones described in the preceding paragraph, since sometimes the activities and the labels attached to them are symbolic rather than real. The authors' last message (2005: 262) is that it is premature to critique the effectiveness and efficiency of the systems developing in local governance, and that some systems designed to ensure accountability could be anti-democratic. Their advice is to scrutinise forms of local government with great care.

In redefining the nature of local leadership, Hambleton (2005: 15) refers to the work of Stone (1989), who discusses the shift away from bureaucracy by legislative ruling towards cooperating partnerships in order to achieve common goals. He sees the potential of collaboration between citizens, councillors and officers; such a tripartite system could create opportunities to develop leadership (2005: 18).

[12] I am not aware that statistics have been compiled in this field.

[13] Full text of the statements in Table 4.1:

49	*Iaith Pawb*, the National Assembly Government's official policy on increasing the number of Welsh speakers, is essential in spreading the network of Ysgolion Cymraeg.
60	The local education authority practises an equal opportunities policy in its provision of Welsh-medium education.
66	A new Welsh Language Law is unnecessary.
50	Documents like *Iaith Pawb* are OK as far as they go; parental pressure is the big influence on providing more Ysgolion Cymraeg.
48	The amount of publicity given by the National Assembly Government in support of Welsh-medium schools is limited.
47	The National Assembly Government has shown considerable political good will in support of promoting Welsh-medium schools.
68	Language minorities suffering from lack of equal opportunities should turn to European law in their fight for justice.
45	The way ahead to increase the number of Welsh-medium schools is through the County Councils' Welsh Education Development Schemes.
65	Parents who believe that the County Council does not treat Welsh-medium schools fairly are extremists.
6	As far as our children in our family are concerned, the Welsh-language chapel/ church has given them the opportunity to speak Welsh, or it will in future. [If there is no such place of worship in your area, write 9 in the score box.]
74	The opinion, attitude and influence of Officers working for the local education authority are an important factor in the process of opening and closing schools.
73	The opinion, attitude and influence of the local County Councillor are an important factor in the process of opening or closing schools.

Source: Thomas (2010a: 312–16).

[14] Full text of the statements in Table 4.2:

1	There's no point in learning Welsh, since everybody in Wales can speak English.
31	Wales is my nation. [If another country, but not the UK, is, in your opinion, your nation, please write 9 in the box.]
2	I hope that our children, when they are themselves parents, will speak Welsh to their own children.
39	There is no place for Welsh at university and college level.
33	I feel wholeheartedly that I am a true Welshman/Welshwoman.
63	Our children deserve the best possible buildings.
35	Having everything in Wales provided in both languages is a waste of time and energy.

Source: Thomas (2010a: 312–15).

Chapter 5

The Articulation of Power

Huw S. Thomas

The first part of this chapter seeks to analyse fundamental societal active processes, particularly the discretion used by individuals to realise a vision. One of the main theses of this volume is that the interdependence of language, identity and education is pivotal in reversing the language shift in Wales. According to Fishman (2006: 92):

> People cannot be tricked into supporting RLS. They must be convinced to accept a definition of their 'best interest' and 'most positive future' that depends upon and derives from RLS . . . The first ones to do so will obviously be pioneers and must be particularly ready to work hard in order to attain very sparse results. All this becomes possible only when the RLS enterprise can count on the participation of maximally dedicated and ideologically oriented individuals.

When one considers the anglicisation of Wales, individuals and their actions within local communities are, according to Colin Williams (1990: 21), a means to influence the combination of interdependent effects, such as patterns of migration and socio-economic changes. The first study below critiques the contribution of individuals within the former Mid Glamorgan, a council at the geographical and political heart of south-east Wales.

MID GLAMORGAN

Between 1974 and 1995 Mid Glamorgan County Council established a new Welsh-medium secondary school every seven years. Keith Price Davies, a former director of education and long serving senior officer of the LEA, spoke proudly of this achievement during an interview (21 June 2006) and offered a detailed explanation. Firstly, the LEA benefited from the services of a series of enlightened directors of education, some, such as John Brace, having a far-reaching vision, and others, such as Aelwyn Jones, possessing a shrewd intellect. All of them cooperated with RhAG through meetings and interchange of ideas and data once a term. Unremitting and assiduous reviews of parental demand were conducted by stalwart campaigners (described in chapter 8), reviews which produced reliable data that in turn strengthened their strategic and practical arguments. According to Keith Price Davies, a tendency for directors of education in the Glamorgan area to be members of the Labour Party (the ruling party), combined with their discussions with the chairperson of the education committee, meant that there was never any objection in the Council to opening a Welsh-medium school. Ken Hopkins, another director of education for Mid Glamorgan, corroborated this opinion when he said in an interview (27 June 2006): 'No, there was no opposition in the Council. We never had anyone opposing in committee. It had been discussed in the Labour group . . . John Brace must have influenced Heycock a great deal. Directors influence chairmen.'

Three weeks after the interview Ken Hopkins wrote to me underlining the contribution made by political leaders in the old Glamorgan and Mid Glamorgan, particularly during the 1970s and 1980s, when their influence was strong, a period 'when support for the language was certainly not a popular or politically helpful position for a Leader to take up'. Hopkins continued (2006b):

> There is no doubt that without their support the campaigns mounted by the Welsh Schools Parent Associations would not have got anywhere.
>
> The contrast in the degree of support for the language between Cardiff and Swansea City and Glamorgan and Mid Glamorgan County Councils is highly significant, and reflects the positive and strong influence of leading councillors like Heycock and Squire. If it were not for them we would certainly not have had Rhydfelen, Ystalyfera, Llanhari and Cwm Rhymni, schools which have clearly played a leading role in saving the language.
>
> Nor should we forget, and it is a significant factor which would have been helpful to the Leaders, that there were several leading Labour councillors but Welsh-speaking who almost daily were telling the Leaders that the council should be supporting the language. I need mention only Joe [Joseph] Williams of Tredegar, Philip Squire's loyal Deputy Leader, and two other senior Welsh-speaking councillors, Will. Llewellyn of Treherbert, Chair of Social Services,

and Ted Davies of Pyle, Chair of the Establishment Committee. Because these were influential councillors, too, the Leaders would know that they could deliver the votes for them of many of their fellow councillors in their valleys at the Labour Group annual elections as well as voting for supportive policies for the language. They were all strong and single minded supporters of the Welsh language and its culture and their influence on the Leaders must have been significant.

In view of such senior elected member support it was not difficult for a succession of Directors of Education to present supportive Welsh language policies.

Every historian shows his bias; Ken Hopkins is no exception. He did not refer to the sit-ins in County Hall and in schools. However, this lacuna does not weaken the significance of his letter which exemplifies the important influence of individual members of the Labour Party on their local leaders and party, *strong and single-minded* supporters of the language (in Welsh one says *caredigion yr iaith* – people in love with the language). It is also interesting that there are two references to 'policies' – advocating, apparently, reacting to parental demand rather than pursuing a proactive policy. Having said that, the 'policies' succeeded, since the county saw a significant increase in provision. In the end, it is the outcome that counts. The sit-ins referred to above were a protest against the council's intention to create Welsh-language units attached to English-medium schools rather than establish Ysgolion Cymraeg. In its annual conference in May 1978, the Welsh Labour Party adopted a policy of establishing Welsh-language units in order to support the principle of the community school (Rawkins 1987: 42, 44). Councillors objected to schools having large catchment areas, which was inevitable in the case of the Ysgolion Cymraeg. Rawkins wrote (1987: 45):

> The degree of hostility exhibited by many councillors toward those who seek to enhance the position of the language appears to reflect politically based prejudice rather than the feelings of their constituents, as the increasing demand from non-Welsh-speaking, working-class parents for Welsh-medium education would appear to attest.

The second feature of Mid Glamorgan's success was the pragmatic, diplomatic and political interface between officers and their fellow-officers and councillors, which meant that an understanding of local politics, coupled with sound data, lay at the heart of planning within County Hall. For example, John Albert Evans was the third interviewee to praise the meticulous information held by Gomer Davies, an officer responsible for buildings. Evans described him as 'an excellent Welsh-speaking Welshman who could see the holistic picture and play a key role in ensuring progress'. Evans in turn would rely on councillors for support on a personal level, rather than for their ideology. When asked what his greatest contribution had been to the growth of the Ysgolion Cymraeg, Keith Price Davies's reply was 'trying to influence officers in County Hall to establish Ysgolion Cymraeg in response to the growth'. He refuted the idea of his using discretion, maintaining that it was more a question of adequate statistics and supporting evidence. Persuading councillors was the main task, together with dealing with parental objections. When officers knew of impending parental objections they would inform the councillors. However, officers could well have neglected to employ strategies and tactics, refusing to deploy their intellectual, educational and professional resources. In that sense, they certainly used their discretion in the critical role played by them in the history of the development of the Ysgolion Cymraeg.

The third feature that facilitated success was the centralisation of Welsh-medium administration in County Hall in Cardiff (geographically outside Mid Glamorgan), rather than in the district offices. A critical mass of specialist knowledge developed in consequence, which ensured a powerful strategic base. It was not so much a case of the central location of people per se but rather that key people were working together. County Hall was also the political power base, one of considerable influence when Llewellyn Heycock (subsequently Lord Heycock of Taibach) was chairman of the Glamorgan LEA at the acme of his illustrious political career.

While LEAs have been criticised for the poor quality buildings they offered to the Ysgolion Cymraeg movement, with few schools established in new, purpose-built accommodation, financial prioritisation has always influenced council decisions. It could be argued that they were (and are) using their power in a democratic process. The vision that existed in the former Glamorgan County Council led to the establishment of a number of schools with very low pupil numbers at their inception. Notable examples are Ynys-lwyd, Aberdâr (1949) 28 pupils; Pont-y-gwaith (1950) 13; Pont Siôn Norton, Pontypridd (1951) 16; Sant Ffransis, Barry (1952) 15; Tonyrefail (1955) 11.

POLITICAL POWER IN CARDIFF COUNCIL

An outstanding example of a local councillor who steered Welsh-medium education firmly and wisely through many a political storm is the late Emyr Currie-Jones. His career was long and distinguished. Amongst his strengths were a clear personal vision, a deep conviction that Welsh and Welsh-medium education would succeed and an ability to persuade fellow councillors and others across political parties to accept his views. When he was elected to the council in 1966, he knew that he was entering dangerous and unchartered waters. Lincoln Hallinan, Recorder of the City of Cardiff, was keen to offer a choice between French and Welsh in the city's secondary schools. Currie-Jones disagreed and persuaded the NUT to back him, along with the Tory spokesman on the Welsh language, Llew Jenkins, a man who, according to Currie-Jones, did pioneering work in support of the language.

Establishing the first Welsh-medium secondary school in Cardiff was a difficult process, with considerable opposition within the Labour group and local councillors campaigning to keep the existing English-medium secondary (Glantaff High) open and not use the buildings for Welsh-medium education, while the powerful lobby of Welsh speakers misunderstood Currie-Jones's political manoeuvring. He was without doubt a pragmatic mover and fixer and for that he needed sound financial resources, a fact which, he maintained, many Welsh-speaking parents appeared not to acknowledge. Currie-Jones referred to a number of recorded quotes to underline the animosity that existed against the Ysgolion Cymraeg, some of which are reproduced here (from *Glantaf, Y Degawd Cyntaf, 1978–88*, Roberts (ed.) 1998):

> The Welsh language is dying and it is a waste of time and money to create Welsh schools!

> Keep Bryntaf open, and in three years there may not be a demand for a Welsh secondary!

> I am against anything which is isolationist . . . It can cause only bitterness.

> Many of the parents demanding Welsh Education for their kids are non-Welsh speakers. I'm very wary of spending money on schools for these.

Currie-Jones prided himself on his honesty and his unwavering support for the Ysgolion Cymraeg. In the political arena, his knowledge of things Welsh outshone that of his opponents, of whatever party. He underlined in an interview (29 August 2006) that there was no rift between the Labour and Tory parties, admitting to differences of opinion on matters of detail, but not on broad policy. He complimented Councillor McCarthy, the Tory chairman, on his support and commitment, a view supported by Rawkins (1979: 63), who describes McCarthy's sensitivity to linguistic friction.

With a continuous focus within the Welsh-medium movement on the reactive policies of LEAs, it is easy to forget or neglect the efficacious contribution made by individuals such as Currie-Jones in influencing their councils to support the establishment of more Welsh-medium schools. It is equally easy to misinterpret or ignore the contribution made by individuals within the main political parties in Wales, which has led, in some cases, to prejudice and the fostering of suspicion and even cynicism. For example, in the mid 1990s Plaid's Owen John Thomas wrote a seminal model of development for increasing the provision of Ysgolion Cymraeg in the capital city, but it became the victim of political and administrative Fabian tactics, brought about to some extent (as it seemed to me, a member of the LEA's Welsh-medium planning group), by anti-Plaid individuals.

POLITICAL PARTIES – VISION AND ACTION, PREJUDICE AND SUSPICION

The Labour Party

'Welsh-medium schools have faced a lot of opposition from local education authorities . . . In Wales, the Labour Party dominates many of the local-government councils and Authorities; it has been traditionally against promoting the Welsh language.' These were Khleif's words (1980: 120), echoed twenty years later by Hopkins (2006b), though in more muted tones. The history of Welsh and Welsh-medium education shows that such sentiments have built philosophical and political walls. Of course, while walls provide shelter, they can easily create fortresses.

Lord Gwilym Prys-Davies's incisive analysis of the growth of Welsh-medium schools in south-east Wales (personal letter to H. Thomas, May

2006) shows a breadth of understanding of linguistic, political, social and cultural influences on the language and education. He balances the image of anti-Welshness within the Labour party fuelled by MPs such as Ness Edwards or George Thomas with the practical vision of individual MPs such as Goronwy Roberts, Jim Griffiths or Cledwyn Hughes. An element of prejudice against the language and Welsh-medium schools still exists within the party, according to Ken Hopkins (interview, 27 June 2006): 'the feeling is still there, but not as strong . . . The existence of the Welsh-medium schools has led to the general feeling of goodwill towards the language.' The influence of the south Wales group of MPs, the political powerhouse of Labour politics, contrasts with that of the trio born into Welsh-speaking families in the west of the country.

At grassroots level, there existed a network of Welsh-speaking county councillors who worked assiduously through the Labour party in support of the language and the Ysgolion Cymraeg: Haydn Thomas of Gilfach Goch, William Llewellyn of Blaenrhondda, Thomas Jones of Coryton, Emyr Currie-Jones of Cardiff, Rose Davies of Aberdâr, Dewi Bonner of Tonyrefail, and Ioan Thomas of Ynyshir. Lord Heycock, the non-Welsh-speaking chairman of the council, was a powerful influence. There is no evidence that they were following any written policy that encouraged the growth of Welsh-medium schools; indeed, that would have been tantamount to political naivety, considering the open hostility of many leading MPs to the language. Pragmatism based on positive reaction to parental wishes was the order of the day. Without the political support of such individuals, it is unlikely that the language shift would have been reversed. One can conclude therefore that support for the Ysgolion Cymraeg came, not from the Labour party, but from individual members of the party at both local and national levels.

Lord Gwilym Prys-Davies's own contribution to the nation's Welshness has been noteworthy. He gave evidence to the Sir David Hughes Parry Committee in 1963 and welcomed the first Welsh Language Act 1967 as an event of enormous symbolic importance, in that for the first time in centuries the state's 'prestige' and power supported the language. However, he does not flinch from criticising his own party for having moved the prime drafter of the act, Cledwyn Hughes, from the Welsh Office in 1968, and replaced him with George Thomas. Thomas opposed any signs that he saw of a national spirit in Wales and would make assertions that some teachers were using the Ysgolion Cymraeg to spread nationalist Plaid Cymru ideology. Against such a vitriolic political background Lord Gwilym Prys-Davies took his stance, being the first ever (in 1982) to take his oath in the House of Lords in Welsh. He subsequently worked assiduously in drafting the second Language Act, which became law in 1993. A recommendation that every person of statutory school age living in Wales should have the right to choose to be educated in Welsh and through the medium of Welsh was rejected. The matter of the individual's language rights is still being debated. The significance of this evidence is that the recommendation was actually made.

While macro politics appeared to deal more with language issues than those of education thorough the medium of the language, still small advances were made which, with hindsight, may have set precedents for greater support for the language and Welsh-medium education. For example, John Morris, as secretary of state for Wales (1974–9), increased the grant to Mudiad Ysgolion Meithrin and insisted that the Treasury accept the principle that the secretary of state for Wales had the right to finance the additional cost of bilingual administration and education. John Morris's personal commitment to the language and Welsh-medium education is acknowledged by Rawkins (1987: 34):

> Indeed, the extent of his commitment to devolution and the language had led a number of his fellow Welsh Labour MPs to hold him in some suspicion, regarding him as a closet nationalist . . . The appointment of a less sympathetic minister, less willing to devote his time to considering how he might best employ his resources to assist the language, or to oblige his officials to give the language in education priority consideration, would certainly have slowed the flow of developments.

Central government macro support for the language and Welsh-medium education, along with a local government meso supportive infrastructure of schools, has shown a slowly evolving line of development due, in the main, to the pragmatic visionaries within ruling parties. So far we have examined the contribution made by the Labour party. Influence and diplomacy were needed during the Labour administration, as they were during the Conservative term of office between 1979 and 1997.

The Conservative Party

As the anti-nationalistic stances of a number of Labour MPs gave rise to deep-rooted doubts and cynicism regarding the party's commitment to the language (doubts which still exist), the traditional Welsh opposition to Conservatism likewise led to grave doubts about that party's policies with regard to supporting Welsh. The idea of a Welsh-speaking Tory MP, Sir Wyn Roberts, was anathema to many. He reminisces (as Lord Roberts of Conwy) in his autobiography, recalling one of Margaret Thatcher's attacks on him during the drafting of the Education Act of 1988 (2006: 221):

> 'You have nothing! You contribute nothing!' she said with great emphasis. I was tempted to say that we had a lot of Japanese companies – more than England – but I refrained. I knew that she would make a mountainous denunciation of our inadequacies from such a reply.
> 'The only Conservatives in Wales are the English who moved in.' I did not let her get away with that – I had hundreds of Welsh-born Conservatives in my constituency and told her so.

Be that as it may, substantial steps were taken during the Conservative administration to strengthen the status of Welsh. The legacy of support for the language owes a great deal to the practical vision of individuals within the party, in particular Nicholas Edwards (Lord Crickhowell), secretary of state for Wales (1979–87) and Wyn Roberts, parliamentary under-secretary of state at the Welsh Office (1979–87) and minister of state at the Welsh Office (1987–94). The following quotation from a lecture given by Sir Wyn (1995: 3) illustrates a number of basic principles, which partly explain the growth in the status of the Welsh language and in the number of Ysgolion Cymraeg:

> In retrospect, the devolutionary process and its progress appears as a smooth continuum from 1964 onwards. There may be some uneven strata here and there but these can hardly be described as the result of volcanic political eruptions but rather as legislative faults and imperfections. There is nothing that can be achieved that improving legislation cannot hone to acceptable levels.

He continues:

> As to the 'force that through the green fuse drives the flower' if I may describe the political and governmental motivation behind administrative

devolution in such poetic terms, there is a consensus across the political parties and within government that there is a uniquely Welsh dimension and what is appropriate for England may be intolerably inappropriate for Wales. There is therefore a predisposition to devolve but, quite rightly, any proposal has to be justified on sound governmental grounds.

Lord Roberts is a historian, having won a history scholarship to Oxford. The concept of a timeline came naturally to him and he appreciated building on previous achievements and refining developments thorough statute. Of considerable significance also was the political consensus across the major parties. From 1964 until 1999 MPs were responsible for shaping policies for Wales that were invariably rooted in the needs of England. Since devolution the range (or absence) of powers and the responsibilities of devolved government have tended to obscure some processes but have given others a sharper focus. For example, though education is one of the major devolved responsibilities, teachers' salaries and conditions of service are not devolved, which makes holistic planning towards policy process in the field of Welsh-medium education difficult. (I mean the demands made by an extended curriculum beyond the statutory school day.) Support for the Welsh language appears to have broad consensus, though the degree of commitment and action depends to a large extent on personal drive and individual discretion. There is proper regard for the needs of two different nations. It has by now become extremely rare to come across the adage 'For Wales, read England', particularly in the field of education. However, even the Welsh Baccalaureate did not develop without consultation with England, and coordinated decisions on assessment matters are spear-headed by Ofqual, 'the new regulator of qualifications, exams and tests in England'. The *statutory regulation of external qualifications (2004) applies to England, Wales and Northern Ireland,* and while DfES is the regulatory body for Wales, the coordinating central role of Ofqual is powerful. The maxim 'justification on sound governmental grounds' takes the agenda beyond ideology to the level of well-researched and dependable argument. Then come the dealing, the debating and the persuading, the stuff of governance.

Lord Roberts's influence on political decisions directly affecting the language and Welsh-medium education were substantial. Joint discussions at formal and informal levels with the schools' inspectorate led to the statutory status of Welsh within the National Curriculum. The well-being of the language was of great concern to Lord Roberts, and he allowed a temporary opting out for a minority of schools, a pragmatic and wise decision. He was at pains to make the right decision to ensure a successful future for the language, as the following extracts from his autobiography reveal:

April 1983
I learnt from Paddy [O'Toole] that it had been a mistake to make Gaelic a compulsory subject in schools in the republic and that the policy had to be abandoned. (2006: 172)

October 1987
Welsh would not be a compulsory subject in all schools in Wales, although there would be a presumption in favour of it. (I had not forgotten what I had been told about the Irish experience with compulsory Irish.) (ibid., 219)

July 1989
I had already persuaded the Welsh local education authorities, much against their will, to set up a special committee to examine the problems relating to the teaching of Welsh in schools . . . I launched our proposals for Welsh in the National Curriculum in July 1989. There was no way that the activists [Cymdeithas yr Iaith Gymraeg/Welsh Language Society] could claim these proposals as their own. But, as well as watching them, I had to keep a wary eye on the prime minister. She . . . had gone out of her way to mention that schools could apply for exemption from teaching the language. Of course, I too referred to this option at the launch, but I expressed the hope that most schools and most children in Wales would take the opportunity to learn their native tongue. I knew I was sailing between Scylla and Charybdis; I had no choice but to negotiate the passage. (ibid., 234)

Gaining Margaret Thatcher's support was not easy for any member of her Cabinet. Though Lord Roberts praises her (1995: 8) for taking 'a keen interest in education' and for keeping 'an eagle eye on preparations, including ours in Wales, for the Education Bill forecast in the Queen's Speech after the election victory in June 1987', nevertheless the opening words of the sentence quoted are: 'There is only one mention of Wales in Margaret Thatcher's autobiography *The Downing Street Years* and that is in connection with housing policy.' One could easily argue that Lord Roberts was Wales's ambassador in Downing Street, where all his diplomatic skills were pushed to the limit. He quotes from a 'contentious meeting' in preparation for the Education Act of 1988 (2006: 220):

'You can do what you like in your Welsh-speaking schools but look here . . .
you define them as schools where "the majority of subjects are taught
through the medium of Welsh". Don't you see that your nationalists will
exploit that definition, use a bit of Welsh in teaching all sorts of subjects and
claim to be Welsh-speaking schools even though their pupils are monoglot
English?'

'Not a chance, Prime Minister. Welsh-medium schools are clearly defined.
You can't change a school overnight as you are suggesting . . .'

Capturing the hearts of people and making Welsh sufficiently attractive
for people to wish to learn the language and use it in every day normal life
was Lord Roberts's vision, not making language issues matters for the law
courts. He was proud of the Conservatives' practical support for the
language, quoting an 800 per cent increase in government grants since they
were previously in power (1970–4). The enhanced status of the language
was described in the *Conservative Campaign Guide 1991* as 'the most far-
reaching ever made by a Welsh secretary of state.' Lord Roberts displayed
discretion in his personal allegiance to the furtherance of the language, and
believed he had been an inspiration to Nicholas Edwards at the time of the
seminal Maenan speech in April 1980. He quotes from a minute sent to
Nicholas Edwards, 'describing our new approach which was to counter the
doom and gloom of Saunders Lewis's *Tynged yr Iaith* broadcast in the
Sixties' (1995: 6–7):

> You may wish to declare at the outset a robustly positive, even aggressive
> approach to the survival of the language as a living tongue. You are after all
> seeking to implement a Party and Government commitment and this
> involves a rejection of the inevitable doom of the language philosophy which
> underlies so much current thinking on the subject.

Lord Roberts was more than a dreamer; he delivered. He ensured the
beginning of an infrastructure by creating new bodies: ACAC, PDAG and
OHMCI. These bodies were properly financed, and grants to voluntary
bodies connected with the language were increased. When he addressed
the RhAG Annual Conference in Pontypridd in 1986, he said (1995: 8):

> In every year since 1980 the level of spending [on direct support for the
> language] has increased to the point where in the financial year 1986/1987,
> we will spend in excess of £2,700,000. A million of this goes directly to the

education authorities but the rest supports a great diversity of organisations and projects.

Pragmatic visionaries have belonged to the major political parties, and it is their personal discretion and drive that advanced the linguistic agenda in Wales. Lord Roberts, in his interview with me, quoted Bradley (a pre-eminent Shakespearean scholar and professor of poetry at Oxford 1901), and applied the thought to his own experience: 'Shakespeare didn't give them what they wanted; he gave them what they hadn't dreamed of.'

Plaid

The Welsh nationalist party is different from the other two political parties critiqued: it is likely that all its members share a common belief in promoting the Welsh language and Welsh-medium or bilingual education. The interpretation of how to deliver those two basic goals will vary according to the linguistic profile of the various areas of the country. In south-east Wales, the party has been in power for comparatively brief periods (1999–2004) in Rhondda Cynon Taf and Caerffili, the latter council also being the only one in the south-east where Plaid held the balance of power between 2008 and the local elections in March 2011. On the whole, therefore, the influence of Plaid councillors (and the party) on the growth of the Ysgolion Cymraeg depends on their gaining political support from the ruling parties. As there is currently substantial good will towards the language across the political parties, it is difficult to make an objective evaluation of Plaid's contribution at local government level to the furtherance of the language and Welsh-medium education. That Plaid councillors have generally taken positive stances on both matters is, how-ever, indisputable.

At national level, Plaid has always been a minority party, and had never held the balance of power until its coalition with the Labour party within the National Assembly for Wales in June 2007. The coalition policy document, 'One Wales/Cymru'n Un' (WAG 2007a), together with political cooperation and expediency, quickly led to significant developments in the promotion of the Welsh language and Welsh-medium education: the acceptance in principle of the Coleg Cymraeg Cenedlaethol (a Welsh-medium university structure) in 2009, the national Welsh-medium Education Strategy in 2010 and the Welsh Language Strategy the following year (Welsh

Government: 2011a). After considerable prevarication a Legislative Competency Order aimed at devolving powers over language legislation to the assembly was passed in the House of Commons in December 2009 and a Welsh-language Measure in late 2010. A referendum was held in 2011 on devolving further law-making powers to the Welsh Assembly Government and received overwhelming support (63.5 per cent in favour, 36.5 per cent against). The opportunity to channel power has been used by Plaid at both local and national levels, and shows, particularly at national level, that making progress when one has the opportunity to do so is critically vital for minorities.

THE CONTRIBUTION OF THE SCHOOLS' INSPECTORATE

The influence of the schools' inspectorate on the growth of the Ysgolion Cymraeg, as on the Welshness of the curriculum, has been noteworthy, but has varied over time. It is fair to emphasise that the role of the inspectorate has changed greatly, particularly since the introduction in 1992 of inspections for all institutions on a six-year basis. For example, the chief inspector wrote in the foreword to her Annual Report for 2005–6 (Estyn 2007b: 1): '[W]e have a unique, independent overview of all education and training in Wales (other than for some parts of higher education). We now work more and more in partnerships with other inspectorates to give us a wider view of all services to children and young people in Wales.'

Little has been published on the influence of the inspectorate on Welsh education, let alone bilingual education, which should be researched in order to fill an important lacuna in the educational history of Wales. One could cite a reference by Baker (1990: 86–7) or quote the following (Baker 2000: 119): 'It is perhaps easy to underestimate the legitimization process effected by OHMCI on the growth of bilingual education in the last three decades. Such a central government agency has played neither a neutral nor an uninterested role.' It is significant that the author interviewed Chief Inspector Ann Keane, (at the time Estyn's head of directorate: Education Providers Directorate), Illtyd Lloyd, a retired chief inspector, and two retired HMIs, Gwilym Humphreys and Owen E. Jones. Ann Keane (interview, 3 July 2006) provided a succinct description of the inspectorate from its inception in 1907. It is not the inspectorate's direct responsibility to create educational policies; that is a matter for government. The first chief inspector, Sir O. M. Edwards, laid the foundations for a truly Welsh inspectorate, where government and the civil service acknowledged that there was something special and different in Wales that called for Welsh education for people who were bilingual. The inspectorate's tradition of being involved with a series of pivotal developments (such as the National Curriculum, compulsory Welsh, and the Welsh Language Acts) has continued for a century, and still does. Ann Keane underlined the high status of Welsh within the inspectorate, pointing out that a senior member of staff, a staff inspector, had been responsible for Welsh for decades. When she was asked about her level of discretion and personal conviction as a key actor within the educational system, her replies were truly professional. However, she failed to hide the enthusiasm in her voice and body language as she felt pride in her 'not insubstantial' contribution to the drafting of 'Iaith Pawb'.

A similar strong conviction that the Welsh language and Welsh-medium education were to be supported (if not promoted) was evident when Illtyd Lloyd, a former chief inspector, was interviewed (6 June 2006). He had high expectations of his staff, of standards of teaching and of pupil achievement and attainment, and was to seize every opportunity to enhance the understanding and support for Welsh and bilingual education, whether in an informal discussion with a headteacher, or when he saw the potential in new legislation. He embraced every chance to make progress whether with ministers, civil servants or local education authorities. He played a pivotal role in adapting the National Curriculum to suit the needs of Wales. Illtyd Lloyd, HMI (1964–71), staff inspector (1972–82), chief inspector (1982–90) is yet another shining example of the pragmatic visionary that emerges as one unravels the influences on the growth of the Ysgolion Cymraeg. Prior to his appointment as chief inspector, some ten schools only were inspected in an annual cycle. He agreed that there was always a sample of schools, but pointed out that it was a personal rather than a statistical one; before the introduction of cyclical inspections, HMIs would note, for instance, themes that were of national importance or matters that they found worrying, and they needed to be salient ones. After deliberation, it was their collective interests and concerns that shaped the sample. Illtyd Lloyd revealed that inspectors were worried about the state of the buildings at Ysgol Gyfun Cwm Rhymni, a concern that led to a full inspection of the school in 1987. Inspecting such a young school (it had been established only six years previously) was an unprecedented step at the time. It appears that the published report was useful in furthering the argument for a replacement building, which was eventually opened fifteen years later in 2002. Illtyd Lloyd's career shows that he went beyond the call of duty, revealing a strong element of professional discretion in order to promote what he believed in.

The line between professional discretion and going the second mile is a fine one to tread. In the case of Owen E. Jones, the inadequate provision for Welsh-medium education had been pressing on him since his experience as an education officer in Tanganyika during the 1960s, when he had realised that the curriculum in that country was alienating the pupils from their roots. Through his unremitting assiduity, he steered the production and publication of some fifty volumes in Welsh on Welsh history, financed by the Welsh Office. A mark of his professional commitment and discretion is that he personally read and redrafted every single volume. Gwilym Humphreys's personal description of life in the inspectorate (1975–83) appears in a rare publication (2000: 113–27), in which he draws attention to the importance of publishing thought-provoking papers on specific educational matters, including Welsh-medium education (2000: 118). Special conferences would be convened to discuss these papers during one of the most productive periods in the history of the inspectorate. This period also saw the formation of a panel specialising in bilingualism under the chairmanship of Gareth Lloyd-Jones, HMI. His brief was to establish an understanding of good practice, consider the main messages emerging from reviews and inspections, and formulate a critique which would inform the Welsh Office on policies and provision for the Welsh language and specifically Welsh-medium education.

The influence of the inspectorate on the development of the Ysgolion Cymraeg has varied over time, and at best can be said to have challenged LEAs to provide new schools in appropriate locations, an exercise founded on detailed research parallel to that conducted by RhAG. Its influence on the production of teaching and learning materials in Welsh, including the establishment of the Resources Centre at Aberystwyth University in 1982, was important at a time when published resources were wholly inadequate in terms of curricular coverage, in spite of the success of the WJEC Welsh

Books Scheme. During the late 1980s it ensured a grant to allow Ysgol Gyfun Cwm Rhymni to experiment with oral homework in Welsh on tapes, a rare experience inspiringly led by Rosalind Williams. Cwm Rhymni was the first secondary school in south-east Wales to be established without the presence of a critical mass of pupils from Welsh-speaking homes. The significance of the success of a school with such a linguistic profile (95 per cent from English-speaking homes) was appreciated by the inspectorate.

INTERIM SUMMARY

This chapter has so far aimed at applying structuration, discretion and agenda-setting to the context of Welsh-medium education, in an attempt to analyse the complex interrelationships between them. The relationship between actors and structures was explored, while the interplay of macro, meso and micro levels of power was used to form a conceptual framework on which to hang empiric research, interpretations of the resultant data and observations based on other sources. The power of individuals, particularly their pragmatic vision, their determination to succeed and their relentless optimism and assiduity were exemplified. The charismatic motivation, drive and persuasiveness of individuals like Douglas Hyde, Ben Yehuda or Bobby Sands in campaigns to reverse language shifts have not received sufficient attention from researchers, an opinion endorsed by Quinn (2007: 5): '[M]ore case studies might enable us to proffer a motivational theory of language revitalization.' Wales could provide a ready field for researchers.

Attention was given to the need for politics and politicians to be involved with the very powers that undermine their credibility. For example, according to Bentley (2001: 10): 'Avoiding this danger, for leaders of all political colours, requires a constant stream of challenging and radical ideas. Governments must be willing to learn, and to accept vigorous debate as a necessity for identifying solutions.' In 1987 Rawkins described the lack of leadership from central government in the promotion of bilingualism through education. In 2004 Colin Williams asked, in a book review (2004a), who was responsible for the development of bilingual education, as it appeared that no one was clear whose responsibility it was to lead and promote it. In 2010, the Welsh Assembly Government published its Welsh-medium Education Strategy and assumed the mantle of potential responsibility. The thesis of this book is that the responsibility has to be a joint, cooperative one between parents and teachers, planners and politicians, and the myriad of other agencies that are part of the provision. Wales has the ability and the opportunity to harness the power that drives the dynamo of language, culture, education and national identity, and at the same time to develop an ideology and rationale across the country's communities, within the institutions, in county halls and in the Senedd, that will deliver the national dream. That is one of the big challenges facing Wales.

THE MOVEMENT IS GREATER THAN THE SUM OF ITS DISCRETE POWERS

After analysing the complex layers of influence on the growth of the Ysgolion Cymraeg in south-east Wales, giving particular attention to a range of powers, the ensuing synergy is presented as aspects of those powers. Nine theses evolved from analysing the empirical research; some were already forming at the outset of the research, but most emerged after that 'quiet, calm deliberation' which 'disentangles every knot.' This section is a synopsis of the main research findings, but with a few examples aimed at making the theses more accessible to a wider audience. The reader will be able to refer to the remainder of the volume and find further evidence that exemplify these theses. The first type of power is arguably the most obvious, being widely quoted by observers of the Welsh-medium school movement.

Parental power has been the main force driving the growth of the Ysgolion Cymraeg. Historically, establishing the Ysgolion Cymraeg in south-east Wales has been a battle, led by individual parents or groups of parents fired with inspiration and enthusiasm. The history of the schools' growth demonstrates how parental determination and perseverance have overcome the power of government, whether local or central. If parents did not choose the Ysgolion Cymraeg, they would close and parental power would weaken. Without any doubt, parental power has been the main force driving the development.

One of the valuable sources of evidence of parental conviction, determination and passion is to be found in recordings that I made as part of my fieldwork. For example, Ann Jones, the headteacher of an English-medium primary school in the Rhymney Valley decided to opt for Welsh-medium education for her own children and was consequently called a traitor in a meeting of her teachers' union. 'Stand up and be counted publicly', she said. In Fochriw, a small village in the same valley, Christine Chater was advised by the headteacher of the local (English-medium) school not to send her daughter to the Ysgol Gymraeg, because doing so would lead to her excommunication from the local community. Her daughter was called a 'Welshy snob' and 'big-headed'. But both mothers overcame the prejudice and intimidation, joined the ranks of campaigners and gained valuable experience in both strategy and tactics. 'You have lots of ties when you've had to fight together for the same things', said Ann Jones.

Like many other parents, Christine Chater was loyal to the cause and was one of the five members of Ysgol Cwm Rhymni's action group, which met one evening a week for three years, preparing strategies and tactics in the campaign for a replacement building. The other core members were Councillor Philip Bevan, a governor, Muriel Bevan, the school bursar, Helen Cook, head of religious studies, and myself as headteacher. Christine Chater would telephone Ron Davies, then the local MP, in his offices in the House of Commons, and would lobby him regularly. He participated with pupils, staff and parents in a protest and publicity march one Saturday morning from Bargod to the lower school site in Aberbargod, one and half miles away, a journey that staff were obliged to make daily. Most memorable and significant for the school's development was the visit in the early 1990s of Sir Wyn Roberts, minister of state at the Welsh Office. The event culminated in the Dickensian-looking rooms on the lower site in Aberbargod where technology was taught. Poetic justice made certain that it was a gloomy November afternoon. In 1995 John Redwood visited the school, when he was secretary of state for Wales. His body language had been carefully studied, and action group members were strategically positioned in the old marching hall ready to signal a change of activity; a video of the debating team winning the Motorola parliamentary competition (for the whole of Britain) was switched off the moment Redwood showed signs of inattention, and the school choir began singing triumphantly.

The Ysgolion Cymraeg create their own identity, a bond of relationship with similar schools, and the confidence that develops with success and being accepted as part of the normal provision. The 'movement' of Welsh-medium schools is micro-centred, in the sense that it campaigns for the next school in the locality. This is a bottom-up influence, from the micro level to the meso or local government level. It is also a counter-negative phenomenon, since parental power is determined to overcome any negativism or indifference on the part of the LEA, or lack of vision by central government.

Parents' main reasons for choosing an Ysgol Gymraeg are a combination of commitment to the Welsh language and the Welsh identity, and the ethos and standards of the schools. However, the combination of reasons is extremely complex. The self-motivated power that emanates from the beliefs and feelings if not the souls of the people is one of the critical forces at work as the Welsh nation fights for the restoration of its language. Without this special power, other powers resulting from the efforts of language planners or politicians would be insufficient to reverse the language shift.

The power of the schools is that they have created a society that focuses parental aspirations on three vital elements: language and identity, a family relationship and ethos, and high standards and expectations. Welsh-medium schools have been distinguished by their high standards in all aspects of school life, culturally, in sports and athletics, academically and in their pastoral care. In the early years, schools had to prove themselves and be at least as good as the schools in their locality. The leadership given by headteachers and the commitment of teachers have been a key factor in ensuring the success of the 'movement'. Eirlys Pritchard Jones's relentless determination to set high expectations and standards at Ysgol Gyfun Cymer Rhondda is but one example of headteacher leadership based on sound educational, social and Christian principles, often against the odds in terms of poor buildings or local hostility to a Welsh-medium school that appeared to have been parachuted into the area. In the early days of development, Ysgolion Cymraeg were socially isolated from their immediate community due to their abnormally large catchment areas. Initially appointed as a deputy head of (English-medium) Cymer Comprehensive School, with responsibility for developing the Welsh-medium school in the same buildings, Eirlys Pritchard Jones was faced with numerous challenges; principally, she needed to change the school ethos, develop a pedagogy that

158

respected the individual pupil, increase staff and pupil expectations, and reduce underachievement. Her success was outstanding, with the school achieving the third highest percentage of A*– C GCSE grades in the whole of Wales in 1997. At the same time she had to overcome prejudice ('it's the back door to private education'), strong opposition ('I don't believe in this Welsh language education nonsense') and intentional negativism. For example, she was denied access to application forms for teaching posts before candidates were interviewed, though she was the senior member of staff responsible for Welsh-medium education.

The more homogeneous and less diversified profile of high academic standards in the Ysgolion Cymraeg has nurtured self-confidence in the sector, and support and pride amongst its parents and pupils, but no educational establishment or movement can survive on the success of its 'brand' nor on its historic achievements. Maintaining the momentum of the flourishing development of the Ysgolion Cymraeg (in terms of growth and standards) could become challenging, as they become accepted as a norm within educational provision.

Political power is one of the supportive forces, which varies in its influence not only during different periods of development but also from locality to locality. Absence of proactive planning by LEAs has been the main hindrance to the growth of Welsh-medium schools. Weaknesses in the planning process reflect lack of vision and political will in some LEAs. However, no homogeneous pattern of support or indifference amongst LEAs exists across south-east Wales, and it is dangerous to generalise about their overall support of the Ysgolion Cymraeg. One could cite, for example, Cardiff's tardiness for decades compared with its current activity in establishing five new primary schools since 2007, as well as its third secondary in 2012. However, one should note that the date for opening the secondary school was postponed several times, even before the current recession and serious cut-backs. Following many years of spearheading Welsh-medium education in south-east Wales, Rhondda Cynon Taf appears to be on a plateau as far as growth goes. Gwent was loath to change its Welsh-medium primary units (attached to English-medium schools) into free-standing schools until the early 1990s, but now has nine primary schools, as well as its own secondary Ysgol Gymraeg. Its latest primary opened in September 2011: Ysgol Gymraeg Bro Teyrnon in Newport. Further expansion is being planned.

Merthyr Tudful's draft Welsh education scheme for 2009–14 (2009) showed that the LEA had decided to 'consider' conducting a survey of parental demand for Welsh-medium provision, a target that was at odds with central government's concurrent draft policy in its national strategy for Welsh-medium education. The Vale of Glamorgan on the other hand has conducted surveys and acted on the needs that emerged from their analysis; two additional Welsh-medium schools opened in 2011. Newport is another good example of conducting parental surveys of demand for Welsh-medium education.

It can be seen therefore that support and encouragement for the Ysgolion Cymraeg vary at local government level when viewed in time and locality. It could be argued that local government's power over school provision has neither increased nor weakened, in spite of the Thatcherian attempts to undermine local government and centralise power. It is rather local government's decisions about how to distribute resources (as argued by Giddens) that highlights that power. During the current recession a dearth of resources will force local government to distribute them with greater care and thrift. This could work in favour of establishing more Ysgolion Cymraeg as demand increases, without the LEA having to build new schools. However, school closures, reorganisation and rationalisation all generate powerful feelings amongst parents and hard political decisions have to be taken. This is a good example of the complexity of tripartite power, as is further exemplified by Michael Jones, Geraint Rees and Rhodri Morgan later in this volume.

Support and encouragement for the Ysgolion Cymraeg also varies within political parties with time and locality, as the history of the former Glamorgan shows. Of course, without success at the polls power is denied political parties: the history of Plaid Cymru in the constituency of Caerffili is a notable example of pushing forward language frontiers through the educational system when conditions were politically in their favour. On the whole, however, the power of the individual within a political party appears to be stronger than the party itself.

The power of the centre to encourage further growth is the substantial potential which should be developed in the near future in order to realise the vision and aims of 'Iaith Pawb'. Substantial potential power lies in what one could term meso-level European politics, that space where people interact and manipulate agenda and action; it can sometimes lie between local and national power. Wales needs to develop an understanding of political forces at the European level and of their impact on language and education within Wales. For example, Wales needs to promote coordinated planning across LEAs, and create a body to oversee provision and growth, according to the European Charter for Regional and Minority Languages. The Welsh-medium Education Strategy and subsequent legislation have set out a detailed rationale for their implementation, but far more work needs to be done on cross-border and consortia structures.

Probably the most challenging development (again featured in the Welsh-medium Education Strategy) is to make planning and action even more effective in order to promote linguistic progression to other language domains, especially further and higher education, the workplace, the family and social milieus. The Welsh Assembly Government's draft Welsh Language Strategy (2010) shows intellectual commitment to developing bilingual social centres where the language may develop as a language for living, and a declared political intention to make its ambitious schemes work. Subsequently, between May and August 2012, Meri Huws, the recently appointed Welsh language commissioner, conducted a widespread consultation on the draft standards (a cornerstone of the measure). In her foreword she said (WLC 2012: 5): 'Some of the proposals in these consultations will appear challenging.' Maintaining a critical mass of speakers in the Bro Gymraeg, moving the frontiers of linguistic attrition back eastwards, and consolidating the increase of speakers in eastern Wales (mainly the result of the education system) by developing the use of Welsh socially are all equally important in a three-pronged strategy for further language success. The potential power of central government and its acceptance of the challenge of reversing language shift could not be more cogently articulated than in the heritage minister's message in the preface to the strategy: 'Despite the last census showing encouraging signs for the language, especially amongst young people, the position of the language remains fragile.'

Central government should develop governance in Wales by enhancing even further the process of joint planning between interested parties. The following four actions are examples of practical steps that need to be taken, all of them inextricably linked with appropriate legislation and central power:

> facilitating the teaching of all subjects on the curriculum through the medium of Welsh by creating legislation that is appropriately anti-negative;

drawing up legislation that is neutral and open to interpretation rather than over-detailed, if that detail is likely to hinder the growth of Welsh-medium schools;

arranging in-service training for the civil service in the field of Welsh-language education and the Ysgolion Cymraeg in order to enhance under-standing of subtle differences in the system;

defining Welsh-medium provision clearly and unequivocally so that there emerges an understanding across pluralistic Wales of the differences in ethos, language of instruction and linguistic outcomes within the country's schools; for this, it is crucial to know what percentage of all assessments of 11 and 16 year-olds are in Welsh.

The power of governance is the apparatus that should be used in order to develop a knowledgeable civic society that could promote a bilingual Wales. The development of a well-informed democratic country should be one of Wales's national aspirations. As civic society becomes more involved in the governance of Wales, one would hope to see emerging a national strategy to promote a wider understanding of the content and implications of reports which are of key significance in shaping the future of the Welsh nation, such as 'Iaith Pawb' (2003) and the 'Report of the Richard Commission' (Commission on the Powers and Electoral Arrangements of the National Assembly for Wales) (2004).

Debate between various levels of government and groups that have an interest in Welsh-medium education needs to be open and enriched with relevant information and data. One outcome of such debate should be further funding of research into the pedagogy of Welsh and bilingual education. Partners need to exchange views and ideas as part of a planned process of promoting the further growth of the Ysgolion Cymraeg. Marketing (by schools, the local press, the media, central and local government) should be based on a coordinated, holistic and agreed strategy. As yet, the power of governance has not been developed to any significant degree within Wales. The possession of relevant information would enable individuals to use that information in order to create a political agenda, form an ideology and a vision before reacting to policies, and contribute to strategic developments. Unfortunately, targets in the Welsh-medium Education Strategy may be met in some areas only by introducing a Welsh-medium education bill to compel some tardy authorities to implement government policy. That is not the best way to encourage governance, but it may be a pragmatic (and Welsh) way to ensure progress. My comments do not detract from central government's positive stance in the draft bill (WG 2012b), which is critiqued by Michael Jones in chapter 8.

The power of the Welsh language and identity is the spiritual force which unites supporters in a long and difficult struggle to save the language. The Ysgolion Cymraeg were the main force that stemmed further decline in the number of Welsh speakers in south-east Wales, and inspired generations of children and adults to learn and use the language. 'Parental Leaps of Faith' was an early title for this volume, and is echoed in Colin Williams's opening chapter. An earlier echo comes from the pen of Dr Eleanor Hartley, writing in 1973 as a non-Welsh-speaking parent from Barry about the family experience of choosing secondary bilingual education at Rhydfelen (Humphreys, 1973: 126):

> The friends and relatives (mostly I regret to say, from North Wales, and Welsh-speaking) who originally warned me of the pitfalls of bilingual education for English-speaking children now re-mustered to prophesy more doom. However, I was not deterred. It seemed logical to continue their education in the way it had started [at Ysgol Sant Ffransis, Barry]. I had faith that those who accepted my children at Rhydfelen would not let them down.

Faith can move mountains, but the Ysgolion Cymraeg cannot save the language on their own, though they were responsible, beyond any other phenomenon, for an initial reversal of the language shift in Wales. A broader understanding of sociolinguistic theories needs to be developed in Wales, along with the intellectual capacity to adapt theories to the country's needs. Wales's traditional pragmatism in the field of RLS has been successful so far, but it is not enough. The fight to save the language has not been won yet, in spite of valiant efforts by generations of campaigners and supporters, and the stances and actions of central government. Reversing language shift is a long and evolutionary process. The Ysgolion Cymraeg are the main symbol of the vision that Welsh people have regarding the future of the language, creating in areas of Wales, particularly the east, the sort of community and relationship (in terms of both Welsh identity and language) that is an essential part of the process of reversing the language shift and preserving the country's traditional culture. The Welsh-language schools form the largest sociolinguistic community in south-east Wales which promotes the fight to save the language. The enthusiasm and commitment of teachers for the success of the Ysgolion Cymraeg and their role in reversing the language shift is still a salient feature during a comparatively early period of language normalisation. The powers of the Welsh language and of the Ysgolion Cymraeg are interdependent. Maintaining and strengthening the right balance between them is essential if we are to enjoy a genuine revival of Welsh, and the future provision and well-being of the Ysgolion Cymraeg should be nurtured and promoted. Nothing should be done to undermine their future.

Potential power – so-called because such power has not yet existed – would make it possible to plan, in a coordinated, holistic way, to serve the linguistic needs of the nation. There has never been a coordinated, holistic approach to language planning in Wales that takes account of the nation's pluralistic language needs; the Ysgolion Cymraeg, for example, grew in their localities in an uncoordinated fashion. The national Strategy for Welsh-medium Education, however, has substantial potential power to plan provision across geographic and political boundaries. This Strategy is historic in that Wales has never before had the opportunity to celebrate such coordinated planning for Welsh-medium education, for all ages and in all parts of the country.

The Welsh-medium Education Strategy accepts that Wales is a land of linguistic pluralism, and that one model does not suit the diverse range of language patterns even within a population of only three million. The sociolinguistic challenges of the east of the country cannot be considered in isolation from the western counties of Wales, particularly when one takes into account the significant loss of intergenerational transmission of the language in the traditional Welsh-speaking west.

A paradoxical feature of the success of the Ysgolion Cymraeg is that parental enthusiasm seems to wane as the normalisation of Welsh-medium provision increases, unless individuals assume the role of language-revival catalysts, prepared to inspire others to campaign for their language rights within education. Consequently, a better understanding by all involved of the flow of power between various strata of structures needs to be developed. A divide between teachers and parents on the one hand and academics and language planners on the other is one that needs to be bridged. A combined and integrated national vision will develop through joint discussion. This is a power that has the potential to generate constructive concepts and ideas as the understanding grows of the complex range of influences on Welsh-medium education and the reversal of the language shift.

The Ysgolion Cymraeg are the most effective means of ensuring language acquisition, and the most sustainable model to make language acquisition effective in the (mainly English-speaking) east of the country. This point is made under potential power since there is a dearth of specialist Welsh-medium teachers, particularly at secondary, FE and HE levels, as well as in the workplace. Their expertise should not be spread too thinly by the development of school models that are unsustainable on a national level, and replicable only in extraordinary circumstances. No criticism is made of individual headteachers whose outstanding vision and application have devised unique provision in their own schools. That is an end result of the power of the individual. The power that will reverse the language shift is the power that is able to plan a national strategy which will replicate a small number of sustainable models in Wales. A national groundswell of goodwill towards saving the language needs to be further nurtured and tied in with language planning in order to combine the most powerful forces of the mind and spirit, and abolish both tokenism and ad hoc development.

The power of the individual is the force that can inspire others to move mountains. The influence of individual parents, councillors, politicians, statesmen, teachers, headteachers and school governors, education officers, civil servants and Her Majesty's inspectors of schools has been one of the important supporting forces during half a century of development of the sector. Within the schools, the enlightened and proactive leadership of headteachers, the unflinching commitment of governors, and the energetic enthusiasm of teachers and support staff have been a powerful force to overcome enormous obstacles. Poor buildings, the challenge of attracting well-qualified staff (and keeping them), and the comparatively narrow (though gradually improving) range of teaching materials have appeared to some as insurmountable obstacles. For the majority, however, they were challenges to be overcome. Within the parent body, individuals have played all sorts of roles: formulating visions and plans, campaigning and debating, conducting missionary and fund-raising crusades, and being inspiring catalysts.

165

Due to their particular vision and action, individuals within political parties have had a greater effect on the Welsh language and on the growth of the Ysgolion Cymraeg than the parties themselves. However, the power of coalition government in progressing language issues has been notable: the Liberal Democrat input into 'Iaith Pawb' and Plaid's insistence on developing a national strategy for Welsh-medium education and the Coleg Cymraeg Cenedlaethol are important examples. There appears to be a move away from individual power to party political power.

The power that has driven the Ysgolion Cymraeg has been multilayered. Parental power remains an immense force, which is fed by other forces, in a plethora of complex combinations. Powers on micro, meso and macro levels interchange according to their context, and interact with one another. Overemphasising the importance of structure or agency is dangerous, without finding and nurturing the source of the power which drives debate and creative action. One advantage enjoyed by Wales is that it is a small country, which facilitates networking, but there is a dire need to improve the debate and make thinking more focused, so that macro, meso and micro levels evolve through the ensuing interaction.

In the previous chapter I discussed the need to avoid polarisation of standpoints and views in moving an agenda forwards. The case of Ysgol Gymraeg Treganna in west Cardiff, as detailed by Rhodri Morgan in chapter 10, provides material illustrative of parental power, practical complexities and political forces all engaged in the sort of complex combination referred to above. Morgan, writing in early July 2011, states that the source of an additional £6 million, the major tranche of the £9 million needed to build a replacement school, was 'shrouded in mystery'. However, it had been reported to the city's executive business meeting on 7 April that the total costs of £9.887 million had been secured (Cardiff Council 2011: par. 114, 122, 123). Party political friction comes to the fore when he claims: 'A further indictment of the Council's competence was that it was the Canton [Labour] councillors, not the Council, who identified the proposed site at Sanatorium Road for the new Welsh-medium primary.' A contradictory statement appears in a blog page ('Syniadau': 5 April 2011): '[B]ut the proposal for a new school was Plaid Cymru's idea and formed part of the Capital Vision document agreed between Plaid and the LibDems after the 2008 election.' Anti-Treganna comments were investigated by the police on the grounds of racism, but an apology was subsequently made (Sharkey:

2009): '[I]n hindsight he should have used the expression "polarisation" rather than "ethnic cleansing"'. However, by the time I wrote these comments (March 2012) there was approval across all political parties in Cardiff for the proposed reorganisation scheme.

Far more important than any analysis is the critical application of that analysis. The next phase of development in the Welsh-medium school movement needs to foster a holistic vision and strategy regarding education, the Welsh language, and the communities of Wales. Gramsci's famous comment (1929), 'I'm a pessimist because of intelligence, but an optimist because of will', would serve us well, as planners at all levels of civic society develop their ideological and practical ideas. The various powers outlined in this chapter need to be applied if Wales is to mature its nascent pragmatic vision: it has reversed the language shift, mainly through education, but now comes the challenge of consolidating that initial success.

Chapter 6

An Evolving Synergy

Huw S. Thomas

This chapter draws on insights, patterns and theses that emerged from empirical research and consequent interpretations of research data, and focuses on what are considered to be some of the key aspects that should inform the future development of Welsh-language education. These aspects are arranged according to micro, meso and macro levels. The micro should be read as the actors and such matters as are of direct importance to them; the meso as the planning for normalisation of Welsh-language education; and the macro as one that encapsulates structuration and governance at global and theoretical levels. The combined effect of micro, meso and macro activities creates a powerful synergy that continues to evolve. It is emphasised that the analysis is of a historical snapshot and it is hoped that the Welsh-medium Education Strategy, along with the Welsh Language Strategy, will enhance an already evolving synergy.

THE MICRO LEVEL

Parents of English-medium Schools, 'the greater portion'
'I believe that the greater portion [of parents] already see [*sic*] the immense advantage of bilingual instruction, and that the number will increase daily with the spread of information.' That was the opinion of Dan Isaac Davies, a pioneering campaigner for Welsh-medium education, when he gave evidence to the Royal Commission on Education in 1887 (Hughes 1984: 206, 134).

Notwithstanding the steady growth of the Ysgolion Cymraeg over the last half-century, most parents have not chosen this medium. Five English-medium schools (three primary and two secondary) were sampled in the county of Caerffili in 2007 and parents were asked to respond to the statement, 'A child will not be admitted into a Welsh-medium school unless at least one of his/her parents is a Welsh speaker.' The response of all seventy-two parents who replied showed that not one of them believed this, a pattern that contrasts with oral evidence based on a survey of parents in the Swansea area and reported in a joint WLB, RhAG and CYDAG meeting in 2006. When asked why they had not chosen Welsh-medium education, the main reasons given by the same Caerffili parents were their own inability to speak Welsh and a genuine concern about their anticipated low level of support for their children's progress and development, particularly with reading and homework. A number of parents quoted difficulties travelling to the nearest Ysgol Gymraeg, the convenient location of the neighbourhood English-medium school and its excellent standards. Two respondents mentioned the importance of social integration with local children and avoiding their being ostracised.

It is significant that eleven respondents volunteered positive comments regarding the Welsh language and Welsh-medium education, such as the following: 'If the local school was Welsh medium we would probably have been more inclined to take Welsh classes and sent him there regardless [that we didn't speak Welsh]. I hope that Welsh schools are more and more, especially in the south-east of Wales.' The parents were also asked to record their fluency in Welsh: of the seventy-two respondents, three said that they were very fluent, four fluent, and seven fairly fluent. The seven fluent/very fluent parents (10 per cent of the sample) and the positive attitudes of the vast majority of respondents towards the Welsh language suggest potential for further growth in the Welsh-medium field. The sample revealed a tendency towards an empathy with Welsh-medium education (36.1 per cent of respondents), a finding which corroborates a comment made by Meirion Prys Jones, chief executive of the WLB (interview 10 July 2006), that there is a threshold of people prepared to choose Welsh-medium schools but that a significant proportion 'just under that threshold' is not sufficiently proactive to send their children any distance in order to be educated in Welsh. Perceived inability to help with homework, he maintained, was the other major hindrance. Interestingly, a telephone homework support service is not widely used. Negative comments against the Welsh language and the Ysgolion Cymraeg were few:

three mentioned the uselessness of Welsh outside Wales, and one argued against compulsory Welsh to the end of key stage 4 (but without arguing against the other compulsory elements in the curriculum).

On the whole, a bright future emerged for the future well-being of the language, which suggests fruitful ground for further development of the Ysgolion Cymraeg. The two following comments by parents from English-medium schools could stimulate further debate:

> Welsh education is a complex subject and being an English woman with a Welsh family I still harbour some reservations about a totally Welsh education for my children. However if it weren't for the English then you wouldn't even have this debate. All schools would still be Welsh and the language would be stronger than ever.
>
> I fully support the existence of Welsh-medium schools. My only concern is that pupils' level (and knowledge) of Welsh to *successfully* cope with GCSEs and A-Levels may not be as sufficient today as it was 15–20 years ago. Should parents enrol their children into the Welsh-medium sector, I feel that they should *also* receive Welsh lessons in order to support their child both on an educational and cultural level. In my locality, the Welsh sector is seen as a means of 'escaping' a 'second-rate' 'non-Welsh' system rather than a deep-rooted desire to educate their children in the nation's language. (A shame.)

Helping with Homework

It is significant that not one parent from Welsh-medium schools responding to an open-ended questionnaire noted Welsh-medium homework as a hindrance to further growth. However, due to the widely perceived challenge of failing to help children with their homework, it was decided to probe attitudes and insights in a subsequent structured questionnaire through the following three statements:

1. In any school, whatever the language of instruction, very few parents indeed are able to help their children with their homework in all subjects and at all levels.
2. It is an advantage that my child has to use the English-Welsh dictionary in order to find the right Welsh word.
3. In the comprehensive school, helping my child with his/her homework in every subject and at all levels is/will be difficult or impossible, since [almost] all the subjects are taught in Welsh. (Thomas 2007: 269–70, 387–9; 2010a: 224–5)

Two important factors to be considered are the way that parents help their children and the support that they give them. Most parental help is given when the children are young, for example helping with their reading. According to Sharp et al. (2001), there is no distinct correlation between the amount of support given by parents and their children's attainment in school. Statement 1 above strongly suggests that the ideal parental model is a polymath. A significant third of respondents appeared to believe in the polymath role. It may be that there were too many layers of concepts included in the statement, and that some new parents' limited experience may have skewed the result to some degree.

Though the next piece of evidence comes from a questionnaire for English-medium schools, it provides a focus for discussion. One parent wrote that learning through the medium of Welsh was an additional burden. Another respondent wrote that her husband had attended a Welsh-medium secondary school and that one was constantly translating everything. The main reason for including statement 2 above was personal knowledge that there was (or had been before a richer provision of teaching and learning materials in Welsh) considerable sympathy with the previous respondent's view. However, pupils are taught the higher skill of using ordinary and technical terms dictionaries, while the skill of trans-languaging has become increasingly better integrated across the curriculum. Most schools also produce their own graded lists of technical terms as an introduction to more comprehensive published volumes. Pupils develop linguistic skills and deepen their understanding of subject matter when they search for the *mot juste*, an experience appreciated by 70 per cent of secondary teachers and over 60 per cent of parents, who realised that the appropriate use of dictionaries was an advantage for pupils. In retrospect, statement 3 has three elements which, when combined, conflate and confuse response and interpretation: the polymath, the medium and the psychology inherent in the status of the Welsh language. Nevertheless, two thirds of all respondents believed that the medium did not hinder parents from helping their children with their homework.

In conclusion, the matter of Welsh-medium homework should be a research project in order to improve pedagogy. The only piece of research on homework in Wales conducted between 1985 and 2005, according to the National Library of Wales's electronic catalogue, was by Gareth Williams (1988), a deputy headteacher at the Welsh-medium Ysgol Gyfun

Cwm Rhymni. His thesis investigated a range of aspects, but not that of the medium, that is homework done in the pupils' second language (over 95 per cent of pupils came from English-speaking homes). His reasoning was that this school was the first Welsh-medium comprehensive with such a high proportion of pupils from English-speaking homes, and he did not wish to suggest to parents that Welsh-medium homework might have been a contentious issue in the school. It was certainly a challenging issue, in part addressed innovatively by the oral homework project on tape; it was never a contentious one.

Hindrances to Further Growth

In order to understand the lower rate of growth in some areas (Rhondda Cynon Taf, for example), parents were asked to list possible factors to account for it. Table 6.1 summarises responses from fifty parents, who wrote profusely and passionately on the subject:

> If those with prejudice and attitude were more open-minded the increase of Welsh speakers from an early educational age would increase dramatically. If only these people could see the lack of harm and instead foresee the benefit of their children being bilingual whilst being educated via the medium of Welsh ultimately speaking Welsh. But unfortunately the majority do not have the vision or inclination to bring about the speedy progression of the Welsh language and this represents a hindrance. It is a question of '*Dyfal donc a dyrr y garreg*' (Constant chipping at the stone will break it).

The main hindrance that emerged was other people's negativity, a factor that strengthens the thesis that the parents are the most important drivers for growth, not only historically but also in the future. It should be noted that these respondents were not ticking boxes but rather investigating their personal experiences and insights.

The most commonly cited hindrances are combined in the following comments by a parent from Newport:

> Accessibility of Welsh-medium schools i.e. the Welsh Primary school in Newport was initially a unit and took a lot of lobbying before the school was opened and then it was located next to Llanwern steel works and many parents were concerned about the quantities of dark smoke belching out on a daily basis – a factor which may have put some people off. Likewise the

TABLE 6.1

An analysis of hindrances to further growth of the Ysgolion Cymraeg – reasons
noted by parents (51) responding to Q3, Spring 2004

Rank order	Description	Numbers	%
1	Negative attitudes of others	16	31.4
2	Travelling/distance between home and school	13	25.5
3=	Insufficient finance	11	21.6
3=	Insufficient opportunities for parents to learn Welsh	11	21.6
3=	Insufficient resources – teachers, teaching and learning materials, the media	11	21.6
6	Opportunities to speak Welsh in the community	9	17.6
7=	Poor publicity/advice	8	15.7
7=	Poor standard of school buildings	8	15.7
9	Weaknesses in leadership/goodwill in local and central government	5	9.8
10	Poor proactive planning by the local education authorities	2	3.1

Source: Thomas (2010a: 226).

school at Trevethin [Gwynllyw, some twelve miles north of Newport] is not
an ideal site, located high up with access via small roads. School buses are
cancelled at any sign of severe weather. So as a cynic the message seems to be
– you can have your school but you may not like where it is. Some parents
may be put off by the site, unless you are committed to Welsh Education and
not borderline.

An expedient decision by the Welsh Assembly Government to facilitate
home-to-school transport was the Learner Travel (Wales) Measure (2008).
The following quotation from a written cabinet statement (14 April 2008)
by Ieuan Wyn Jones AM, deputy first minister and minister for the economy
and transport, shows a positive attitude towards Welsh-medium schools.
Time will reveal the efficacy of the measure:

I have been eager to encourage the continued provision of transport to
Welsh- medium schools whilst recognising that, given the varied patterns of

provision of Welsh-medium education and the differing conditions that apply throughout Wales, there cannot be one size that fits all answers. I am also mindful that all local authorities, in accordance with the Welsh Language Act 1993, prepare, as part of their Welsh Language Schemes, Welsh Education Schemes which set out how they will promote the learning of Welsh generally, whether through Welsh-medium schools or second-language teaching in other settings. I have decided to complement the above with a new duty (section 10 of the Measure) on local authorities and on Welsh Ministers, when exercising their functions under the Measure, to promote access to education and training through the medium of Welsh.

It does not follow that the most frequently mentioned drivers are necessarily the most powerful ones. For example, while the Welsh language was by far the most important reason quoted by parents in two question-naires for choosing the Ysgol Gymraeg, two respondents in a third noted that the image of the Welsh language was a hindrance: 'Welsh language perceived by many as "elite", especially in white working-class areas.' Some parents wrote succinctly and with considerable insight. The following quotation is an example showing breadth and depth of understanding: 'Lack of knowledge of availability of this type of education – parents have to want a Welsh education and seek it out rather than this format being the default medium; number of schools and places available; number of teachers; geography – how far to the nearest school; a potential of parliaments to cap growth.'

Lack of proactive planning by LEAs was the main criticism made by activists and educationists. Ironically, only two respondents referred to this weakness, but the following quotation by a parent born in Birmingham encapsulates the frustrations and determination of campaigners. She apologised for writing at length, but she 'felt so passionately about it':

If the council showed genuine foresight and planned to develop W.M.E. in the future there would be no need for endless parental pressure groups and campaigns to set up new schools . . . The truth is there is *no* high school for my child at present – Glantaf [in Cardiff] is full and there is a danger of Porta-cabins on site while a new site is 'identified' and made ready – the same cycle repeats and it is left to parents to push the process forward and we are sick of it. Obviously if there is no choice we will campaign – but it is unfair to expect us to be the ones ensuring buildings are built or sites are identified when the council are paid to do exactly that.

Her fears were realised when four temporary classrooms arrived in Ysgol Gyfun Gymraeg Glantaf a few years later. Another decision by the council was to spend £17 million on extensions for Glantaf and its sister school, Plasmawr. This appears to be an expedient move brought about by the delayed reorganisation of secondary school places within the capital city and the consequent late opening of its third Welsh-medium secondary school. At the same time, the extensions will extend the provision of specialist accommodation and are an improvement on the generally poor fabric of the original buildings.

The previous parental quotation is in stark contrast to the next. Both provide important evidence in that they exemplify a range of opinions and experiences by parents from different areas of south-east Wales. It appears that the successful establishment of Ysgol Gyfun Bro Morgannwg in Barry (Vale of Glamorgan), without overt political opposition, is responsible for the positive tone of the statement. The respondent generalises about LEAs on the basis of his personal experiences:

> During my time as a parent of children involved in Welsh-medium education, I have seen the infant/junior school double in size, and I have been involved with the establishment of two new Welsh-medium Secondary schools. I therefore have seen the hindrances which *used* to exist, as lack of will on behalf of local authorities, change into excellent support from local authorities.

Publicity
Publicity is examined from the point of view of parents and prospective parents, and focuses on its relative impact on their decision to opt for an Ysgol Gymraeg. It is the final section within the micro level of analysis. Lack of publicity was cited by 15.7 per cent of respondents to a questionnaire as a hindrance against further growth, a view corroborated by parental response to the following question: 'Before you decided to send your child/children to a Cylch Ti a Fi or Cylch Meithrin or Ysgol Gymraeg, what support or advice or guidance did you receive from public bodies or institutions or groups or individuals?' No support was offered to 85 per cent of families in the sample of sixty-five. Rather than write 'nothing', it is significant that almost a half of respondents volunteered their reasons for choosing the Ysgol Gymraeg. They felt a responsibility to contribute towards the research (and by implication the growth of the Ysgolion Cymraeg) and showed commitment to the movement and an eagerness to relate their

story. Table 6.2 analyses the advice that was given to a minority of prospective parents. The positive message that emerges is the range of sources of information, to which could be added the WLB web information (2003a, 2003b), literature published by Twf, or Baker's handbook (1995). However, it is not a paucity of sources that needs to be addressed but rather the need for a publicity campaign to inform prospective parents that such information is readily available.

TABLE 6.2

The support, advice or guidance received by prospective parents from public bodies, institutions, groups, or individuals before they opted for an Ysgol Gymraeg (65 respondents)

Nature of advice, etc.	Number of times noted
Schools	15
Head of primary school	6
School visit	3
Mudiad Ysgolion Meithrin	2
Parents of the Nursery School/class	2
Non-Welsh-speaking parents	2
Other people	5
Word of mouth	1
Neighbours	1

Source: Thomas (2007: 352).

Table 6.3 shows that the main source of information was the schools themselves and people associated with the schools. Printed evidence seems to have had little influence, while an excellent inspection report seems to be related by word of mouth. Later research revealed strong agreement (83.1 per cent) with the statement that 'having an excellent report [from Estyn] attracts prospective parents'. Oral transmission seems to be a key factor.

Respondents believed that one of the outstanding qualities of the Ysgolion Cymraeg is the way they nurture a range of talents innate to individual pupils. This is an aspect that could be marketed, especially since four out of every five parents noted this as a reason for choosing an Ysgol

TABLE 6.3
Main sources of information for prospective parents

Type of source	Number of sources	Percentage
Friends/MYM/parents	15	60%
Other people	5	20%
Published evidence	4	16%
Other (county council)	1	4%

Source: Thomas (2010a: 230).

Gymraeg. A high quality of pastoral care was another facet that scored highly with both parents and teachers. One mother who responded quoted five sources or reasons that she and her husband had considered before opting for an Ysgol Gymraeg. Her list (in order of importance) is a good example of comprehensive evidence:

1. On a personal level my husband and I have always regretted not being able to converse fluently in Welsh and if given the choice we would both have wished to have Welsh-medium education.
2. Documentation from the school itself was very compelling particularly regarding external exam results in a league table against other primary schools.
3. I read articles published in the press regarding Welsh-medium education and its advantages.
4. I spoke with mothers of other children already in the school and asked them about various aspects of the school.
5. Personal experience of teaching and the experience of other teachers in Welsh-medium schools.

One of the most memorable pieces of advice recorded was the following: 'We were informed by another parent just because you can't play the piano or swim are you going to stop your child doing it?'

With regard to the question of how advice should be promoted, there was unanimity amongst the three groups of respondents (parents, secondary and primary teachers) that parents should be given advice. Yet over a half of parents thought that seeking that advice should be the parents' own responsibility, a view possibly reflecting their personal experience. Another explanation could be that the eagerness to campaign has weakened. At the same time, over 80 per cent of teachers thought that advice should be provided for parents, without the onus lying on the parents themselves. Teachers' strong opinions on this matter compared with parents' responses is typical of the general indications from the research data; teachers appear to be more aware of the significance of strategies and of the psychological influence of feelings about and attitudes to the success of the Ysgolion Cymraeg and their continued development than are the parents.

THE MESO LEVEL

Suggestions for Marketing

The advice available for prospective parents is good; its distribution and marketing are not. A concerted effort is needed by individual parents, individual schools, voluntary bodies, LEAs, central government and the office of the language commissioner to create consensually a detailed marketing strategy. This is essential in order to maintain the growth of the Ysgolion Cymraeg and, in parallel, to reverse the language shift. A similar proposal has been made in the Strategy for Welsh-medium Education (2010a) and it needs to be implemented. Various agencies need to market appropriate aspects of Welsh-medium education but they should refer to the holistic strategy in order to deepen parental understanding of minority-language education in both national and international contexts. In 1999 the WLB offered advice for marketing Welsh-medium education, but very little action was taken. One of its recommendations (Baker and Jones 1999: 27) was 'to market Welsh medium provision at strategic points during an individual's progression through the system, for example, at the end of primary, beginning of secondary, at year 9, 11 and 13, and also in FE and HE.' A comprehensive range of data such as that collected by Thomas (2007: 344–613) could provide a sound platform for formulating the marketing programme. Parental motives should be a central theme. While the pedagogy of Welsh-medium and bilingual education needs much more research, considerable tact and wisdom will be needed in its implementation, as outlined by Baker (2000: 112–16):

> Bilingual schools need to emphasize specifics in the value-addedness of
> bilingual education. If these value-added attributes are clearly articulated

and monitored with qualitative and quantitative evidence, it can be shown whether the extra aims and objectives of bilingual education are being delivered.

Three major considerations are implied by 'tact and wisdom'. Firstly, the political context of school comparisons appears to be in a fluid state; while so-called league tables have been abolished in Wales, Estyn, the schools' inspectorate, has (since 2007) published tables of inspection scores in such a way that school-by-school comparison is unavoidable. The tables of secondary school examination results and value added data published in June 2011 need to be critiqued intelligently. Secondly, political and psychological sensitivity will need to be applied to avoid direct comparison between Welsh-medium and English-medium schools leading to a rift between them. Thirdly, as Thomas has shown (2007), the complex combination of reasons why Welsh-medium schools have flourished needs to be taken on board. Baker made a similar point (1990: 79): 'The development is likely to be the result of complex educational, political, economic and social factors.'

The marketing needs to be based on further research by an institution whose academic standards are held in high regard. The nature and style of marketing also needs to be built on firm principles such as those outlined by Jones and Dafis (2000: 163–73). Parents (and many others) are unclear what the different linguistic labels attached to schools actually mean. The term 'bilingual' in particular is so multi-faceted that the linguistic outcomes of pupils attending such schools (as well as schools that are mainly Welsh-medium or English-medium) need to be articulated lucidly. For example, how bilingual is a school where only a miniscule percentage of external examination papers are taken through the medium of Welsh? Joined-up, coordinated planning of the marketing programme by educators, language planners, policy makers and parents should lead to what Baker called (2000: 120) an 'idealistic conclusion', with 'a mature, logical, rational and smooth evolution in bilingual education' rather than the 'gentle revolution' (Baker, 1990: 79) that has happened since 1950.

Planning

Status, corpus, language acquisition, provision of school places, additional learning needs, teacher supply, the sustainability of Welsh-medium education, provision within further and higher education and academic research all need careful planning, evaluation, and development. An overview only is provided of these aspects.

The status of the Welsh language needs to develop contemporaneously on all possible fronts, a view which goes against Fishman's tenet that language developments have to be prioritised. While prioritisation, it may be argued, suggests pragmatism, classification of developments into varying degrees of importance raises issues of modernity, lack of modernity, and relative importance. The challenge of status planning was well enunciated by Baker (2003: 107–8):

> An argument can be made for preserving (and increasing) everything that affects the status of the Welsh language. Nothing becomes unimportant. Such components of language status exist in delicate interactions and combinations and not as separate, isolatable influences. Remove a few bricks and the public may believe that the castle is beginning to crumble.

Corpus planning is meant to ensure that terminology exists to support a developing range of usage (information technology, for example). In the past, Welsh-medium teachers had to create technical terms, supported by disparate (and often contradictory) lists published by the University of Wales. The *Termiadur* (a technical terms dictionary, Prys et al.: 2006) has standardised usage and is a good basis for further development. A language has to develop if it is to survive, and the services of Canolfan Bedwyr (University of Bangor), which spearheads work in contemporary terminology, have to be consolidated by sound central funding. It is remarkable that the Welsh language is responding so quickly to a rapidly developing world, without the support of substantial funding. The Welsh Assembly Government's consultative document 'A living language: A language for living' (2011a: 30) states that 'The Government agrees that a National Standardisation Body for the Welsh Language should be established', a most welcome development.

Language acquisition cannot be allowed to develop according to the vagaries of existing speakers of the language. In spite of impressive efforts by the Ysgolion Cymraeg and some English-medium and bilingual schools, which were accompanied by considerable success, the frequency of normal everyday usage is nevertheless disappointing. Jeni Price's analysis (chapter 11) is an illuminating example of what can be achieved. Promoting the social use of Welsh is the language's biggest challenge, involving intergenerational transfer (or rather tackling the lack of it), further improvements in Welsh for adults, the development of Welsh-medium and bilingual education, and an enhanced range of opportunities to use Welsh in the community. All of these challenges are well documented in the WAG draft Welsh-language Strategy (2010c: 2011).

The proactive planning of sufficient places in Ysgolion Cymraeg[1] has been highlighted as a priority in the Welsh-medium Education Strategy (2010a). It is generally acknowledged that past planning has been reactive, often slow, with schools established in inappropriate geographical locations. A new education act needs to ensure that central policies can be supported by legal structures that facilitate cross-border planning of school places. Current planning and the actual provision are too patchy, in spite of attempts by some LEAs to measure (successfully) the demand for Welsh-medium places. Owen John Thomas (2008: 51–62) has analysed good and bad practice in fourteen LEAs which have fewer than 20 per cent of Welsh speakers; Newport, Wrecsam and Swansea are examples of growth or of substantial potential for growth. Michael Jones too provides a critique of LA planning in his chapter and in an article (Jones 2012) in which he seeks to link the degree of parental pressure in each local authority area with the degree of progress of Welsh-medium education there. Caerffili County Borough Council, for example, shows committed forward planning, particularly in measuring the demand for Welsh-medium education, and in its strategy for planning provision. It is reassuring that the local authority has prioritised the proper funding of the Ysgolion Cymraeg, based on what appear to be sound research methodologies and a well-balanced response to the demand shown. The data provided in its draft Welsh education scheme (2009: 47) are encouraging, showing a steady growth in parental requests for the Ysgolion Cymraeg:

Children born in the 2004/05 academic year	21.6%
Children born in the 2005/06 academic year	22.4%
Children born in the 2006/07 academic year	26.8%

The annual increase of over four percentage points in the final year exemplified is significant, in that the overall percentage equates to over a quarter of the pupils within the LEA being likely to be educated in the Ysgolion Cymraeg in the foreseeable future. It is also encouraging that the LEA has decided to develop the model of Welsh-medium education that best suits south-east Wales, namely the Welsh-medium school, the Ysgol Gymraeg. This practice reflects the view of the draft Welsh-medium Education Strategy (2009a: 42): 'In the south-east and north-east, designated Welsh-medium education is the most successful means of producing fluent Welsh speakers, and it needs to be maintained and strengthened.'

Conversely, pupil numbers in the Welsh-medium sector in the County Borough of Merthyr Tudful have decreased steadily. Its draft Welsh-education scheme showed little determination to improve the situation; it stated that during 2009–10 the local authority would (2009: 5) *consider* surveying parents to assess the demand for Welsh-medium education, while one of its targets (2009: 35) was to '*assess the need to survey* parents on demand for Welsh-medium education' (my italics). The national draft Welsh-medium Strategy, on the other hand, was vigorously proactive (2009a: 46):

> The centrality given to Welsh-medium education provision at Welsh Assembly Government level should be reflected within local authorities and across consortia. Appropriate methods will be determined for placing a statutory duty on local authorities to establish a Welsh-medium education forum within each authority . . . With the aim of ensuring that policy developments in education take full account of the needs of the Welsh-language sector as a matter of course across all authorities, mechanisms will be put in place for annual meetings of local authority representatives to be arranged, chaired by the Minister for Children, Education, Lifelong Learning and Skills, to monitor progress on Welsh-medium provision and planning.

New provision within the Welsh-medium primary sector has often created further difficulties for local council planners in that the schools quickly become oversubscribed. Demand for places grows and outstrips the provision. Flexibility needs to be incorporated into the size of classes in order to cope with fluctuating demand, and avoid children from the same families having to attend different primary schools. LEAs may redefine catchment areas annually, thereby allowing them to satisfy the law, which has provided that Welsh-medium education shall be available for all who request it, but not necessarily in the immediate neighbourhood of all pupils. In a word, proactive, well-thought-through planning is essential.

Additional Learning Needs (ALN) provision in Wales provides a good example of tension between structure and agencies. The SEN and Disabilities

Act (2001), the Code of Practice (2002), LEA and school policies, and the SEN Tribunal for Wales provide a comprehensive structure for provision. However, the review of SEN policy (WAG 2004) highlighted a serious shortage of staff appropriately trained in the wide range of SEN (ALN) needs. While the review recommended that the Welsh Assembly Government should publish a timetable for implementing their recommendations (ibid., 46), Welsh does not appear in the Labour party's proposed *Legislative Competence Order Additional Learning Needs* (SEN) 2007 (icNetwork 2007: 20–1 and Welsh Affairs Committee, House of Commons 2007). Though SEN (ALN) integration into mainstream education has happened, essential building blocks, especially the supply of appropriately trained and qualified staff, are still in an unsatisfactory state. Pressure through effective governance needs to be developed as a priority.

Planning for the growth of a trained Welsh-speaking teaching and ancillary working force needs to be fully implemented to complement the overall growth in Welsh-medium provision. Sustainability of the workforce is essential. The Furlong review (2006) of initial teacher training in Wales, commissioned by the Welsh Assembly Government, neglected to research Welsh-medium issues. A subsequent commission was given to London Economics, which presented a report on the matter in 2007. It is too early to evaluate the long-term effect of its recommendations. In the meantime a vigorous annual evaluation of training and professional development needs to be carried out, and schemes which have been initially successful in increasing the supply of teachers (the Welsh Language Sabbatical Scheme, for example) are to be refined and their application made more comprehensive and better tailored to the individual needs of schools and colleges (Arad Research 2011). Continuing support for the Sabbatical Scheme (£6 million over three years) was announced by the minister for education and skills, Leighton Andrews, in June 2011, which is most encouraging.

Statistics compiled by Thomas (2007 354–5) showed that across the curriculum three times as many applications were made for English-medium vacancies as for Welsh-medium ones. Statistics produced by the General Teaching Council for Wales suggest that the pool of Welsh-medium teachers is bigger than it actually is, since there is no way at the moment of avoiding double or triple accounting. According to Gruffudd (2005: 1), some 120 applications were made for 7 posts in a newly established Welsh-medium secondary school. This does not mean that over 110 teachers were unemployed after the interviews, since many would have been in post already in other schools. Thomas showed that in 2005 some 3 applications were made for every Welsh-medium vacancy (apart from PE), compared with about 11 in English-medium schools in Wales.

The sustainability of Welsh-medium education, particularly the Ysgolion Cymraeg, leads to a consideration of alternative models of schools. The Ysgolion Cymraeg have been a successful model for educating the whole child and producing fluent bilingual speakers. It is appropriate to trial alternative school models in Wales, particularly when one considers the country's pluralistic and complex linguistic patterns. With outstanding leadership and specialist staff any model may succeed. However, the experimentation and liberalism that are the mark of pushing forward the frontiers of alternative provision have to ensure sustainability on a national level. I would suggest that David Hawker's far-reaching vision (chapter 7) needs to be viewed in the light of the short- and mid-term reality that I describe in this paragraph. It is the Ysgolion Cymraeg (with adjunct provision for latecomers) that is the only sustainable model in the foreseeable future. Political dogma and linguistic inclusiveness have to be compromised in Wales's relentless fight to reverse the language shift. Nothing should be done to weaken the position and status and efficacy of the Ysgolion Cymraeg, particularly in south-east and north-east Wales. At the same time, the loosely used adjective 'bilingual' needs intellectual probing and serious debate within civic and educational society. All too often the word is thrown into discussion with little understanding of its ramifications and implications. Baker's volume, *Foundations of Bilingual Education and Bilingualism* (2006) is an excellent introductory textbook, providing an overview of 'the major concerns in bilingualism and bilingual education with a future perspective' (2006: xiii).

Within further education, the number of courses available in Welsh is extremely low, compared with a pleasing level of Welsh-medium courses in the country's sixth forms (Thomas 2007: 351). Starting from a low base makes it difficult for planners to create an impetus, in spite of valiant efforts by individual members of staff or college principals. Within higher education, while it is possible to take initial and higher degrees completely though the medium of Welsh, the number of courses, modules, and combinations available is severely limited. For many years, students, staff and pressure groups (such as the Welsh Language Society) have campaigned for a substantial improvement in provision, but progress has been painfully slow. Cooperation between institutions has been lethargic, patchy at best but improved somewhat as a result of planning by the University of Wales Welsh-medium Teaching Committee and the coordinated approach of Mantais.

Parents and teachers supported overwhelmingly (90.5 per cent) the view that the number of Welsh-medium courses in the colleges and universities of Wales should expand substantially. Ninety-four per cent of respondents disagreed with a parallel statement that there was no place for Welsh-medium courses in further and higher education. It is notable that parental support, which has been critical in the growth of Welsh-medium schools, has not been tapped at HE and FE levels. Parents should become part of the appropriate democratic and political processes. The over-whelmingly positive response that emerged from the empirical data reflects the clear vision that parents and teachers have of a healthy future for the language. Campaigners and language planners should combine this optimism with arguments for modernism and incisive intellectualism. 'Without a vibrant intellectual culture the Welsh language will wither. To be a language in the modern world, Welsh must continue to develop so that individuals and communities can express their experiences of that world in its idiom' (Richard Wyn Jones et al. 2002: 15).

A report on HE Welsh-medium developments (Williams: 2009) supported, with ministerial approval, the setting up of what was called a Federal College. The tight timetable, with the college (subsequently termed the Coleg Cymraeg Cenedlaethol) to be fully operational by September 2011, was a further indication of Welsh Government's commitment to the development of Welsh-medium education at all levels. According to the Centre for Welsh-medium Higher Education (2010):

> The mission of the Coleg is to maintain, develop and oversee Welsh medium provision in higher education in Wales. It will not have a single geographical entity nor be a degree awarding body in its own right, but would work in partnership with and through the existing higher education (HE) institutions in Wales.

The planning of academic research to inform pedagogy within the Ysgolion Cymraeg needs to be implemented as a priority within the national Welsh-medium Education Strategy, and to complement Bangor University's

Bilingual Project and the research conducted by the Language, Policy and Planning Research Unit at Cardiff University. The lacuna within research into pedagogy, particularly research based on classroom activities, is even more glaring when one considers the outstanding contribution of the Ysgolion Cymraeg to the reversal of the language shift. Planning and implementing research is essential in developing a critical and holistic understanding of the pluralistic influences not only on the Welsh language but on RLS on a global level, particularly within the ever-shifting linguistic scene in Europe.

Finally, all planning needs to be seen as an essential aspect of a holistic grand plan, with an understanding by all actors of the complex ramifications of reversing language shift. Actors need to be representative of a good cross-section of interested parties, so that planners and practitioners work in tandem. Fishman, for example (2000: 130) wrote that '[L]anguage planning is conducted by elites that are governed by their own self-interest'. He spoke these words in a conference in Cardiff on reversing language shift where representation was as follows: Higher Education Wales 32; Welsh institutions 24; other individuals 9; rest of the world 7 (Thomas and Mathias, 2000: 759–63). Not one of the listed conference members was from the numerous Welsh-medium schools in the area. Ironically, Sir Wyn Roberts, minister of state at the Welsh Office stated in his keynote speech, 'The mainstay of the Government's Welsh-language policy has . . . been driven by education' (Thomas and Mathias 2000: 2).

THE MESO/MACRO LEVEL

As is apparent from the evidence of preceding chapters, the micro, meso and macro levels, with their variable definitions, have an effect on one another and are often interchangeable. One could, for example, consider the European Union as a macro power, but the political power of the European meso should not be underestimated. Sharpe (Keating et al. 2004: 529) considers that developing the meso is one of the most important institutional changes seen in the modern state in twenty years, while Mény (1986: 1) argues that it is one of the most radical ever. An emerging challenge on the European meso level is the perceived hegemony of 'largely governmental' organisations such as NPLD (NPLD: 2011), or FUEN ('the largest umbrella organisation of the autochthonous, national minorities in Europe, with 86 member organisations in 32 European countries' (FUEN 2011). Following the demise of the European-funded EBLUL, there is a danger that the role of NGOs representative of bottom-up movements could be weakened by more top-down bodies, and that consequently their very genuine and informed opinions and demands are not voiced at EU levels. France, for example, has not ratified the Charter for Regional or Minority Languages, thereby making it politically challenging for 'largely governmental' organisations to argue the case of, for example, Breton or Occitan against their own state and constitution. My own argument is that both strata are needed, with productive interaction between them as they strive for the same goals. In other words, filling a perceived European lacuna with a body such as ELEN (established in 2011) is consistent with my views on greater cooperation at the Welsh level. Numerous language NGOs do exist at a pan-European level, but they do not network success-fully, as the following quotation shows (CSPM 2011 27):

> The Platform [a body set up by the European Commission in October 2009 to promote multilingualism in Europe in the areas of culture, media and non-formal education] is of the opinion that a simple network is not adequate, but that it would be beneficial to create a permanent platform of network organisations (network of networks) as an instrument of dialogue between the European policy level and the local, regional and national language policy level and social reality. In the current economic and political climate, this appears to be a more feasible solution than the creation of a European Agency.

Globalisation, Europe and the English Language

The political, economic and cultural implications of globalisation and the expansion and integration of the European Union will become more pronounced in future as language policies are developed in its countries or regions. One of the fundamental aspects of the linguistic cauldron will be the formulation (or not) of language policies aimed at protecting minority languages and language rights. Crystal is one commentator who argues (1997: 21) that lesser-used languages will flourish or die according to political history (Galician in Spain, for example). His view of the future of lesser-used languages is, on the whole, optimistic, arguing that since the middle of the last century identity, nationhood and campaigning have all strengthened their status and future well-being:

> [T]he typical scenario is one where a language has come to be threatened by the emergence of a more dominant language. It may take a long time for people who speak the threatened language to respond: in the case of Welsh, the reversal of several hundred years of English domination has begun to show real results only recently, starting with the Welsh Language Act of 1967. Similar movements can be seen in Ireland, Hawaii, New Zealand and Quebec. Inevitably, in such cases, there is a secondary reaction, with English-users finding themselves – often for the first time – on the defensive.

Phillipson is an author who discusses the implications of European multi-lingualism and the possibility that English could develop as the dominant continental language. His critique of the ideological and structural factors that contribute to the more comprehensive use of English in Europe (2003: 64–7) provides an important initial focus for studying the possible effects on attitudes towards the language in a bilingual Wales. One should not be overly optimistic or pessimistic as one recalls two factors: the varying rise and fall in the fortunes of languages across the centuries and the supremacy of linguistic hegemonies. One is reminded of Voltaire's letter to Catherine the Great, 26 May 1767: 'Je ne suis pas comme une dame de la cour de Versailles, qui disait: c'est bien dommage que l'aventure de la tour de Babel ait produit la confusion des langues; sans cela tout le monde aurait toujours parlé français' ['I am not like a lady of the court of Versailles who used to say "it's a frightful pity that the trouble at the Tower of Babel produced such a confusion of languages; but for that everyone would always have spoken French"'].

The growth of the Ysgolion Cymraeg has been pivotal in increasing the number of fluent Welsh speakers and has thereby stimulated the processes, planning and policies of RLS in Wales. In future, in planning for a multilingual Wales as part of Europe, it will be necessary to be sensitive to the increasing domination of English in foreign countries. While continental Europe adds English to its linguistic portfolio there is a danger that it could intensify that hoary argument that Welsh is unnecessary since 'everybody' understands or speaks English. English is incrementally becoming an inseparable ingredient in the globalisation of trade, politics, military matters, science, education and the media (Phillipson, 2003: 64).

The hegemony of English appears, unsurprisingly, in the opening paragraphs of a report on trilingual primary education in Europe (Beetsma 2002: 6):

> Most member states of the European Union are bilingual or multilingual. English is the second language for a large number of Europeans, but there are several regions in the European context where English is the third language. In regions where three languages are spoken in daily life, English is even the fourth language. The people in these regions already speak the national or majority language(s) and the regional or minority language(s).
>
> Now that English has become the most important language for global science and technology and is the number one international means of communication, it is expanding into many countries where it is not spoken traditionally (Cenoz and Jessner 2000). It can therefore be considered important to teach English in primary education in the European member states. However, English is not the only language important in education.

A close analysis of this report shows that in the sample of 202,053 pupils (from twelve regions or countries), English was the third medium of study in seven areas, accounting for over 80 per cent of all learners, while French accounted for over 15 per cent (mainly in Luxembourg, for which compare Colin Baker's comments in his foreword to this volume), and Francoprovençal, German, Italian and Frisian for 1.3 per cent. Pupils from the Basque Country with English as their third medium accounted for 77.6 per cent of all learners in the sample.

According to Mackey (2003: 78), most models of language planning do not, on the whole, represent the multidimensional nature and the multi-functional dynamics of language. Historically, according to Tonkin (2003: 324), the rise and fall of languages and their interrelationship with economic, political and military matters were considered as local and regional phenomena. There has been a shift to a more world-wide context. It is generally acknowledged that cultural diversity is desirable and that a pan-global language is developing, with English at the forefront for the present. Planning, says Tonkin (ibid., 326) is needed for linguistic diversity. The planning for such diversity will need to be holistic and coordinated, and to take into account the possible effects of individual policies (health, private services, education and the emphasis placed on learning foreign languages) on the basic, holistic policy. In Wales, which has tended to follow the British tradition of incremental growth, considerable wisdom will be needed in order to maintain equilibrium between interested sectors.[2] Understanding the difference between planning for a bilingual Wales and a Wales with linguistic diversity will be crucial.

The argument made is not against the teaching of foreign languages in primary and secondary schools. The argument is that one has to be aware of the vagaries of public policies and of superficial attitudes, particularly amongst those who have little understanding of or sympathy with the Welsh language. Saving a language is a long and difficult process, calling for patience and clear milestones, some to be reached fairly quickly, some over considerable time and the remainder in the unforeseeable future. Wales will need to be prepared to avoid polarised arguments based on a superficial assumption that developing multilingualism is liberal-minded whilst developing Welsh is narrow-minded. The current bilingual mantra (Welsh and English) could easily become a different mantra (modern foreign language and English). Continental European countries have invested heavily in teaching English in their educational institutions, and the trend is growing. Wales will need to understand to a greater depth and with more intellectual maturity how the patterns of speaking a variety of languages are changing in Europe and across the world. It is never too early to shape sound arguments.

One way of developing a national critique of the role of English in Wales would be to debate a number of ideological reasons for the growing hegemony of English. Phillipson, for example, notes four main reasons (2003: 65). Firstly, a pan-European pattern is emerging of a shift towards dominant languages, especially English. Secondly, there are substantial ideological differences between the EU countries with regard to their awareness and understanding of language policies and language matters, as well as of their motivation to learn additional languages. Thirdly, English is becoming increasingly more attractive as a language of communication, 'connoting success, influence, consumerism, and hedonism.' Fourthly, 'Ranking languages for their purported qualities or limitations, through processes of glorification and stigmatization, correlates with hierarchies and their hegemonic rationalization.'

Another challenge will be to avoid confusing liberal modernism with reality, since there is in fact 'a pecking order of languages' in the European Commission, the Council of Ministers and the Senate, 'with English at the top and French near the top' (Phillipson 2000: 270). This has happened in spite of the agreement that every 'official' language has equal status. ('Official languages' and 'every-day working languages' do not mean the same thing within these institutions.) It is also significant that in the Council of Europe Steering Committee for Human Rights (CE 2005b: par.13) Philip Blair underlined the lack of awareness of minority and regional languages and the low incidence of teaching them. The EU Civil Society Platform on Multilingualism (CSPM) published its policy recommendations in June 2011 and underlined the lack of equality between languages within the EU (CSPM 2001, 26):

> The EU has evolved an *ad-hoc* language policy based on the official status of Member State languages. It is time to consider an EU language plan and policy. The plan should set targets and timelines and would act to implement the rights and obligations set out in the CFR, and together work towards making a reality of the statement that 'all European languages are equal'.

Finally, European cooperation and cross-fertilisation need to be developed in many areas dealing with lesser-used languages, as pointed out by Colin Williams (2000a: 353–4). The WLB and CAER have shown considerable initiative in this field, and now need to influence European partners of the more frequently used languages. In Wales, as in any country, one has to be careful before grafting ideas from foreign countries on to the educational system. This caveat is developed in the next section with specific reference to two European case studies.

Cymru (Wales), Latvia and Euskadi (the Basque Country)
Ideally one would compare the political, economic and historical contexts of the three countries, but space is limited. Nevertheless, the general principle stands that it is unsound to select facets from foreign contexts that suit one's own agenda and disregard the holistic home context. Apposite adaptation of ideas and policies according to the special needs of one's own country has to be a more balanced way forward.

A salient difference at the macro level is the way that governments use their power in implementing language policies through the education system. Latvia, for example, decreed that, from September 2004, all schools had to teach a minimum of 60 per cent of the curriculum through the medium of Latvian. Initially, some readers may find it easy to empathise with such a policy in a country which has only one official language, Latvian. However, Russian is the mother tongue of half of the citizens of the capital city, Riga; it is also the mother tongue of over 80 per cent of communities bordering with Russia, and here there is considerable opposition to central government's policy. According to Gabrielle Hogan-Brun (2004):

> [T]he process of the implementation of the . . . educational reform is framed in different ways by the (Latvian and Russian) press at macro level . . . The transmission of their values impacts on the polarized social groups (the Latvians and Russians), who are framed in the background . . . The picture that emerges highlights the discrepancy in present-day Latvia between language policy (as laid down by law) and actual beliefs, needs and practices.

Learning foreign languages, particularly English, is popular in Latvia: English is needed to 'get on in the world', which echoes popular sentiments in Welsh-speaking Wales half a century ago (not that it does not hold true today, particularly in west Wales). Fewer families bring up their children to speak Russian, though the argument that Russian is needed for middle-management posts is often heard. One could interpret such an argument as an example of the power of a country and of a dominant language persisting long after the fall of the Berlin Wall. If one were to advocate adopting Latvia's positive stance on learning foreign languages within Wales's education system, rather than adapting it, one would have to bear in mind that Latvia is slowly changing its definition of bilingualism from Latvian and Russian to Latvian and English (in the main). One has to develop both Welsh and English within Wales, and establish them on a firm footing. Only then can Wales afford to turn to multilingualism.

The revival of the Basque language (Euskara) is often quoted as good practice in reversing language shift, and the country's success is a source of inspiration for others who have a similar vision. Significant variations between different parts of the country are features of the linguistic map of Euskal Herria: Euskadi, or Comunidad Autónoma Vasca (CAV) (the Basque Autonomous Community); Iparralde, the area to the north of the border between Spain and France (Northern Basque Country); and Nafarroako Foru Komunitatea (Navarre). Since 84 per cent of Euskara speakers live in the CAV, the discussion will focus on policies in that part of the Basque Country.

Euskadi's linguistic profile is that approximately a quarter of the population is actively bilingual (speaking Euskara well or rather well). An additional 11 per cent is passively bilingual (speaking Euskara with difficulty or not at all, though with a good understanding of it or the ability to read it fluently). Details are given in Table 6.4.

TABLE 6.4
Linguistic profile of the Basque Country

Description	Numbers	Percentage
Population	2,496,836	–
True bilingual speakers with predominance in Basque	177,790	7%
True bilingual speakers	177,009	7%
Bilingual speakers with predominance in Spanish or French	278,955	11%
Passive bilingual speakers	263,498	11%
Monoglot Spanish or French speakers	1,599,584	64%

Source: *lll Carte Sociolinguistique 2001*, Eusko Jaurlaritzaren Argitalpen Zerbitsu Nagusia (2005), *passim*.

At the beginning of every calendar year families with children who are two years of age receive a letter from the government of the CAV reminding them that they need to register their children in a nursery school, ready for admission the following September. The government advocates applying for the Basque-medium school (D model). This is the model that has been most popular and shown the most consistent growth, while the Spanish-medium model (A model) has been diminishing in popularity. There has been a substantial drop in population for a number of years, leading to the closure of A-model schools, with pupils having to attend an alternative school, either bilingual (B model) or the Basque-medium school. Parents have rejected the bilingual model and adopted the Basque-medium schools to a significant degree. In Wales, when the various models of schools in the Basque Country are discussed, parental wishes and government persuasion are two vital themes often missing from the argument. Wales does not have a tradition of being proactive nor of central government advocating the Ysgolion Cymraeg (corresponding to the D model). In fact, even 'Iaith Pawb' (2003) was loath to refer to them; instead it praised the contribution of Welsh-medium education in reversing

193

the language shift. The onus has been on the meso level of government (local government), rather than on the macro (central). Historically, therefore, macro power has had little influence on the growth of the Ysgolion Cymraeg. In future, macro government needs to consider linguistic development in a holistic way, rather than being selective in its adoption of ideas from overseas.

On a global level, transnational frameworks are being developed by people such as Risager (2007), in order to develop a pedagogy for language and culture which will be suitable for world citizens. This will be another challenge for Wales as academics and advisers offer their ideas for yet another change of policies. Wales's biggest challenge will be to maintain a firm grip on its vision of a bilingual Wales, with all citizens able to speak Welsh, and adapt according to the specific needs of that vision.[3]

Linguistic and Educational Rights
Wales does not have a tradition of using human rights legislation in its campaigning for Welsh-medium education, though *battle* is a popular word in discussions about the history of the 'movement'. For example, the word *right* is used once in the draft strategy for Welsh-medium education (2009a: 26): 'The 1944 Education Act first gave pupils the right to be educated in accordance with the wishes of their parents.' The word *rights* appears three times.[4]

It is worth noting the difference between the pragmatism and slow but steady evolution of statute and policy in Wales (but not in the field of rights) and the substantial theorising by numerous thinkers across the world in the field of minority rights. According to Skutnabb-Kangas (1999: 58): 'Linguistic human rights in education are a prerequisite for the maintenance of the diversity in the world that we are all responsible for.' Having said that, there is a danger that overdependence on rights embodied in statute could lead to a preponderance of lawsuits; however, the converse danger of not having rights embodied in law is that there could be an increase in campaigning leading to the exhaustion, physical and intellectual, of the campaigners. When all other arguments and strategies for justice have failed, knowing that one may argue on the grounds of legal rights is positive support for campaigners.

It is to be hoped that individuals, groups and countries all learn from each other's efforts to protect minority languages and cultures, though different people will place different emphases on different aspects. Success in these activities will safeguard the differences between the varying identities of countries and nations across the world. That variety is the essence of the richness of civilisation. With the proliferation of pan-European policies there is a cogent argument that a more incisive national understanding of linguistic rights could facilitate the growth of the Ysgolion Cymraeg.

Some critics might argue that the devolution of power from Westminster to Cardiff is enough to promote further growth in the number of speakers of Welsh and in the availability of Welsh-medium schools, notwithstanding a strong degree of convergence in the British political agenda. However, while one cannot depend solely on international agreements in order to support minorities, nevertheless it is necessary to institutionalise and legitimise language as part of the process of normalising language and identity within Wales, as in any other country. A basic weakness in the Welsh Language Act (1993) was that it did not acknowledge the rights of the individual, a weakness that convinced many of the need for a new Language Act, incorporating those rights. In spite of considerable lobbying, individual rights were missing from the Welsh Language (Wales) Measure (2011) (WG 2011c). It appears that Wales has moved from a tolerance-oriented stance towards the language and evolved a more promotion-oriented stance (Thomas 2007: 139–41).[5] Historically, the critical contribution of Welsh-medium education in reversing the language shift has been acknowledged by central government, both pre- and post-devolution, but central government has been comparatively neutral in its own efforts to promote Welsh-medium education (compared, say, with Catalonia's dynamism in driving forward the normalisation of Catalan). Wales has been reactive to parental wishes and to local government provision.

However, the Welsh Assembly Government's Welsh-medium Education Strategy (2010a) shows considerable vision on how to make progress, though it is arguable whether it has sufficient legislative powers to accomplish all that it sets out to do. It is an ambitious programme with tight implementation schedules, in spite of criticism that its numerical targets are weak. Wales needs to act concurrently on a number of fronts, building on its traditional pragmatism, to secure a sufficient workforce of civil servants to accomplish the tasks enumerated; ensure sufficient funding to support progress; train the civil service in the basic and finer aspects of Welsh-medium education; and make sure that it has the necessary legislative powers to allow it to execute the details of the strategy. These are the imminent steps that need to be taken in the fight for linguistic and educational minority rights.[6]

CONCLUSION

'[N]ecessity is supposed to be the mother of invention and we can suppose that over the next decade we shall learn to find breathing space for . . . reflection and proposals. It certainly behoves us to: those who wish for a comfortable modus vivendi (not moriendi) for our weakened little native tongue (as for thousands of others world-wide) have a lot at stake.' These words of Mikel Zalbide (2005: 27) conclude his paper outlining the Basque vision for the future of lesser-used languages. Language planners, campaigners and deliverers in Wales are daily confronted with challenges, directly or indirectly. Schools are challenged by the pressure to raise or maintain standards, adapting to new curricula and skills, developing partnerships, coping with ever-growing demands on the ever-insufficient fiscal pot, nurturing the use of Welsh in social domains, improving buildings, campaigning for additional schools, and so on indefinitely. The greatest challenge for planners, campaigners and deliverers will be to guarantee that they have time to think and develop an ideology that will help promote the Ysgolion Cymraeg.

It appears that Wales has won an important battle, namely that the nation is now on course towards normalisation of the Welsh language. Significantly, support for Welsh appears to go against the trend that Fishman sees (or has seen) across the world (1995: 60): 'It is unfortunately true that very few people (including most of their own speakers) care about the impending demise of small languages.' Fulfilling the vision of a bilingual Wales is still far away, but it is important to use 'Iaith Pawb' and successive versions of it as an intellectual focus point within the wider European and global contexts in order to ensure more genuine rights, embodied in legislation and with strict regulatory powers. But that is not enough. The greatest challenge facing Wales is to strengthen positive attitudes towards Welsh-language education by a three-pronged cohesive development: turning the pragmatic vision in the strategy for Welsh-medium education into reality; ensuring the practical cooperation of politicians, locally, nationally and internationally, whatever their political party; and increasing involvement and enthusiasm amongst parents for Welsh-medium education. That is the process. The first annual report on the Welsh-medium Education Strategy (WG 2011b: 2) was promising and highlighted 'progress in developing a new planning system for statutory education; further developments in the planning of post-16 provision; and a focus on practitioner development to ensure a Welsh-medium workforce with high-quality Welsh-language skills'. The potential outcomes are far more important: fostering generations of Welsh people able to achieve their potential through the medium of Welsh and achieve the highest possible standards. They will use Welsh increasingly in their every day lives, develop into bilingual and multilingual citizens, and enrich the governance of Wales. Wales has firm foundations on which to develop as it journeys towards its educational, linguistic and civic dream.

Success calls for balance between actors and structures, for a spiritual optimism of the will and an incisive intellectual pessimism. Gramsci's well-known quotation serves us well as thinkers at all levels develop our philosophical, ideological and practical ideas. The preceding chapters aimed at analysing the variety of complex reasons for the success of the Ysgolion Cymraeg, and at unravelling a range of interrelationships at micro, meso and macro levels. The conclusion was that people have been more responsible than ideology for Wales's flourishing development, as teachers and parents, supported by advisers, inspectors, officers, civil servants and politicians, have all used their power to stimulate the evolution. But where would Welsh-language education be without parental leaps of faith? The parents are the main dynamic influence on the road to the normalisation of the Welsh language, primarily through the education system, particularly the Ysgolion Cymraeg.

Notes

1 For further reading, refer to Thomas (2008: 53–61).
2 Cf. Phillipson (2003: 65):

> Responsibility for language policy in each country tends to be shared between ministries of foreign affairs, education, culture, research, and commerce. They each tend to have a little experience in language policy, and between them there is inadequate coordination, if any. In countries with a federal structure, responsibility is even more diffuse.

3 Gardner (2008: 50) makes a similar point. It is always dangerous to transplant the solutions found in one context into another without first making a measured assessment of the exact conditions under consideration.
4 There are two references to the United Nations Convention on the Rights of the Child and one to 'Children and Young People: Rights to Action – Stronger Partnerships for Better Outcomes' (Welsh Assembly Government 2006).
5 Tolerance-oriented and promotion-oriented language and education rights and international law are critiqued by May (2001: 184–93), who acknowledges Kloss's seminal works (1971; 1977). Tolerance-oriented rights include allowing individuals to speak their first language in private and public (nongovernmental) domains, to assemble, to organise meetings, 'to establish private cultural, economic and social institutions wherein the first language may be used, and the right to foster one's first language in private schools. The key principle of such rights is that the state does 'not interfere with efforts on the part of the minority to make use of [their language] in the private domain' (Kloss: 1977: 2).' (May 2001: 185).

Promotion-oriented rights cover a wide spectrum of promotion in the legislative, administrative, and educational domains, from 'the publishing of public documents in minority languages' to the 'recognition of minority languages in all formal domains within the nation-state' including 'the provision of state-funded minority-language education *as of right*.'

In Wales, some observers would maintain that in the past central government has done little more than react to pressure from the minority (for example, on road signs, the Ysgolion Cymraeg, official forms and establishing S4C, the Welsh-language television channel). These are a few examples of language campaigning during the second half of the twentieth century. Other observers would see progress as tolerance-oriented attitudes and/or rights under the guise of promotion.
6 For further reading, see Skutnabb-Kangas (2000); Lewis (2008); Thomas (2010b).

Chapter 7

Future Prospects for Welsh-medium Education: Reflections from a Recent Migrant

David Hawker

One of the things which I found rather inexplicable when I was approached to apply for the post of director general in the Welsh Assembly Government was that the ability to speak Welsh, or a willingness to learn it, was not included in the job description. Apparently, civil service rules meant that, in order to attract a high-quality field, Welsh could be at best an optional extra – nice to have, but certainly not needed. As someone applying for the key post responsible for leading the Welsh education system, this struck me as extremely odd, as it did almost all my friends and colleagues in England. Suffice to say that, as someone who enjoys a challenge, I decided to learn the language anyway. Looking back over my two years in Wales, I am glad I made the effort. It has been an immensely enriching experience, both professionally and personally.

For me, the failure to mention Welsh in the job description came to symbolise the deeply ambiguous attitude which most Welsh people adopt towards their own language. Indeed, when I joined the staff of WAG, I found that, far from being prized as the country's most precious asset, the language was viewed as 'difficult' and something of a millstone, because of the need to produce all documents bilingually and pay for interpreting services at large meetings and conferences. I was told that maintaining a bilingual education system inevitably means inefficient use of funding, leading to poorer quality provision, lower standards and a generally third-rate educational experience for children.

Such views are not new; they were famously promulgated in the late nineteenth century by the chief schools inspector, Matthew Arnold, who appeared to believe that the very existence of the language was responsible for educational underachievement in Wales and needed therefore to be stamped out.

Continuing in the anecdotal vein for the moment, after I had accepted the job and knew I was going to work for WAG, I asked a business friend who owns a couple of tourist shops in Barmouth what he thought the government should do to improve things in Wales. He immediately said 'get rid of the Welsh language from signs and documents – it's a waste of money'. I suspect he is not alone in having such views.

So while there is this mixture of apathy and incomprehension in (some) official circles, and downright opposition from a range of people through from academics to businessmen, the Welsh language will continue to need determined, intelligent individuals with fire in their belly to advocate and fight for it. The educational field is one where many of the key battles have been fought and won over the past fifty years, and there is no more doughty a fighter than Huw Thomas. It was with great pleasure, therefore, that I accepted the invitation, after I had left WAG to go on loan to the Department of Education in London, to contribute my own reflections on the development and future prospects of Welsh-medium education, drawing partly on his excellent analysis of its growth in south-east Wales over the past two generations (Thomas: 2010).

HOW DOES THE FUTURE CONNECT WITH THE PAST?

Welsh education is more deeply rooted in the centuries-long struggle for the language than almost any other modern education system. As a language, Welsh has been under threat ever since the Act of Union of 1536 banned its use for legal and governmental purposes. The first Welsh translation of the Bible not many years afterwards guaranteed its preservation, indeed development, as a living literary and cultural language. The curious juxtaposition of English officialdom and Welsh religion and culture meant that the soul of the nation was represented not by the nobility but by the *gwerin*, the ordinary people. From the sixteenth century on, education, religion and culture in Wales were an essentially grassroots endeavour. It is no accident that the last line of the national anthem refers specifically to the *hen iaith* – there are few places where defence of the national identity has historically, and for so many centuries, been bound up with defence of the language.

One of the proudest moments in history, in terms of Welsh-medium education, came in the eighteenth century, with the circulating schools of Griffith Jones, a nonconformist preacher. In a remarkable thirty year period, Jones established 3,495 schools and saw almost half the population of the country – some 158,000 people – through their doors, in the first truly mass education movement the modern world had seen (Welsh Biography Online). By contrast, in the late nineteenth century the Victorians sought to suppress the language entirely in their new public elementary school system. The very first annual report submitted to the Board of Education by Matthew Arnold in 1852 dealt very precisely with the question of Welsh education. In his view Welsh, while it might be of some 'philological and antiquarian' interest, was no language for the modern world, and should therefore not be used in schools (Marvin 1908: 11). 'It must always be the desire of a government to render its dominions, as far as possible, homogeneous', he wrote. 'Sooner or later the difference of language between Wales and England will probably be effaced . . . an event which is socially and politically desirable.'

The struggle to re-establish Welsh as a language of everyday literacy and learning began in the early years of the twentieth century, led by pioneering figures such as Sir Owen M. Edwards, founder of the *Cymro* newspaper, and the educationalist John Phillips, who established what could be called one of the first Welsh-medium primary schools in Cilfynydd, Pontypridd in the early 1930s (Iolo Wyn Williams 2003: 21). Had it not been for courageous figures such as these, the Welsh language might today have been reduced to little more than a folk curiosity.

The reintroduction since then of Welsh as a medium of instruction, particularly in south-east Wales, through the Ysgolion Cymraeg, has been widely hailed as a success, and so it is. But as the title of Huw Thomas's book implies (*Brwydr i Baradwys?* – 'A Battle towards Paradise?'), it has been a struggle. Moreover, it has depended on the lifetime efforts of a number of key figures, such as my own Welsh teacher John Albert Evans, who, brought up in an exclusively Welsh-speaking village in Cardiganshire in the 1940s, spent most of his career supporting the reintroduction of Welsh in the schools of Mid Glamorgan (Evans: 2010).

So for now, Welsh-medium education is in a better position than it has been since the eighteenth century. But how will it fare in the future? Will the future be the same as the past? Of course not. The world has moved on, and with modern population mobility, it is no longer realistic, even in traditionally Welsh-speaking areas, to expect Welsh to be the sole, or even the dominant language. The present day patriarchs – John Albert, Huw Thomas and their colleagues – know that the way forward is not to try to recreate the comfortable language communities of the past, but to fight for a more fully bilingual future, where Welsh is a language of everyday communication alongside English, not just in its traditional heartlands, but in the 'reclaimed' English-speaking areas.

However, for that to happen, a critical mass must be reached in the education system. In my view, the proportion of children who are educated wholly or mainly in Welsh will need to double, from the current 20 per cent plus, to around 40 per cent, if Welsh is to have a secure future as a genuine *lingua franca*. This is a tall order, and rather beyond the target of 30 per cent set out in the Welsh-medium Education Strategy (Welsh Assembly Government 2010).

What are the drivers which will bring this about?

THE LEVERS OF POWER – PARENTAL DEMAND AND POLITICAL WILL – BUT WILL IT LAST?

Undoubtedly the most powerful lever in the system at the moment is the demand from parents for a Welsh-medium education for their children. Some of this, as we know, is fuelled by middle-class aspirations, and a perception that Welsh-medium schools (alongside church schools) are better disciplined and achieve better results. The fact is that any school which attracts more motivated parents is likely to get better results, pound for pound, from its pupils. However, there is also a deeper motivation driving the demand for Welsh-medium education. It is a pride in the language itself, a sense of patriotism towards the history and culture of Wales, and an awareness that bilingualism is good for the brain.

Sadly, the political vision in some local authorities has not always matched these aspirations, with the result that they tend to lag behind parental demand in creating new Welsh-medium schools and housing them in decent accommodation. If hope deferred makes the heart sick, there is a danger of some communities losing their enthusiasm for Welsh-medium education simply because of the barriers in the way to achieving it. This is why one of the key planks of the government's Welsh-medium education strategy is a challenge to local authorities to become more ambitious in planning their Welsh-medium provision, on the basis that when the provision appears, the demand often increases as a result. By the same token, if there is a lack of such planning (perhaps due to lack of resources for building or converting schools), there is a danger that the impressive growth in provision which we have seen over the past fifteen to twenty years will slow to a standstill.

THE SOUL OF THE NATION – IS IT SECURE?

That is one of the reasons why the future is far from secure. Another reason is that there is still little real understanding among senior main-stream educationalists about why the language is so important. Those who advocate the language generally do so from the position of an interest or lobby group, and the temptation for policy makers has been to listen politely, but then put it in the 'difficult' box. When I became head of DCELLS in 2008 it was clear to me that there was little trust between my department and the leaders of the Welsh-medium educational community, who had come to the conclusion (probably rightly) that we didn't under-stand their concerns, and that we tended to regard them, quite frankly, as a bit of a nuisance. The Welsh Language Board was reluctant to consider handing over its education responsibilities to DCELLS because of this perception. The in-house Welsh Language Development Unit was seen as rather marginal to the main work of the department, and leading organisations such as CYDAG and UCAC felt frustrated at our apparent suspicion towards them.

To me, this only illustrated the distance we needed to travel as a department, and possibly the wider system with us, if we were to really get in tune with the aspirations and concerns of the Welsh-medium sector. The fact that our attitudes reflected the general ignorance and apathy in the wider community did not make our position any better. For me, as an outsider, it felt as if we had a double problem. Wales as a whole, for all its patriotism, appeared to have little real awareness of its historical and cultural roots, including the fact that the soul of the nation is indivisible from its language. And the department I had joined did not appear to be showing the leadership needed to make a difference. So I made it a personal objective to show by example how this could change. I took lessons, eventually passing my Intermediate exam, and made a point of communicating as much as I could and as often as I could in Welsh. I tried to dispense with the interpreter when I was in meetings, and even gave a couple of speeches in Welsh. Did this make any difference? I would like to think so. I fear that until a greater proportion of the department are Welsh speakers, it will be difficult to shift the underlying culture.

A trivial incident early on brought the problem home to me. Soon after I took up my post, I joined a very friendly (and partly bilingual) choir which rehearsed every week in Howells School in Cardiff. At one rehearsal I noticed an impressive-looking history frieze on the wall of the playground. Good, I thought, the pupils are learning history while they play. But when I looked more closely, I saw that the frieze started with Alfred the Great, featured William the Conqueror, Henry VIII and all the great figures of English history. No mention at all of the very different history of Wales. Of course, I immediately went back to my department and asked why a school in Wales (albeit an independent school) should be teaching English history, and whether we didn't have a Welsh frieze for them to use instead. Sadly, it appeared that we didn't.

There is, and always has been, a battle for the soul of the nation, and the battle is won or lost in the schools. The school curriculum is not just about reading, writing and arithmetic. It is also, crucially, about handing on the values, stories and culture of a proud people and their language.

A DISTINCTIVELY DIFFERENT SYSTEM – DOES WALES HAVE THE CONFIDENCE TO STAND ON ITS OWN TWO FEET?

Wales made a good start to its devolved responsibilities, with the abolition of national school tests and league tables, and the determination to uphold the values of collaboration and quality education for all, rather than engage with the increasingly competitive atmosphere which developed in England. In this respect Wales was behaving true to its roots as an egalitarian, even communitarian society, which valued learning for its own sake and shunned elitism. The belief was that this would lead to better results and greater well-being for both individuals and communities.

It has not completely turned out like that, however, and in recent years Wales has suffered from a crisis of confidence, as results at GCSE and A Level have fallen behind England, and the country has slipped further down the economic league table. The suggestion that Wales should lower its ambition and become 'happy but poor' does not cut much ice (nor should it) in a competitive world where parents aspire to the best for their children.

The temptation would be to emulate the approach taken by England a decade or so ago, and focus exclusively on literacy and numeracy, with schemes dictated by the government, and schools being held to account for the improvement gained by their pupils on these rather narrow measures. England's experience shows that this approach works. But equally, it can miss out large chunks of important educational experience which are vital to young people gaining a deep understanding of their country, culture and language, and the self-confidence to succeed in a complex and confusing world. Wales needs to endow her children with this self-confidence, but it can do so only if it has that confidence itself. Rather than trying to copy others, it needs to recognise the unique value of its own inheritance, and use its own resourcefulness to build on it. For example, the new frameworks for inspection and school effectiveness place the emphasis on schools developing professional learning networks – a deliberately collaborative approach to improvement. Longer term, this approach is likely to produce more motivated, skilled teachers, and therefore better all round results for the students, than one which relies on heavy systems of accountability. It is an approach rooted in the democratic instincts of the nation which reach back over the centuries.

BRIDGING THE GAP – WHAT IS THE ROLE OF THE YSGOLION CYMRAEG IN THE WIDER SYSTEM?

So where do the Ysgolion Cymraeg fit in?

I believe they have a vital role to play in addressing two key challenges facing the system as a whole. The first is how to preserve the distinctiveness of Welsh education while raising standards, and the second is how to improve and extend the population's regard for, and competence in, the Welsh language as a secure foundation for a bilingual society.

The advantage of Welsh-medium schools is that they cannot help being totally distinctive from all other schools in the UK, and indeed the world. (The Foreword, however, draws the reader's attention to parallel provision across the world.) And while they are consistently achieving better results as a sector than English-medium schools, their success will continue to provide a good basis for building a distinctively Welsh educational offer. However, for that to happen, they need to be confident in their ability to continue to develop the Cwricwlwm Cymreig and to engage in debate about it with their English-medium counterparts. It should never be a question of first developing a curriculum in English and then translating it, as if into a foreign language. The curriculum needs to be developed primarily in Welsh, by Welsh teachers working in Welsh schools, imbued with the spirit of Welshness, and then taken out and applied in the English-speaking context. Of course, this is not to belittle the many thousands of excellent English-speaking teachers who are just as Welsh as the Welsh speakers – I would never for a moment suggest that they have less of a stake in developing a distinctively Welsh curriculum. But I do believe the centre of gravity, in terms of the overall design and content of the curriculum, should lie closer to the Ysgolion Cymraeg than it currently does.

The second way in which the Ysgolion Cymraeg need to play a more active leadership role in the wider system is in helping to improve the quality of Welsh teaching in the English-medium schools, which is consistently criticised by Estyn as the weakest part of the school curriculum. We currently have the ludicrous situation where it is possible to have, in one town, a Welsh-medium school where every pupil is fluent in Welsh (many from English-speaking homes), while in another part of the town an English-medium school can barely muster a handful of rather poor GCSEs in Welsh as a second language. Why can't the two schools work together to improve the Welsh second-language provision, by giving the pupils in the English-medium school intensive immersion experiences, and by working with the teachers to build up their fluency and language-teaching techniques? It is a big challenge, but unless the sector as a whole is willing to grasp it, there will be little or no improvement in the quality of Welsh taught in the English-medium system, and the ultimate goal of a bilingual nation will remain as far off as it is today.

THE CHALLENGE OF SUSTAINABILITY – WHAT STRUGGLES LIE AHEAD FOR WELSH-MEDIUM EDUCATION?

These are hard messages for the sector, and I am conscious that there will be many who disagree with me, saying that it is not yet strong enough to take on such a challenge. I would respond by saying that it certainly needs courage, but I believe that rising to the challenge will actually make the sector stronger and more successful in the long term. There are already encouraging signs of a readiness within the system for this to happen. In the new Foundation Phase there is a growing emphasis on bilingualism, with many lessons being taught in Welsh even in English-medium schools, and this trend is moving upwards through the primary sector. The challenge is to build on this trend by deepening the experience both for learners and for teachers, and to move it up the age range into the secondary sector. In both of these respects, I believe the Welsh-medium sector has a key role to play.

As things stand at present, the future of Welsh-medium education is uncertain, and there is a very long way to go before the tipping point of 40 per cent penetration is reached. Until then, the position will remain fragile. But, on the basis that the best form of defence is attack, my recommendation is for the sector to take the initiative and develop a plan to build stronger links with the English-medium sector as part of the School Effectiveness Framework, targeting curriculum development and improvements in the teaching of Welsh as priorities, and accepting its leadership role in the system as a whole.

There are many struggles ahead, and I have touched on many of them already. Resources will become scarce and parental interest may start to tail off. The Ysgolion Cymraeg must rise to the challenge of the new collaborative 14–19 arrangements without diluting their own offer. In parts of the country where a bilingual policy is being introduced, the challenge is to ensure that the culture and ethos in those schools are strongly Welsh, with the language nurtured and used in every context. There will continue to be challenges in recruiting and training high calibre Welsh-speaking teachers at all levels. The pipeline to Welsh-medium further and higher education needs to be opened up further. The leadership of some local authorities, and of the Welsh Government itself, needs to be supported and challenged to do better in terms of strengthening Welsh-medium provision. And all this needs to be done alongside strengthening the links between the English-medium and Welsh-medium sectors – it is one education system, not two.

There is no doubting the fervour and commitment of the leaders of the Ysgolion Cymraeg to the cause of further Welsh-medium education. Nor indeed is there any doubting their strategic vision for the future. What is needed now is for the bridges to be built more strongly between the sectors, and for the Welsh-medium sector to have greater confidence in itself as an engine of change for the system as a whole.

Chapter 8

Parent Power

Michael L. N. Jones

A consideration of the historical contribution of parents to the development of Welsh-medium education since the 1930s leads a lawyer such as the writer to place the parents into two classes derived from legal philosophy, those whose contribution was a *sine qua non*, an underlying cause of development, an essential circumstance and those whose contribution was a *causa causans*, an exciting cause of development.

1. THE POWER OF PARENTS *SINE QUA NON*

Undoubtedly in quantitative terms, the first class is the more important. By 2013 these are the thousands of parents who, in local authorities throughout south-east and north-east Wales and in Powys and to a lesser extent in the three counties of Dyfed, choose Welsh-medium education for their children, which in most cases is a choice adhered to until school leaving age at 16 or 18. (In Gwynedd and Ynys Môn Welsh-medium primary education is almost universally compulsory; alas in secondary education, allowed a belated choice, pupils mostly elect for English-medium education.) Without these many acts of choice each year their children would be deemed to have taken the default option, namely English-medium education in a community school. Without these thousands of parents Welsh-medium education would not include over 20 per cent of the children of Wales, and continuing growth means that the percentage of children starting Welsh-medium education in September 2010 was substantially greater than the total percentage of children in Welsh-medium education over the whole age range of 4–18.

For example, until 2005 there was one Welsh-medium primary in Newport receiving a one-stream entry. Since then Ysgol Gymraeg Casnewydd has become a two-stream school and a second school, Ifor Hael, was opened with one stream in 2009 but had to be expanded to two streams for September 2010. and a third school (Bro Teyrnon) opened in 2011. Thus Welsh-medium education in Newport is a pyramid with one stream of thirty at the top expanding to a current total of 120 at the foot. Seven schools with a total of eight streams (places for 240 pupils per annum) have opened in Cardiff since 2000 and all but two of the eight streams were fully subscribed by 2010.

If Welsh-medium schools are conveniently available there is a supply of parents, so far not exhausted, willing to make the choice that contributes to the growth of Welsh-medium education and the contribution of these parental choices forms the essential substratum for the continuing growth and development of Welsh-medium education.

However, there are local authorities where the exercise of the parental choice in favour of Welsh-medium education is not a simple matter. Every local authority in Wales has at least one designated Welsh-medium primary school. By no means all have a designated Welsh-medium secondary school but those authorities lacking their own Welsh-medium secondary will more or less willingly arrange for children in their area to receive Welsh-medium secondary education in an adjacent area. Some local authorities do not consider it their duty to ensure that Welsh-medium provision corresponds to Welsh-medium demand. Rhondda Cynon Taf, an authority in an area with an excellent historical record for Welsh-medium provision (when the LEA was Glamorgan County Council, up to 1974 and thereafter until 1996 Mid Glamorgan County Council) and having more designated Welsh-medium secondary schools (four) than any other local authority in Wales, has carried out surveys of demand for Welsh-medium education in two areas, namely the catchment of Ysgol Gymraeg Aberdâr and the catchments of Ysgolion Cynradd Garth Olwg and Castellau. In each case it has established a demand for an extra stream but declines to make provision, pleading recently the difficulty of appointing headteachers in Welsh schools in the Rhondda. Other local authorities with a poor record are Swansea, Neath and Port Talbot, Bridgend, Merthyr Tudful and Blaenau Gwent. In those authorities there undoubtedly reside parents who would choose Welsh-medium education if there was a school within a reasonable distance of home or if such a school had sufficient places available, not the case in Aberdâr, Beddau and the villages adjacent to Ysgol Garth Olwg. In such cases class 1 parents are deprived of a choice.

2. THE PARENTS WHO MAKE THINGS HAPPEN

The expansion of opportunities for parental choice by parents in class 1 has very largely depended on the energy of the far smaller number of parents falling into class 2, those who first secured the agreement of the local authority to open a Welsh-medium school and those who have ensured that local authorities have continued to expand Welsh-medium provision and to do so in a way which experience has shown to be the most effective method of Welsh-medium education. Parents of class 2 have proceeded in many different ways to secure their ends from gentle but persistent pressure at one end of the spectrum to civil disobedience eliciting from local authorities threats of imprisonment and deprivation of parental rights for alleged child neglect at the other. The class 2 parents have therefore had to display far more persistence, resolution, bravery and tactical and strategic ability in the course of long campaigns to secure their aims than is the case in completing a form electing Welsh-medium education that is more or less freely available, all-important though such elections continue to be.

i. *The Parents who Founded the First Primary Schools*
Back in the 1930s there were no Welsh-medium schools in the anglicised areas of south-east and north-east Wales though 'traditionally Welsh schools' existed in Gwynedd, Dyfed, rural Montgomeryshire and the Swansea Valley. Since these 'traditionally Welsh' elementary schools had to prepare their brighter pupils to move to English-medium grammar schools at eleven they clearly were involved to a greater or lesser degree in English-medium instruction also. There were parents in Welsh-speaking families concerned about the anglicisation provided by education in the areas where English was the majority language, and pioneers like Ifan ab Owen Edwards in Aberystwyth and Gwyn Daniel and his friends in Cardiff took the first steps to press for the establishment of Welsh-medium schools, for which no statutory provision existed. Faced with an inflow of evacuees

to Aberystwyth schools, Edwards and his friends set up a full-time fee-paying Welsh-medium school in Aberystwyth, Ysgol Lluest, which continued as a private school from 1940 to 1952 when it was at last taken over by the county council.

Gwyn Daniel's efforts in Cardiff suffered grave interference from the threat of bombing raids on Cardiff, which led to many Welsh-speaking children being sent off to safer addresses in the country. It was 1942 before Ysgol Fore Sadwrn (Saturday morning school) started to give some Welsh instruction to add to the English-medium instruction of the local authority schools. Again this was a voluntary arrangement. Gwyn Daniel had more success in correspondence with the then minister of education, R. A. Butler, one of the surprising heroes of Welsh-medium education who was persuaded to insert into his 1944 Education Act a section – s76 – which provided that children should be educated in accordance with parental wishes. The act did not specify how such wishes were to be ascertained, much less lay down how parents were to secure the compliance of local or other authorities with their wishes however expressed. At best s76 provided a statutory foundation upon which a willing local education authority could erect a Welsh-medium school.

LEAs did not rush to open Welsh-medium primary schools. It took a lot of parental agitation, leadership from local ministers of religion and backing from senior Education Ministry officials to secure in 1947 the opening of the first LEA Welsh-medium school, Dewi Sant in Llanelli. The second school followed two years later in Maesteg, where parental agitation failed to obtain action by the LEA. The parents therefore decided to open a private school in a chapel vestry. This was basically a working-class enterprise, not like Ysgol Lluest, the project of middle-class academics. After several months of private enterprise (heading towards early insolvency) the local authority was shamed into taking the venture over and a county school was opened in September 1949 with five others all over Wales but mostly in Glamorgan.

The common feature of all these early schools was total dependence on parental action 'to prove the need'. Names of prospective pupils had to be collected. Deputations of local worthies in support had to attend on local authority representatives, very often in company with Ifan ab Owen Edwards, who could of course speak as founder of Ysgol Lluest and recount its continuing success to establish that a Welsh-medium school was viable.

Often a preparatory school had to be set up like the Ysgol Fore Sadwrn in Cardiff, both to show local support and to illustrate how a Welsh-medium school could proceed. Sometimes, as in Maesteg, it was actually necessary to open a school privately to convince councillors that real parents would abandon 'their' schools and send their children to be educated in this old-fashioned language incapable of expressing modern ideas.

Without pressure from pioneering parents willing to take a risk on these wholly unproven new schools Welsh-medium education would not have got off the ground, except only in Flintshire, where Welsh-medium schools were opened without parental pressure but rather because the director of education and his deputy thought that Welsh-medium schools were needed in the county, so close to the magnetic anglicising effect of Liverpool.

Between 1947 and 1956 thirty Welsh-medium schools were opened, of which twelve were in the county of Glamorgan. It should be emphasised that these schools were intended for use by the children of Welsh speakers and had a purely preservative function, to assist in the transmission of Welsh from one generation of Welsh speakers to the next, and no missionary function, to enable children of English speakers who might well be grand-children of Welsh speakers to revert to the language of their ancestors. To exclude interlopers many LEAs sent officials soon after pupils started in Welsh-medium schools to check that all children already spoke Welsh.

By 1952 parents of children in Welsh-medium schools decided to found a federation of the parents' societies in each Welsh-medium school under the name Undeb Rhieni Ysgolion Cymraeg – The Welsh-medium Schools Parents' Union with the objects of:

1. backing efforts to found more Welsh-medium schools
2. expressing parental views on pertinent subjects for submission to the Ministry of Education, the WJEC, Welsh LEAs and professional bodies
3. proposing the foundation of Welsh-medium schools and nursery schools and to support existing establishments.

Through the union parents were able to exchange experiences and copy successful efforts to obtain the opening of schools. Importantly, the union led the way in establishing nursery schools for would-be pupils in Welsh-medium schools. In such schools children from non-Welsh-speaking homes where the parents were enthusiastic for their children to have Welsh-medium education could be taught enough Welsh to pass muster as

Welsh-speaking children when the LEA officials visited their Welsh-medium school to ensure that only Welsh-speaking children were being taught. Thus did those parents who favoured missionary efforts to extend the reach of the language get round the rule that all children had to be able to speak Welsh before starting to receive Welsh-medium education. Eventually the efforts of the union in connection with nursery schools passed to a separate organisation founded in 1971, Mudiad Ysgolion Meithrin. Now very many nursery schools are in fact provided by the LEAs and it is wholly accepted that Welsh-medium education is on offer to every parent, Welsh-speaking or not, and the vast majority of Welsh-medium pupils come from non-Welsh-speaking homes. In 1981, at a national level, the name of Undeb yr Ysgolion Cymraeg was changed to Rhieni dros Addysg Gymraeg (RhAG) – Parents for Welsh-medium Education.

ii. The Founding Parents Move on to Secondary Schools

All the early Welsh-medium schools were primary schools and for some time numbers were so small that it was clear that sufficient numbers did not exist to support a viable Welsh-medium secondary. Yet again the education officers of Flintshire led the way by opening a Welsh-medium secondary in Rhyl, Ysgol Glan Clwyd, just in time to receive the first children to have received Welsh-medium primary education in the area (that is in 1956), seven years after the first primary was opened. Glan Clwyd subsequently moved to St Asaph and was joined by Maes Garmon in Mold in 1961.

Meanwhile in south-east Wales children were moving from Welsh-medium primaries to English-medium secondary schools, but not without opposition from the parents of the Welsh Schools Union under the leadership of Gwyn Daniel, fighting what was to prove his last campaign, the success of which he did not live to see. The committee of parents to campaign for a Welsh-medium secondary school was founded in June 1959 by representatives of parents' societies from eight Welsh-medium primaries in east Glamorgan and Monmouthshire. The usual pattern followed – deputations to see the director of education of Glamorgan (Dr Emlyn Stephens, distantly related to Gwyn Daniel and also Welsh-speaking), to persuade Cardiff Education Committee to send on their Welsh-medium primary children to a Glamorgan secondary, the collection of names of prospective pupils, and efforts to set up more feeder primaries. Much of the work had been completed by the time Gwyn Daniel died in October 1960 but the efforts continued after his death to reach a successful conclusion in March 1962, when Glamorgan announced their intention of opening a secondary school at Rhydyfelin, Pontypridd, in September 1962.

Ysgol Glan Clwyd, owing its foundation to the far-sightedness of two education officers, has one school as its offspring. Rhydfelen's original catchment area of Pontypridd, stretching from the Neath Valley in the west to Monmouthshire in the east, has seen that catchment divided and sub-divided in the ensuing period of nearly fifty years so that it is now (September 2012) served by at least eleven additional secondary schools with another three near to opening (Caerffili's second, Port Talbot, and Newport). All of these have followed from pressure by parents for additional provision with less distance to travel for pupils and in many cases for better buildings to replace the educational slums that disfigured the early days (and years) of Rhydfelen, Cwm Rhymni and Gwynllyw. The parental efforts in this area were less obvious than in relation to primary education because the children that were needed to justify further schools always existed in the primary schools and could not therefore be dismissed as the fantastic ideas of Welsh-language zealots. Also the most important factor was often an ultimatum from local authority A that its school was needed for its children and local authority B had better open its own school. Such an ultimatum from Mid Glamorgan led to the foundation of Glantaf in Cardiff and that from Cardiff led the Vale of Glamorgan to found Ysgol Gyfun Bro Morgannwg.

iii. The Parents who Secured the Second Generation of Schools
Blessed now with a proper succession of educational provision from nursery schools to the sixth form of secondary schools and with evidence that Welsh-medium education produced well-educated children in all subjects, the Welsh-medium system proved increasingly attractive to more and more parents. The primary schools founded in the 1950s and 1960s, or often the Welsh streams in English-medium schools, became increasingly overcrowded. What were nominally Welsh streams in an English school became so large that the building or buildings housed a Welsh school with a small number of English classes but local authorities declined formally to close the English 'school' to make more room for Welsh-medium pupils and equally declined to consider further Welsh-medium provision.

There ensued a struggle which led to the foundation of the second generation of Welsh-medium primaries in the areas of the three education authorities which covered south-east Wales from 1974 onwards, when Glamorgan County, Merthyr Tudful County Borough, Cardiff City, Monmouthshire County and Newport County Borough were succeeded by Mid Glamorgan, South Glamorgan and Gwent, where the battles between parents and councillors took different forms in each authority.

(a) Open War in Mid Glamorgan, with Strategic Planning to Follow
In Mid Glamorgan the professional officers, under the leadership of John Brace, the director, were broadly favourable to Welsh-medium education but the Labour majority of councillors could not see why the existing network of schools and streams needed further expansion. Some professional staff in the county favoured extension of Welsh-medium provision by opening new streams, while parents on the whole favoured free-standing Welsh schools where numbers could not be limited to protect the English side. From the foundation of Mid Glamorgan there was some growth in response to parental pressure with units (Welsh streams) being opened in Penderyn (formerly in Breconshire), Creigiau, Rhyd y Grug (Quakers' Yard) and Llanbradach (infants only) and schools at Bodringallt (Ystrad Rhondda) and Llantrisant.

However, the parents were not satisfied with this limited growth and in May 1980 they responded to the problems which had arisen in particular in relation to Pont Siôn Norton School, Pontypridd, by holding a meeting of representatives of all the parents' societies of the Welsh-medium schools of Mid Glamorgan; a working party was set up, initially to give support to the Pont Siôn Norton parents and subsequently to carry out research into Welsh-medium provision in the six divisional executive areas of Mid Glamorgan. The Chairman of this committee was Revd Eric Jones and its secretary was a local solicitor, Wyn Rees (now His Honour Judge Wyn Rees). Other leading members were the lecturer Cennard Davies (subsequently Councillor Davies of RCT), Gareth Miles, secretary of UCAC and a distinguished playwright and novelist, Margaret Francis (Pontypridd), Allan James (Maesteg), Gwyn Griffiths (Caerffili) and Councillor Phil Bevan (also of Caerffili). Additionally, Councillor Bevan would organise annual Ysgolion Cymraeg festivals, which generated enjoyment for the participants and excellent publicity for the movement. Teachers, parents and their children would parade though town and city centres and carry banners in the tradition of the mining communities, and distribute leaflets conveying information about the nature and purpose of education in Welsh-medium schools and exactly where they were located.

Ysgol Pont Siôn Norton had opened as a unit in 1951 with fifteen children. By 1964 it had 190 pupils who had increased to over 250 when Mid Glamorgan became the LEA in 1974. The site contained three buildings and by 1980 the 'Welsh stream' had exclusive occupation of two of them and two classrooms in the third building, which also housed 'the English school' with fewer than thirty pupils. Mid Glamorgan decided to limit the 'Welsh stream' to three hundred with effect from the start of the school year 1980/81 and refused to admit eight children in excess of that number while making no alternative Welsh-medium provision for them. The parents decided to protest by occupying a classroom at the school overnight and continued to do so until the LEA admitted the children. Further protest meetings were held in a number of locations. The LEA responded by proposing to open 'Welsh units' elsewhere but parents (and teachers) demanded further provision of 'stand alone' Welsh schools. The parents were confirmed in their opinion that Welsh units were inferior to Welsh schools by the refusal of the county council to declare Ysgol Pont Siôn Norton a Welsh school with an English unit of thirty pupils, even though that was manifestly the actual situation on the ground. The protest continued. On 30 September 1980 the county sent a lawyer to take the eight children at the centre of the dispute into care in the English section of the school. The parents responded with threats of violence against county officials.

On 3 November 1980 the eight children were allowed to join a class with those of the same age but without being registered at the school. The nightly occupation by parents continued until 26 November. Finally on 29 January 1981, the local authority formally surrendered to parental pressure by registering the eight children, thus admitting them to the school. This was not the end of the war of Pont Siôn Norton. The authority decided to close the school to pupils of infant age (5–7), thus restricting it to junior children. Infant children were to be taught in a number of 'infant Welsh units', losing thereby the benefits of total immersion in Welsh-medium education. At the start of the academic year 1981/82, 310 children were registered and nineteen refused admission. Mudiad Ysgolion Meithrin organised a private school for these children and their successors over four years thereafter. At last however Mid Glamorgan recognised that it must make further provision and opened a second Welsh-medium school for the Pont Siôn Norton catchment at the old Mill Street building in Pontypridd town centre in September 1985 under the name Ysgol Evan James (author of the words of 'Hen Wlad fy Nhadau', the Welsh National Anthem). At last on 26 July 1990 the last few English-medium pupils (fewer than twenty) said a final farewell to Norton Bridge CP School and in September 1990 Ysgol Gynradd Gymraeg Pont Siôn Norton was legally recognised as such.

The war of Pont Siôn Norton led to territorial gains for Welsh-medium education outside the area of the Pontypridd Education District, particularly when combined with the meticulous research into the true demand for it marshalled by Wyn Rees and presented in one report after another to the Mid Glamorgan Education Committee. In the Cynon Valley this led to the opening of Ysgol Gymraeg Abercynon in 1989. In the Rhondda two more schools were added to the three existing, Ysgol Llyn y Forwyn, Ferndale (1985), and Ysgol Bronllwyn, Gelli (1990). Outside the Pont Siôn Norton area another school, Ysgol Castellau, was opened in 1985 at Beddau. In the Bridgend area two schools were opened, in 1982 Y Ferch o'r Sgêr at Corneli to serve Porthcawl and Pyle and in 1988 Ysgol Cwm Garw to serve the Ogmore and Garw valleys. In Caerffili an infant unit was opened in Tir-y-berth in 1984, which matured into a full primary school, Ysgol Bro Allta, Ystrad Mynach, in 1993. Likewise the Llanbradach infant unit was from 1977 developed into Caerffili town's second Welsh-medium primary: Ysgol y Castell opened in 1994. Only in Merthyr Tudful did the war bear no fruit, but a gain of nine schools is a fair reward for the sacrifice of the Pont Siôn Norton parents who did battle over three months and for the careful research and well-argued reports of the RhAG working party.

Alas, when Mid Glamorgan was abolished as an LEA in 1996, to be succeeded by authorities for Bridgend, Rhondda Cynon Taf, Merthyr Tudful and Caerffili, the Mid Glamorgan County Committee of RhAG also ceased to exist. In RCT the consequence is that no Welsh-medium primary school has been opened there since 1990. In Bridgend parental efforts have concentrated (successfully) on securing a local secondary school (Llangynwyd) and Merthyr has continued to be a place where a deaf ear is turned to calls for further Welsh-medium provision. Caerffili illustrates the difference made by a hard-working RhAG local committee of parents. The area acquired two schools by boundary changes but in addition new primary schools have been opened at Aberbargod (Bro Sannan), Gelligaer (Penalltau) and Oakdale (Cwm Derwen), others are under discussion, and a second comprehensive will open in 2013.

(b) Forensic Battles in South Glamorgan with Strategic Monitoring to Follow
In Mid Glamorgan the parents resorted to direct (and certainly illegal) action. In Cardiff the parents had to weather protests (certainly illegal) against Welsh-medium education and one parent had to conduct a series of legal battles, supported by other parents, the successful outcome of which has certainly changed the atmosphere for Welsh-medium development permanently for the better.

In 1974 Cardiff City was merged with Cardiff and Cowbridge Rural Districts, Cowbridge and Barry Boroughs and Penarth Urban District to form South Glamorgan County, whose council became the LEA. Cardiff had one Welsh-medium primary, Bryntaf, while Penarth and Cowbridge each had a Welsh-medium primary. Barry uniquely had a Welsh-medium infants and a Welsh-medium junior school.

Bryntaf had moved to its third site in 1972 after outgrowing its second site in Highfields, Llandaff and failing to secure a suitable larger site. Instead it was moved to the site of a disused secondary school, Viriamu (William in Polynesian) Jones, located on the Mynachdy council estate in Gabalfa, which had the reputation of being a 'sink estate'. The Mynachdy residents gave the new children a warm welcome, shouting and jeering at them and even spitting on them. The children came from all over Cardiff and necessarily many of them by bus. They were dropped at the edge of the estate, which had narrow roads easily blocked by the residents who objected to buses on 'their' roads. The children therefore had to run the gauntlet of verbal abuse and worse for three years until the council at last found alternative accommodation in the disused Cardiff High School for Girls in September 1975. Here there were no unpleasant local residents, although the building was run down and unsuitable. By now Bryntaf was in excess of a three-form entry school, admitting ninety-two pupils in September 1975 to the reception class. The parents kept up an unceasing barrage of correspondence to the LEA and its members and one of the least pleasant duties of the chairman of the education committee was to face the infuriated parents *en masse* at annual meetings of the PTA, following which he would complain of the headteacher's lack of control over 'his' parents. 'They are your electors' was the response to this Tory chairman.

Shortly after Labour took control Emyr Currie-Jones became chairman of the education committee, which in 1979 decided that Bryntaf was to be closed and replaced with four schools in the west, north-west, north-east and east central district of the city. Accommodation was found by closing two-stream infants' schools on council estates where the child population had fallen as the estates grew older, sending the infants into the junior schools to become primary schools, thus leaving the infants' schools to become one-stream Welsh schools. The first school was opened in 1980, the second and third in 1981 leaving the children from the east central district still in the old Bryntaf, hastily renamed Y Parêd after the street in which it stood. After a good deal of parental protest the children of Y Parêd were moved to a school in Rumney on the far east of Cardiff, a good way from where most of the children lived.

Meanwhile the other three schools, all more or less central to the district served, had rapidly been seen as more attractive than Bryntaf, far away in the city centre in a crumbling building, and increasing numbers of parents chose Welsh-medium education. The deputy director of education, with special responsibility for Welsh-medium education (rather than the Welsh-speaking director), had expressed the view that the provision of 120 places a year was excessive and would never be needed; three schools with a little short-term overcrowding would have been better. By 1986 the number admitted had risen to 172 from 107 in 1980, with the excess over 120 accommodated by hastily opening a second stream in Bro Eirwg, the eastern school which had been blessed with an excess of rooms and by opening a 'free' class in an English school (Lansdowne), from which Ysgol Treganna grew. Meanwhile Mr Pearce, the deputy director of education, coped with his problems by placing new children wherever it was convenient to him: that is where there was space.

In September 1983, Mr Pearce decided that it would be convenient to him for Catrin, the four-year-old daughter of Dafydd Hywel (Evans) to be admitted to Bro Eirwg where there was room. Dafydd Hywel lived in Pontcanna on the western side of the Taff and his son was already attending Coed y Gof, the Welsh-medium school for western Cardiff. Bro

Eirwg lies on the eastern bank of the river Rhymney about six or seven miles from Pontcanna and until 1946 was actually in Monmouthshire. Dafydd Hywel insisted that his daughter should go with her brother to Coed y Gof to which school she was taken on the first day of term. The head, Mr Tom Evans, was quite willing to admit her but the decision was not his but reserved to the director of education under a special rule applicable only to Welsh-medium schools. English-medium heads were trusted to decide their own admission policies. The deputy director, ignoring the fact that he had already exceeded the proper admission number of thirty by admitting thirty-four, refused to admit one more. Dafydd Hywel continued to take Catrin to Coed y Gof. He was sent an official letter prohibiting him from entering school land. He took the child to the gate and trusted his son to escort her the five yards to the school door where the staff declined to leave her unattended on the doorstep.

Emyr Currie-Jones endeavoured to persuade his colleague, the chairman of social services, to treat Catrin as abandoned and appropriate to be taken into the care of the local authority. To his credit the chairman of social services refused to have anything to do with such a step. The education department then sought a High Court injunction to restrain Dafydd Hywel from procuring that Catrin should trespass on the land of Coed y Gof school. The application came before Mr Justice Michael Davies sitting in Cardiff, who dismissed the application as unfounded in law. He added that as a grandfather he entirely sympathised with Dafydd Hywel in his wish that both children should attend the same school and in his view that a school six or seven miles away was inappropriate. He recommended however an end to direct action and resort to an appeal to the appropriate admissions appeal committee.

Dafydd Hywel took the judicial advice and appealed to the admissions committee where he lost because the committee wrongly placed the burden on him of proving that the admission of his daughter would not prejudice the education of other children and would not be a waste of educational resources. The argument of his RhAG lawyer (the writer) to the contrary was dismissed. RhAG agreed to support Dafydd Hywel's application for judicial review heard in London by Mr Justice Forbes in 1984 when the writer's legal submissions were upheld, the order of the appeal committee quashed and the appeal ordered to be reheard with the burden of proof on the county. The only witness who could prove prejudice was a teacher in Coed y Gof and the county persisted in resisting the appeal notwithstanding that their witness, Mr Tom Evans, the head, declared his view that there would be no prejudice and that his school could educate thirty-five in a class just as well as thirty-four. Mr Evans was cross-examined (most improperly) by the county solicitor for a prolonged period but would not change his evidence, and the committee finally had no option but to allow the appeal. Dafydd Hywel was awarded costs in the High Court and with QCs instructed on both sides the county's own costs and those of the applicant came to about £20,000. South Glamorgan learnt an expensive lesson. Thereafter they (and Cardiff and the Vale of Glamorgan after re-organisation in 1996) have operated a policy of close consultation with RhAG as parents' representatives, meeting at least once a term, and taking care to ensure that the supply of places in Welsh-medium education has met or exceeded the demand. Thus over the ensuing twenty-six years from 1984 the numbers of children admitted to reception classes has risen fourfold to over 600 in 2010 and the number of primary schools in Cardiff from four one-stream schools in 1983 to seventeen with a total of twenty-three streams over the same period with an increase to twenty-five by 2011. Consequentially the secondary provision in what was South Glamorgan has risen from one, Glantaf, opened in 1978 to four (three in Cardiff and one in the Vale).

It should be noted that South Glamorgan's changed attitude was felt also in the Vale of Glamorgan area where a second Welsh-medium school (Sant Curig) was opened in 1992. Shortly after coming into existence the Vale opened a 'starter class' in 1996, which after some vicissitudes became Barry's third school as Gwaun y Nant in 2000. In 2009 the Vale carried out a survey of unmet Welsh-medium need, found it to be considerable and within a month of publication had proposed a Welsh-medium development plan involving the expansion of the schools at Penarth and Cowbridge and the opening of two new schools, one at Llantwit Major (Dewi Sant) and a second as Barry's fourth Welsh-medium primary (Nant Talwg). The county committee of RhAG was closely involved in these developments.

Dafydd Hywel's legal battle in the courts with the support of RhAG has, like the direct action at Pont Siôn Norton, been a true *causa causans* bearing fruit and illustrating how parent power has effected the growth of Welsh-medium provision.

(c) Organised Parental Pressure and a Decisive Legal Victory

In Monmouthshire too parent power had a direct effect on the development of Welsh-medium education, which lagged behind that in east Glamorgan. Only in Rhymni, a curious enclave of surviving natural Welsh speakers, was there established a Welsh-medium school of the first wave in the 1940s and 1950s. Otherwise parents in anglicised Monmouthshire had to work hard to obtain the establishment of Welsh-medium classes or at best units from 1967 onwards and these were badly treated, being moved from one English-medium school to another to suit the LEA's convenience and not that of the children. For example, after ten years in the lower Ebbw Valley the unit at Risca was peremptorily moved, not to the next valley, but to a building at Pengam in the next but one, the Rhymney Valley. Likewise the unit at High Cross in the north-west of Newport was moved to a new building in south-eastern Newport. When at last a secondary school was opened for Gwent children in a former primary school in Abercarn in the lower Ebbw Valley, it was expected after a few years to move to a disused secondary school on top of a mountain outside Ponypool, twelve miles away.

The parents, under the leadership of a dedicated county committee of RhAG, persisted through all vicissitudes, at last encountering an Anglo-Irish director of education (Geoffrey Drought, 1985–93) who could not understand the unremitting hostility of Labour councillors with strong Welsh accents to Welsh-medium units and who worked with the county committee to win over Mrs Anita Lloyd, the chair of the education committee, to support Welsh-medium education by the conversion of six units into full Welsh-medium schools in the 1990s and by the opening as a school from the outset of Ysgol Gymraeg Y Fenni at Abergavenny in 1994.

The division of Gwent into four LEAs in 1996 was a blow to Welsh-medium education. Nonetheless, parents worked hard to secure the foundation of a second school in Monmouthshire (the name given to the rural new authority in very anglicised east Monmouthshire). This was to be opened in Caldicot but at the last minute a county councillor with an undeclared personal interest voted the proposal down. The parents invoked the aid of RhAG, who again resorted to the remedy of judicial review. Service of the papers led to the collapse of opposition to the proposal. The new school was opened as Ysgol y Ffin and the local government ombudsman ordered the county to pay RhAG's legal costs.

Again parent power was vindicated in the courts and local authorities obliged to have proper regard for parental opinion.

In Newport RhAG formed an effective committee to represent parental opinion and under parental pressure the county agreed to carry out a survey to ascertain the truth of RhAG's assertions that there was an unmet need for proper Welsh-medium provision apart from the badly sited Welsh-medium school that had opened in 1993. When at last the survey was carried out the city of Newport found that RhAG's assertions were fully justified and that a second school was called for in addition to the oversubscribed Newport Welsh School. This second school was opened in 2009 on the northern side of Newport under the name of Ifor Hael. Such was the demand for places that by 2010 it was doubled to a two-form entry, as was the original school, and a third school, Bro Teyrnon, was established in west Newport in 2011.

In Torfaen parental pressure has led to the opening in 2010 of a third Welsh-medium primary in Griffithstown as Ysgol Panteg, with a fourth under consideration to be the second Ysgol Gymraeg in Cwmbrân. In Blaenau Gwent Ysgol Gymraeg Brynmawr has at last been moved from its ruinous building in Brynmawr to a new building near Nantyglo in the Ebbw Fach. There has been some pressure for a school to open in Ebbw Vale itself following the visit of the National Eisteddfod to the town in 2010.

3. CONCLUSIONS

Parental power may manifest its importance in different ways, but without such manifestations the continuing expansion of Welsh-medium provision by the exercise of individual parental choice becomes a chimera; a parent cannot exercise a choice to take up a place that does not exist or has already been taken by a parent who made his or her choice earlier. In the catchments of Castellau and Garth Olwg (Cynradd) it pays to notify Rhondda Cynon Taf (RCT) of election for Welsh-medium education shortly after the birth of a child, such is the competition for places in the nursery classes connected with those two schools, which a child joins shortly after becoming three years of age. Such an absurd situation arises because the local authority has not been under any real parental pressure for nearly twenty years. This may be compared with the position in Cardiff where orderly growth, at a rate of 10 per cent a year for the last five years, has been secured without open conflict once parental power had proved itself by the victory in the case of Dafydd Hywel. In RCT the fruits of the victory at Pont Siôn Norton have withered on the vine without the constant quiet pressure of parents. Without that parental concern there is even a real threat of closure of some existing Ysgolion Cymraeg. The contrast is particularly vivid between RCT and Caerffili, both formerly in Mid Glamorgan, where in the latter area continued parental interest has secured continuing expansion of Welsh-medium provision. Such further provision simply does not come without parental pressure because the default option for educational administrators, English-medium provision, is much less trouble.

ADDENDUM 1

Since writing this chapter some months ago, events have occurred in Rhondda Cynon Taf which are a very clear illustration of parent power, and the editors have kindly agreed that I may add this short account.

Between 1974 and 1996 the area now within Rhondda Cynon Taf County Borough Council was part of the area under the authority of the Mid Glamorgan County Council. I have referred above to the battle of Pont Siôn Norton and to the very active county committee of RhAG in Mid Glamorgan, which between 1980 and 1996 was instrumental in providing evidence of parental demand that led to the opening of nine new Welsh primary schools in the area of Mid Glamorgan. Five of these schools fell into the area subsequently under the authority of RCT; the last to be opened (in September 1990) was Ysgol Bronllwyn in Gelli Rhondda.

Broadly speaking there were four successor education authorities to Mid Glamorgan, of which the largest by far, but also the most divided by its geography, was RCT. RhAG endeavoured to establish four successor county committees and succeeded with three but failed with RCT. Caerffili, the largest, was the most successful of the heirs of Mid Glamorgan RhAG, bringing to a successful conclusion the efforts (instigated, in the opinion of the editors, by the Cwm Rhymni action group) to secure a proper, modern building for the Welsh comprehensive, opened in 2002. Caerffili RhAG also

225

continued to battle for more local primary schools, a campaign that led to three new foundations as well as new and bigger buildings for existing schools. In Bridgend the committee concentrated on securing a Welsh-medium secondary within the boundary of the authority, achieving a successful outcome in 2008. The undaunted committee in Merthyr Tudful has so far secured no more than a new building for one of the two primaries, where the LA carefully did not include one extra place.

In RCT however the county committee did not come into effective existence. Although local agitation by individual PTAs did secure new school buildings (in Aberdâr and Ynyswen) and some additional accommodation in existing schools, no new primary school was brought into existence for a period of twenty-one years. In 2010 the LA threatened to close every sixth form in the area, concentrating all the sixth form students, English and Welsh-medium, in one sixth form college, probably to be located in Nantgarw. The college would of course be 'bi-lingual', that is with classes through the medium of English and Welsh but with administration, ethos and all common services through English 'as it is understood by everyone'. The parents rose against this idea, came to RhAG for help and at last, fourteen years late, formed an effective county committee with an agenda including not only co-coordinating the fight against a sixth form college but also the implementation of plans to act upon the need shown by the LA's own surveys for extra schools in the Cynon Valley and the area of Church Village.

The sixth form threat has faded away because finance is lacking but the county committee has continued to be active on the need for the development of primary education, securing a meeting with the new acting director of education early in 2011. In March it became clear that there was no sufficient provision of Welsh-medium education within the catchments of Ysgolion Cymraeg Llantrisant and Llwyncelyn (Porth), where upwards of fifteen sets of parents in each school were told that there was no room and that the parents should look elsewhere for places in Welsh or English-medium schools without any attempt by the authority to offer places at any specific school. The reason for this became apparent; no such places existed, as the adjacent schools were equally full to capacity. After a good deal of parental pressure through RhAG the authority agreed to provide a terrapin at Llantrisant to cope with the immediate problem, but far more dramatically also agreed to open an additional Welsh primary in

September 2012 by using spare accommodation at Llanhari Welsh-medium comprehensive, not required because Bridgend no longer sends its Welsh-medium pupils to Llanhari for secondary education. This answer to the problem had been suggested to the director at RhAG's meeting in January but not then taken too seriously. The LA has further promised to bring forward a revised plan for development of Welsh-medium education. Local and vocal parents have secured a complete about-face on the part of the LA and the growth of the provision of Welsh-medium education in RCT is once again under way.

ADDENDUM 2
PARENTAL CHOICE TO BE GIVEN
STATUTORY RECOGNITION

In April 2012 there occurred the most crucial step in the legal recognition of parental choice in Welsh-medium education since the passage of the Education Act of 1944, s76 of which provided that children should be educated in accordance with the wishes of their parents. This provision legally had only a moral effect, since no legal mechanism was enacted whereby parents could in court oblige a local authority to provide the type of school in which their choice of education would be available. Since 1944 parents have had to rely on persuasion and, in fairness, warm words of support from HM Inspectors of Education and other officials and ministers, first in the Department of Education, then the Welsh Office and finally the Department of Education within Welsh Government.

Part 4 of the School Standards and Organisation (Wales) Bill (WG 2012b) will give a statutory mechanism for enforcing recognition of parental wishes upon the twenty-two local authorities of Wales. Part 4 contains four sections, ss85–8, which will be fleshed out by statutory regulations to be made under their authority. The Welsh Government is empowered by s87 to make regulations requiring local authorities to assess parental demand for Welsh-medium education and setting out how often this exercise shall be undertaken; s87 replaces the exhortation contained in ministerial circular letters recommending that such assessments be under-taken, which some local authorities have complied with but some have not. Each local authority is required by s85 to prepare a Welsh-in-education strategic plan (WESP), to keep it under review and to revise it when necessary. This replaces a provision in the Welsh Language Act 1993, which gave the Welsh Language Board (now abolished) the power to demand a similar plan from local authorities once every three years, starting in 1995. Plans were ultimately extracted from mostly unwilling LEAs over the period 1998–2002. The second round of plans was never fully obtained and the WLB was very reluctant even to threaten to use its reserve statutory powers to obtain plans from recalcitrant authorities. It certainly never used those statutory powers and never publicly condemned LEAs which had not carried out the plans for Welsh-medium development which had been promised. Latterly the minister of education exhorted local authorities by circular letter to improve Welsh-medium provision after carrying out surveys of unmet need, and these exhortations had a dramatic effect in those authorities that complied with them, most particularly Newport, Torfaen and the Vale of Glamorgan.

For the last eighteen months the present minister of education has been warning authorities unimpressed by exhortation that he would take statutory powers and he has now taken the first step to doing so; his ministerial statement in support of the draft legislation makes it clear that he sees the new statute as the means whereby he will see that local authorities 'respond to demand' and take steps to 'increase the number of people fluent in Welsh', and to ensure that 'more children of the age of seven are being educated through the medium of Welsh'. The whole purpose of the legislation is to put into effect 'strategic planning to facilitate growth' and for 'improving provision' of Welsh-medium education.

It is unfortunate therefore that s85(1) (a) requires that the WESP includes only proposals to 'improve the planning of the provision of [WM] education' and 'to improve the standards of WM education' without a third most necessary requirement, namely to ensure as far as may be practicable that the provision of Welsh-medium education in its area shall be sufficient to meet the demand in that area as shall be assessed pursuant to s87 hereof. It seems clear that the draftsmen of Part 4 have not put into statutory language the intentions of the minister as clearly set out in his statement quoted above. It is required under s86 that each WESP be sumitted to the minister, who can approve, modify or reject it and call for a better plan. The plan must then be published and implemented. Under s88, the minister is given power to make detailed regulations as to the content of a WESP, for consultation in its preparation, for review of the plan during its operation and other matters.

With the one exception highlighted this is an excellent statutory scheme which at last gives s76 of the Education Act 1944 the teeth which it has lacked for nearly seventy years.

Multum in parvo

Parents favouring Welsh-medium education must always make a nuisance of themselves, enough of a nuisance to make it easier and cheaper to provide enough Welsh-medium places than not to do so.

[Editorial comment: the editors requested the author to write a second addendum for a number of reasons: to provide expert opinion on a draft bill which is of considerable legal, historic and pragmatic significance to the themes developed in this book, to illustrate the dynamic power of expanding Welsh-medium provision, and to exemplify Fishman's tenet of constant vigilance.]

Chapter 9

Local Authorities and Welsh-medium Education

Geraint Rees

It is now well over a century since the planning of educational provision for children and young people was put into the hands of local authorities. Consequently, it is right that local authorities are praised or criticised in turn when their provision is excellent or inadequate. Prior to the development of local authorities, it was the established church which took on much of the responsibility for education and it is during that era that it became the norm for education to be provided in English – to a nation for whom it was, in the main, a foreign language. It would be interesting to speculate as to which would be Wales's dominant language today had the largely Welsh-speaking nonconformist denominations, with their huge grip on Welsh society, taken the opportunity to provide formal education for the children of Wales after the Treason/Treachery of the Blue Books in 1847. The commission which led to the publication of the Blue Books had been called for by William Williams, the Carmarthenshire-born MP for Coventry, who believed that Wales needed a reformed education system so that it would lead in time to the Welsh 'instead of appearing a distinct people, in no respect differ from the English' (Hansard 1846: vol. 84, c.854). It seems reasonable to speculate that had the nonconformist denominations ventured into such provision they would have normalised education through the medium of Welsh in an age of highly literate peasantry, widespread political change and prolific publishing in Welsh. However, our history is as it is, and the development of a universal educational provision in English established that language, for the first time in our history, as the strongest language in Wales. Consequently, a common theme throughout the last century has been the effort to improve the status of our indigenous language in our own schools – not only from the perspective of language learning, but also from the perspective of curriculum content and medium of delivery. It is in that context that we should assess the progress of Welsh in our education system and evaluate the contribution of individuals who have often led the campaigns to give our language its due status in our own education system.

THE LOCAL EDUCATION AUTHORITIES

Apart from the diocesan boundaries of the Church in Wales and the archdiocesan boundaries of the Catholic education authorities, the boundaries of our education authorities, as things stand, follow those of the twenty-two local authorities in Wales. In 2010, the term local education authority was formally abolished in Wales. In their last year of existence, the LEAs spent an average of £5,429 on each pupil in 2009–10 and, despite being £527 per pupil less than the corresponding spend in England, it is nevertheless a significant amount annually. This spend is of course administered in conjunction with other significant budgets managed by those authorities as they discharge their responsibilities for children's services in Wales.

The last quarter century of the twentieth century was characterised by great structural and geopolitical change within Wales. From 1973 to 1998 most of the Welsh population was affected by the reorganisation that befell local government. In that time, most Welsh citizens lived in three different counties – even without moving house. In 1972 the town of Neath was in Glamorgan. From 1974 to 1996 it was in West Glamorgan and since 1996 it has been in the County Borough of Neath Port Talbot.

The fortunes of Welsh-medium education during these years have depended heavily on the balance achieved within each authority. Because there was no statutory requirement for local authorities to provide education through the medium of Welsh, the development of that sector has depended heavily on a complex set of relationships between prominent politicians, the interest and ingenuity of individual senior education officials and the demands made by parents in each area.

While depending on such dynamics, it would be fair to note that the growth in Welsh-medium provision lost some of its momentum at times as the UK government (via the Welsh Office) set about reorganising Welsh local government twice in a quarter century. For example, the County Borough of Merthyr Tudful started its life in 1996 with only two Welsh-medium primary schools. Sixteen years later it has not added to that number. Previously, Merthyr Tudful was part of Mid Glamorgan, a county which made enormous strides in providing education through the medium of Welsh. In the last days of the old Glamorgan in 1974, plans were afoot to open Ysgol Gyfun Llanhari in addition to Ysgol Gyfun Rhydfelen and Ysgol Gyfun Ystalyfera, which had been opened over a decade earlier. In 1974, the old Glamorgan was divided into three counties, with Swansea and Neath becoming the main towns of West Glamorgan, Barry and Cardiff becoming the main areas of South Glamorgan, whilst the old coal-mining communities from Merthyr to the Vale and from the Rhymney Valley to Maesteg formed Mid Glamorgan. In Mid Glamorgan, the next fifteen years experienced a considerable growth in Welsh-medium demand, with the authority making considerable strides to meet that demand. Welsh-medium primary schools were opened in communities across the county, and, by the time the authority was abolished in 1996, there were five Welsh-medium secondary schools; Ysgol Gyfun Llanhari in the west, Ysgol Gyfun Rhydywaun in the north, Ysgol Gyfun Cymer Rhondda and Ysgol Gyfun Rhydfelen at the centre and Ysgol Gyfun Cwm Rhymni in the east.

Following the Conservative Government's reorganisation of local government in Wales in 1996, Mid Glamorgan was divided into four new authorities – Bridgend, Rhondda Cynon Taf, Merthyr Tudful and Caerffili. Some boundaries were drawn in unexpected ways, leading to communities being handed to neighbouring authorities, for example, the semi-rural communities of Creigiau, Pentyrch and Gwaelod-y-garth which, under the new arrangements, fell into the new authority of Cardiff County Council.

It was during this reorganisation that four posts were created for directors of education to succeed Keith Price Davies, who had been the last director of education for the larger Mid Glamorgan County Council. It was noted at the time that the new directors had jurisdiction over areas that were considerably smaller than Keith Price Davies's area, and significantly they also lacked his understanding and appreciation of the dynamics of bilingualism within valley communities. The fact that their sizes were so much smaller than the previous Mid Glamorgan gave each council a smaller budget, but also a far smaller critical mass in the minority world of Welsh-medium education. Following a sharp growth from one to five Welsh-medium secondary schools in the area of the old Mid Glamorgan, there followed a break of twelve years before any of the new authorities opened a new Welsh-medium secondary school, with that one being in Bridgend CBC, under the name of Ysgol Llangynwyd, in 2008. Not only did the momentum for growth slow down, but also it has been argued repeatedly that the opening of Ysgol Gyfun Llangynwyd in Bridgend CBC (in an area formerly part of Mid Glamorgan) was based upon the needs of one small local authority and did not form part of any regional strategic plan, showing that planning regionally for Welsh-medium education was still not in place, despite the existence of a national assembly. Such lack of cross-border or trans-authority planning is reaffirmed by critics who believe it accounts for the fact that the former Gwent, with its one Welsh-medium secondary school in Torfaen (Ysgol Gyfun Gwynllyw) providing for all of the old Gwent authorities, has suffered from a slow response to the rapidly rising numbers at that school – a growth in numbers that was in danger of leading to chronic over-subscription.

THE SITUATION IN 2012

By 2012 the situation had changed considerably. The devolutionary process had stabilised and the Welsh Government had published, launched and is monitoring its Welsh-medium Education Strategy. Coupled with the election of a new Conservative/Liberal Democrat government in Westminster from May 2010 and the impetus in Wales for LAs to work together in regional consortia during a time of growing financial pressure likely to last until 2014 and beyond, planning educational provision in Wales requires some imaginative remodelling. The regional consortia are being expected to deliver better coordinated and more cost-effective outcomes, in keeping with the 'Making the Connections' agenda that has been clear since 2006. The need to deliver the components of the Welsh-medium Education Strategy during a period of financial constraint will prove to be a considerable challenge for many local authorities. The stability that has been established since the reorganisation of local government in 1996 has witnessed, in many areas, a consistent coordinated growth in

Welsh-medium provision. It will be interesting to see whether introducing the new dynamic of regional consortia hinders or facilitates further growth. Past experience suggests that growth in the Welsh-medium sector is better achieved during periods of stability.

THE NEW DYNAMIC AND THE PLANNING
OF WELSH-MEDIUM PROVISION

For local authorities in Wales, this century has been characterised by new significant factors which are impinging on their administrative systems and planning processes. At a national level, they work with the Welsh Government, and at local level they contend with the development of Children and Young People's Partnerships (CYPPs). These partnerships have had variable but sometimes major impacts locally in terms of forward planning of services for children and young people. They were intended to bring about more coordinated forward planning between various providers in the public, private and third sectors. Evidence from organisations such as the Mentrau Iaith and Mudiad Meithrin suggests that the partnerships have not eased the development of provision in Welsh for young people. Before they were established, the main contributors towards the development of Welsh provision for the young were the education departments of local authorities. Even in areas which had been largely anglicised, the teams planning education provision were generally mindful of their responsibilities and often had a good understanding of the needs of parents and schools in the Welsh-medium sector. Schools were generally opened and supported in line with parental demand. As far east as the Severn Tunnel, Welsh-medium provision was developed, with the opening of Ysgol y Ffin in response to parental demand. As new schools were opened, local authorities would be required to put in place the associated infrastructure to support them, and gradually individuals were appointed to positions in those authorities to support Welsh-medium schools and their development. There is considerable evidence to suggest that local authorities grew in terms of their empathy for the Welsh-medium sector, and much of the hostility reported in the 1970s could be seen as a thing of the past. During this time, prior to the establishment of CYPPs, there does not seem to have been a corresponding growth in Welsh-medium provision for children in other areas of public service such as the NHS, Leisure or Children's Services. Under the Children Act which introduced Children and Young People's Partnerships in Wales (2004) it was expected that all partners would work together to ensure that all provision for young people was properly planned and coordinated. By 2011, these partnerships had become highly resourced, well-connected groupings with far-reaching responsibilities. It is ironic that in several parts of Wales, many of those working through the medium of Welsh with young people report that their partnerships show very little empathy with the needs of young people who are attempting to live their lives in Welsh. This is coupled with the accusation that the partnership-funded activities for children in Welsh are miniscule in comparison with those activities available in English. It seems that, despite the significant expenditure allocated to Welsh-medium education and channelled through the local authorities, putting planning in the hands of Children and Young People's Partnerships has once again destabilised the growth of Welsh-medium provision as new partners have been introduced into the planning equation, many of whom have not previously considered the language needs of young people – especially if that language is Welsh. This has certainly been true in south-east Wales and much work is required to ensure that young people and their parents can have genuine equality of opportunity in all aspects of their lives in our native language.

LOCAL AUTHORITIES AND THEIR PLANNING OF SCHOOL PLACES

The educational responsibilities placed on LAs range widely, including ensuring fair funding of schools, offering support and challenge regarding their management of pupil outcomes, ensuring support for pupils with Additional Learning Needs, managing admissions arrangements and planning sufficient school places. Parents do not have a statutory right to a Welsh-medium education, and such a right has not been enshrined in the Welsh-medium Education Strategy of 2010. It should also be noted that there is no enshrined right in Wales to an education through the medium of English either. Within this grey area, LAs are expected to plan ahead to ensure sufficient school places. Such forward planning is easier when LAs are able to ascertain what kind of educational provision parents would prefer – if such a choice can be made available. However, under the protocols established relating to data protection, there is variation across Wales in terms of the exchanging and sharing of data to assist with language planning. A local authority can expect its local health authority to share data on live births or GP registrations with it, so that it can plan for sufficient school places. However, where the choice is available, a local authority needs more than global numbers in order to plan the balance between English-medium and Welsh-medium early years provision; it needs to be able to contact parents to ascertain whether they would like provision for their child to be in Welsh or in English. The legislation, passed by Westminster, can work effectively for local authorities in England, where all provision is in English. A local authority in England needs only to provide sufficient places for children under its jurisdiction, but in Wales, if Welsh-medium provision is to be made available for all who want it, further flexibility is needed so that proper provision can be put in place. A significant challenge facing many authorities in Wales over recent decades (Cardiff, for example) has been the recorded growth in demand for Welsh-medium provision, coinciding for a decade with a general decline in the numbers of children born in the city. The available population data suggested that the authority needed fewer school places. It would have been particularly helpful for the LA if it had been able to know what choices parents would have made if they had been given the opportunity to express a preference for Welsh- or English-medium education. The inability of the LA to access data which would have enabled it to contact the parents of infants to ascertain their language preference for their child's education for many years undermined smooth and timely planning. Instead, the LA was forced to plan for each September on the basis of requests for places submitted the previous January coupled with a predictive model that it used to asess future demand. Put simply, in Cardiff the LA would receive approximately 4,000 forms annually in January showing parental choices of primary education for their three-year-old children for September of that year. In order to respond in such a short time-frame to the rising demand for Welsh-medium provision each September, the LA deployed a technique first used in the 1950s. In a two-year period from 2008–10, Cardiff Council opened five Welsh-medium 'starter classes'. Different terms are used in different parts of Wales (e.g. seed schools) to describe these arrangements. Under such arrangements, a

Welsh-medium class is opened on the site of an English-medium school. A headteacher of a neighbouring Welsh-medium school will usually be asked to take responsibility for the starter class and to ensure an effective link between that class and its nearest Welsh-medium school – the 'mother school'. Such arrangements can be put in place at quite short notice, which allows such temporary measues to provide the new capacity required whilst the LA goes through statutory processes for the longer-term future of a new school. In this way, the starter classes established on the sites of English-medium primary schools such as Oakfield, Bryn Celyn, Gabalfa and Holy Family R.C. Primary are in due course growing into fully fledged primary schools with their discrete sites, known as Ysgol Pen y Pîl, Ysgol Pen y Groes, Ysgol Glan Ceubal and Ysgol Nant Caerau. The successes achieved in establishing these schools went largely unnoticed, mainly because of the very public difficulties over resolving the challenges of rapidly rising Welsh-medium numbers in the Canton area and the significant difficulties faced by Ysgol Treganna, which became a cause célèbre throughout Wales, and is discussed elsewhere in this volume.

Local authorities need access to relevant and detailed data and the freedom to use it to ensure that they can plan adequately for the needs of both English- and Welsh-medium education. It is helpful that Leighton Andrews is a pivotal politician in Wales and that he is both the Minister for Education and Skills, and also has the responsibility for the Welsh language. That high-profile role, coupled with a clear Welsh-medium education strategy produced under his leadership, should ensure that linguistic planning is accorded proper status within both the national assembly and local authorities across Wales over the coming years.

LOCAL AUTHORITIES AND THEIR WIDER CONTRIBUTION TO THE DEVELOPMENT OF WELSH-MEDIUM PROVISION

Because of the high profile given to the statutory consultation processes necessary to plan for the opening or closing of schools, it is easy to under-estimate the significant wider contribution made by local authorities to the well-being of the Welsh language. The local authority contribution is crucial, not only in its planning and provision of sufficient school places, but also in its role in supporting leadership and management of schools, staff development, school transport and a plethora of other key roles. The development of regional consortia offers very exciting opportunities in relation to Welsh-medium provision. Those opportunities are particularly obvious in developing 14–19 provision and specialist provision for pupils with Additional Learning Needs.

As far as the Welsh Government's Transformation Agenda is concerned, in relation to 14–19 provision, local authorities and their further education partners are seeking to deliver far-reaching structural change in the way that the curriculum is provided to young people in their areas. The clear intention is to enhance the curriculum and the wider experiences offered to pupils. As things stand, it appears that different authorities are taking different approaches to these challenges. In some authorities, change is being delivered by moving towards a more explicitly tertiary model (i.e., schools will be the main providers of education up until the age of 16, whilst FE colleges will lead on provision after that age). On the other hand, some authorities are seeking to develop a more complex set of arrangements where schools, FE colleges and work-based learning providers will offer, in their turn, a wide range of options to enable the learner to make informed choices in a mixed economy. In these local authorities, it should become the norm for young people to receive their education in more than one institution in the course of a typical week. Within the Transformation Agenda lie a whole host of opportunities and risks for Welsh-medium provision. Young people may receive a wider range of opportunities to study in Welsh, intended to satisfy the economic and social needs of Wales, but also to satisfy our young people's individual needs. Several challenges face Welsh-medium providers. Firstly, the transformation will be achieved for pupils in Welsh-medium settings only if their schools commit to cooperating in ways in which they have not done in the past. Such cooperation has been inhibited historically by the distances between the institutions and, significantly, by the inability of partner organisations (such as FE colleges and work-based learning providers) to provide adequately for young people in Welsh. This leads to the second challenge facing providers. FE colleges in Wales will need to commit to proper provision in Welsh (in keeping with their declarations in 2010) in order to ensure that the Learning and Skills (Wales) Measure (2009) can be delivered for all young people in Wales – in their language of choice.

A third challenge facing public bodies in Wales as they seek to support Welsh-medium provision is how to meet the global challenge facing minority languages with regard to matters such as the internet and the availability of global learning resources available in the world's dominant languages. With the proliferation of materials available in English, a challenge facing providers in Welsh in future will be how they make use of those resources. The pattern of education over the centuries has been that students would access most of their information from a small number of available texts. In such a world, the availability of a major text in Welsh would have been sufficient to allow the student to be able to access that entire subject in Welsh. The move towards digital media has led to a proliferation of available materials. The challenge now is not the production of a standard traditional text book in Welsh, but has more to do with how students using a minority language can use that language in the midst of the vast number of global subject resources available. Of course, therein lies a great opportunity for Welsh-medium education. Ensuring that core resources are available in Welsh, side by side with the plethora of global materials, should lead to young people in Welsh-medium education continuing to be truly globally focused, bilingual and multilingual learners and citizens.

ADDITIONAL LEARNING NEEDS (ALN) AND SPECIAL EDUCATIONAL NEEDS (SEN) PROVISION IN WELSH

Over the last three decades there has been a significant growth in the number of Welsh speakers under the age of thirty in south-east Wales. In a recent interview, the solicitor Miles Richards from Church Village noted that he was one of only six pupils in Pontypridd Boys' Grammar School able to speak Welsh during his time at the school in the 1940s. That would have contrasted significantly with the majority who would have been Welsh-speaking only half a century earlier. This sharp decline and the desperately small numbers of Welsh-speaking teenagers in the 1940s led in due course to a very small number of Welsh-speaking families in south-east Wales for the following twenty-five years. The situation was transformed initially by an influx of young Welsh speakers from the rest of Wales during the 1960s and 1970s. Subsequently, that influx has been matched by a growth in the numbers of young people who have graduated from the

239

Welsh-medium sector and who have stayed in south-east Wales to make their way in life. In combination the migrants and the Welsh-medium graduates have generated an enormous change in the numbers of young couples who are today raising their children as natural Welsh speakers in south-east Wales. Whilst this is likely to fuel a further growth in demand for Welsh-medium education, it is also likely to lead to a significant growth in demand for ALN and SEN Welsh-medium places in the region, where provision in Welsh for pupils with significant special needs has at best been 'adequate'. The lack of a critical mass has led to LAs dealing with the needs of Welsh-speaking pupils with significant special needs on a case-by-case basis. There is no special school in south-east Wales providing fully in Welsh for children with SEN. The changing population dynamic and the expectation that LAs engage in regional planning should lead to a significant improvement in the provision in Welsh across the region over the coming years – or else there will almost certainly be a high-profile test case about the rights of a Welsh-speaking child with a disability to be provided with a full education in his mother tongue in his own country.

Welsh-medium education stood at a crossroads. In the past, the main challenge facing the LAs had been to do with the provision of sufficient numbers of places in Welsh-medium schools. At the start of this new century, both agenda and expectations have changed. Local authorities and their partners need to plan for more than a sufficiency of school places – the wide range of statutory and non-statutory targets included in the Welsh-medium Education Strategy now needs to be achieved. On a regional level, it is imperative that the 14–19 provision meets the needs of employers and students and that ALN/SEN provision offers equality of access for a child from a Welsh-speaking or an English-speaking home. Local authorities and their health partners need to ensure that they are offering education or therapies in the appropriate language for the child. These are now national expectations, but satisfying these expectations will require regional partnership working within multidisciplinary and multilayered frameworks. Joint working is being encouraged and expected at a time when there is great insecurity regarding the relationships between our local authorities. The challenge will be to ensure that structural change does not, as it seems that it did in the past, slow down the growth in Welsh-medium education. This challenge will be a considerable one to overcome. However, for the first time in our history, we can say that Wales has a national government with a legislative toolkit to manage our educational system and sustain our language, a Minister with a commitment and a strategy to ensure the effective implementation of that government's wishes, and local authorities charged with delivering Welsh-medium education in keeping with a national agenda for effective educational provision and equality of opportunity for all our young people.

Chapter 10

School Reorganisation:
A Lesson in How Not to Do It.
The Case of Canton, Cardiff West

Rhodri Morgan

INTRODUCTION: TOO MANY CHILDREN FOR SCHOOL?
THE LONG AND WINDING SEARCH FOR A SOLUTION

One of the best, if not THE best day of my constituency life in twenty-three years as an elected public representative for the Cardiff West constituency, either as a member of parliament or as an assembly member, was 26 May 2010. This was the day when the Welsh Assembly Government, in the person of the first minister, Carwyn Jones, put an end to several years of speculation over the possible closure of Lansdowne Primary School. In upholding the appeal by the parents, teachers and children of Lansdowne Primary to keep their school open, in effect he announced the rejection of the Liberal Democrat/Plaid Cymru administration's proposals for school reorganisation in western Cardiff. Since that date, the campaigners' decision to stand firm in opposing the council's various flawed proposals to deal with the surplus places in English-medium schools and the lack of places for Welsh-medium primary education in the west of Cardiff has been totally vindicated. Carwyn Jones's decision has also been totally vindicated despite the council's threat of seeking a judicial review.

It had been four long years since Cardiff Council councillors and officers first dipped their toes into what were to become extremely choppy waters over school reorganisation. Since then, children, staff, parents and politicians suffered a long and winding sea journey chock full of rocky reefs and sandbanks combined with captains half asleep at the wheel. What is more, by late spring 2011 we were still not 100 per cent sure where we would end up. It is crucial to remember that this is not, and never has been a case of favouring one school over the other, or prioritising Welsh-medium education over English-medium or vice versa. Sadly, when politicians are playing politics, this will always be the motive imputed to your opponents.

What needs to be remembered, but is sometimes forgotten in the heat of battle, is that it was the Labour-controlled South Glamorgan Council that decided to open Ysgol Treganna, Canton's first Welsh-language primary school, in the mid 1980s. The chair of education was Labour councillor Emyr Currie-Jones and it was the then newly elected Labour councillor, Mark Drakeford, who was the founding chair of governors during the school's first and formative years. Both were instrumental in bringing Ysgol Treganna into being.

It is inexcusable that four and a half years after the first proposals to reorganise primary school education in inner city western Cardiff, we were by December 2010 back to square one, with no clear fully funded solution agreed. All were united in recognising the urgent need to resolve the overcrowding issues at Ysgol Treganna and provide adequate facilities for the pupils at the school. Why had it taken four years to circumnavigate the globe and come back to the same starting place, with the Treganna children no nearer a solution?

PLAN No. 1: PROPOSAL TO CLOSE RADNOR ENGLISH-MEDIUM PRIMARY

Rumours before the Proposal Announced?
The original proposal to close Radnor Primary was put forward as a part of the City-Wide Investment Plan (CWIP) which was made public at the beginning of April 2006. Many dubbed this the council's attempt at a 'Big Bang' approach to school reorganisation. It prompted widespread objections and a shocked reaction to the raft of proposed school closures across the city.

One part of this city-wide school reorganisation plan was to close Radnor Primary and to extend Ysgol Treganna to take over the whole site. Treganna currently occupies the old infants department and Radnor occupies the rather larger old junior and secondary modern building. The proposed closure of Radnor Primary would have seen its children split up and dispersed across the various surplus places in other schools across Canton and Riverside. That prospect was unacceptable to many of the Radnor parents, let alone the staff and the three local Labour councillors. The opposition was extremely vocal and well-organised.

The population figures on which the council based their closure proposal for Radnor showed that the school was not full. There were only about 210 children on the school roll. However, by late 2010 the school was close to capacity, with the younger classes already at capacity, acting as a reliable marker of what would happen next, with the increase in the birth rate feeding through into class sizes in a sustainable way.

The proposals were also flawed in focusing too much on the demand for Welsh-medium education in Canton whilst ignoring the growth in demand from Grangetown to the south. The council may have been seeking too keenly to get Welsh-medium primary education on to a single site, as there was (and is) a theory about Welsh-medium thriving better when not on a shared site. Whatever the reasons, on 27 April, one month after its announcement, the council announced that it was abandoning that plan.

PLAN No. 2: THE LANSDOWNE AND TREGANNA SAGA

Following the stymied Radnor proposals, an alternative proposal to close Lansdowne Primary was initially considered by the schools sub-committee on 9 November 2007. It was a proposal that was again designed to make way for Ysgol Treganna's expansion on to a single site. There were in effect two options (of which more below) put forward by the council in an attempt to combine reducing the surplus places for English-medium schools at the same time as addressing the lack of space for Welsh-medium schools in Canton.

Once again there was an outraged response from the parents, teachers and children at Lansdowne Primary. Canton's three Labour councillors, Ramesh Patel, Cerys Furlong and Richard Cook, spoke out against the plan. The previous year the council had backed off the Radnor solution to the Treganna problem in the face of a vociferous and well-organised campaign but had presumably calculated that closing Lansdowne Primary would, in some mysterious way, be 'easier', because the parents would be less likely to be so well-organised and articulate. That was a disastrous miscalculation. The psychological effect of being perceived by the council as easier targets than the Radnor parents was to galvanise the Lansdowne parents into action. 'We'll show 'em!' was the watchword. When developing their plans, the underlying flaw in the council's decision was its failure to consider the significant shifts in the birth rate and the demographics of inner city Cardiff West. The birth rate in the whole of Wales had shown a trend to decrease from 1990 to 2001, when it had started to increase, but this was particularly marked in the Canton-Riverside area.

Following the EU enlargement in 2004, which saw ten new members join the EU (including eight eastern European states), there were significant flows of migrant workers to all parts of the UK, including Wales. Cardiff was one of five local authorities in Wales that attracted some of the largest numbers of these new migrants. Between 2004 and 2008 the number of employed Welsh residents born outside the UK increased from 52,000 to 74,000 (42 per cent). This means that by 2008 5.5 per cent of all employed residents were foreign-born (WAG 2009c). Moreover, consideration does not seem to have been given to likely future changes to family formation in Cardiff West, including the proposed development of the former Arjo Wiggins Paper Mill, which had been earmarked as a site for the development of 900 new homes in the catchment area of Lansdowne Primary School.

Prior to the Welsh local elections in May 2008, the council was run by a minority Liberal Democrat administration which slowed the progression of the council's plans for school reorganisation, probably due to an understandable reluctance to rock the boat ahead of the local elections. Progress therefore stalled in the run up to the election. However, following the elections the political picture shifted when the Liberal Democrats formed a coalition with Plaid Cymru. Without the pressure of the election, attention again turned to progressing the plans for closing Lansdowne Primary School. On 6 November 2008, following widespread objection to the council's plans for the closure of Lansdowne, a supplementary proposal was announced in which the council's executive recommended officers to go back out to consultation on a second proposal for a brand new one-form entry school for Lansdowne to be established on spare land on the site of Fitzalan High School. This was pitched to 'buy off' community opposition to the total closure of Lansdowne Primary School.

However, the council made it quite plain that it had no funds to build this new school, so the proposal never really got off the ground.

Following the collapse of the proposed new single-form entry Lansdowne on the Fitzalan site, on 30 April 2009 the council's executive approved the publication of statutory notices for the closure of Lansdowne Primary school, the closure of Treganna's feeder school unit in Grangetown (Ysgol Tan yr Eos), the transfer and expansion of Ysgol Treganna and Tan yr Eos on to the Lansdowne site and the establishment of Radnor Primary as a two-form entry with nursery.

WHERE NEXT FOR YSGOL TREGANNA: A NEW WELSH-MEDIUM SCHOOL IN CANTON?

The Welsh Assembly Government's decision to reject those proposals was announced by First Minster Carwyn Jones AM on 26 May 2010.

Since the first minister's upholding of the appeal by Lansdowne School against the threat of closure, Cardiff Council completely changed its strategy on Welsh-medium education in the Canton, Riverside and Grangetown area. The council has now accepted that the demand for English-medium education is sufficient to keep four primary schools fully occupied in the future, given the recent rise in the birth rate. The four are Severn Road, Kitchener, Radnor and Lansdowne. Ninian Park Primary in north Grangetown (which also hosts Tan yr Eos) is absolutely full. In this part of Wales, human nature has removed the surplus places issue.

However, following the first minister's appeal decision, Ysgol Treganna teachers and parents have campaigned in order to put pressure on the Welsh Assembly Government in particular for special help to alleviate the overcrowding issue. In September 2010, Cardiff Council announced its proposed solution to the overcrowding and cramped conditions at Ysgol Treganna by outlining plans to build a new £9m Welsh-medium primary school in Canton. The new school would be built on council-owned land off Sanatorium Road. The new building would match demand for Welsh-medium education in the area. A consultation on the procedure was carried out in the spring of 2011, and the proposals were cautiously welcomed by local councillors. A further indictment of the council's competence was that it was the Canton councillors, not the council, who identified the proposed site at Sanatorium Road for the new Welsh-medium primary, despite the fact that the land belongs to the council and would have been patently obvious on its land register.

According to Cardiff Council's submission to the '21st Century Schools Programme' (Cardiff Council 2010):

> Cardiff has seen accelerated growth in the demand for Welsh-medium education over the last ten years and particularly between 2004 and 2008 with demand increasing from 12 per cent to 15 per cent. If this rate of growth were to be sustained year on year, it is anticipated that by 2018, up to 25 per cent of the total population (maximum figure) could be requesting Welsh-medium education. The authority has two well-established Welsh-medium High schools – Ysgol Glantaf and Ysgol Plasmawr, which are at 100 per cent occupancy. The authority has embarked upon an investment programme of £15.6m in these schools in order to meet their increase in numbers and deliver the curriculum needs of their students. In addition, the recent announcement by the Welsh Assembly Government to provide capital funding for the new St. Teilo's Church in Wales secondary school and the refurbishment of the existing St. Teilo's school to create a third Welsh-medium secondary school enables the authority to respond to the immediate pressures of primary pupils requiring secondary education in 2012. How-ever, the need for a fourth Welsh-medium secondary provision is acknowledged and will be part of the authority's planning for future investment.

What is interesting is that in putting forward these proposals for Welsh-medium education in Cardiff West, the council's estimates have gone from needing to expand from the present provision of three-form entry (two forms at Pwll Coch and one at Treganna) up to four-form entry (two at Pwll Coch and two at the new Treganna on the Lansdowne site), then up to five-form entry via the new three-form entry school at Sanatorium Road. Most recently they have upped that from five-form entry to six-form entry, with the latest projected need being a three-form entry school in Sanatorium Road and the addition of a third-form entry to the existing two at Pwll Coch.

By early 2011 what remained unclear and a question that urgently needed to be answered was how exactly the council would pay for a new-build three-form entry school on the Sanatorium Road site. On 10 December 2010 the council submitted its bid for funding for Cardiff Schools for 2012–15 under the Twenty-first Century Schools Programme, which included a bid for the necessary funds for the proposed new Welsh-medium school at the Sanatorium Road site. No particular priority was attached to the bid for funds for the new Treganna. It was an undifferentiated shopping list of school expansions, refurbishments and new builds.

The other concern was that Councillor Rodney Berman (leader of the council) had admitted that this proposed new school would take at least three years to bring about a solution to Treganna's overcrowding. It was therefore by no means an 'urgent' solution. The minimum of three years delay is explained as follows. If the full council approved the council leadership's proposal, a period of consultation would follow. If that went well (which it did), the council would then include the £9 million total cost, or the residual £6 million the council said it had not yet found from its own resources, in its bid to the Welsh Assembly Government – the capital expenditure programme under the Twenty-first Century Schools Programme. This was the stage we had reached by late spring 2011.

Cardiff Council already had a large number of bids in and had done well in getting bids approved during the period I am critiquing; for example, the £38 million cost of the new St. Teilo's Church in Wales secondary school and upgrading the present St. Teilo's into the new third Welsh-medium secondary school for eastern Cardiff. After digesting all the new bids, a mammoth task, Welsh Government has to go back to the council before final design and European procurement procedures and actual tendering and construction can start. Adaptations to the building of this third Welsh-medium secondary school are not likely to be completed until 2013, making it seven years since it first appeared in the City-Wide Investment Plan in 2006. That was for a school proposal which has not encountered that much opposition and had gone comparatively smoothly, but it still took seven years. Can Treganna wait seven years?

What was not clear was whether the council planned to make any changes in its capital programme to get the new Sanatorium Road Welsh primary for Canton higher up the order of priority, because that would take something else down the list. Approval in the capital programme would mean showing why the proposed new school was the best solution to the problem, given the urgency of the overcrowding at Treganna, the surplus places problem elsewhere in the city's primary school system and the difficulty the council would have in finding the total cost from capital receipts etc.

In its consideration of the proposal the city council scrutiny system now needed to go into overdrive, scoring it on (a) how quickly it solved Treganna's overcrowding; (b) what chances the city had of finding the other £6 million from capital receipts; (c) what other school capital projects already submitted for assembly funding would be lower in priority than the new school, if indeed there were any candidates for lower priority? We also needed to know what Plan B and C (and even maybe D or E) the city council had and how they scored on the same three key tests. Then we would be able to see whether the new school proposal really was the only possible solution, albeit very slow. The case didn't just need to be strong. It had to be cast-iron.

The council leader then took the plunge and put a bid for the new school forward into the all-Wales capital programme competitive bidding system, taking its chances relative to all the other bids from Cardiff and all other twenty-one local authorities in Wales. What was difficult was that this seemed to be based on an assumption that the assembly government somehow owed Cardiff a financial favour or two because of the first minister's decision to uphold the appeal on Lansdowne School. There seemed to be an element of gambling on the part of the council that the Welsh Assembly Government would look favourably on an application for £6 million simply because the first minister's decision had frustrated the council's original intentions. That assumption appeared at the time to be utterly unrealistic.

Set against the backdrop of the most difficult settlement for Wales since the beginning of devolution, with the assembly's budget under pressure from every direction but especially on capital, there could have been absolutely no guarantees that it would be in a position to fund the council's plans for a new-build school on Sanatorium Road. If there had been no likelihood of the special allocation of £6 million, did the council have any other alternative means of financing a new school? Prudential borrowing seemed to be the likeliest source, but the council claimed that it was unwilling to increase its indebtedness, although it did have headroom for further borrowing without breaching its prudential borrowing limit (Cardiff Council 2010: 31). Canton Councillor Ramesh Patel did table such a question to the full council meeting on 18 November 2010, asking if the Council would access the prudential borrowing schemes that were available to it if the funding from WAG was not available, The Lib Dem/Plaid administration refused to answer the question. If the council was unwilling to increase its use of borrowing and the assembly had run out of capital, were the children of Treganna going to face years more of overcrowding? The council's belief, oft-expressed, that they had lived with overcrowding for that many years that they wouldn't object to a few more, only applied if there was a reasonable prospect of a new school at the end of it.

On 29 November 2010 Leighton Andrews AM, the Welsh Assembly Government education minister, launched a major new consultation which had the potential to change significantly the school reorganisation process in Wales. The consultation was designed to garner views on a wholesale overhaul of the school reorganisation process and to make future decisions more efficiently, quickly and with more local input. The key points in the consultation included establishing a local appeal mechanism, to prevent proposals being referred to ministers other than in exceptional cases; ensuring that, in line with existing best practice, all local authorities were required to publish consultation documents to ensure that parents, teachers and interested parties were kept fully informed; and changing the threshold for objections so that a single objection could no longer delay the proposal. In extreme circumstances, the assembly could be given powers to close schools with few or no pupils. The consultation on these new proposals ran until 18 February 2011.

There were still a number of loose ends which were the fallout from the council's botched proposals for Canton. For instance, Cardiff Council was doggedly refusing to remove the threat of judicial review which at the time of writing was still looming over Lansdowne Primary. We all know that a judicial review challenge can realistically only be mounted within the first thirteen week after the minister's decision. After that, it can be done only by making a special application to the judge and offering a watertight justification for why a judicial review application was not lodged within the normal thirteen-week window. So with the prospect of a judicial review all but dead in the water, the council still allowed the threat to hang over Lansdowne, presumably in a spiteful attempt to blight the school. The teachers, parents, and above all the children of Lansdowne School, almost 400 of them, deserved to continue to get the best education without any further threats to their continued existence created by Cardiff Council's refusal to withdraw the threat of judicial review.

CONCLUSIONS: CLEAR AS MUD AND NO PLAN B?

The council failed to spot the change in the demographic trends. The council used to employ a small team of expert demographers. They would have spotted the change. The amount of time wasted trying to kill two birds with one stone, the surplus places bird and the rising demand for Welsh-medium bird, has been an abysmal failure. It might well work in other areas of Cardiff where the birth rate remains low but not in the inner city, where the birth rate has been rising sharply since 2001–2.

The obsession with Welsh-medium needing single site schools may well have added to the planning difficulties in coping with the rise in demand because of the loss of flexibility in the siting of provision.

Grown-up attitudes as to how to deal with funding issues and negotiate with the assembly government, combined with the threat of judicial review, seem to show remarkable immaturity for a capital city. All in all, this has been a very sad episode of circular futility where the children of Treganna have been the victims; but then so, for a while anyway, were the children of Radnor and Lansdowne.

The most remarkable aspect of this entire episode was the resolute refusal of the parents in the Lansdowne catchment area to withdraw their children from the school or not send them to the school in Year 6, despite the closure announcement. They stuck like limpets to their school. Thank goodness they did!

The final chapter in the Treganna saga came when the chief education officer issued a new notice in May 2011, indicating that the city was now going to proceed with the new three-form entry school on the Sanatorium Road site. The £6 million which the city council had claimed not to have, had now come to hand, and there was no financial impediment any longer holding the council back from being able to proceed.

Although the announcement (closing the present Treganna and the Tan-yr-Eos starter unit in Grangetown) had to be put out for consultation, resulting in two objections compared with 281 in support (Evans 2011), the council was remarkably confident that, late in 2011, it would be able to start work with a view to pupils moving into the new school in September 2013. Everyone assumes that the adjoining English-medium primaries will take over the buildings released by the construction of the new school, Radnor taking over Treganna and Ninian Park taking over Tan yr Eos.

Where the £6 million came from was shrouded in mystery. The council's education department claims that underspends in their capital building programme, caused by delays in getting other school building projects to the starting gate on time, enabled them to put a case to the assembly government education department for some easement in getting the £6 million freed up. 'Reprofiling' is the favoured term for this process. It is a handy device for face-saving for a council which was absolutely adamant that it could lay hands on only £3 million out of the £9 million required for the new school to be built. It claimed that it was holding a gun to the Welsh Assembly Government's head in issuing a demand for the £6 million. It did after all believe that the first minister's decision not to allow the closure of Lansdowne to proceed meant that the assembly owed Cardiff Council a favour. The council thought it held the high moral ground.

Wherever this 'reprofiled' £6 million came from, it certainly came in the nick of time. The likelihood of any major objections to the proposal to build the new school is very low. The estimates for the population growth of Cardiff issued on 30 June 2011 still look very healthy. The city's population is rising by 1.5 per cent a year, despite the recession. This 1.5 per cent implies a growth of 5,000 a year. It is not caused directly by net migration coming into the city but by the excess of births over deaths. This excess of births over deaths continues to be concentrated in the inner city in a belt running from Victoria Park in the west through Canton and Riverside and to Roath Park in the east via the Docks and Splott.

On that basis, the likelihood of surplus school places recurring in inner-city Cardiff over the next decade is very low, although the problem remains in outer-city Cardiff and in most of the rest of Wales. It is a really strange paradox, and difficult to explain, that the inner and outer circles of Cardiff are behaving in such contrasting ways. It means that when the council sets out to look at a solution for the surplus school places issue, they will need to be much more scientific and surgical in deciding which areas to study. 'One size fits all' cannot work, when Cardiff is divided into two concentric circles of resurgent child population and stable child population. That is what has saved Lansdowne but it may not save other schools threatened.

Chapter 11

The School Phenomenon: Encouraging Social Language Use Patterns in Welsh-medium Education

Jeni Price

Welsh-medium education doubles the percentage of fluent Welsh speakers, compared to the percentage speaking Welsh at home (Jones 2010). However, the apparent success of the Welsh-medium education system in creating more speakers has not been matched by an increase in social use of the language by young people outside the classroom (WLB 2008). To an extent this has been compounded by the increased uptake of Welsh-medium education by children from non-Welsh-speaking families. Baker (2006) recognises that one of the limitations of the immersion education system is that, for many students, the second language (Welsh in this case) can become a school phenomenon, rarely used in contexts other than the formal academic. However, there is also evidence from schools in areas with higher proportions of Welsh speakers to suggest a marked decrease in the use of Welsh socially amongst pupils. Clearly this decline is at risk of undermining the whole purpose of Welsh-medium education as the main vehicle for creating a truly bilingual country.

My own experience as a product of the Welsh-medium education system in an area with a low proportion of Welsh speakers in the community[1] who was raised in a largely English-speaking home mirrors the experience of many thousands of others. Welsh was the language of my education in every subject between the ages of 3 and 18, and was also the language of informal discourse with teachers at all times. However, English was more often than not the language of any informal discourse with friends outside the classroom, especially during the secondary years, and was also the language of any social interactions in the wider community, apart from those with family members who were able to speak Welsh.

This trend is not exclusive to the Welsh-medium immersion system. A recent research report by Comhairle na Gaelscolaíochta (Ó Riagáin et al. 2008) highlights the following key finding: although minority-language communities may be successful in increasing the number of children in immersion-language education programmes and in developing high standards in written skills, there is a concern that 'social' use of the language in out-of-school contexts is not developing satisfactorily.

ACADEMIC AND SOCIAL LANGUAGE PROFICIENCY

One of the most notable and debated distinctions between types of language proficiency was introduced by Cummins (1979). Cummins's distinctions (often referred to as BICS and CALP) differentiate between the basic interpersonal communicative skills (BICS) and cognitive academic language proficiency (CALP). Pauline Gibbons (1991) also outlines the differences in types of language which she terms *playground* language and *classroom* language. The importance of opportunities to develop equally and simultaneously both types of language to ensure linguistic fluency is widely recognised. Gibbons (1991: 3) also highlights the importance of playground language to academic achievement:

> The language of the playground is not the language associated with learning . . . nor does it normally require the language associated with the higher order thinking skills, such as hypothesizing, evaluating . . . Yet these are the language functions which are related to learning and the development of cognition . . . and without them a child's potential in academic areas cannot be realized.

It could be argued that those pupils for whom Welsh is the language of the home and community develop the social aspect of their language outside the school. However, where this is not the case, the responsibility for developing the social language of pupils must also lie with the immersion-schooling system, if that system is to achieve its objective and create fluent and confident fully bilingual pupils. This paper therefore, explores ways of supporting and encouraging social language use within the school.

SUPPORTING SOCIAL LANGUAGE USE AT SCHOOL

As a result of the growth in Welsh-language education, Welsh-medium schools have shown increased concern about the lack of use of the language in social contexts. As a result, many schools have developed innovative ideas to try and encourage increased social language use. Following the publication of the Welsh Language Board's Youth Strategy in 2005, the board began work to establish a project in conjunction with CYDAG (the Association of Schools for Welsh-Medium Education) and other board partners. The project looks in detail at the factors influencing young people's choice of social language use patterns and explores strategies to change them, whilst also encouraging and supporting an increase in the use of Welsh socially outside the classroom.

The research already carried out in relation to language use (WLB 2008) and student choices in terms of their medium of study (Nicholas 2008) highlighted lack of linguistic confidence as one of the most important influences on the choices made. Therefore it was essential to consider methods of tackling the lack of confidence by offering informal opportunities to increase the use of the language among school pupils. As the project evolved, it became evident that there was a need for two components – a pupil-organised project, led by older pupils, to arrange activities and structured opportunities to influence and support greater social use of Welsh amongst younger pupils, and more in-depth work, piloted in three schools, to explore wider whole-school approaches to encourage greater use of Welsh socially outside the classroom. The methodology of each component is summarised below, followed by further discussion of some of the key developmental issues and influences. These include raising pupils' confidence, tackling negative approaches to language use, focusing on language use rather than pupils' sense of national identity and the role of teachers and support staff. Current indications are that both elements have been successful in promoting increased use of the language socially by pupils in the target schools.

PRELIMINARY RESEARCH

In order to build a current picture of the attitudes towards the Welsh language and its social use, workshops were held in the ten schools in south-west Wales chosen to pilot the project. They were intended as a means of providing information to enable schools to plan the project's activities better, as well as offering a baseline from which to assess the impact of the project.

Workshops were held with two groups of pupils from years 7, 9 and 11, with one group including pupils from non-Welsh-speaking backgrounds and the second including pupils from Welsh-speaking backgrounds. Approximately 500 pupils were seen in total, with between 7 and10 pupils attending each workshop. The groups included a range of gender, academic ability and general attitudes towards the Welsh language. The aim of the workshops was to obtain a better understanding of the following:

- The factors influencing the pupils' language use
- General attitudes towards the language
- What has led to developing these attitudes
- What would make the Welsh language more appealing to them and their friends.

KEY FINDINGS

Across the ten schools, it became apparent that language patterns were established during the final two years (Y5–6) of primary school, but were then rooted soon after arriving at secondary school. It was noted that from secondary school onwards, the Welsh language was linked more with learning, structure, order, routine and enforcement, whereas the English language was linked with contemporary culture, media, web-chatting and socialising.

Although not a major factor, it was possible to identify differing attitudes and varying patterns of language use in pupils from urban and rural areas; between boys and girls; and according to their linguistic background. The use of Welsh outside school in different situations was more frequent among pupils from Welsh-speaking backgrounds and those in rural areas, with these pupils more likely to use the Welsh language in the community, during private lessons, and in various clubs and societies.

The influence of the Mentrau Iaith in the urban areas and the Young Farmers' Clubs, mainly in the rural areas, was also acknowledged.

SIXTH FORM

It was evident that pupils saw the process of transferring to a new period in their educational career path as an opportunity to reconsider some of their ideas and presumptions regarding the language, and consequently, change their language practices. The sixth form was seen as a family or community where new and more mature groups of friends were formed. There was certainly a general feeling amongst the young people involved in the focus groups that they now had more responsibility. This period, therefore, was viewed as a chance to change the language practices established in the previous years. With a more mature attitude towards teachers and school life (as the senior members) and looking to the future, many noted that they either expected to see or had seen an improvement in their attitudes towards the Welsh language and an increase in its use.

PUPIL-ORGANISED PROJECTS

In order to utilise the influence of senior pupils noted above and the potential for change during the latter 'transitional' part of pupils' compulsory education, responsibility was given to senior pupils to lead and organise the activities within their schools to promote language use, with a view to influencing their own language use patterns, and establishing positive language use patterns with their peers and with younger pupils.

A wide variety of activities was offered, among them music workshops, podcasts, radio stations, talent shows, trips and various weekly clubs for specific target audiences. The most popular included School of Rock 'Sgol Sŵn', a series of workshops which entailed composing and performing songs; *Pod Nwdl*, a series of fortnightly podcasts; school radio stations broadcasting during lunchtimes and break times; and the weekly clubs for specific years. However, these were not individual activities; rather they were activities that ensured that there were regular and continuous opportunities to increase use of the Welsh language. Evidence that these activities contributed to placing the pupils' use of Welsh into different contexts, developed a relationship between the schools' senior and junior pupils and established the language use pattern in that relationship is subsequently evaluated.

MEASURING IMPACT

In order to be able to measure the impact of the activities offered to pupils, a series of 'Language Use Actions' were prepared jointly with the schools' teachers. There are ten stages which summarise the different levels in attitude towards the Welsh language and its use, from stage 1, which states 'I speak Welsh in class and outside class with teachers and pupils. I see that the Welsh language has a purpose in every situation and I try to encourage other pupils to speak Welsh.' to stage 10, which notes 'I speak English with everyone – teachers and pupils, in class and outside class. I do not see that the Welsh language has any purpose at all'.

This self-assessment tool is used to measure attitude and use of the target audience at the beginning of the project's activities and once more at the end of the year. During the evaluation days, which are held each year at the end of the project, the use of these actions was discussed. A number of schools reported that the percentage of pupils at the higher 6–8 stages had reduced, and there had been an increase in the percentage of pupils at lower stages. We can gather from this that the project's activities have had a generally positive effect on the language use and attitudes of the target audience. The other interesting aspect of these findings was the general desire among the pupils to increase their use of Welsh.

WHOLE-SCHOOL APPROACHES AND STRATEGIES TO ENCOURAGE SOCIAL LANGUAGE USE

Despite the influence of the activities, it was felt that closer consideration needed to be given to whole-school approaches to promoting language use, and that the wider role of the school should be explored. This included examining and developing the necessary structures and attitudes to create an environment that stimulates change in pupils' language use patterns.

258

METHODOLOGY

Full analysis of the schools' policies and other documents was required in order to ascertain the current approach towards issues involving informal language use. Focus groups were then arranged with a range of stakeholders, including the senior management team, auxiliary staff, parents and pupils, in order to gain more evidence about the situation and to identify the possible roles and influences of these groups on pupils' language use. The aim of the work carried out with the pupils was to build upon the initial research work already discussed, and analyse it further in the context of the whole-school approach.

Quantitative analysis of parents' expectations and attitudes towards pupils' informal language use was also used. The findings of this exercise have been very valuable in empowering and giving confidence to the staff of one school, where research showed that 71 per cent of parents felt that it was 'very important' that their children speak Welsh outside class, and 93 per cent noted that they would like to know if their children were not using Welsh at school. This gave the school the confidence to act positively by strengthening the procedures for informing parents about any lack of Welsh-language use at the school.

All the quantitative and qualitative data collected through the above methods provided a foundation to the subsequent work of preparing a whole-school framework which would identify formal and informal opportunities of influencing the language use of pupils. Additionally, individual school action plans would identify specific targets to be achieved in order to develop a whole-school approach aiming to increase informal language use around the school.

THEMATIC FINDINGS
AND DEVELOPMENTAL NEEDS

The intention of this section is to give constructive critical consideration to the thematic findings of both elements of the project so far, and to identify and discuss the developmental needs.

LINGUISTIC CONFIDENCE

As noted above, lack of confidence has been highlighted as one of the main obstacles preventing pupils from using Welsh naturally and informally around the school. The work of this project so far has consistently reinforced this finding, with direct evidence from pupils underlining the need to consider the matter in greater detail. In the intensive work, it was seen in one specific school that this lack of confidence becomes apparent in two ways. Firstly, a lack of confidence among those pupils who speak Welsh as a first language in establishing that the conversation will take place in Welsh, and secondly, a lack of confidence among those from a non-Welsh-speaking or mixed homes in venturing to speak Welsh in the first place. As a result of the experiences of the entire project, we suggest that lack of confidence becomes apparent in two general ways, a lack of confidence with regard to using the language, and a lack of confidence in their linguistic abilities.

Firstly, it is clear that this project has offered experiences and opportunities for pupils to use Welsh in a variety of different contexts, and to do so within the school. By offering regular, attractive opportunities to pupils, a slow yet purposeful change of attitude towards Welsh can be seen, with the language being associated with enjoyment and having fun. On the basis of the evidence, it could be noted that this project has succeeded in associating the Welsh language with events and activities that reflect those things that appeal to pupils outside school, for example podcasts, rock and rap music workshops and beauty clubs. This was done within the context of the formality of the school, and the effect was clear with regard to increasing the pupils' confidence and normalising the use of Welsh.

Secondly, and linked with the above, is a lack of confidence in their linguistic abilities. It is very often reported through the evaluation process, that pupils have extensively varying perceptions of their individual linguistic resources, and of course this is reflected in the findings of wider research work regarding adults' attitudes towards their linguistic ability. This point has also been reinforced in the research work conducted as part of the intensive work, where it became apparent from the auxiliary staff, parents and pupils that the standard and formality of the language used around the school sometimes inhibits them from interacting with the school in Welsh; for example, parents who are fluent Welsh speakers noted that they chose not to receive Welsh-medium reports as the standard of the language in them is too formal and incomprehensible to them.

One group decided to consider this finding directly, choosing a target audience within Y7 that had lower than average reading ages. Weekly clubs were held with these pupils, where they were offered purposeful games that would enrich the pupils' vocabulary and linguistic abilities. The atmosphere of these sessions was very informal and the older, leading pupils felt that having fun and holding informal sessions with such a specific intention would increase pupils' confidence in their language use. The clubs proved to be extremely popular, and the evidence from interviews with the pupils submitted in the evaluation meeting proves that they enjoyed them and had expanded their vocabulary. This particular activity seems to reinforce Gibbons's relationship between the development of what she calls 'playground' language and the ability to access the academic formal language, thus increasing educational achievement.

BALANCING NEGATIVE AND POSITIVE METHODS OF ENCOURAGEMENT

Another possible reason, cited during the preliminary work, for apparent lack of confidence in their language ability was that pupils felt that they were constantly being 'tested' linguistically (spelling, mutation, speaking, etc.). In many schools it is natural for teachers to correct oral use of the language in informal discourse, outside the classroom, during break and lunchtimes. It is fair to argue that there is an emphasis within schools on ensuring the accuracy of the language across the curriculum for the purpose of educational achievement. It is possible, nonetheless, that this emphasis is at the expense of ensuring that pupils have the ability and confidence to use the language in informal contexts. Further work would need to be carried out to experiment with implementing a regular policy of correcting formal language (in writing and orally in formal situations, such as presentations), but not informal language (in the corridors and in extracurricular activities). However, we note that there would be a need to ensure appropriate role models for pupils, via staff and other pupils, in order to concentrate on drawing attention to the use of informal language in a positive way, while avoiding correction.

As already acknowledged, many schools already implement innovative ideas to try and encourage language use. However, use of the Welsh language at all times during the school day is a fundamental expectation in the designated Welsh-medium schools and is intrinsic to their very purpose and vision. Pupils may therefore be rebuked and disciplined in line with general school disciplinary procedures for any use of English. The long-term effects of the implementation of such measures on attitudes towards language use has not been formally researched and documented. However, evidence gathered during this project suggests that in the short term, pupils do not generally respond, in terms of changing their language use, to such measures. The project has therefore identified a need for schools to strike a balance between disciplinary actions due to lack of language use on the one hand and constructive, reinforcing and supportive systems to encourage language use on the other. The work of creating and piloting such a framework and support structure, with the aim of breaking the constant cycle of disciplining and rebuking pupils for speaking English, and nurturing a healthy relationship between the pupils and their Welsh language use, is currently underway as a continuing element of this project.

The framework also identifies the relationship between both issues in the school's procedures and defines the roles and responsibilities of members of staff and pupils at every stage. However, it is already predicted that the success of any such manageable and robust framework to achieve a balance between 'punishment' and support methods aimed at increasing the use of Welsh will depend on ensuring that all the support mechanisms are in place. All stakeholders, including staff, both teaching and auxiliary, governors, parents and pupils must be fully aware of their roles and responsibilities and take ownership of the operational procedures.

Schools already seem very keen to develop this framework as a central part of their campaign to promote informal use of the Welsh language in the school, and have identified the potential for it to lead to further discussions on creating a National Welsh-Language Quality Mark in schools.

THE ATTITUDES OF TEACHERS AND AUXILIARY STAFF AND THEIR LANGUAGE USE

One very distinct feature noted during the initial research period in the three schools was the influence of the attitudes and language use of teachers and auxiliary staff on pupils' language use. A number of comments were made about the lack of informal use of Welsh among teaching staff, and these issues should be discussed openly, sensitively and yet unambiguously. It is clear that there is further work to be done in the schools to increase staff awareness of their duties and responsibilities with regard to their use of Welsh. It would be interesting to conduct a case study and further research on these teachers' attitudes towards Welsh, and the importance of Welsh in their lives outside school. An obvious question arises as to the relationship between the fact that Welsh has only been the 'language of school/education' for a significant number of the current workforce in our schools, and their own use of Welsh as teachers, in informal situations within the school.

The importance of the role of auxiliary staff at the school in promoting language use also emerged. Interesting and comprehensive discussions were held with these stakeholders during the work, and it was found that they were generally not familiar with discussing whole-school issues. Neither did they have any clear responsibility for reinforcing the school's commitments in relation to language use. A number of schools, especially those in non-Welsh-speaking areas, employ auxiliary staff who are themselves not able to speak Welsh fluently. The fact that they were not fluent themselves however, was not seen as a significant barrier to enhancing their role in the general encouragement of the use of Welsh among pupils. Many also expressed an eagerness to learn the language, and this should be harnessed and addressed at an individual school level, with appropriate provision. Should this particular cohort act and take responsibility for promoting and increasing pupils' use of Welsh around the school, we believe they can become, especially at lunchtime and break time, the regular and constant influence needed in order to change language practices. The need was identified to offer specific 'training' or awareness sessions to this cohort and to ensure their participation in whole-school discussions on the issue.

THE INFLUENCE OF ROLE MODELS AND OLDER CATALYSTS

During the preliminary research, specific reference was made to the influence of significant people on pupils' language use; these included family members

– grandmother and/or grandfather specifically; teachers (sports specifically); senior pupils; community officers; employers and sport/music stars. Although these individuals were not given the title 'role model', the pupils acknowledged that, indirectly and almost semi-consciously, they had increased the pupil's confidence and ability in Welsh. In the case of public figures, it was suggested that this was because they extended the contexts and remit of a language that for many was and sadly is, only a language of education. In these cases, the Welsh language was secondary to their relationship and was not the reason for their appeal.

During the pupil-organised activities, the nature and motivation of the pupils who lead them is key to the success of this project. Where the pupils were influential and popular characters generally within the school and reflected the vast majority of the school population with regard to their linguistic background, their interests and their abilities, the younger pupils could be seen to identify with them, and as a result developed a closer relationship with them. Their influence was also more apparent on the younger pupils, thereby ensuring, among other things, that Welsh was a language both accessible and attractive to the majority of the pupils, and not only a language used by the most able pupils and those from Welsh-speaking backgrounds. In addition, other pupils in their year also expressed interest in being a part of the organising committee, thereby also ensuring that the Welsh language was within their reach. It was interesting to note this year that only eight pupils who attended the evaluation day in south-west Wales (which included five pupils from every school, a total of fifty-five pupils) were studying Welsh as an AS subject, which is very different from the situation at the beginning of the project where the vast majority of pupils were studying Welsh.

Language practices are established at a very early stage; it is quite a challenge to change the language of the sixth-form common room over-night, as the pupils have developed their language use practices over six years at the school. However, it is certain that the responsibility given to these groups has changed their language practices with each other, and has established positive language practices between them and the target pupils who attended the activities. Of course this was at its most evident where the group had chosen a regular target audience and saw them on a weekly basis. The nature of the relationships formed between the senior pupils and the target audience goes beyond merely establishing language practices;

it also includes pastoral characteristics; they become 'buddies' and con-fidants for any general worries the younger pupils may have during their first few years at a new school.

PROMOTING WELSHNESS VERSUS PROMOTING LANGUAGE USE

During the intensive work, there was a great deal of discussion on the difference between promoting Welshness and the feeling of belonging to the Welsh community, and promoting the practical use of the Welsh language. There is no doubt that maintaining and developing pupils' Welsh identity is a crucial aspect of their development and educational experiences, and it could also certainly be argued that it contributes to increasing pupils' desire to use the Welsh language. However, this work concentrated on promoting the use of the Welsh language in particular. This was discussed with pupils during the focus groups, and it appears clearly and regularly that pupils did not often have opportunities to discuss language use and identity within the current educational system.

CONCLUSION

If the Welsh-medium education system is to continue to be the main vehicle for creating a truly bilingual country, where everyday use of the language becomes increasingly common across all areas, then it has a specific and vital role to equip pupils with the necessary skills and con-fidence to use the language for both formal and informal purposes.

This project showed that better planning is required for the social use of the Welsh language among school pupils in order to change some of the practices that had been embedded since primary education. It was possible to use some of the aspects identified as negative during the discussions of the focus groups and put them to positive use as the basis for specific projects. For example, the possibility that the school's senior pupils would want to change language practices offered the opportunity for them to be project leaders. In this way, they became effective role models. They could create fun, with informal activities leading to a more continuous use of informal language levels and vocabulary. In addition, an opportunity was recognised to look at the attitudes of the schools' management team, teaching and auxiliary staff and to prepare suitable methods of supporting the use of informal language. As a result of all this, a change in attitude was noticed and an increase in the use of the Welsh language within the social interplay of the pupils at the project's schools.

However, this project has not found all the answers, and it remains to been seen how other schools, and, more importantly, the pupils in those schools respond to the methods and resources which will derive from the intensive work.

Notes

[1] The census figures for 2001 showed that 11.2 per cent of the inhabitants in my home authority of Caerffili were Welsh speakers.

Chapter 12

Transforming Strategies: Pathways to an Integral Education System

Colin H. Williams and Meirion Prys Jones

In the title of his inaugural lecture to open the Bangor University Centre for Language Studies (1988), Williams posited a seminal question, 'Bilingual Education for Wales or Education for a Bilingual Wales'? The implications of adopting either axiom as a central plank of future education planning were then spelt out. In the intervening period 1988–2012, having secured the recognition of Welsh-medium education as a legitimate choice for a substantial number of parents and their children, we are now on the verge of repositioning such choices as an integral, fully mainstreamed part of the educational provision. In the conclusion of this volume we will be arguing that this is an exciting opportunity and one which needs careful thought in terms of its scholastic integrity, curriculum aims and occupational skills development.

First we need to identify what are the key issues in Welsh-medium education before moving on to an analysis of the principal structural elements which influence the success or otherwise of Welsh-medium institutions within public life and civil society writ large. This is essential if Welsh-medium education is to be fully embedded within the socio-economic system, rather than seen as an exceptional, add-on element to the routine, 'normal' English-medium system. It is also essential if Welsh is to be conceived as a public good, rather than situated within the context of a 'minority discourse' which is counterintuitive and constantly having to justify its existence within an intellectual framework which privileges English as the rational choice for enlightened residents in Wales. This conceptualisation both limits the analysis and conditions the possibility which appears to be open to us to break old boundaries and seek newer, more attuned ways of behaving and organising our educational provision. This is especially pressing if Welsh is to secure its place in the emerging European order, where various EU strategies seek to encourage an admixture of languages both as a medium of instruction and as a subject in a broader curriculum,

When Baker and Jones (2000) surveyed the state of bilingual education a decade ago they argued that neither the aims nor the vision for bilingual education had been clearly defined and they offered a strategy for revitalisation which offered a more coherent basis for language acquisition planning and curriculum design. Some elements of this strategy are now being realised as a consequence of a more robust educational policy which is discussed in the middle section of this chapter. However, we are acutely aware that educational strategies are only part of a broader set of social, economic and political impulses. Consequently the articulation of new initiatives, welcome as they are, has to be evaluated by reference to how successfully they are implemented as a social fact.

KEY ISSUES IN
WELSH-MEDIUM EDUCATION

1. The history and psychology of the nation has had an inordinate influence on our level of ambition and on our expectations. Despite the devolution of powers to a National Assembly for Wales in 1999, we have yet to overcome or tackle head on the impact of many centuries of being treated as a conquered nation. In consequence, what role the language can play in our educational system is always calibrated by reference to an alternative model which exists both within anglicised Wales and within England writ large.

2. Dualism and inconsistency have been a dominant characteristic of language-related strategy and educational provision in Wales. So many of the failings of past initiatives have been due not to the quality of the thought or precept involved but to their inconsistent application as social practice. Thus a great deal of energy has been dissipated in securing long-term succession of educational gains, revisiting programmes that have been cancelled as the political mix of particular local government changes. Education, far more than most public goods, is an ideologically infused service and Welsh-medium education adds an extra frisson to the debate.

3. The prevailing discourse is an admixture of evidence, propaganda and hype. What are needed are clear, well-reasoned messages which advance the cause of Welsh-medium education within an increasingly plural and multilingual context both within Wales and globally. Typically such arguments have been made in relation to parental choices and to prospective students, but this message needs to be rearticulated so that it is taken on board by politicians and decision makers and to business people, the probable employers.
4. Succession is a major problem at all levels after primary education is completed. Were the same number of pupils to be enrolled in senior secondary and post-18 courses as are enrolled as 5- or 7-year-olds, our educational system and capacity to use Welsh as a real language of choice within social and commercial life would be revolutionised. The reasons for this lack of succession were enumerated by Baker and Jones (2000) and are revisited by us below.
5. The sustainability of Welsh-medium posts in colleges and universities offers a more positive note. The development of the Coleg Cymraeg Cenedlaethol is likely to improve as a result of recent strategic changes and policy reforms. Williams (2010) has argued for the need for such posts to be guaranteed for the long term and not serve as short-term expedients only. There is some disquiet in several university departments at the manner in which assembly-driven policy is changing the nature of Welsh universities, making them both more accountable and more responsive to targets set by the national assembly in a whole host of fields, only one of which is Welsh-medium professional and higher education.
6. Ideology and conventions. Much of the discourse reflects a post-Thatcher quasi-Blairite concern with meeting demand, viewing education as a free choice exercised by customers in a relatively closed market. There is little discussion of measuring need, or considering the logical questions which arise in post-18 education if a larger proportion of the statutory 5-16 age group receive a Welsh-medium education. A positive sign is the realisation that civil society needs to be engaged in the discussions, and not just as parents, and that Welsh may be treated increasingly as a public good and not as a political football.
7. The balance between the sectors. The greater emphasis on Welsh for Adults in the new strategy is essential, as is the wider role of learning beyond the school more generally in formal and non-formal settings.
8. Skills development and training for the workplace accord with UK and EU priorities and encourage knowledge transfer and occupational mobility.
9. Teaching and research/scholarship are essential if Welsh education is to benefit from British and international perspectives. There is a tendency to treat Welsh-medium education in many of our universities as an

add-on feature and not integral to the institute's remit and mission. Given the new initiatives mentioned above, this marginalisation could be compounded if Welsh is seen as a service-teaching language only and not also as a language of scholarship within an international perspective. Currently many pressures related to international peer review evaluation, citation indices, impact and ranking, the influence of the UK's Research Excellence Framework (REF) on university financing and organisation conduce to publishing and researching in English and other major languages rather than within Welsh or other Celtic languages.

It is evident then that many simultaneous influences are having a cumulative impact on the remit and capacity of Welsh-medium education to deliver a robust service. A plethora of initiatives and new policy strategies is emerging and at times it is necessary to stand back and critique their real import. In order to decouple rhetoric from practice it is essential to know what the relevant significant variables are which influence the passage of new policies into social practice. Williams (2008; 2009) has discussed this issue in relation to organisational change in the Basque Country and Northern Ireland, but his analysis is equally relevant to Wales. There follows an a priori checklist of reasons why reformed language and educational policies are not necessarily fully implemented in organisations at various levels:

- Personal competence – the individuals working within an organisation may lack the requisite language skills, or lack confidence in their actual language skills.
- Team competence – the team of individuals delivering a given service within or on behalf of the organisation may lack the requisite language skills or lack confidence in their actual language skills, or they may have the appropriate skills as individuals but these are not deployed – due to historical practices, job descriptions, work locations – in such a manner as to make use of them.
- Organisational culture – those working for the organisation may perceive it to be defined by a culture which is inimical or not suited to the embedding of the new language; this may include conventional, historical practices in the dominant language, institutional prejudice, ownership (e.g., corporate centre versus service providers, and services delivered by third parties on behalf of the organisation).
- Personal prejudice – the attitudes of the individual, whether a speaker of the new language or not, may be driven by prejudice against the new target language.

- Availability of financial resources – the organisation, or sections within the organisation, may face real financial constraints and competing budgetary pressures and priorities; this could include the procurement of translation services and facilities, the recruitment of additional staff with new language skills and other required competences.
- Technical capacity – the organisation, or sections within the organisation, may be confronted by real difficulties in the realm of technical capacity; this could include services that are delivered electronically, and are thus cumbersome, time-consuming and expensive to revisit (e.g., personnel management system, information management system).
- Limitations of current specialist vocabulary and software – there is often a huge gap between the developed vocabulary and software of the dominant language in contradistinction to those of the new language.
- Trade union or professional reluctance to differentiate between members – often the most ardent opponents of a linguistically segmented work-force are the trade unions and the professional bodies which govern entry, determine core curricula, monitor standards of behaviour and search for a flat pay structure which is opposed to paying a bonus for a particular set of linguistically related skills.
- Politics, representation and interest group power differentials – for organisations with directly elected members the new language may be a politically contentious area and therefore risky for the careers of officers; also the institutionalisation of a new language can become mired in political correctness, thus losing sight of the language customer, with a drift toward tokenism and ghettoisation.
- Leadership – where leadership at chief executive officer level is equivocal regarding the new language (despite or in contrast to public rhetoric) it generates and energises challenges (reasonable and unreasonable) to the institutionalisation of the new language at all levels within the organisation. Equivocation may be driven by a range of complex and interrelated factors – personal experience of the language, response to the nature of the organisation, perception of a political dimension to the organisation, the nature of the relationship between the chief executive (and deputies in the management structure) and the elected leader (and cabinet) of the organisation.
- Change – a general issue that can impact upon language institutional-isation is resistance to change of any sort; a new language can be perceived as yet another new task which interferes with the day-to day job and gives preference to minority group members.
- Generic versus distinct civil service – a major issue for language and governance is the emergence of a regionally distinct civil service within multinational or multiregional states. Core values of a state-wide civil service are often challenged by the 'alternative' orientation of a linguistically

distinct jurisdiction. This raises organisation and loyalty implications for customer service, entry qualifications and relative attractiveness of certain positions, career development, training and retention of staff as either generalists or specialists. (Williams 2008).

Having surveyed the key issues and the organisational filters which influence the transmission of policy into practice let us now turn to the broader context wherein education acts as the prime instrument of language revitalisation and cultural choice.

LANGUAGE REVITALISATION
AND CULTURAL CHOICE

Language revitalisation and its associated promotional campaigns rightly give due prominence to the acquisition of new linguistic and communicative skills. The emphasis on acquisition has been accompanied by the need to create new opportunities within which the skills so assiduously developed can be utilised. Thus there has been a focus on extending the outreach work of Urdd Gobaith Cymru, on developing the young people's remit of Mentrau Iaith, and on providing bridges between the Welsh-medium and Anglo-Welsh or anglicised cultural milieus. Many commentators have argued that Welsh culture is increasingly suffused with English values, patterns and genres, leading in the most extreme case to claims that what we have is an English culture mediated through the Welsh language. But there is ample evidence, albeit on a smaller scale, to argue that the anglicised culture of Wales is also imbued with references and interlocking links with Welsh culture.

Welsh-medium education has developed on the basis of the principle that learning a language goes hand in hand with learning to appreciate its associated culture. Pupils and their parents, on the whole, accept this. In fact, for many parents, non-Welsh-speaking and Welsh-speaking alike, the emphasis placed in schools on cultural aspects of the Welsh language and of Wales engenders great pride, and it is one of the strengths of the system. We are familiar with the common manifestations of this 'culture': music, sport, the varied activities provided by Urdd Gobaith Cymru, and the events of the Welsh calendar. Over the years, schools throughout Wales have carried out exemplary work, promoting access to particularly rich cultural opportunities and experiences. They have done so by developing an awareness of Wales's traditional cultural character whilst at the same time offering opportunities of experiencing contemporary Welsh culture.

It would be difficult to dispute the value of this contribution to the total package of educational and extracurricular experiences which have enriched the lives of pupils for decades. Nevertheless, perhaps the time has now come for us to re-evaluate what we mean when we refer to 'two cultures'? In fact, the same question could be formulated differently by asking how easy it is now to actually define the cultures of the Welsh language or of Wales. How would someone describe or define this culture: Anglo-Welsh? Anglo-American? European? The truth of the matter is that contemporary Wales offers a tapestry of cultures, values, languages and linguistic practices. Neither is this merely an urban phenomenon, reserved for the metropolitan cores and densely settled valley communities of the south and north-east. Due to technology and the pace of knowledge transfer, rural communities also form part of these global trends. Social communication and IT advances have created both integrated space economies and new types of communities. This technology accelerates a trend identified a generation earlier whereby new communities are being formed in such a way that 'community without propinquity', to cite Webber's (1963) memorable description of the modern age, is a more prominent feature of social life. The virtual reality is becoming commonplace, but are the opportunities to access information, education and other services equally available and distributed? Further we could ask not just about the salience of two cultures, defined by language, but of all other cultures which currently operate in Wales. How related the one to the other are the discourse and practices of planning for a bilingual society and those concerned with managing a plurilingual social system? This is no trivial fancy, for at its heart lie the conjoined issues of power, engagement and information.

PLANNING FUTURE GROWTH: MAINTAIN THE STATUS QUO OR BREAK NEW GROUND?

How should one interpret the significance of this increasingly pluralistic situation in terms of the viability of the Welsh language? The cornerstone of language planning in Wales is the aim of normalisation of the Welsh language and the extension of its use across the widest possible range of spheres of activity – that is, ensuring that use of the Welsh language becomes the 'norm' rather than the exception, and that it becomes an increasingly integrated element in the lives of a growing number of speakers.

This raises new issues. It is a cause for celebration and optimism that the appeal of Welsh-medium education has now extended to embrace a range of linguistic and social backgrounds. As the school population base expands, our Welsh-medium schools face a particular challenge: how to embrace diversity whilst remaining true to one of the core principles of the Welsh-medium system, namely to foster interest and pride in the culture of Wales. As we look to the future, one may wonder whether it might be appropriate for us to take a step back and accept that we might need to change course in certain respects.

In responding to this question we dare to suggest that some basic values are just as valuable today as they were half a century and more ago, at the time when the first Welsh-medium schools were established. However, the Welsh-medium education system, and all those involved in its planning and provision, also have another function which is equally important: to respond positively and creatively to the diversity which is now such a central facet of the cultural experiences and needs of our children and young people.

This dichotomy between maintaining and sustaining familiar values on the one hand, and defining a new direction on the other, is not merely relevant in the cultural dimension. The values and circumstances that characterised the growth of Welsh-medium education in the 1960s and 1970s are not necessarily relevant to the twenty-first century. Although the Welsh language enjoys privileges these days, it also faces quite different challenges. The education system has seen far-reaching changes in terms of objectives, structures and approaches. The role of parents and their contribution to their children's education has also evolved, as discussed above. What are the implications of these changes for the Welsh-medium education system?

LANGUAGE NORMALISATION: LEARNING TO LET GO?

We have seen in this volume that the growth of Welsh-medium education since the 1960s has produced a number of significant themes: the vision and influence of prominent individuals; the support of a comparatively small nucleus of parents growing to embrace a far wider circle, including non-Welsh-speaking parents. Central to these considerations was the power of grassroots activity, a willingness to volunteer, and action founded on conviction. As Welsh-medium education developed and became more integrated, these characteristics have tended to diminish in their influence. It is worth noting that the Welsh language, in this sense, has taken a similar path to that of a large number of the world's so-called lesser languages. As a lesser language gains recognition within official spheres, and as efforts to strengthen it become formalised, personal commitment and responsibility tend to be displaced by a more professional, sometimes mainstreamed, avowal by the local state to promote and regulate a language.

This leads us to another dichotomy: on the one hand, the desire for change drives action based on goodwill and conviction, whilst on the other hand, as time progresses, a desire for professionalisation and normalisation develops. Deeply embedded in this transfer of responsibility and direction is the question of engagement. What now are the relative roles of parents, teachers, local authorities and national government in setting the agenda and implementing strategy?

Let us consider the current policy context for Welsh-medium education in Wales. In April 2010, the assembly government's Welsh-medium Education Strategy (WAG 2010a) was published. In the government's own words, this was a 'historic milestone in the history of Welsh-medium education'. For the first time ever, the government gave a formal commitment to lead from the centre the process of planning provision and to support a coherent system from early years to higher education provision and lifelong learning, with an emphasis on continuity and sustainability.

Between December 2010 and February 2011, consultation took place on the government's strategy for the Welsh language, 'A living language: A language for living' (WAG 2010c). The final official version of the document provides a strategic framework for the support and promotion of the Welsh language in all aspects of our lives, within the family, in the community, at work and at leisure. Successful implementation of numerous proposals in this strategy will complement both the principles and the objectives of the Welsh-medium Education Strategy. Both strategies could make a valuable contribution to the linguistic experiences and opportunities of our children and young people, as they progress through their educational careers and extend their use of the Welsh language into the wider community. In February 2011, the passing of the Welsh Language Measure (Wales) marked another milestone in the history of the Welsh language. In terms of policy and legislation, therefore, one can justifiably argue that the Welsh language has never been in such an advantageous position.

The Welsh-medium Education Strategy was published following years of pressing upon the government the importance of planning for Welsh-medium education as an integrated part of educational provision in Wales. The document clearly sets out the responsibilities of central government and those of local authorities and schools, based on six principles: national direction, shared responsibilities, integrated planning, quality, sustainability and equality of opportunity. Having witnessed years of neglect of Welsh-medium education or its merely being bolted on during the final steps of policy development, it is extremely heartening to see commitments such as the following:

> The Welsh Assembly Government is responsible for determining and leading national policy for Welsh-medium education and training. It will set the national strategic direction and establish and maintain the supporting structures. (3. 1: 10)

> The Welsh Assembly Government expects that the characteristics and contribution of Welsh-medium education will receive early and thorough attention in all policy developments at national, regional and local level. (2. 3: 11)

Therefore, there is cause for celebration. However, as a new interpretation of responsibility develops, and as the Welsh language becomes mainstreamed, a new concern arises. Are we ready to let go, and accept that the time has come to stop treating Welsh-medium education as if it is something 'apart'? The weakness of the former system was that Welsh education was always a 'special case'. The strength of that system, however, was that a small group of committed individuals, activists and experts were prepared to care for, nurture and pay particular attention to the needs of the Welsh language and its speakers. Are we prepared for this intensive care to become a more 'normalised' overview? When is the right time to let go?

WELSH-MEDIUM EDUCATION IN THE FUTURE: WHAT ARE THE CHALLENGES?

Our response to this question will depend partially on our perception of the nature of the challenges facing the Welsh-medium system today, and the challenges it is likely to face in future.

PLANNING THE PROVISION

No one can deny that a lack of strategic planning continues to hamper the development of Welsh-medium education in many parts of Wales. Those parents and communities in areas where the provision is inadequate would hardly accept that the system is now the subject of long-term purposeful planning. This was clearly manifest in the differing responses of parents, politicians and advisers to the need for reforming the provision of Welsh-medium primary education in Cardiff. We saw this from both sides of the argument, as it were, in relation to the quite variant perspectives being advanced by parents involved in the Lansdowne Road Primary School decision described by Rhodri Morgan above.

However, it is fair to say that local authorities, on the whole, have adopted an increasingly strategic approach towards Welsh-medium education provision. Through policies such as their Welsh Language Education Schemes, and comparatively recent steps to systematically measure demand amongst parents, local authorities have demonstrated an increasing willingness to plan ahead and consider Welsh-medium education as an integrated element of educational provision as a whole. Things *have* changed since the 1960s and the 1970s, but we have a long way to go to reach a position where all authorities act firmly and with vision when planning future provision. Clearly the vision has to be transformed into a mission and this in turn should be constantly informed by the latest data on the demand and supply of the constituent educational, teacher-training and demo-lingusitic elements.

DEVELOPING WELSH LANGUAGE SKILLS AND CREATING
OPPORTUNITIES FOR THEIR USE

We have already mentioned how the population base of our Welsh-medium schools has expanded substantially over the years. In addition, the cultural and linguistic influences which form an intrinsic part of the experiences of our children and young people are both complex and diverse. Two significant challenges face the Welsh-medium education system: equipping our pupils with the appropriate linguistic resources to achieve academically and extracurricularly through the medium of Welsh, and attempting to ensure that these pupils contribute to the viability of Welsh and collateral languages beyond the confines of the classroom.

To a certain extent, the issues relating to these challenges are manifest in geographic trends. One of the most difficult challenges facing the western areas of Wales, the traditional heartland of Welsh-speaking communities, is to ensure that those pupils whose Welsh may not be so fluent can become confident bilingual speakers within their communities. Current work in Carmarthenshire and Ceredigion by Hywel Lewis (2010) has demonstrated in a succinct manner several of the underlying difficulties facing predominantly Welsh-speaking local authorities and has drawn attention to the most serious implication, which is that students who do not perform satisfactorily are not given more intense, supportive Welsh language tuition (e.g., *gloywi iaith* = language improvement lessons), but are rather encouraged to pursue their studies and formal examinations in English. Although at times pragmatic, this seems to be a self-defeating outcome of an ostensibly Welsh-medium education system. Lewis has identified several structural weaknesses which characterise the current practice of local authorities in predominantly Welsh-speaking regions of Wales. The most important concerns the language of instruction and the language of formal assessment. There is some variety in this relationship for, despite the fact that education authorities seek to guarantee Welsh-medium linguistic and curriculum succession, at times it is the formal examination only which is in Welsh, not the whole of the teaching input. Very often the external final assessment is in English, with pupil choice of medium. The proportion of Welsh-medium assessment is low in comparison with the Welsh-medium school, the Ysgol Gymraeg, in north-east and south-east Wales. This practice is interpreted as 'bilingual education', even though there is no clear methodological definition of the aims and outcomes of such education. Thus two issues interact, the first is succession rates, the second is the language of assessment versus the language of instruction debate. A third situation arises where the formal assessment may be in English whereas the teaching may have followed bilingual precepts.

Lewis has also argued that some secondary school 'models' in predominantly Welsh-speaking areas, such as Carmarthenshire and Ceredigion, do not cater for the full potential of second-language students. Consequently a great deal of solid, preparatory work undertaken in honing language acquisition skills at the primary level is not realised or fulfilled by the secondary-level experience. Consequently, this particular 'model' tends not to be 'cost-effective'. Because such schools do not always succeed in integrating pupils from a non-Welsh-speaking background, it is possible that English becomes the default language of social exchange among the first-language Welsh speakers. Typically, the school-based patterns of discourse and language switching become reproduced in the wider society and anglicisation is more prevalent. The advantage of Category 1 and 2a models (all or most subjects, apart from English, taught through the medium of Welsh) is that they can adopt robust and unambiguous language policies which are not a characteristic of the other so-called 'Welsh-medium' schools. In consequence, non-Welsh-speaking migrants to such areas can demand English-medium education for their children at the expense of the provision made for local Welsh-speaking families. (Lewis 2010)

Because of the way Welsh-medium education has developed in Wales, pupils from diverse linguistic backgrounds with quite different linguistic needs may receive their education in the same classroom. Meeting these diverse linguistic needs within the same classroom in numerous schools in the north-west requires sophisticated, prudent and flexible learning methods.

Quite a different picture emerges when one considers school provision in the south-east and the north-east. For a substantial proportion of pupils in these areas, school provides their principal, if not their only contact with the Welsh language. It must be ensured that their grasp of the language is firm enough for them to be able to develop academically and intellectually through the medium of Welsh. In addition, they must be equipped with the necessary linguistic skills for them to use the Welsh language as a medium of expression in their social and cultural lives.

Nevertheless, we should avoid interpreting these circumstances purely on the basis of geography. Providing for a range of linguistic needs within the same classroom is a challenge for schools throughout Wales (Lewis 2008). Similarly, convincing pupils of the value of the Welsh language, and ensuring appropriate opportunities for them to use it, is as much a priority for schools in the north and the west as it is for the areas in the south and south-east. At times, we can easily lose sight of the importance of the link between fluency and language use. According to the results of the Welsh Language Review (2004) published by the Welsh Language Board in 2006, 88 per cent of those who spoke Welsh fluently spoke the language daily. Of those who did not speak Welsh fluently, only 26 per cent spoke it daily (WLB 2006).

Pupils need a spectrum of linguistic experiences to develop the full range of linguistic resources and registers. Who is responsible for ensuring that pupils are able to receive these experiences, which will enable them to use the language both confidently and effectively? There is certainly a role for schools, and it is important that we recognise the commendable work done throughout Wales to provide opportunities for pupils to reinforce their linguistic experiences in informal contexts. The Welsh Language Board's Language Practices' Support Project has demonstrated the value and potential of such activities. The aim of the project, established in 2007–8 with a group of schools in the south-west, is to provide informal activities to increase pupils' use of the language. The findings of these projects demonstrate the importance of giving the pupils themselves the responsibility for action. This work has also highlighted how important it is to provide appropriate opportunities for pupils to gain a better under-standing of those factors which influence their linguistic behaviour – whether it be a lack of confidence or ownership, or their attitude toward the Welsh language (Lewis and Smallwood 2010).

However successful the efforts of schools prove in encouraging, through formal or informal structures, the use of the Welsh language, one must accept that the education system is in no position to foster fluency and confidence without external support. The responsibility extends far beyond the walls of the classroom and the school gate. We see in the government's Welsh-medium Education Strategy, and even more so in the proposed strategy 'A living language: A language for living', a real effort to ensure that the Welsh language becomes embedded as a means of communication and an intrinsic part of the community in the social and cultural life of our children and young people.

When discussing the challenge of convincing young people of the value of using the Welsh language, some may argue that the problem is that the language is irrelevant to their lives, that it is not 'cool'. There may be an element of truth in this. But perhaps we are in danger of being slightly naive, simplistic even, in our assumptions. For many young people, discovering that phrases and responses do not flow as smoothly in Welsh as they do in English can be just as much of an obstruction to using Welsh as any perception that the language is irrelevant to their interests. This brings us back to the essential link between confidence and use, and the importance of ensuring that our young people possess the necessary linguistic skills, before we criticise their reluctance to use them.

PLANNING FOR GROWTH:
SUSTAINABLE PLANNING

Over the years, many of our efforts have concentrated on attracting pupils and their parents, convincing them of the advantages of Welsh education, and lobbying local authorities to increase provision and facilitate access. This has been done for the best reasons. Ensuring an increase in early years Welsh-language provision is totally central to the aim of encouraging growth. However, perhaps on occasions we lose sight of what lies beyond this aspiration of seeing an increase in numbers. Perhaps we should be looking more perceptively and more critically at how to get the best from our pupils, and how to help them realise their potential as they progress through the system. The salient question then becomes, how does one plan a sustainable system and also at the same time continue to raise educational standards?

Fostering Welsh-language skills is a process which develops over time, and requires long-term investment. For many years now, rates of continuity have been a cause for concern in some areas of Wales, almost exclusively so in western parts of the country. It is a familiar picture: pupils choosing to pursue fewer subjects through the medium of Welsh as they transfer from primary to secondary education (and during their secondary education career), or choosing to change track and study Welsh as a second language as they progress to Key Stage 3. The root reasons for these trends are numerous and complex and tend to relate to a combination of factors linked to attitudes and aspirations, principles and policy guidance, and structural and practical considerations in schools. It is heartening that specific projects, under the supervision and guidance of the Welsh Language Board, have succeeded in influencing continuity rates in many areas of Wales during recent years, demonstrating the value of working in close partnership with local authorities, schools and parents. Detailed guidance for local authorities and individual schools was issued by Welsh Government in February 2012 (WG 2012a). These projects have demonstrated that detailed planning, purposeful dialogue and the careful measuring of progress can effect change and realise the potential of this investment. To what extent is this consistent with the aim of mainstreaming Welsh-medium education? Careful and prudent steps are required to ensure that individual attention and a willingness to discuss specific circumstances are not sacrificed.

It might be tempting to point a finger at parents and criticise them for their unwillingness to allow their children to continue developing their Welsh-language skills as they progress through their education. This is especially acute when it comes to the natural desire of parents to help their children with their homework and preparation for formal assessment and examinations. In circumstances where a majority of parents are often non-Welsh-speaking, it becomes a difficult calculation to weigh the benefits of a Welsh-medium education over and above the often frustrating inability of parents to 'manage' their children's learning experiences and trajectory outside the school.

Equally germane is the assumption made by many parents that a Welsh-medium primary school education would give their children a sufficient grounding in bilingualism, so that they may be safely removed to an English-medium high school, without necessarily jeopardising these fundamental skills. Then it would be up to the student to choose the degree to which he/she wished to maintain fluency in Welsh in the teenage years or adulthood. This becomes a progressively 'rational' assumption, it is argued, as more and more ostensibly English-medium high schools offer a wider range of Welsh-medium subject options.

From our perspective we would argue that a large number of the doubts harboured by parents regarding the quality or standard of their children's Welsh-language skills are often based on unsound assumptions. Thus it is critical that we convince both pupils and their parents that their Welsh is totally acceptable. At the same time, however, it is our duty to listen to the concerns of these parents and respond constructively and responsibly. Kind words and encouragement and telling people not to worry about the 'quality' of their Welsh are not always the best response. Their concerns regarding the strength of skills are often likely to be totally genuine, and we might need to consider a combination of issues in order to provide solutions: the intensity and structure of Welsh-language provision, the school's linguistic ethos, educational methodologies, the competence and experience of teachers. Our willingness to accept and face these challenges will provide the best evidence of the maturity of a system we have fought to develop.

It is comparatively easy to generate enthusiasm and momentum amongst parents when they initially decide to opt for Welsh-medium education for their children, but we must ask ourselves whether everything possible is being done to sustain this. The Welsh language is a skill, and a valuable resource in a range of fields, including the workplace. It is one advantage amongst many cited in the effort to attract parents and their young children in the early years, and on the whole, it is a principle which gains acceptance for a certain time. However, we are not succeeding as well as we should in terms of keeping this message alive as pupils progress through their educational career. One of the great challenges facing the education and training system is to develop a strategic means of expressing and reinforcing consistent messages about the value of the Welsh language in the workplace. This requires partnership between numerous sectors, including training providers, skills sector councils and careers services. Most important of all, perhaps, is the message conveyed by the workplace itself. It is the reality of the world of work from day to day, and clear messages about the status and usefulness of the Welsh language as a medium of internal administration and service provision for the public, that will effect real change.

WIDER DEVELOPMENTS IN THE WORLD OF EDUCATION IN WALES AND THEIR IMPLICATIONS FOR WELSH-MEDIUM EDUCATION

Without a doubt, the education system in Wales is now facing exciting but challenging opportunities. When one considers the impact of these developments on Welsh-medium provision, one realises that it is no longer really an option for us to continue in the same vein as we did in the past.

In general, the introduction of the Foundation Phase for 3–7-year-olds has been welcomed in Wales. Many of the core principles of the Foundation Phase offer favourable conditions which support that which has been at the root of immersion education in Wales for decades: learning through doing and discovery, and utilising skills through interaction and communication. Whilst welcoming these developments, however, it is also important to consider how the implications of the Foundation Phase might highlight new questions regarding the linguistic experiences of young children. How much and what kind of linguistic input or guidance is provided by teachers and class assistants as the children lead and define their own activities? Are we confident that there will be an adequate number of teachers and class assistants with the necessary Welsh-language skills available to support this provision? Another consideration which continues to be a serious cause for concern for some is the way in which the role of the Welsh language in Foundation Phase provision is interpreted in those settings which do not provide Welsh immersion or Welsh-medium education. One cannot but welcome the new emphasis on learning and use of Welsh in active contexts across all the pupils' learning experiences. Implemented effectively, this development could provide a favourable and positive foundation for linguistic progress in the Welsh language, facilitating attainment far more satisfactory than that which has generally been achieved by second-language provision in the past.

However, a word of caution is advisable. The success of such a venture depends totally on providing thorough training for teachers and assistants, appropriate resources and purposeful planning, in order to ensure appropriate continuity as pupils progress from the Foundation Phase to the subsequent stage. We will also need to be aware of another possible consequence, the understandable tendency for some parents to assume that Welsh language provision at such schools is in fact immersion provision. Not all parents will be familiar with the aims and objectives of their local schools in terms of developing bilingual skills. Where there are choices to be made regarding a school's provision, it is essentially important that parents have access to clear information about what is being offered, and what they can expect in terms of linguistic outcomes for their children. It is not only in the Foundation Phase that this clarity regarding language provision in schools is required. Despite a reluctance in some quarters to accept the categorisation of language provision in primary and secondary schools (WAG 2007c), the basic principle of ensuring greater clarity in terms of what pupils and their parents can expect is to be welcomed.

Children between the ages of 3 and 7 are not the only ones to experience the impact of substantial changes to educational provision. The introduction of Learning Pathways for 14–19-year-olds has increased choice and expanded opportunities, and there is now far more emphasis on equipping pupils with a range of skills for further and higher education and for the workplace. In terms of Welsh-medium provision, the developments could easily be mainly seen as a threat: the enormous challenge of offering a sufficient range of options and opportunities through the medium of Welsh and the related risk of seeing pupils turning their back on Welsh-medium provision if those courses they find attractive are not easily accessible. However, it is not all doom and gloom. The need to provide courses, including vocational courses in relatively unfamiliar fields in terms of Welsh-medium provision, has encouraged the establishment of effective and creative partnerships between providers. Countless schemes have been set up to improve access to courses and to reinforce the infrastructure of the provision through collaboration. However, it is a continuing challenge, and the need for appropriate resources and for materials and assessment methods emphasises the constant pressure on Welsh-medium provision to keep pace with English-medium provision.

CONCLUSION: 'TWO CULTURES', AND MORE?

We referred at the outset to the fact that 'the key to two cultures' has been and remains one of the core characteristics of Welsh-medium education for a large number of pupils and their parents. We have also seen, however, how the system fulfils a more complex and varied function in a society which is increasingly multicultural – or for others perhaps uniformly Anglo-American.

The key aim of the education system is to enable our children and young people to thrive intellectually and to contribute constructively to their communities. The wider aim of the Welsh-medium education system is to nurture speakers who are fluent and confident enough to use the Welsh language in their everyday lives, both socially and in the workplace.

This requires enormous investment, in terms both of resources and of individual and organisational commitment. It requires effective partnership between the education system and all those structures which provide a context for the language in the community and in the world of work. It also requires a willingness to acknowledge that recognising gaps is a sign of maturity rather than of weakness.

Within this context, another extremely significant development is afoot: the process of linguistic normalisation, meaning that Welsh-medium education is that much nearer being seen as an integral part of the education system in Wales. This leads us to the dichotomy between the desire to sustain the status quo on the one hand, and the recognition that we need to break new ground on the other.

Three major developments are of the utmost significance. The first is the extra energy, drive and attention being paid to Welsh-medium education at all levels as a consequence of the implementation since 2010 of the strategy for Welsh-medium education. Quite challenging targets are set out in the document, targets which will require government and local authorities to be very proactive if they are to be met. The 2012 Draft Education Measure (WAG 2012b) sets out the expectations of the government as to how the system will oblige and promote these new initiatives.

A second development has been the establishment, within the education department of the Government of Wales, of a subdivision which has been given overall responsibility for the Welsh language. This subdivision has sections which are responsible for Welsh-medium education, for all policy areas in the context of the language and also for all aspects of increasing the usage of Welsh within families and in communities throughout Wales. Again this is a significant development in terms of holistic planning and is a very obvious sign that the Government of Wales in now taking on full responsibility for the promotion of the Welsh language and for ensuring its sustainability in the future. Strategic planning for the promotion of Welsh and Welsh-medium education now becomes an integral part of the role of the Government of Wales.

These new requirements will call for the further development of a body of civil servants who have the skills and knowledge to plan this new and exciting phase in the history of the regeneration of the Welsh language in Wales. Parents, personalities and power interact at many levels, but the critical anchor is a determined official policy, directed by convinced politicians and supported by capable and skilled public servants.

The third critical development is the interrelationship between the promotional and regulatory aspects of language policy. The current policy is enunciated in the strategy document 'A living language: A language for living', which outlines the government's proposals for the future development of the Welsh language itself. It follows a recent tradition in Wales of producing robust and detailed plans which outline the policies and practical strategies which are required to safeguard the future of the Welsh language. 'A living language: A language for living' follows on from two strategic documents produced by the Welsh Language Board in the late 1990s, and, more recently, the publication of 'Iaith Pawb' (Everyone's language) in 2003 by the Welsh Assembly Government. The main impact of 'A living language: A language for living' is that the Government of Wales has taken full and active responsibility for the planning, funding and monitoring of the comprehensive language planning process. Consequently it will be possible to measure the success of the government's strategies against the targets and goals that have been set by the government itself in this important strategic document.

If promotion is one side of the coin, the other is regulation. The passage of the Welsh Language (Wales) Measure (2011) and the establishment of the office of Welsh language commissioner in April 2012 herald the dawn of a new legislative language regime. The commissioner will determine and monitor national standards for bilingual service delivery systems, most critically in the domains of education, health and local government services. In time it is anticipated that the commissioner will develop a suite of language rights in accordance with the official status which Welsh now enjoys. The commissioner will also act as a champion for the language and in consequence the statutory foundations of the office offer a far more robust legal framework for the implementation of Welsh-medium services than existed previously.

We are on the cusp of an exciting period in the history of the Welsh language, and there are heartening developments in terms of Welsh-medium education bearing fruit. At times like this, it is appropriate that we stop for a moment to re-appreciate those principles and values we need to safeguard. It is just as essential, however, that we feel confident enough to know when to let go, to venture and push boundaries. The underlying structures act as an operative framework, but as we have seen throughout this volume, it is parents and key decision makers within the political realm and the field of education who are the drivers of change.

Bibliography

Abley, Mark (2005). *Spoken Here: Travels among Threatened Languages*, London, Arrow Books.

ACCAC (2003). *Developing the Curriculum Cymreig*, Cardiff, Awdurdod Cymwysterau Cwricwlwm ac Asesu Cymru.

Adler, J. (2001). *Teaching Mathematics in Multilingual Classrooms*, Dordrecht, Kluwer.

Aitchison, John and Carter, Harold (1985). *The Welsh Language 1961–1981: An Interpretative Atlas*, Cardiff, University of Wales Press.

— (1987). 'The Welsh language in Cardiff: A quiet revolution', *Transactions of the Institute of British Geographers*, new series, vol. 12, no. 4, 482–92.

— (1988). 'The Welsh language in the Cardiff area', Rural Surveys Research Unit, Monograph 1, Aberystwyth, Department of Geography, University College of Wales, Aberystwyth.

— (1994). *A Geography of the Welsh Language 1961–1991*, Cardiff, University of Wales Press.

— (2000). *Language, Economy and Society: The Changing Fortunes of the Welsh Language in the Twentieth Century*, Cardiff, University of Wales Press.

— (2003/04). 'Turning the Tide?', *Agenda*, Winter, 55–8.

— (2004). *Spreading the Word: The Welsh Language 2001*, Talybont, Y Lolfa.

Aldekoa, Jasone and Gardner, Nicholas (2002). 'Turning knowledge of Basque into use: Normalization plans for schools', *International Journal of Bilingual Education and Bilingualism*, vol. 5, no. 6, 339–54.

Ambrose, John and Williams, Colin H. (1980). 'On the spatial definition of "minority": Scale as an influence in the geolinguistic analysis of Welsh', in E. Haugen et al., *Minority Languages Today*, Edinburgh, Edinburgh University Press, 53–71.

Arad Research (2011). 'Research work into the Welsh-language Sabbatical Scheme for education practitioners: The use of Welsh made by ex-participants in their place of work', final report, June, Cardiff, Arad Research.

Archer, Margaret Scotford (1995). *Realist Social Theory: The Morphogenetic Approach*, Cambridge, Cambridge University Press.

Baker, Colin (1985). *Aspects of Bilingualism in Wales*, Clevedon, Multilingual Matters.

— (1987). 'Bilingualism and bilingual education', *Special Issue of Education for Development*, vol. 10, no. 3.

— (1990). 'The growth of bilingual education in the secondary schools of Wales', in W. G. Evans (ed.), *Perspectives on a Century of Secondary Education in Wales*, Canolfan Astudiaethau Addysg, Cyfadran Addysg, Coleg Prifysgol Cymru, 77–96.

— (1993). *Foundations of Bilingual Education and Bilingualism*, Clevedon, Multilingual Matters.

— (1995). *A Parents' and Teachers' Guide to Bilingualism*, Clevedon, Multilingual Matters.

— (2000). 'Bilingual education: Three perspectives on bilingual education policy in Wales: Bilingual education as language planning, as pedagogy and as politics', in R. Daugherty, R. Phillips and G. Rees (eds), *Education Policy-Making in Wales: Explorations in Devolved Governance*, Cardiff, University of Wales Press, 102–23.

— (2003). 'Language planning: A grounded approach', in J-M. Dewaele, A. Housen and L. Wei (eds), *Bilingualism: Beyond Basic Principles*, Clevedon, Multilingual Matters, 88–111.

— (2006). *Foundations of Bilingual Education and Bilingualism* (4th edition), Clevedon, Multilingual Matters.

Baker, Colin and Jones, Meirion Prys (1999). *Continuity in Welsh Language Education*, Cardiff, Welsh Language Board.

— (2000). 'Welsh language education: A strategy for revitalization', in Colin H. Williams (ed.), *Language Revitalization: Policy and Planning in Wales*, Cardiff, University of Wales Press, 116–37.

Baker, Colin and Jones, Twm Prys (2003). 'Addysg cyfrwng-Cymraeg fel system', in G. Roberts and C. Williams (eds), *Addysg Gymraeg – Addysg Gymreig*, Bangor, Prifysgol Cymru, Bangor, 66–84.

Balsom, Denis (1985). 'The three-Wales model', in J. Osmond (ed.), *The National Question Again*, Llandysul, Gomer Press, 1–17.

Beetsma, Danny (ed.) (2002). 'Trilingual primary education in Europe: Inventory of the provisions for trilingual primary education in minority language communities in the European Union', Ljouwert/Leeuwarden, Mercator-Education, *http://www. mercator-research.eu/fileadmin/mercator/publications_pdf/tpee_report.pdf* (downloaded 13 April 2012).

Bentley, Tom (2001). 'It's democracy, stupid: An agenda for self government', London, Demos, *http://www.demos.co.uk/files/itsdemocracystupid.pdf?1240939425* (downloaded 5 March 2011).

Blake, Aled (2006a). 'Welsh medium education is a victim of its own success', icwales, *http://icwales.icnetwork.co.uk/.../tm_objectid=16583107&method=full&siteid=5008 2-name_page.html - 82k* (downloaded 29 August 2006).

— (2006b). 'Welsh Medium Schools Storm', Questia Online Library, *http:// www.questia.com/PM.qst;jsessionid=G25BJ0yVQTN7ZpHFfJKTnr6xZM5h1v1s9 zmbT2yYwskSgtpzHC2N!161906379?a=o&...* (downloaded 29 August 2006).

Boyce, S., Browman, C. P. and Goldstein, L. (1987). 'Lexical organization and Welsh consonant mutations', New Haven, Haskins Laboratories, originally published in *Journal of Memory and Language*, 26, 419–52.
http://www.haskins.yale.edu/sr/SR088/SR088_01.pdf (downloaded 11 April 2012).

Brace, John (1982). 'The educational state of Wales: The debate reviewed', *Education for Development*, vol. 7, no. 2, 63–72.

Bridgend County Borough Council (2006a). 'Welsh Education scheme 2006–2011', final draft for consultation, Bridgend, Bridgend County Borough Council.

— (2006b). 'Minutes of a meeting of the Bridgend County Borough Council, 11 October 2006', *www.bridgend.gov.uk?Web1/groups/public/coduments/minutes/ 017569.doc* (downloaded 16 May 2007).

Bush, Eluned (1979). 'Bilingual education in Gwent: Parental attitudes and aspirations (unpublished MEd thesis, Cardiff, University of Wales).

Bush, Eluned, Atkinson, Paul, and Read, Martin (1981a). 'Addysg trwy gyfrwng y Gymraeg mewn ardal Seisnig: Nodweddion ac ymagweddau'r rhieni', *Education for Development*, vol. 6, no. 3, 42–50.
— (1981b). A Minority Choice: Welsh Medium Education in an Anglicised Area – Parents' Characteristics and Motives, Cardiff, Sociological Research Unit, Departments of Sociology, University College, Cardiff.

Caerffili County Borough Council (2009). 'Welsh education scheme 2009–14', draft, Ystrad Mynach, Caerffili County Borough Council.
Campbell, Cefin (2000). 'Menter Cwm Gwendraeth: A case-study in community language planning', in Colin H. Williams (ed.), *Language Revitalization: Policy and Planning in Wales*, Cardiff, University of Wales Press, 247–91.
Cardiff Council (2010). 'Strategic outline programme 21st century schools', submission by Cardiff Council, Cardiff Council.
— (2011). 'School organization planning: Provision of Welsh medium and English medium community primary schools in and around Canton', report of Corporate Director (People), 7 April, Cardiff, Cardiff Council.
Carter, Harold (2002). 'The Future of the Welsh language', *Planet*, 152, April/May, 44–51.
— (2010). *Against the Odds: The Survival of Welsh Identity*, Cardiff, Institute of Welsh Affairs.
Cenoz, Jasone and Jessner, Ulrike (2000). *English in Europe: The Acquisition of a Third Language*, Clevedon, Multilingual Matters.
Centre for Welsh Medium Higher Education (2010). 'Coleg Cymraeg (Welsh medium national College)', *http://www.aucyfrwngcymraeg.ac.uk/en/about-us/coleg-ffederal/* (downloaded 5 March 2011).
Civil Society Platform on Multilingualism (2011). 'Policy recommendations for the promotion of multilingualism in the European Union', Brussels, Civil Society Platform on Multilingualism.
http://ec.europa.eu/languages/pdf/doc5088_en.pdf (downloaded 21 September 2011).
Cohen, Ira J. (1989). *Structuration Theory: Anthony Giddens and the Constitution of Social Life*, London, Macmillan.
Commission on the Powers and Electoral Arrangements of the National Assembly for Wales (2004): 'Report of the Richard Commission', Cardiff, Commission on the Powers and Electoral Arrangements of the National Assembly for Wales.
Council of Europe (1992). 'European charter for regional or minority languages', Strasbourg, 5.XI.1992, ETS no. 148, Strasbourg, Council of Europe. *http:// conventions.coe.int/treaty/en/Treaties/Html/148.htm* (downloaded 30 November 2005).
— (2004). 'European charter for regional or minority languages – application of the charter in the United Kingdom', ECRML (2004) 1, Strasbourg, Council of Europe.
— (2005a). 'European charter for regional or minority languages – second periodical report presented to the Secretary General of the Council of Europe in accordance with Article 15 of the charter, supplement to second periodical report from the United Kingdom correcting, updating and supplementing the information already provided on the Welsh language', MIN-LANG/PR (2005) 5 Addendum 1, Strasbourg, Council of Europe.

— (2005b). 'Meeting report, 10–12 May, 2005', Steering Committee for Human Rights DH-MIN(2005)008rev. Strasbourg, Council of Europe, *http://www. coe.int/…/2._documents/1PDF_DH- MIN(2005)008_1st_Mtg_Report_rev_ang.pdf* (downloaded 4 January 2007).

— (2007). 'European charter for regional or minority languages – application of the charter in the United Kingdom', ECRML (2007) 2, Strasbourg, Council of Europe, *http://www.coe.int/…/2_Monitoring/2.3_Committee_of_Experts'_Reports/ UK_2nd_report.pdf* (downloaded 8 April 2007).

Coupland, N. (ed.), in association with Alan R. Thomas (1990). *English in Wales: Diversity, Conflict and Change*, Clevedon, Multilingual Matters.

Coupland, N., Bishop, Hywel, and Garrett, Peter (2006). 'One Wales? Reassessing diversity in Welsh ethnolinguistic identification', *Contemporary Wales*, vol. 18, no. 1, 1–27.

Craib, Ian (1992). *Anthony Giddens*, London, Routledge.

Crystal, David (1997). *English as a Global Language*, Cambridge, Cambridge University Press.

— (1999a). 'The death of language', *Prospect*, November, 56–8.

— (1999b). 'Death sentence', *Guardian*, 25 October, G2, 2–3.

— (2000). *Language Death*, Cambridge, Cambridge University Press.

Cummins, Jim (1979). 'Cognitive/academic language proficiency, linguistic inter-dependence, the optimum age question and some other matters', *Working Papers on Bilingualism*, no.19, 121–9.

Currie-Jones, Emyr (1988). Cyfarchiad yn Bethan Roberts (ed.), *Glantaf, Y Degawd Cyntaf, 1978–88*, 4–5, Caerdydd, Ysgol Gyfun Gymraeg Glantaf.

Daugbjerg, Carsten and Marsh, David, (1998). 'Explaining policy outcomes: Integrating the policy network approach with macro-level and micro-level analysis', in D. Marsh (ed.), *Comparing Policy Networks*, Buckingham, Open University Press, 52–71.

Daugherty, Richard, Phillips, Robert and Rees, Gareth (eds) (2000). *Education Policy-Making in Wales: Explorations in Devolved Governance*, Cardiff, University of Wales Press.

Davies, Gwilym Prys, Lord (2001). *Darlith Goffa Gwyneth Morgan*, Caerdydd, Cronfa Glyndŵr yr Ysgolion Cymraeg.

— (2006). Personal letter to the author, 14 May 2006.

— (2008). *Cynhaeaf Hanner Canrif: Gwleidyddiaeth Gymreig 1945–2005*, Llan-dysul, Gwasg Gomer.

Davies, Janet (1993). *The Welsh Language*, Cardiff, University of Wales Press.

Davies, John (2007). *A History of Wales*, London, Penguin Books.

Denters, Bas and Rose, Lawrence E. (eds) (2005). *Comparing Local Governance: Trends and Developments*, Basingstoke, Palgrave Macmillan.

Department for Education and Skills (2004). *2003 KS2 to GCSE Value Added Pilot*, London, Department for Education and Skills, *http://www.dfes.gov.uk/performance tables/va1_03/docB.shtml* (downloaded 7 December 2006).

Dewaele, Jean-Marc, Housen, Alex and Wei, Li, (eds) (2003). *Bilingualism: Beyond Basic Principles, Festschrift in honour of Hugo Baetens Beardsmore*, Clevedon, Multi-lingual Matters.

Dwyer, Denis J. and Drakakis-Smith, David (eds) (1996). *Ethnicity and Development: Geographical Perspectives*, Chichester, Wiley.

Eastman, Carol (1984). 'Language, ethnic identity and change', in J. Edwards (ed.), *Linguistic Minorities, Policies and Pluralism*, London, Academic Press, 259–76.
Edwards, John, (1984a). 'Language, diversity and identity', in J. Edwards (ed.), *Linguistic Minorities, Policies and Pluralism*, London, Academic Press, 277–310.
— (ed.) (1984b). *Linguistic Minorities, Policies and Pluralism*, London, Academic Press.
— (1985). *Language, Society and Identity*, Oxford, Basil Blackwell.
— (1994). *Multilingualism*, London, Routledge.
Edwards, Viv K. and Newcombe, Lynda Pritchard (2003). 'Evaluation of the efficiency and effectiveness of the Twf Project, which encourages parents to transmit the language to their children', final report, December, Cardiff, Welsh Language Board.
Estyn (2003). 'The annual report of Her Majesty's Chief Inspector of Education and Training in Wales, 2001–2002', Cardiff, The Crown.
— (2004). 'The annual report of Her Majesty's Chief Inspector of Education and Training in Wales, 2002–2003', Cardiff, The Crown.
— (2005a). 'Report by Gareth Wyn Roberts, Ysgol Gyfun Gymraeg Glantaf – April 2005, Cardiff, The Crown.
— (2005b). 'The annual report of Her Majesty's Chief Inspector of Education and Training in Wales, 2003–2004', Cardiff, The Crown.
— (2005c). 'Y Cwricwlwm Cymreig: Progress made by schools in implementation of guidance issued by ACCAC in 2003', Cardiff, The Crown.
— (2006a). 'The annual report of Her Majesty's Chief Inspector of Education and Training in Wales, 2004–2005', Cardiff, The Crown.
— (2006b). 'A report on Welsh immersion and intensive language teaching pilot projects in schools', Cardiff, The Crown.
— (2001–2006). 'Reports under Section 10 of the Schools Inspections Act 1996' (186 in total), Cardiff, The Crown.
— (2007a). 'An evaluation of performance of schools before and after moving into new buildings or significantly refurbished premises', Cardiff, The Crown.
— (2007b). 'The annual report of Her Majesty's Chief Inspector of Education and Training in Wales, 2005–2006', Cardiff, The Crown.
— (2011). 'Supplementary guidance for inspecting additional learning needs', Cardiff, The Crown.
Eusko Jaurlaritzaren Argitalpen Zerbitzu Nagusia (2005). *Ill Carte Sociolinguistique 2001*, Donostia-San Sebastián, Servicio Central de Publicaciones del Gobierno Vasco.
Evans, Gareth (2011). 'Assembly funding for Welsh-medium primary school', 5 April, Cardiff, South Wales Echo, *http://www.walesonline.co.uk/news/local-news/cardiff/2011/04/05/assembly-funding-for-welsh-medium-primary-school-91466-28458986/#ixzz1SSrfnELK* (downloaded 18 July 2011).
Evans, John Albert. (2010). *Llanw Bwlch*, Llandysul, Gwasg Gomer.
Evans, Siôn Wyn (2007). 'Differential performance of items in mathematics assessment materials for 7-year-old pupils in English-medium and Welsh-medium versions', *Educational Studies in Mathematics*, vol. 64, no. 2, February, 145–68.

Evans, W. Gareth (ed.) (1990). *Perspectives on a Century of Secondary Education in Wales, 1889–1989,* Aberystwyth, Canolfan Astudiaethau Addysg, Cyfadran Addysg, Coleg Prifysgol Cymru.

Evas, Jeremy (1999). 'Rhwystrau ar lwybr dwyieithrwydd' (unpublished PhD thesis, Cardiff, University of Wales).

Fase, Willem, Jaspaert, Koen, and Kroon, Sjaak (eds) (1982). *Maintenance and Loss of Minority Languages,* Amsterdam, John Benjamins Publishing Company.

Federal Union of European Nationalities (2011). 'FUEN', *http://www.fuen.org/show.php* (downloaded 10 July 2011).

Fforwm Iaith Genedlaethol (1991). 'Strategaeth Iaith, 1991–2001', Aberystwyth, Fforwm yr Iaith Gymraeg.

Fishman, Joshua A. (1991). *Reversing Language Shift: Theoretical and Empirical Foundations of Assistance to Threatened Languages,* Clevedon, Multilingual Matters.

— (1994). 'The truth about language and culture (and a note about its relevance to the Jewish case)', *International Journal of the Sociology of Language,* vol. 109, issue 1, 83–96.

— (1995). 'On the limits of ethnolinguistic democracy', in T. Skutnabb-Kangas and R. Phillipson (eds), *Linguistic Human Rights – Overcoming Linguistic Discrimination,* Berlin, Mouton de Gruyter, 49–61.

— (1997). 'Review of C. H. Williams, *Called Unto Liberty: On Language and Nationalism', Journal of Sociolinguistics,* vol. 1, no. 1, 145–9.

— (ed.) (1999). *Handbook of Language and Ethnic Identity,* Oxford, Oxford University Press.

— (2000). 'Critiques of language planning: A minority languages perspective', in P. W. Thomas and J. Mathias (eds), *Developing Minority Languages,* Llandysul, Gwasg Gomer, 130–7.

— (2001). *Can Threatened Languages be Saved?* Clevedon, Multilingual Matters.

— (2006). *Language Loyalty, Language Planning and Language Revitalization, Recent Writings and Reflections from Joshua A. Fishman,* ed. by Nancy H. Hornberger and Martin Pütz, Clevedon, Multilingual Matters.

Furlong, John, Hagger, Hazel, Butcher, Cerys and Howson, John (2006). 'Review of initial teacher training provision in Wales: A report to the Welsh Assembly Government', Oxford, University of Oxford Department of Educational Studies.

Galligan, Denis J. (1997). 'Discretionary powers and the principle of legality', in *Administrative Discretion and Problems of Accountability,* ; *Twenty-fifth Colloquy on European Law Conference Proceedings,* Strasbourg, Council of Europe Publishing, 11–35.

Gardner, Nick (Nicholas) (2008). 'The Basque Experience', in *Creating a Bilingual Wales: The Role of Education,* Cardiff, Institute of Welsh Affairs, 39–50.

Gardner, Nicholas, Puigdevall i Serralvo, Maite and Williams, Colin H. (2000) 'Language revitalization in comparative context: Ireland, the Basque Country and Catalonia', in Colin H. Williams (ed.), *Language Revitalization: Policy and Planning in Wales,* Cardiff, University of Wales Press, 311–61.

Gibbons, Pauline (1991). *Learning to Learn in a Second Language,* Newtown, New South Wales, Primary English Teaching Association.

Giddens, Anthony (1979). *Central Problems in Social Theory: Action, Structure and Contradiction in Social Analysis*, London, Macmillan.

— (1984). *The Constitution of Society, Outline of the Theory of Structuration*, Cambridge, Polity Press.

— (1985). *Contemporary Critique of Historical Materialism, Vol. 2: The Nation-state and Violence*, Cambridge, Polity.

Gingrich, Paul (2000). *Structuration Theory*, http://uregina.ca/~gingrich/f300.htm. (downloaded 7 March 2006).

Goldsmith, Michael (1997). 'The changing patterns of local government', *ECPR News*, vol. 9, no. 1, Autumn, 6–7.

Gorard, Stephen (1997). 'Two perspectives on parental choice of school', working paper 25, Cardiff, School of Education, Cardiff, University of Wales.

— (1998). 'Four errors . . . and a conspiracy? The effectiveness of schools in Wales', *Oxford Review of Education*, vol. 24, no. 4, 459–72.

— (2000). 'A re-examination of the effectiveness of schools in Wales', in Daugherty, R. Phillips, R. and Rees, G. (eds), *Education Policy-Making in Wales*, Cardiff, University of Wales Press, 127–48.

Gregory, Derek (1982). *Regional Transformation and Industrial Revolution*, London, Macmillan.

Grenoble, Lenore A. and Whaley, Lindsay J. (1996). 'Endangered languages: Current issues and future prospects', *International Journal of the Sociology of Language*, 118, 209–23.

— (1998). *Endangered Languages, Language Loss and Community Response*, Cambridge, Cambridge University Press.

— (2006). *Saving Languages, An Introduction to Language Revitalization*, Cambridge, Cambridge University Press.

Gruffudd, Heini (2005). 'Anghenion hyfforddi ar gyfer athrawon yng Nghymru: Darpariaeth cyfrwng Cymraeg', sylwadau RhAG i adolygiad Llywodraeth Cynulliad Cymru o'r ddarpariaeth ar gyfer hyfforddiant cychwynnol athrawon, *www.RhAG.net/hyfforddiathrawon.doc* (downloaded May 13, 2007).

Gutstein, Eric (2007). 'Multiple language use and mathematics: Politicizing the discussion', *Educational Studies in Mathematics*, vol. 64, no. 2, February, 243–6.

Hambleton, Robin (2005). 'New leadership for democratic urban space', presentation to the Life in the Urban Conference, Gothenburg, Sweden, 1 June. *http://www.urbanlife2005.com/proceedings/keynotes/Robin_Hambleton.pdf* (downloaded 29 October 2005).

Hansard (1846). 'Education in Wales: Commons sitting: House of Commons debate', 10 March vol. 84, c. 854, *http://hansard.millbanksystems.com/commons/1846/mar/10/education-in-wales* (downloaded 27 June 2011).

— (1992). 'House of Commons Hansard Debates for 20 January', Sixth Series, Fifth Volume of Session 1991–2, vol. 202, c.11, *http://www.publications.parliament.uk/pa/cm199192/hansrd/1992-01-20/Orals-1.html* (downloaded 27 September 2006).

Hart, Herbert L. A. (1963). *Law, Liberty and Morality*, Oxford, Oxford University Press.

Haugen, Einar, McClure, J. Derrick and Thomson, Derrick (1980). *Minority Languages Today*, Edinburgh, Edinburgh University Press.

Hederman, Miriam and Kearney, Richard (eds) (1982). *The Crane Bag Book of Irish Studies 1977-81*, Dublin, Blackwater Press.

Higgs, Gary, Williams, Colin and Dorling, Danny (2004). 'Use of the census of population to discern trends in the Welsh language: An aggregate result', *Area*, 36.2, 187–201.

Hodges, Rhian Siân (2010a). 'Tua'r Goleuni: Addysg Gymraeg yng Nghwm Rhymni – rhesymau rhieni dros ddewis addysg Gymraeg i'w plant' (unpublished PhD thesis, Bangor University).

— (2010b). ' "Tua'r Goleuni": Rhesymau plant dros ddewis addysg Gymraeg i'w plant yng Nghwm Rhymni', *Gwerddon*, rhifyn 6.

— (2011). 'Towards the Light/Tua'r Goleuni: Welsh medium education for the non-Welsh-speaking in south Wales: A parent's choice', *Journal of Estonian and Finno-Ugric Linguistics*, 2–1, 303–14.

Hogan-Brun, Gabrielle (2004). 'Framing educational debates in Latvia: Language and the future of Europe: Ideologies, policies and practices', 8–10 July, Southampton, Centre for Transnational Studies, University of Southampton, *http://www.lang.soton.ac.uk/lipp/abstracts/hogan.rtf* (downloaded 6 April 2007).

Holson, David and Holt, Dan (1994). 'Joshua Fishman interview on preserving cultural and linguistic resources conducted by California Department of Education', *http://www.cde.ca.gov/iasa/fishman.html*, updated 27 December 2001 (downloaded 3 January 2005).

Hopkins, Ken (2006a). *Achub Ein Hiaith/Saving our Language*, Cardiff, Institute of Welsh Affairs.

— (2006b). Personal letter to H. Thomas, 14 July 2006.

Huber, John D. and Shipan, Charles R. (2002). *Deliberate Discretion? The Institutional Foundations of Bureaucratic Autonomy*, Cambridge, Cambridge University Press.

Hughes, J. Elwyn (1984). *Arloeswr Dwyieithedd: Dan Isaac Davies, 1839–1887*, Caerdydd, Gwasg Prifysgol Cymru.

Humphreys, Gwilym E. (gol.) (1973). *Rhydfelen: Y Deng Mlynedd Cyntaf*, Llandysul, Gwasg Gomer.

— (1987). 'Polisi iaith Awdurdod Addysg Gwynedd: Adolygu a gweithredu ym 1986', *Education for Development*, vol. 10, no. 3, 7–23.

— (2000). *Heyrn Yn Y Tân: Atgofion Addysgwr*, Caernarfon, Gwasg Pantycelyn.

icNetwork (2007). *Labour Minority Government Stability Agreement with Plaid Cymru*, *http://images.icnetwork.co.uk/docs/icWales/B9B3297D-E958-C2F2-75CB77 C1C1B0C6FA.doc* (downloaded 27 May 2007).

Irvine, Fiona, Roberts, Gwerfyl, Spencer, Llinos, Jones, Peter and Tranter, Siobhan (2008). 'Twf and onwards: Impact assessment and the way forward', Cardiff, The Welsh Language Board.

Jenkins, Geraint H. and Williams, Mari A. (eds) (2000). *Let's Do Our best for the Ancient Tongue: The Welsh Language in the Twentieth Century*, Cardiff, University of Wales Press.

John, Peter (2001). *Local Governance in Western Europe*, London, Sage.

Jones, Alan Wynne and Dafis, Llinos (2000). 'Why should the devil have all the good tunes? Marketing: A valuable discipline in language planning,' in P. W. Thomas and J. Mathias (eds), *Developing Minority Languages*, Llandysul, Gwasg Gomer, 63 –73.

Jones, Dylan Vaughan (1997). 'The assessment of bilingual pupils: observations from recent Welsh experiences', paper presented at the British Educational Research Association Annual Conference, 11–14 September 1997, *http://www.leeds.ac.uk/educol/documents/000000387.htm* (downloaded 27 September 2006).

Jones, Dylan Vaughan and Martin-Jones, Marilyn (2004). 'Bilingual education and language revitalization in Wales: Past achievements and current issues' in J. W. Tollefson and A. B. Tsui (eds), *Which Agenda? Whose Agenda?*, Mahwah, NJ, Lawrence Erlbaum, 43–70.

Jones, Gareth Elwyn (1997). *The Education of a Nation*, Cardiff, University of Wales Press.

Jones, Glyn E., Hughes, Medwin, Jones, Delyth, Council of Europe (1996). *Y Lefel Drothwy: Ar Gyfer y Gymraeg (The Threshold Level for Welsh)*, Croton-on-Hudson, New York, Manhattan Publishing Company.

Jones, Glyn E. and Williams, Colin H. (2000). 'Reactive policy and piecemeal planning: Welsh-medium education in Cardiff', in Colin H. Williams (ed.), *Language Revitalization: Policy and Planning in Wales*, Cardiff, University of Wales Press, 138–72.

Jones, Hywel M. (2008). 'The changing social context of Welsh: A review of statistical trends', *International Journal of Bilingual Education and Bilingualism*, vol.11, no.5, September, 541–57.

— (2010). Unpublished analysis by Hywel Jones, statistician Welsh Language Board, on the basis of 2001 census data and national curriculum assessments.

— (2012). 'A statistical overview of the Welsh language/Darlun ystadegol o sefyllfa'r Gymraeg', Cardiff, Welsh Language Board.

Jones, Hywel M. and Williams, Colin H. (2000). 'The statistical basis for Welsh language planning: Data, trends, patterns, processes' in Colin H. Williams (ed.), *Language Revitalization: Policy and Planning in Wales*, Cardiff, University of Wales Press, 48–82.

Jones, Michael L. N. (2012). 'On target for seven-year-old Welsh speakers reaching 25% by 2015', *Agenda*, Spring, no. 46, 40–3.

Jones, Richard Wyn, Morris, Delyth, Roberts-Young, Dilwyn, Popkins, Gareth, and Young, Einir (2002). 'Keeping Up Appearances', *Planet*, 154, August/September, 7–15.

Jones, R. Morris and Ghuman, Paul (eds) (1995). *Bilingualism, Education and Identity*, Cardiff, University of Wales Press.

Jones, W. R. (1966). *Bilingualism in Welsh Education*, Cardiff, University of Wales Press.

Keating, Michael (ed.) (2004). *Regions and Regionalism in Europe*, Cheltenham, Edward Elgar.

Khisty, L. L. (1995). 'Making inequality: Issues of language and meanings in mathematics teaching with Hispanic students', in W. G. Secada et al. (eds), *New Directions for Equity in Mathematics Education*, New York, Cambridge University Press, 279–97.

Khleif, Bud B. (1980). *Language, Ethnicity and Education in Wales*, The Hague, Mouton Publishers.

King, Lid, Byrne, Nick, Djouadj, Imke, Lo Bianco, Joseph and Stoicheva, Maria (eds) (2011). *Languages in Europe: Towards 2020: Analysis and Proposals from the LETPP Consultation and Review*, London, The Languages Company.

Kingdon, John W. (2003). *Agendas, Alternatives and Public Policies*, New York, Longman.

Kloss, Heinz (1971). 'The Language Rights of Immigrant Groups', *International Migration Review 5*, 250–68.

— (1977). *The American Bilingual Tradition*, Rowley, Mass., Newbury House.

Krauss, Heinz (1992). 'The world's languages in crisis', *Language*, vol. 68, no. 1, 4–10.

Lewis, E. Glyn (1981). *Bilingualism and Bilingual Education*, Oxford, Pergamon Press.

Lewis, Emyr (2004). *Minority Languages in the New Europe – a bit of a headache for those who believe in order?*, Annual Lecture of the Law Society delivered at the National Eisteddfod of Wales, Newport and District, Law Society. It is currently available at *http://www.lawsociety.org.uk/documents/.../annuallecture2004eng.pdf*

Lewis, Gari and Smallwood, Jeni (2010). 'Pobl ifanc: Ymbweru er mwyn gweithredu', in Lewis, Hywel Glyn and Ostler, Nicholas (eds), *Reversing Language Shift*, Bath, Foundation for Endangered Languages, 141–7.

Lewis, Gwion (2008). *Hawl i'r Gymraeg*, Talybont, Y Lolfa.

Lewis, Hywel Glyn (2010). 'A yw ysgolion dwyieithog yn llwyddo?', *Golwg*, 9 December, 11.

Lewis, Hywel Glyn and Ostler, Nicholas (eds) (2010). *Reversing Language Shift: How to Re-awaken a Language Tradition: Proceedings of the Conference FEL Xiv, 13–15 September 2010, Carmarthen Wales – Proceedings of the Foundation for Endangered Languages,* Bath, Foundation for Endangered Languages.

Lewis, Saunders (1962). *Tynged yr Iaith*, darlith flynyddol y BBC yng Nghymru, BBC, Llundain. English translation by G. Aled Williams available at *http://quixoticquisling.com/2012/02/fate-of-the-language/*

Lewis, W. Gwyn (2008). 'Addysg drochi yng Nghymru: Methodolegau a sialensau', in *Creu Cymru Ddwyieithog: Rôl y Gymraeg mewn Addysg*, Cardiff, Sefydliad Materion Cymreig, 7–16.

London Economics Wales in association with Professor Peter Dolton and Professor Geraint Johnes (2007). 'A review of the statistical issues underlying Welsh medium initial teacher training intake planning', final report for Department of Education, Lifelong Learning and Skills Welsh Assembly Government, Cardiff, London Economics Wales.

Loyal, Steven (2003). *The Sociology of Anthony Giddens*, London, Pluto Press.

Lucanovic, Sonja Noval and Mikolic, Vesna (eds) (2012). *Applied Linguistics*, Ljubljana, Institute of Ethnic Studies.

Mackey, William F. (2003). 'Forecasting the fate of languages', in J. Maurais and Michael A. Morris (eds), *Languages in a Globalising World*, Cambridge, Cambridge University Press, 64–81.

Mac Giolla Chríost, Diarmait (2003). *Language, Identity and Conflict: A Comparative Study of Language in Ethnic Conflict in Europe and Eurasia*, London, Routledge.

Mac Giolla Chríost, Diarmait and Aitchison, J. W. (1998). 'Ethnic identities and language in Northern Ireland,' *Area*, 30.4, 301–9.

Mar-Molinero, Clare (2011). 'Language normalization', *Encyclopedia of Contemporary Spanish Culture*, http://www/bookrags.com/tandf/language-normalization-tf/ (downloaded 20 June 2011).

Mar-Molinero, Clare and Smith, Angel (eds) (1996). *Nationalism and the Nation in the Iberian Peninsula: Competing and Conflicting Identities*, Oxford, Berg Publishers.

Marquand, David (2004). *Decline of the Public: The Hollowing-out of Citizenship*, Cambridge, Polity Press.

Marsh, David (ed.) (1998). *Comparing Policy Networks*, Buckingham, Open University Press.

Marvin, F. S. (ed.) (1908). *Reports on Elementary Schools 1852–1882 by Matthew Arnold*, new edition with additional matter and appendices and with an introduction by F. S. Marvin, London, Board of Education, HMSO.

Maurais, Jacques and Morris, Michael A. (eds) (2003). *Languages in a Globalising World*, Cambridge, Cambridge University Press.

May, Stephen (2001). *Language and Minority Rights, Ethnicity, Nationalism and the Politics of Language*, Harlow, Longman.

— (2005). 'Language rights: Moving the debate forward', *Journal of Sociolinguistics*, vol. 9, issue 3, 319–47.

Mény, Yves (1986). 'The political dynamics of regionalism: Italy, France, Spain', in R. Morgan (ed.), *Regionalism in European Politics*, London, Policy Studies Institute, 1–28.

Merthyr Tydfil County Borough Council (2009). 'Welsh education scheme 2009–2014', draft for consultation, Merthyr Tydfil, Merthyr Tydfil County Borough Council.

Mitchell, Lisa (2009). *Language, Emotion, and Politics in South India: The Making of a Mother Tongue*, Bloomington and Indianapolis, Indiana University Press.

Montaña, Benjamin Tejerina (1996). 'Language and Basque nationalism: Collective identity, social conflict and institutionalisation', in C. Mar-Molinero and A. Smith (eds), *Nationalism and the Nation in the Iberian Peninsula: Competing and Conflicting Identities*, Oxford, Berg Publishers, 221–36.

Morgan, Iorwerth W. (1969). 'A study of parental motivations and home interaction in the social milieu of a Welsh-medium school (unpublished MEd thesis University of Leicester).

— (2003). 'The early days of Welsh-medium schools', in Iolo Wyn Williams (ed.), *Our Children's Language: the Welsh-medium Schools of Wales, 1939–2000*, Talybont, Y Lolfa, 21– 41.

Morgan, Prys (ed.) (1991). *Brad y Llyfrau Gleision*, Llandysul, Gwasg Gomer.

Morgan, Roger (ed.) (1986). *Regionalism in European Politics*, London, Policy Studies Institute.

Morris, Steve (2000). 'Adult education, language revival and language planning' in Colin H. Williams, *Language Revitalization: Policy and Planning in Wales*, Cardiff, University of Wales Press, 208–20.

Moschkovick, J. N. (2002). 'A situated and sociocultural perspective on bilingual mathematics learners', *Mathematical Thinking and Learning*, vol. 4, nos. 2 and 3, 189–212.

National Assembly for Wales (2000). 'A Better Wales', *www.betterwales.com.*
— (2001). 'Welsh Medium Secondary Education, Examination and Attendance Data', 2000, SDB 30/2001, Cardiff, Statistical Directorate.
— (2003–6). 'Summary Data on Schools', National Pupil Database, Cardiff, Statistical Directorate, *http://www.npd-wales.gov.uk/index.cfm* (downloaded 10 December, 2006).
— (2006a). 'Welsh in Schools 2004 and 2005', Statistical Bulletin SB4/2006, Cardiff, Statistical Directorate, *http://new.wales.gov.uk/topics/statistics/headlines/schools-2006/hdw200601264/?lang=cy* (downloaded 22 December 2006).
— (2006b). 'Schools in Wales: General Statistics 2005, SDR7/2006', Cardiff. Statistical Directorate, *http://new.wales.gov.uk/topics/statistics/publications'swgs 2005/?lang=en* (downloaded 16 August 2006).
— (2007). 'Welsh in Schools 2006', Statistical Bulletin SB2/2007, Cardiff, NAW, Statistical Directorate, NAW, *http://new.wales.gov.uk/topics/statistics/headlines/ schools2007/hdw200701181/?lang=en* (downloaded 1 February 2007).
— (2009). 'Statistics for Wales, Value-added Guidance', Cardiff, *http://www.schools. wales.gov.uk/vaguidance-e.htm* (downloaded 17 February 2009).
National Library of Wales. 'Ymgyrchu! – The Welsh Language – Broadcasting – Act . . .', *http://www.llgc.org.uk/ymgyrchu/Iaith/Tyngedlaith/index-e.htm* (downloaded 18 May 2012).
Nelde, Peter H., Labrie, N., Williams, Colin H. (1992). 'The principles of territoriality and personality in the solution of linguistic conflicts', *Journal of Multilingual and Multicultural Development*, vol. 13, no. 5, 387–406.
Nelde, Peter H., Strubell, Miquel and Williams, Glyn (1996). *Euromosaic: The Production and Reproduction of the Minority Language Groups in the European Union*, Luxembourg, Office for Official Publications of the European Comminities.
Network to Promote Linguistic Diversity (2011). 'Why join the NPLD?', *http://www. npld.eu/aboutus/membership/pages/whyjointhenpld.aspx* (downloaded 10 July 2011).
Nicholas, Gari (2008). 'Llwybrau Dysgu 14–19: Prosiect ymwybyddiaeth iaith (Hydref 2007–Mawrth 2008): Adroddiad terfynol', Pontyberem, Llanelli, Menter Cwm Gwendraeth mewn partneriaeth â Chyngor Sir Gaerfyrddin.
Northover, M. and Donnelly, S. (1996). 'A future for English/Irish bilingualism in Northern Ireland?', *Journal of Multilingual and Multicultural Development*, vol. 17, no. 1, 33–48.

Ó Murchú, Máirtín (1982). 'Whorf and Irish language politics', in M. Hederman and R. Kearney (eds), *The Crane Bag Book of Irish Studies 1977–81*, Dublin, Blackwater Press, 326–30.
Ó Néill, Diarmuid (ed.) (2005). *Rebuilding the Celtic Languages: Reversing Language Shift in the Celtic Countries*, Talybont, Y Lolfa.
Ó Riagáin, Pádraig and Ó Gliasáin, M. (1984). 'The Irish language in the Republic of Ireland 1983: Preliminary report of a national survey', Dublin, Institiúid Teangeolaíochta Éireann.
— (1994). 'National survey on languages 1993: Preliminary report', Tuarascail Taighde 18, Dublin, Institiúid Teangeolaíochta Éireann.

Ó Riagáin, Pádraig, Williams, Glyn and Mila i Moreno, F. Xavier (2008). 'Young people and minority languages: Language outside the classroom, Dublin, Trinity College, Centre for Language and Communication Study,
— and Williams, Glyn, Mila i Moreno, F. Xavier (2009). 'Young people and minority languages: Language outside the classroom, Dublin, Trinity College, Centre for Language and Communication Study, *http://www.comhairle.org/PDFs/publications/Young People and Minority Languages.pdf* (downloaded 1 March 2011).
Osborne, David and Gaebler, Ted (1992). *Reinventing Government: How the Entrepreneurial Spirit Is Transforming the Public Sector*, New York, Plume.
Osmond, John (ed.) (1985). *The National Question Again: Political Identity in the 1980s*, Llandysul, Gomer Press.

Pertot, Susanna, Priestly, Tom M. S. and Williams, Colin H. (eds) (2009). *Rights, Promotion and Integration Issues for Minority Language in Europe*, Basingstoke, Palgrave Macmillan.
Phillipson, Robert (ed.) (2000). *Rights to Language, Equity, Power and Education*, London, Lawrence Erlbaum Associates.
— (2003). *English-Only Europe? Challenging Language Policy*, London, Routledge.
Prys, Delyth, Jones, J. Prys Morgan, Davies, Owain and Prys, Gruffudd (2006). *Y Termiadur: Termau wedi'u safoni/Standardized Terminology*, Cardiff, ACCAC.

Quinn, Brid (2005). 'Governance and democracy – vacillation and vicariousness', paper to be presented at the EGPA Annual Conference Bern, 31 August–3 September. *http://www.egpa2005.com/workshops/abstracts_sg4/Paper_quinn.pdf* (downloaded 29 October 2005).
Quinn, Eileen Moore (2007). *Can This Language be Saved? http://www.cs.org/publications/csq/csq-article.cfm?id=1288* (downloaded 7 May 2007).

Rawkins, Phillip M. (1979). *The Implementation of Language Policy in the Schools of Wales*, Strathclyde, Centre for the Study of Public Policy, University of Strathclyde.
— (1987). 'The politics of benign neglect: education, public policy, and the mediation of linguistic conflict in Wales', *International Journal of the Sociology of Language*, Amsterdam, Mouton de Gruyter, 66 (1987), 27–48.
Rees, Gareth (2004). 'Democratic devolution and educational policy in Wales', *Contemporary Wales*, vol. 17, no. 1, 28–43.
Reynolds, David, Bellin, Wynford, and ab Ieuan, Ruth (1998). *A Competitive Edge: Why Welsh Medium Schools Perform Better*, Cardiff, Institute of Welsh Affairs.
Rhodes, R. A. W. (1997). *Understanding Governance: Policy Networks, Governance, Reflexivity and Accountability*, Buckingham, Open University Press.
Rhondda Cynon Taf County Borough Council (2006). 'Single education scheme, September 2006–8', Abercynon, Department of Education and Lifelong Learning, Rhondda Cynon Taf County Borough Council.
— (2008). 'Welsh Education Scheme 2008–13', consultation draft, Abercynon, School and Community Directorate, Rhondda Cynon Taf County Borough Council. *http://www.rhondda-cynon-taff.gov.uk/stellent/groups/Public/documents/relateddocuments/022389.pdf* (downloaded 28 January 2009).

— (2009). 'Strategic outline case for school transformation', Abercynon, School and Community Directorate, Rhondda Cynon Taf County Borough Council.

Risager, Karen (2007). *Language and Culture Pedagogy: From a National to a Transnational Paradigm* (Languages for Intercultural Communication and Education), Clevedon, Multilingual Matters.

Roberts, Bethan, (ed.) (1988). *Glantaf, Y Degawd Cyntaf, 1978–88*, Caerdydd, Ysgol Gyfun Gymraeg Glantaf.

Roberts, Gareth and Williams, Cen (eds) (2003). *Addysg Gymraeg – Addysg Gymreig*, Bangor, Prifysgol Cymru, Bangor.

Roberts, Gwyneth Tyson (1998). *The Language of the Blue Books: The Perfect Instrument of Empire*, Cardiff, University of Wales Press.

Roberts, Wyn (1986). 'Education in Wales: Looking ahead/Addysg yng Nghymru: Edrych ymlaen', speech delivered by Mr Wyn Roberts, MP, Under-Secretary of State for Wales, at the Annual Conference of Parents for Welsh-medium Education, Pontypridd, 19 April 1986, Cardiff, Welsh Office.

— (1995). 'Fifteen years at the Welsh Office/Pymtheng mlynedd yn y Swyddfa Gymreig', Welsh Political Archive lecture, Aberystwyth, National Library of Wales.

— (2006). *Right from the Start: The Memoirs of Sir Wyn Roberts, The Rt. Hon. Lord Roberts of Conwy*, Cardiff, University of Wales Press.

Saunders, Lesley (1999). '"Value added" measurement of school effectiveness: A critical review', Slough, NFER.

Setati, M. (2005). 'Learning and teaching mathematics in the primary multilingual classroom', *Journal for Research in Mathematics Education*, vol. 36, no. 5, 447–66.

Sharkey, Moira (2009). 'Police investigate Coun. Ramesh Patel's "ethnic cleansing" school remarks', Cardiff, *South Wales Echo*, WalesOnline, 6 February, *http://www.walesonline.co.uk/news/education-news/2009/02/06/police-investigate-coun-ramesh-patel-s-ethnic-cleansing-school-remarks-91466-22867298/* (downloaded 24 July 2011).

Sharp, Caroline, Keys, W. and Benefield, P. (2001). 'Homework: A review of recent research', Slough, NFER, on-line summary, *http://nfer.ac.uk/research-areas/pims-data/summaries/hwk-review-of-studies-on-homework.cfm* (downloaded 13 April 2007).

Sharpe, L. J. (1993). 'The European meso: An appraisal', in M. Keating (ed.), *Regions and Regionalism in Europe*, Cheltenham, Edward Elgar, 529–67.

Skutnabb-Kangas, Tove (1999). 'Education of minorities', in J. Fishman (ed.), *Handbook of Language and Ethnic Identity*, Oxford, Oxford University Press, 42-59.

— (2000). *Linguistic Genocide in Education – or Worldwide Diversity and Human Rights?*, Mahwah, New Jersey, Lawrence Erlbaum.

Skutnabb-Kangas, Tove and Phillipson, Robert (eds), in collaboration with Rannut, Mart (1995). *Linguistic Human Rights – Overcoming Linguistic Discrimination*, Berlin, Mouton de Gruyter.

Smolicz, Jerzy J. (1979). *Culture and Education in a Plural Society*, Canberra, Curriculum Development Centre.

— (1993). 'The monolingual myopia and minority rights: Australia's language policies from an international perspective', *Muslim Education Quarterly* 10, 44–61.

— (1995). 'Australia's language policies and minority rights: A core value perspective', in T. Skunabb-Kangas et al., *Linguistic Human Rights – Overcoming Linguistic Discrimination*, Berlin, Mouton de Gruyter, 235–52.

Stoker, Gerry (2004). *Transforming Local Governance: From Thatcherism to New Labour*, Basingstoke, Palgrave Macmillan.

Stone, Clarence (1989). *Regime Politics: Governing Atlanta, 1946–1988*, Lawrence, University Press of Kansas.

Stones, Rob (2005). *Structuration Theory*, Basingstoke and New York, Palgrave Macmillan.

Syniadau (2011). 'Ysgol Treganna', 5 April, Syniadau blog, *http://syniadau--building anindependentwales.blogspot.com/2011/04/ysgol-treganna.html* (downloaded 18 July 2011).

Thomas, Gerran and Egan, David (2000). 'Policies on schools' inspection in Wales and England', in R. Daugherty, R. Phillips and G. Rees (eds), *Education Policy-Making in Wales*, Cardiff, University of Wales Press, 149–68.

Thomas, Huw S. (gol.) (1979). *Geiriadur Lladin–Cymraeg*, Caerdydd, Gwasg Prifysgol Cymru.

— (2005). 'Submission by CYDAG to the Delegation of the Committee of Experts, Cardiff, December 6' (unpublished paper).

— (2007). 'Brwydr i baradwys? Y dylanwadau ar dwf ysgolion Cymraeg de-ddwyrain Cymru' (unpublished PhD thesis, Cardiff University).

— (2010a). *Brwydr i Baradwys? Y Dylanwadau ar Dwf Ysgolion Cymraeg De-ddwyrain Cymru*, Caerdydd, Gwasg Prifysgol Cymru.

— (2010b). 'Hawliau addysgol a ieithyddol', *Contemporary Wales*, vol. 23, 201–18.

Thomas, Owen John (2008). 'Strategic action for creating a bilingual Wales', in *Creating a Bilingual Wales: The Role of Welsh in Education*, Cardiff, Institute for Welsh Affairs, 51–62.

Thomas, Peter Wynn (1996). *Gramadeg y Gymraeg*, Caerdydd, Gwasg Prifysgol Cymru.

— and Mathias, Jayne (eds) (2000). *Developing Minority Languages*: Proceedings of the Fifth International Conference on Minority Languages, July 1993, Cardiff, Wales, Llandysul, Gwasg Gomer.

Thurber, James A. (2003). 'Foreword', in J. W. Kingdon, *Agendas, Alternatives and Public Policies*, New York, Longman.

Tonkin, Humphrey (2003). 'The search for a global linguistic strategy', in J. Maurais and M. A. Morris (eds), *Languages in a Globalising World*, Cambridge, Cambridge University Press, 319–33.

Tua'r Goleuni (2007), papur bro Cwm Rhymni, rhifyn 96, Chwefror.

Webber, M. M. (1963). 'Order in diversity: Community without propinquity', in L. Wirigo (ed.), *Cities and Space*, Baltimore, John Hopkins University Press, 22–54.

Welsh Affairs Committee House of Commons (2007). 'The proposed Legislative Competence Order in Council on additional learning needs: Government response to the Committee's second report of session 2007–8', London, Stationery Office Limited.

Welsh Assembly Government (2001). 'Plan for Wales', Cardiff, Welsh Assembly Government.

— (2003). 'Iaith Pawb: A national action plan for a bilingual Wales', Cardiff, Welsh Assembly Government.

— (2004). 'Policy review of special educational needs. Part I: Early identification and intervention', report by the Education Lifelong Learning and Skills Committee, Cardiff, Welsh Assembly Government.

— (2005). 'School governance and improvement in Wales: Executive summary', DfTE Information Document no. 057–05, Cardiff, Welsh Assembly Government.

— (2006). 'Canllawiau ar gyfer gwerth ychwanegol, Cyhoeddiadau Allweddol Ystadegau Cymru', Caerdydd, Cyfarwyddiaeth Ystadegol.
http://www.ysgolion.cymru.gov.uk/index.asp (downloaded 7 December 2006).

— (2007a). 'One Wales: A progressive agenda for the government of Wales', an agreement between the Labour and Plaid Cymru groups in the National Assembly, Cardiff, Welsh Assembly Government.

— (2007b). 'Bilingual statistics for the post-16 learning sector in Wales', Cardiff, Welsh Assembly Government, Department of Education, Lifelong Learning and Skills.

— (2007c). 'Defining schools according to Welsh-medium provision', October 2007: 023/2007, Cardiff: Welsh Assembly Government.

— (2008). 'Learner travel (Wales) measure 2008: Cabinet statement by Ieuan Wyn Jones, AM (Deputy First Minister and Minister for Economy and Transport)', Cardiff, Welsh Assembly Government Cabinet Statements.
http://wales.gov.uk?about/cabinet/cabinetstatements/2008/learnertravel/?lang=en (downloaded 7 December 2009).

— (2009a). 'Welsh-medium education strategy: Draft Consultation', consultation document no. 067/2009, Cardiff, Welsh Assembly Government.

— (2009b). 'The Welsh-medium education strategy: Analysis of the responses to Consultation', Cardiff, Welsh Assembly Government.
http://wales.gov.uk/docs/dcells/consultation/091120wmesanalysisen.pdf (downloaded 9 December 2009).

— (2009c). 'Statistics on migrant workers in Wales', Cardiff, Welsh Assembly Government, *http://wales.gov.uk/docs/statistics/2009/090827sa28en.pdf* (downloaded 10 December 2010)

— (2010a). 'Welsh-medium education strategy', information document no. 083/2010, Cardiff, Welsh Assembly Government.

— (2010b). 'Schools in Wales: General statistics 2009', Cardiff, Welsh Assembly Government.

— (2010c). 'A living language: A language for living: A Strategy for the Welsh language': Consultation document 13 December 2010–4 February 2011, Cardiff, Welsh Assembly Government.

— (2011). 'A living language: A language for living: A strategy for the Welsh language', draft, Cardiff, Welsh Assembly Government.

Welsh Biography Online. 'Griffith Jones Llanddowror', *http://yba.llgc.org.uk/en/s-JONE-GRI-1683.html* (downloaded 1 March 2011).

Welsh Government (2009). 'Schools in Wales: General statistics 2009', Cardiff, Welsh Government.

— (2011a). 'A living language: A language for living. A strategy for the Welsh Language', Cardiff, Welsh Government.

— (2011b). 'Welsh-medium Education Strategy: Annual report 2010–11', Cardiff, Welsh Government.
— (2011c). Welsh Language (Wales) Measure, Cardiff, Welsh Government.
— (2012a). 'Promoting linguistic progression between Key Stages 2 and 3', Cardiff, Welsh Government.
— (2012b). 'School Standards and Organisation (Wales) Bill 2012 (draft)', Cardiff, Welsh Government.
Welsh Language Board (1999). 'A strategy for the Welsh language: Targets for 2000–2005', Cardiff, Welsh Language Board.
— (2003a). 'Y Gymraeg a'r Teulu', *http://www.bwrdd-yr-iaith.org.uk* (downloaded 27 November 2003).
— (2003b). 'Addysg cyfrwng Cymraeg neu ddwyieithog – o'r ysgol gynradd i'r ysgol uwchradd. Be Nesa ? Y dewis naturiol', Caerdydd, Bwrdd yr Iaith Gymraeg.
— (2003c). 'Welsh speakers by age group: 2001 census', Table S133, *http://www. bwrdd-yr-iaith.org.uk/cynnwys.php?pID=109andnID=149andlangID=2* (downloaded 20 December 2006).
— (2003d). 'Documents of the 62nd WLB meeting, Hirwaun, 16 May, document 62/4, language action plans', Cardiff, Welsh Language Board.
— (2004). 'Reports on 1901, 1911, 1921, 1931, 1951 Censuses', *http://www.byig-wlb.org.uk/english/publications/pages/index.aspx?drillmode=title&alpha=p;q;r* (downloaded 7 May 2007).
— (2006). 'Language Use Survey 2004', Cardiff, Welsh Language Board.
— (2008). 'The Welsh Language Use Surveys of 2004–6', Cardiff, Welsh Language Board.
Welsh Language Commissioner (2012). 'Standards and the Welsh language: What are your views?', Cardiff, Welsh Language Commissioner.
Welsh Office (1980). 'General Statistics, Schools, Section 5', Cardiff, The Crown.
— (1985). 'General Statistics, Schools, Section 5', Cardiff, The Crown.
— (1990). 'General Statistics, Schools, Section 7', Cardiff, The Crown.
— (1998). 'Digest of Welsh historical statistics 1974–1996, Statistics of Education in Wales, no.1; Statistics of education and training in Wales: Schools, no.3', Cardiff, The Crown.
Williams, Cen (2003). *Cyfrwng Cymraeg mewn Addysg Uwch – Tueddiadau a Dyheadau*, Caerdydd, Prifysgol Cymru.
Williams, Colin H. (1982). 'Agencies of language reproduction in Celtic societies', in W. Fase et al. (eds), *Maintenance and Loss of Minority Languages*, Amsterdam, John Benjamins Publishing Company, 306–29.
— (1988). 'Addysg ddwyieithog yng Nghymru ynteu addysg ar gyfer Cymru ddwyieithog? Bilingual education in Wales or education for a bilingual Wales?', Bangor, Cyfres Darlithoedd Canolfan Astudiaethau Iaith, Bangor, 1, 1–28.
— (1990). 'The Anglicisation of Wales', in N. Coupland, *English in Wales: Diversity, Conflict and Change*, Clevedon, Multilingual Matters, 19–47.
— (1994). *Called unto Liberty: On Language and Nationalism*, Clevedon, Multilingual Matters.
— (1995). 'Questions concerning the development of bilingual Wales' in R. M. Jones and P. Ghuman (eds), *Bilingualism, Education and Identity*, Cardiff, University of Wales Press, 47–78.

— (1996). 'Ethnic identity and language issues in development', in D. J. Dwyer and D. Drakakis-Smith (eds), *Ethnicity and Development: Geographical Perspectives*, Chichester, Wiley, 45–85.

— (1999). 'Bilingual education in the service of democracy', *Annales di Studi istriani e mediterranei*, Koper, ZRS, vol. 10. no. 1, 89–110.

— (ed.) (2000a). *Language Revitalization: Policy and Planning in Wales*, Cardiff, University of Wales Press.

— (2000b). 'Restoring the language', in G. H. Jenkins and M. A. Williams (eds), *Let's Do Our Best for the Ancient Tongue*, Cardiff, University of Wales Press, 657–81.

— (2000c). 'On recognition, resolution and revitalization', in C. H. Williams (ed.), *Language Revitalization: Policy and Planning in Wales*, Cardiff, University of Wales Press, 1–47.

— (2001). 'Y Cyngor Cenedlaethol – ELWa: Adroddiad dysgu cyfrwng Cymraeg a dwyieithog/National Council – ELWa: Report on Welsh medium and bilingualism learning', 1–25.

— (2004a). Adolygiad o *Addysg Gymraeg – Addysg Gymreig*, from *http://www.gwales.com*, by permission of the Welsh Books Council. *http://www.gwales.com/reviews/?newsize=100andtsid=1* (downloaded 30 April 2007).

— (2004b). ' *Iaith Pawb*: The doctrine of plenary inclusion', *Contemporary Wales*, vol. 17, Summer, 1–27.

— (2005). 'The case of Welsh/Cymraeg in Wales', in D. Ó Néill (ed.), *Rebuilding the Celtic Languages*, Talybont, Y Lolfa, 35–114.

— (2008). *Linguistic Minorities in Democratic Context*, Basingstoke, Palgrave Macmillan.

— (2009). 'Governance without conviction', in S. Pertot et al. (eds), *Rights, Promotion and Integration Issues for Minority Languages in Europe*, Basingstoke, Palgrave Macmillan, 89–122.

— (2010). 'Linguistic diversity and legislative regimes', in *Lenguas Minoritarias en la Administración*, Vitorio-Gasteiz, Parlamento Vasco, 23–50.

— (2011). 'Constrained ambition: Reflections on the Welsh model of bilingual education', in S. N. Lukanovic and V. Mikolic (eds), *Applied Linguistics*, Ljubljana, Institute of Ethnic Studies, 238–63.

Williams, Colin H. and Evas, Jeremy (1997). 'The community research project', Cardiff, Welsh Language Board.

Williams, Colin H. and Evas, Jeremy (1998). 'Community language regeneration: Realising the potential', Cardiff, Welsh Language Board.

Williams, Gareth J. (1988). 'An investigation into homework in a comprehensive school' (unpublished MEd thesis, Cardiff, University of Wales).

Williams, Glyn (ed.) (1987). 'The sociology of Welsh', *International Journal of the Sociology of Language*, vol. 66.

— (1999). 'Language and ethnicity: The sociological approach' in J. Fishman (ed.), *Handbook of Language and Ethnic Identity*, Oxford, Oxford University Press, 164–80.

Williams, Glyn E. and Morris, Delyth (2000). *Language Planning and language Use: Welsh in a Global Age*, Cardiff, University of Wales Press.

Williams, Heulwen (2005). *Memories of Ysgol Gymraeg Rhymni 1950s–1960s*, private publication by the author.

Williams, Iolo Wyn, (1987). 'Mathematics and science: The final frontier for bilingual education', *Education for Development*, vol.10, no. 3, 40–54.

— (ed.) (2002). *Gorau Arf: Hanes Sefydlu Ysgolion Cymraeg, 1939–2000*, Talybont, Y Lolfa.

— (ed.) (2003). *Our Children's Language: The Welsh-medium Schools of Wales, 1939–2000*, Talybont, Y Lolfa.

Williams, Jac L. (ed.) (1973). *Geiriadur Termau/Dictionary of Terms*, Cardiff, University of Wales Press.

Williams, Robin (2009). 'Y Coleg Ffederal: Adroddiad i'r Gweinidog dros Blant, Addysg, Dysgu Gydol Oes, a Sgiliau', *http://wales.gov.uk/docs/dcells/publications/090622ColegFfederalReporten.pdf* (downloaded 1 August 2009).

Williams, Sian Rhiannon (1992). *Oes y Byd i'r Iaith Gymraeg*, Caerdydd, Gwasg Prifysgol Cymru.

— (2002). 'Review of *Gorau Arf*, *Welsh Journal of Education*, vol.11, no. 2, 120–2.

Wirigo, L. (ed.) (1963). *Cities and Space*, Baltimore, MD, Johns Hopkins University Press.

Zalbide, Mikel (2005). 'A Basque perspective on the future of lesser used languages in education', paper presented at CAER's 2005 conference, Mikel Zalbide, *huieusk@ej-gv.es*, Department of Education, Basque Government, Spain.

Index

A number of entries appear only under their generic heading, for example 'County Councillors', 'Local Authorities', 'politicians', 'schools'. People, places or institutions that have multi-roles appear under their own names as well.

307

Index

levels (structural) macro, meso, micro
    generic principles 98, 100, 108–9, 136,
        155, 166, 168, 197
    macro 73, 81, 85, 136
    meso 73
    micro 73, 106, 136
    see also influences
Lewis, E. Glyn 90
Lewis, Emyr 88
Lewis, Gari 280
Lewis, Gethin 54
Lewis, Hywel G. 278–9
Lewis, Saunders xxx, 150
Lewis, W. Gwyn 280
Liberal Democrats see political parties
liberalism, liberality 3–5, 22–3, 184, 190
lingua franca 14, 89, 202
linguistic
    apartheid 56
    attrition 70, 94, 161
    background of Ysgolion Cymraeg in
        south-east Wales 7, 27, 34–40, 51,
        56, 155, 256, 264, 274, 279
    confidence 20–1, 71, 92, 255, 259–65,
        270, 278, 280–1, 285
    continuum 11
    disruption see GIDS
    diversity xxi, 5, 86, 189–90, 274
    fluency see fluency
    functions 83, 91–2, 254, 256
    genocide 201
    human rights (LHR) xxiv 12, 25, 31,
        68, 87, 134, 146, 164, 187, 194–5,
        211, 240, 287
linguistics xxviii
literacy 78, 89, 128, 201, 205, 230
    see also language across the curriculum,
        oral homework
Liverpool (Lerpwl) 213
Llais Gwynedd xxviii, 68
Llanbadarn Fawr 4
Llanbradach 216, 218
Llandaf 219
Llanelli 28, 212
Llanelwy (St Asaph) 214
Llanilltud Fawr (Llantwit Major) 222
Llangynwyd 127

Llantrisant 216
Llantwit Major (Llanilltud Fawr) 222
Llanwenarth 28
Llanwern 172
Lloyd, Anita 223
Lloyd, Illtyd 152–4
Llundain (London) xxi, 26, 106, 123, 200,
    221
lobbying 33, 87, 134, 143, 157, 172, 195,
    203, 281
Local (Education) Authorities xxiv, xxviii,
    1–2, 14–19, 23, 27, 33, 87, 122, 124–5,
    174–5, 181–2, 202–3, 207, 209–12, 215,
    224, 227–8, 230–41, 245, 249–50,
    275–8, 281–2, 286
    Blaenau Gwent xviii, 32, 35–6, 38,
        44–5, 210, 224
    Bridgend xix, 8, 16, 31–3, 35–6, 38,
        44–5, 81, 112–14, 127, 210, 218,
        226–7, 232–3
    Caerffili xviii, 16, 29–32, 35–6, 38,
        44–6, 113, 127, 151, 160, 169, 181,
        215, 218, 225, 232, 266
    Cardiff xvii, xxi, 10, 17–19, 29, 87–8,
        110–13, 125, 127, 143–4, 159,
        166–7, 174, 210, 214–15, 219–22,
        225, 236, 242–52, 277
    Cardigan see Ceredigion
    Carmarthen 68, 74–6, 92, 94, 105,
        278–9
    Ceredigion (Cardigan) 74–5, 90, 201,
        229, 278–9
    Dyfed 209, 211
    Flint 2, 10, 26, 213–14
    Glamorgan 2, 4, 23, 30–1, 33–4, 110,
        140, 142, 160, 210, 212–26, 223,
        231–2
    Gwent xviii, 28–30, 32, 34, 45, 110, 125,
        159, 216, 223–4, 233
    Gwynedd v, 2, 90, 94, 209, 211
    Merthyr Tudful xx, 32, 35–6, 38, 44–5,
        160, 182, 210, 216, 218, 226, 232
    Mid Glamorgan xviii–xx, 10, 29–31,
        34, 39, 43, 110, 139–42, 201, 210,
        215–19, 225, 232–3
    Monmouthshire xviii, 32, 34–6, 38,
        44–5, 214–16, 221, 223

319

methodology
    research 24, 50, 53, 100–1, 183, 255–9,
        279,
    teaching 1, 42, 253–66, 279, 283
    see also research
micro *see* levels
migration x, 5, 19, 25–6, 68, 70, 77, 86,
    89–90, 139, 199, 239–40, 245, 252, 279
Mila i Moreno, F. Xavier 254
Miles, Gareth 216
ministers
    European 190, 198
    of religion 23, 212
    UK government 146–7, 149–50, 153,
        157, 186, 212–13, 227
    Welsh Government xxi, 11, 14, 18, 91,
        121–2, 128, 161, 173–4, 182–3, 185,
        227–8, 237, 241–2, 246, 249–50,
        252
Ministry of Education 212–13
minority cultures, groups xxi, 20, 27, 57,
    65, 67, 69, 73, 75–7, 84, 88, 103, 134,
    149, 151, 194, 196, 198, 233, 245, 254,
    267, 271
minority language communities xxviii, 9,
    35–6, 73, 75–8, 84, 86, 94, 254, 273, 277
minority rights *see* rights
mission 51, 185, 213–14, 270, 277
Mitchell, Lisa 64
Modality 101
models (schools) of language delivery ix, x,
    7, 26, 103, 165, 184, 189, 193, 279
modernity 8, 67–8, 93, 180
Mold (Yr Wyddgrug) 214
momentum (to facilitate development)
    107, 135, 159, 202–3, 231–3, 283
Monmouthshire (Sir Fynwy) (before 1996)
    28, 34, 90, 214–16, 221, 223
monoglot *see* monolingualism
monolingualism x, xxvii, 23, 66, 68, 75,
    131, 150, 193, 202
Montaña, Benjamin Tejerina 128
Montgomeryshire (Sir Drefaldwyn) 211
moral, morality 11, 99, 109, 134, 221, 252
Morgan, Gwyneth 81
Morgan, Iorwerth 30, 43, 80, 102
Morgan, Prys 91

Morgan, Rhodri, The Right Honourable,
    MP, AM, Former First Minister xxi,
    17–20, 88, 160, 166, 242–52, 277
Morgan, Trefor 81
Morris, Delyth 20, 185
Moschkovich, J. N. 97
mother tongue 8, 40, 56, 72–3, 75, 95, 132,
    192, 240
Motorola 157
'movement' (belonging to the Ysgolion
    Cymraeg) x, xi, 9–10, 12, 25, 132–3,
    135, 142, 144, 156, 158–9, 167, 175, 194
MP (Member of Parliament) *see* politicians
Mudiad Meithrin, Mudiad Ysgolion
    Meithrin (MYM) 2, 27, 125, 127, 146,
    176–7, 214, 217–18, 234
multiculturalism xiv, xxi, 66, 68, 285
multi-ethnicity 68
multilingualism xxiii, 3, 12, 22–3, 68,
    187–92, 197, 239, 268–9
music 4, 157, 204
mutations xxviii, 261
MYM *see* Mudiad Ysgolion Meithrin
Mynachdy 219
Mynwent y Crynwyr (Quakers['] Yard)
    216
myths 47, 60

Nafarroako Foru Komunitatea 192
Nantgarw 226
Nantyglo 224
national
    Assembly for Wales (NAfW, NAW)
        xxiv, 7, 91, 96, 123, 132, 151–2, 162,
        233, 237, 268
    Curriculum xxvii, 37, 81, 87, 123,
        148–51, 152–3, 206–7, 238
    Grid for learning (Wales), NGfL
        Cymru xxiv, 79
    Health Service 77, 116, 189, 235–6, 240,
        287
    institutions 31, 69
    Library of Wales xxx, 171
    self-confidence, self-respect *see*
        confidence
    Standardisation Body for the Welsh
        Language 180